979.403　　　　　　　　　　　154549
　Zam
　Har
　　　Harding.
　　　Don Agustin V. Zamorano.

THE
CHICANO
HERITAGE

This is a volume in the Arno Press collection

THE CHICANO HERITAGE

Advisory Editor
Carlos E. Cortés

Editorial Board
Rodolfo Acuña
Juan Gómez-Quiñones
George F. Rivera, Jr.

*See last pages of this volume
for a complete list of titles.*

Don Agustin V. ZAMORANO

GEORGE L. HARDING

ARNO PRESS

A New York Times Company

New York — 1976

LEARNING RESOURCES CENTER
NAZARETH COLLEGE

154549

Editorial Supervision: LESLIE PARR

Reprint Edition 1976 by Arno Press Inc.

THE CHICANO HERITAGE
ISBN for complete set: 0-405-09480-9
See last pages of this volume for titles.

Manufactured in the United States of America

Library of Congress Cataloging in Publication Data

Harding, George Laban, 1893-
  Don Agustin V. Zamorano.

  (The Chicano heritage)
  Reprint of the ed. published by the Zamorano Club,
Los Angeles.
  Bibliography: p.
  1. Zamorano, Agustin Juan Vicente, 1798-1842.
2. California--History--To 1846. 3. Printing--
History--California. I. Title. II. Series.
F864.Z262H37 1976   979.4'03'0924 [B]   76-1269
ISBN 0-405-09505-8

DON AGUSTIN V. ZAMORANO
STATESMAN, SOLDIER, CRAFTSMAN,

AND

CALIFORNIA'S FIRST PRINTER

Self-portrait and signature of Agustin V. Zamorano

Don Agustin V. ZAMORANO

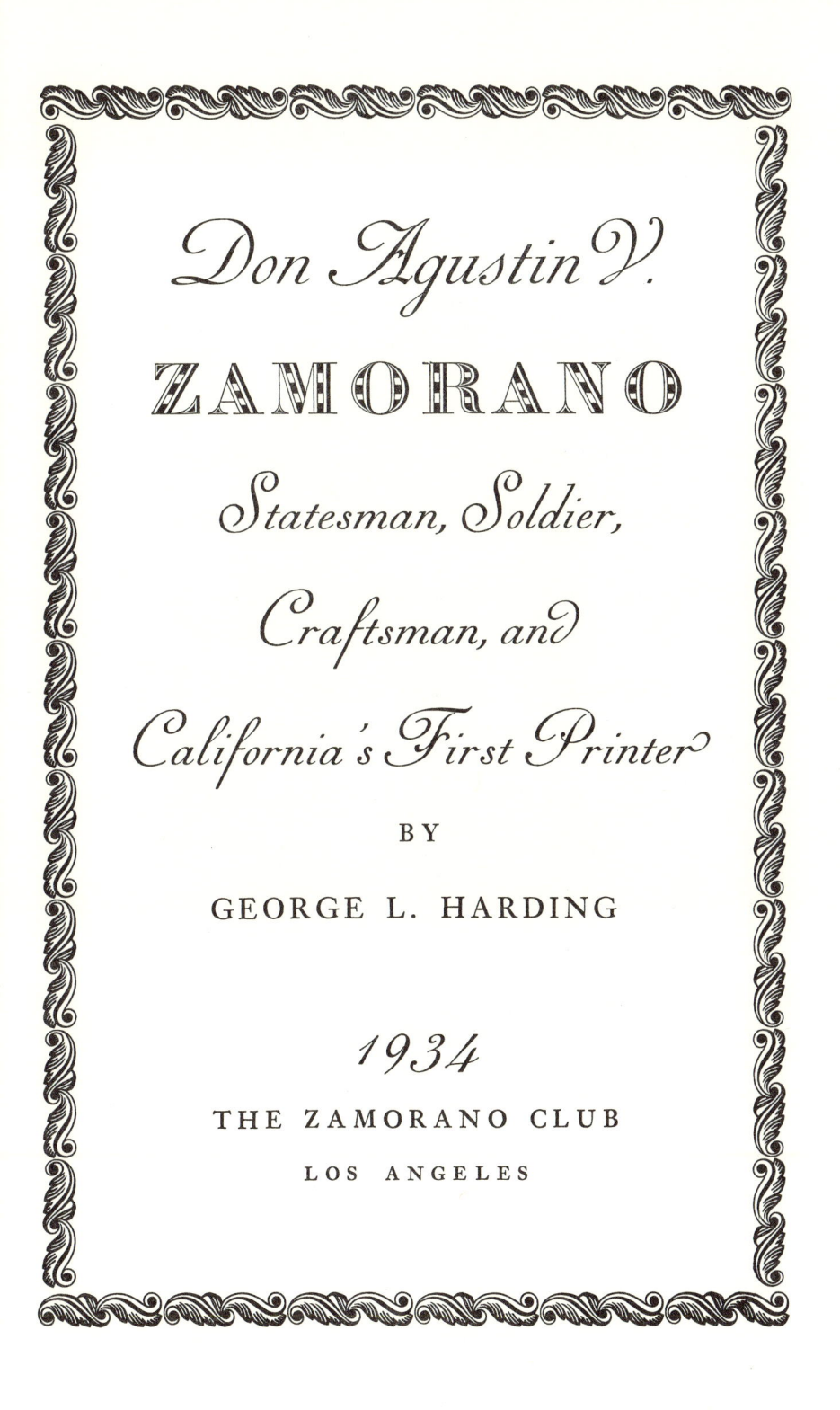

Statesman, Soldier, Craftsman, and California's First Printer

BY

GEORGE L. HARDING

1934

THE ZAMORANO CLUB

LOS ANGELES

*Copyright 1934
by
George L. Harding*

DEDICATED TO THE MEMORY OF

Edward C. Kemble

THE FIRST HISTORIAN OF

CALIFORNIA'S PIONEER PRESS

Preface

THIS book has but one purpose: to give the reader the life history of the man who introduced the art of printing into the territory within the boundaries of the modern American State of California.

Don Agustin Vicente Zamorano was a Mexican army officer who served in California during the period that territory was a part of the Republic of Mexico. He came in 1825 as the executive secretary of the Territory of Alta California. He served in that capacity for eleven years and as such was the second administrative officer in the territorial government. In addition, he was, for six years, commandant of the most important military post within the Territory, the *presidio* at Monterey. He was also acting governor for approximately one year. However, he has not been remembered for these services. These services to California have been recalled only by historians and by them in a curiously colored light. The cause of this neglect, as will be demonstrated, was that Zamorano, although not a Mexican by birth, did not consider his Mexican citizenship lightly and, consequently, was never in sympathy with or a party to the continual political intrigues carried on by those native Californians who achieved prominence in later years and supplied in great part, in dictated memoirs and histories, the materials from which American historians have written the history of California.

As an incidental private act, possibly solely for his personal satisfaction, Zamorano imported the first printing press to be set up west of the Rocky Mountains and on it caused to be printed the series of small books and official proclamations that are today the rarest of California imprints. For this he has been remembered.

These imprints, however, have preserved the name only of Agustin Vicente Zamorano. This study will attempt to rebuild the events of Zamorano's life, to recast the written history of his public services, and to give the history of the introduction of printing into California.

In the gathering of material for this study I have had the help of many persons. Their names and courtesies are so numerous as to make a detailed statement of them here impractical. I have credited them, wherever it was possible to do so, with their individual assistance in the footnotes. To all these, individually and collectively, I give my sincere thanks for the time and patience they have devoted to the cause.

There are, however, a few whose help has been much more than incidental and it would be ungracious not to state specifically the debt I owe them.

To Mr. Henry R. Wagner, of San Marino, belongs the credit, in a very large measure, for this study having been undertaken and, once started, brought to completion. Long a distinguished student, historian and bibliographer of the Spanish Southwest, Mr. Wagner has given without stint of his knowledge, time and energy in the search for source material. As this work lies within his chosen special field, his help has been invaluable. He has advised, criticised, found sources, remembered the project on his travels, read my manuscript, arranged for its publication, and proved himself generally a rare friend. My indebtedness to him is indeed great.

If I have succeeded in restating the history of Zamorano's public services in a more adequate manner, it is due to the assistance I have had from Dr. George Tays, of Berkeley. Most of the year 1929 was spent by Dr. Tays, under a Native Sons of the Golden West Traveling Fellowship in Pacific Coast History, in a search of the archives of the Mexican Government for historical material relative to the period in which Zamorano was so prominent a figure. His efforts were richly rewarded in the discovery of documents that throw a new and completely different light on those years. These I have described in considerable detail in my statement of sources. Dr. Tays has generously placed his copies of this material at my disposal and aided me in the translation of those I have quoted. He has also read my manuscript and given me the benefit of many helpful criticisms.

It is but fair to both Mr. Wagner and Dr. Tays to state that the organization of the material, the opinions stated and the conclusions drawn are my own. I assume full responsibility for them.

Preface

The descendants of Don Agustin have given me every assistance within their power. Mrs. Francis H. Throop, *née* María Anaís Estudillo, of San Luis Obispo, a granddaughter, possesses the largest collection of family documents available and placed them at my disposal without restrictions. She has also been energetic and faithful in the search for other sources. In addition, Mr. Agustin Vicente Zamorano 3d, of Azusa, the late Mr. Joseph Russell Henry Dalton, also of Azusa, Doña Luisa Ana Zamorano de Gilbert, of Tijuana, Baja California, all grandchildren of Don Agustin, and Mr. George Henry Dalton, of Tucson, Arizona, a great-grandson, have given me every assistance possible.

To Dr. Herbert E. Bolton and Dr. Herbert I. Priestley, Director and Librarian, respectively, of the Bancroft Library, University of California, Berkeley, and to Mr. Joseph J. Hill, late Assistant Librarian, I am beholden for innumerable courtesies and privileges over a long period of time. I am also indebted to Miss Mabel Gillis and Miss Caroline Wenzel, of the California State Library, Sacramento, and to Mr. Leslie E. Bliss and Mr. Willard O. Waters, of the Henry E. Huntington Library, San Marino, for many courtesies.

I am obliged to Mr. Henry H. Taylor and Mr. Edwin E. Grabhorn, two thoroughly experienced San Francisco printers, who, independently, verified my typographical findings and thereby rendered this study a unique service. Mr. Oscar Lewis, of San Francisco, has earned my thanks for his many helpful criticisms and suggestions.

Lastly, I am grateful to the members of The Zamorano Club, Los Angeles, for making the publication of this study possible.

George L. Harding

Palo Alto, October 1, 1934

Contents

PREFACE vii

CHAPTER I. California's History, 1769 to 1831. 1
    I. California's History.

CHAPTER II. Zamorano's Antecedents. 10
    I. Don Gonzalo Zamorano y González.
    II. Guanajuato.
    III. To California.

CHAPTER III. Echeandia's Administration, 1825 to 1830. 22
    I. San Diego.
    II. Santa Barbara.
    III. Monterey.
    IV. The Ship *Franklin*.
    V. San Diego Again.
    VI. The Solis Revolt.
    VII. Don José María Padrés.
    VIII. Monterey Again.

CHAPTER IV. Victoria As Governor, January to December 1831. 45
    I. Echeandia's Secularization Decree of January 6, 1831.
    II. Victoria's Rule.
    III. The Plan of San Diego.
    IV. The Battle at Cahuenga Pass and Its Results.
    V. Don Romualdo Pacheco.

CHAPTER V. Zamorano and the Plan of San Diego, December 1831 and January 1832. 70
    I. Zamorano Rejects the Plan of San Diego.
    II. Echeandia Intimidates the Legislature.

CHAPTER VI. Zamorano As Acting Governor, February 1832 to January 1833. 90
    I. The Monterey Council of February 1, 1832.
    II. Echeandia Refuses to Recognize Zamorano.
    III. The Negotiations between the Rival Claimants.

IV. Zamorano as Governor.
  V. The Arrival of Brigadier General Figueroa.

Chapter VII. Figueroa, Gutiérrez, Chico, and again Gutiérrez as Governors, January 1833 to November 1836.   157
  I. Brigadier General Don José Figueroa.
  II. Lieutenant Colonel Don Nicolás Gutiérrez.
  III. Colonel Don Mariano Chico.
  IV. Lieutenant Colonel Gutiérrez Again Acts as Governor.

Chapter VIII. The Printing Press Arrives in California.   178
  I. Contemporary References to the Press.
  II. Printing in Alta California before June 1834.
  III. The Ship *Lagoda*.
  IV. The Press and Its Equipment.
  V. Zamorano's First Printer.
  VI. Zamorano's Second Printer.

Chapter IX. Zamorano's Remaining Years in California, November 1836 to the Spring of 1838.   211
  I. San Diego's Opposition to Alvarado.
  II. Zamorano Again Serves as Acting Governor.
  III. The Campaign of 1837.
  IV. Don Carlos Antonio Carrillo Claims the Governorship.

Chapter X. Zamorano's Last Years, 1838 to 1842.   251
  I. In Mexico.
  II. Brigadier General Don Manuel Micheltorena.
  III. Zamorano's Death.

Chapter XI. Zamorano's Family: Conclusion.   258
  I. Doña Luisa.
  II. Zamorano's Children.
  III. Don Agustin V. Zamorano.

Sources   275

Appendix. Genealogy.   285
  I. The Family of Don Agustin V. Zamorano.
  II. The Ancestry of Don Agustin V. Zamorano.
  III. The Ancestry of Doña María Luisa Argüello de Zamorano.

Index   295

Illustrations

Self-Portrait of Don Agustin V. Zamorano — *Frontispiece*

Plaza of St. Augustine, Florida — *Facing Page* 14

Monterey in 1829 — 30
From an unfinished pencil sketch by Alfred Robinson

Plano del territorio de la alta California del Capitan de Fragata D. José María Narvaez. Año de 1830. — 32
From original manuscript map in Bancroft Library

Letterheads printed from wood-blocks, 1826-1829 — 184

Letterheads printed from type, 1830 — 186

Sealed-paper headings, 1831-1834 — 188

Printed endorsement on Mexican proclamation, May 1834 — 190

Aviso al Publico, Imprenta de Zamorano y Ca., 1834 — 196

Small Pica No. 1, Specimen of 1846, Boston Type and Stereotype Foundry — 198

Governor Chico's *Discurso* of May 27, 1836 — 206

Chapter 1.

CALIFORNIA'S HISTORY, 1769 TO 1831.

IN 1825, the Territory of Alta California was expecting a new governor. The Secretary of War and Marine, in Mexico, had written to Acting Governor Don Luis Antonio Argüello on February 1, that the President had appointed Lieutenant Colonel of Engineers Don José María de Echeandia to the civil and military commands of both the Californias.[1] Again, on May 11, the Secretary had written Don Luis that Señor Echeandia was on his way[2] and this news had been transmitted to the *presidios* and *pueblos* of the Territory in a circular letter dated July 28.[3]

Therefore, the commandant of the *presidio* at San Diego was not taken by surprise when he received a letter from the new general commandant, written on October 8 at San Vicente in Baja California, advising him that he expected to reach San Diego soon and asking that fresh horses and mules be sent down the trail to meet him.[4] A corporal and his squad, with the needed animals, left hurriedly and soon disappeared in the dust to the south.[5] Excitement and confusion reigned in the rambling and dilapidated *presidio* atop the hill overlooking the harbor of San Diego as quarters were cleaned, uniforms mended and gear polished, while speculation ran on as to what the new governor would be like and as to the identity of the young officers said to be with him. On about the 16th of October, the cavalcade

---

[1] Pedraza to Argüello, Mexico, February 1, 1825, in *Sup. Govt. St. Pap.*, MS., III, 3.
[2] Castro to Echeandia, Mexico, May 11, 1825, forwarding copy of letter to Argüello, *idem*.
[3] Argüello, Circular letter to *presidios*, Monterey, July 28, 1825, in *Dept. Rec.*, MS., II, 37.
[4] Echeandia to Commandant of San Diego, San Vicente, October 8, 1825, *ibid.*, II, 4.
[5] Hittell, *History of California*, II, 83-4, giving his source as *Dept. St. Pap., Ben.*, LIV, 46-7; these items were not included in Bancroft's transcripts of the provincial archives.

was sighted.[6] Captain Don Francisco María Ruiz drew up his command before the *presidio* gate and the women and children hurried to windows and other vantage points from which to get a glimpse of the great man.

In Señor Echeandia they were destined to disappointment. He was a tall gaunt individual, physically exhausted from the hardships of the march overland from Loreto, shivering and complaining of the cold and desiring, for the present, only a place to rest and recuperate his strength. In his party, however, were many to offset the first unfavorable impression of the new chief—especially in the eyes of the *señoritas*. The wear and accumulated dust of a long march across mountains and deserts could dim but not conceal the youth and dash of the group of officers with him.

There were Ensign Don José María Ramírez, a cavalry officer, Ensign Don Juan José Rocha, Ensign Don Rodrigo del Pliego, Ensign Don Patricio Estrada, who commanded a detachment of infantry from the battalion known as *Fijo de Hidalgo*, and Lieutenant Don Miguel González, with his platoon of artillerymen. There was the general commandant's aide-de-camp, Ensign Don Romualdo Pacheco, who was tall and slight, with the most courtly manners. And there was the latter's bosom friend, Ensign Don Agustin Vicente Zamorano, fair skinned, blue eyed, with jet black hair and of medium height, slightly inclined toward stoutness, who was coming as the executive secretary of the Territory.

I. California's History.

Originally, the name "California" was applied to the entire northwest coast of New Spain. In time it was used more specifically as the name of the peninsula we know today as Baja, or Lower, California. After the establishment of missions and colonies there, the frontier lands to the northward became known first as "Nueva," or New, and then as "Alta," or Upper, California. For our purposes, the boundaries of California may be considered as coincident with those of our present state of that name.

---

[6] Echeandia to Commandant of Monterey, San Diego, October 18, 1825, in *Dept. Rec.*, MS., II, 5.

In 1769, at the instance of Don José de Gálvez, *Visitador General* of New Spain, the first expedition of colonists set out from Mexico for Alta California. This party, under the leadership of Captain Don Gaspar de Portolá, California's first governor, and the famous head of the missionaries, Fr. Junípero Serra, O.F.M., reached San Diego in July. There, on July 16, 1769, the first mission in Alta California was dedicated to San Diego de Alcalá.

Forthwith, an expedition set out overland, under Portolá, to explore the northern coast and to locate the harbor of Monterey. This expedition reached Monterey, camped there, and passed on, without recognizing it. On October 31, from the ocean shore on the southern part of the San Francisco peninsula, the Farallones and Point Reyes were sighted. A detachment, under Sergeant José Francisco Ortega, was sent forward to reach Point Reyes. During their absence, soldiers from the main body, while hunting, climbed the nearby hills and saw, for the first time, San Francisco Bay. Ortega's detachment soon returned as they were unable to pass the Golden Gate. In a short time, the expedition turned south again and returned to San Diego. Another trip was made in the next year. This time Monterey Bay was recognized and the mission of San Carlos Borromeo founded on its shore. Thereafter, there was a generally rapid progress in the exploration and settlement of Alta California. By the end of the eighteenth century there were eighteen missions with a neophyte Indian population of approximately thirteen thousand, under the tutelage of forty friars.

As the missions were the outstanding feature of California's history under both Spanish and Mexican rule, it is well that we consider their purpose and progress. The mission system was an integral part of the mechanics of Spanish expansion in the new world. Since the King was, in fact, the head of the Church, as well as of the State, in the Spanish dominions, the Cross usually accompanied the Sword. Missions were promptly founded on nearly every frontier as a second line of defense. Under the care and direction of the missionaries, a flourishing community would arise where none had been before. When the aborigines had absorbed sufficient European civilization, the mission became a parish, its church was turned over to the secular priesthood and the missionaries then moved on to a new frontier to establish new outposts of civilization and the Christian faith. Thus to the untiring and pious efforts of the missionaries is due, in large measure, the credit for the rapid and thorough conquest of Spanish America. Through the centuries, in an ever widening circle, this cycle of events went on until Alta California, the last frontier, was reached.

In all, twenty-one missions were finally established in Alta California. These through years of labor on the part of the Indian neophytes under the careful, frugal and devoutly earnest administration of the missionaries built up great estates of orchards, vineyards, grain fields, flocks of sheep, and herds of cattle and stood in startling contrast to the progress made on the *ranchos reales* run, supposedly, for the support of the military stationed at the *presidios*. No grants of land, in a legal sense, were ever made or promised to the mission establishments. They were spiritual institutions entrusted with the instruction of the neophytes and holding in trust the property that should be given or produced for that purpose against the time when the Indians should acquire sufficient training to accept and discharge the duties and responsibilities of citizenship.

Great indeed was the material progress from the missionaries' labors. As much can not be said, however, for their work in the cause of true spiritual progress in California. In this field the permanent results attained were extremely meager. In fact, nearly every trace of the spiritual labors of the friars disappeared with their passing from control. This was due not to lack of zeal on the part of the missionary fathers and not to the methods employed, which had been proven successful in other parts of Spanish America, but to the inferiority of the Californian Indian, since classified by anthropologists as being among the dullest and lowest of the Indians that inhabited the United States.[7] The energy and devotion expended by the missionaries did not, could not civilize their wards but only made them hopelessly dependent.

There can be no question as to the sincerity of the motives of the friars. There can be no doubt that their intentions were humane as well as pious. They gladly labored and gave their lives in the service

---

[7] Hodge, *Handbook of American Indians*, 191, 895. *Cf.* also Kroeber, *Handbook of the Indians of California*.

of their neophytes. Therein lies the tragedy of the California missions. "But after all, upon this whole toil of the missions, considered in itself, one looks back with respectful regret, as upon one of the most devout and praiseworthy of mortal efforts, and, in view of its avowed intentions, one of the most complete and fruitless of human failures."[3] The significance of the missions lies not in their spiritual conquests but in their beginning and making possible the colonization of California.

Not only missions, however, but also *presidios*, garrisoned by Spanish soldiers, and *pueblos*, inhabited by Spanish colonists, were included in the plan for colonizing Alta California. The country was divided into four military districts, each with its *presidio*. The first two of these were founded at the same time as the first two missions —in 1769, at San Diego, and in 1770, at Monterey. The third, that of San Francisco, was also established at the same time as its mission, in 1776. The fourth *presidio*, that of Santa Barbara, was founded in 1782, four years before the mission. The first *pueblo* to be established was that of *San José de Guadalupe*, founded in November 1776, with an original population of fourteen families. The second was that of *Nuestra Señora la Reina de los Angeles*, founded in September 1781. Its original population was twelve families, forty-six persons in all.

The first foreign visitor to California was La Pérouse, the Frenchman, in 1786. In 1792, Captain George Vancouver stopped in California on his visit to the coast. The first American ship, the *Otter*, of Boston, appeared at Monterey in 1796. The first Russian ship came to San Francisco Bay in 1806. On board was Nikolai Petrovich Rezánof, chamberlain of the Russian Court, seeking grain and supplies for the starving Russian colony at Sitka. Commercial intercourse with foreigners was strictly forbidden but the Russian gained his point after tedious negotiation with the governor and making successful love to Doña Concepcion, the beautiful young daughter of Captain Don José Darío Argüello, commandant of the *presidio* at San Francisco. Rezánof sailed under a solemn promise to return and marry his new beloved as soon as possible. He died while on his way across Siberia. The news of that sad event did not reach his betrothed until many

---

[3] Royce, *California*, 16.

years later; meanwhile she waited patiently for his return. Out of this incident came California's most famous romance of Spanish days, immortalized in Bret Harte's poem and Mrs. Atherton's novel.

With political events of the period of Spanish government we have no need to deal. Mexico, in 1821, achieved her independence of the Spanish Crown and fell heir to Alta California. All that, however, happened far away and meant little and brought no immediate change to the Californians. In the following year, a commissioner in the person of a worldly and dissolute clerical, Canónigo Agustín Fernández de San Vicente, was sent from Mexico to see that the new order of things was properly installed in California. He arrived at Monterey September 26, 1822. Three days later, a few Californians stood in silence as the red and gold ensign of Spain was struck and the green, white and red standard of Emperor Agustín I, of Mexico, was hoisted in its place. Don Pablo Vicente de Solá, the last governor of California under Spanish rule, felt it necessary to explain to the emissary of the new government, "They do not cheer because they are unused to independence."[9] Alta California had become a Mexican province. The first provincial *diputacion*, or legislature, was called into being in November. That body, at the instigation of the commissioner, chose Don Luis Antonio Argüello, a native of California, son of a former governor, and commandant of the *presidio* of San Francisco, to be the first Mexican governor and he assumed office on November 22.

Canónigo Fernández and his retinue, according to the accounts left by the older Californians, immediately upon their arrival gave themselves up to a merry life. Gambling was their favorite diversion but they were skilled in all the vices. On their visit to Mission Santa Clara, Father Magin, a man of austere and exemplary habits, was so shocked at what his eyes beheld that he gave his guests a polite but insistent invitation to depart. Such conduct was not lost on the Indians and lower classes to the horror of the Californians. The departure of the commissioner brought a feeling of relief and Don Luis Argüello is said to have remarked to one of his officers, as he stood on the beach at Monterey and watched the vessel disappear, "If those are the great

---

[9] Vallejo, *Historia de California*, MS., I, 287-9.

men of Mexico, what are the ragamuffins?"[10] The change of flags, however, was but an incident; life went on as before and the four years of Argüello's rule passed peacefully and quickly.

The empire of Agustin I of Mexico did not long endure and was followed by the Republic, organized under the Constitution of 1824. In 1825, the central government of the Mexican Republic sent a new governor to Alta California to succeed Argüello. With his arrival, the Spanish period in California's history came definitely to an end; the golden pastoral age was over. A period of turmoil and strife soon began that did not end until Alta California, some twenty years later, found peace under the flag of the United States. The change from the conservative and paternalistic system of Spain to the careless and unstable administration of Mexico cost California a terrible price and gave her very little in return. The years of Mexican rule completely destroyed the economic structure of her missions and demonstrated the unfitness of her inhabitants for self-government.

During the years of Echeandia's administration, the province gradually grew toward the Mexican ideals of republicanism and the secularization of the missions. In these years the seeds were germinated of the strife that was to become endemic in California. The first of these was the instability of the national government of Mexico. From the very day of independence, Mexico fell on evil ways; liberalism contended with conservatism, federalism with centralism, and internal dissension became a habit. Constitutions followed plans and plans followed constitutions as Iturbide, Victoria, Guerrero, Bustamante, and a long line of others succeeded each other in the presidential chair. Radical and supposedly republican ideas became the vogue as every effort was made to copy the language and usage of the French Revolution. The old and dignified address of *Don* became *Ciudadano*, that is Citizen, and, by legislative enactment in 1827, all official letters and documents were required to be closed with the Voltairean phrase, *"Dios y Libertad"*—"God and Liberty," rather than with the time-honored Spanish, Old Christian, *"Dios le guarde muchos años"* —"God keep you many years." All of this had its repercussions in far off Alta California where they disturbed the missionaries and older

[10] *Ibid.*, I, 327.

rancheros but were accepted eagerly by the younger generation as progress.

The second cause of California's unrest during the Mexican period of her history was the problem of secularizing the missions. The original intention of Spain, as we have seen, was to use the missions as an instrument in the civilization of the indigenes and the settlement of the land. The failure of the Californian Indian to show capacity for civilization was ignored by republican Mexico; the missions had long passed their allotted years under the missionaries and must be secularized. The efforts of the friars to explain the true state of their wards were misconstrued as a worldly reluctance to surrender the control of the wealth and temporalities under their jurisdiction. When the regular annual remittance of funds from the Spanish Royal Treasury ceased with Mexican independence, the missions proved the only economic support of the military. The lack and suffering of the troops, relieved only by contributions from the missions, served as a constant reminder of the wealth and independence of these to the military and civil authorities. Echeandia early gave his attention to plans for secularization. In 1826, he issued a decree that provided for the partial removal of the neophytes at Missions San Diego, Santa Barbara, and San Carlos Borromeo from the authority of the friars. In 1830, he brought before the legislative body a secularization plan which was approved and forwarded to the central government for confirmation before being placed in operation. The anti-mission party came into being under Echeandia and found in him a willing tool. Before turning over his office to his successor, in January 1831, fearing a reversal or modification of his policies, he rashly attempted, by trickery, to put his scheme into immediate effect. Thenceforth, secularization was an important and bitter issue. In the struggle that ensued the missions bore the brunt of the vacillating policy of the national government and the rapacity and greed of the local politicians. In the end, they were not secularized but rather plundered to their ruin by politically appointed administrators, their buildings finally confiscated and sold to supply governmental funds, and their neophytes turned out to shift for themselves.

A third cause of the unrest prevalent during this new period was the influx of undesirable immigrants from Mexico. Before independence, the population of Alta California was homogeneous and its people contented in the life they led. For some time after the Mexican Revolution, California, because of its remoteness, was looked upon as a proper place for exile and penal servitude. There came *vaqueros* from Sinaloa and Sonora, gangsters from the interior cities, and convicts in the guise of soldiers under officers with characters but little better than those of their men. To be sure, there came also men of substantial worth, but they were in the minority.

A fourth cause of the turmoil and strife that became habitual in California was a group of native sons—*hijos del pais*, who were just coming to maturity and were anxious to play a part in governmental affairs. They were from the older families, sons of men who had died or grown gray in the service of Spain, and were born to the best social position in the Territory. They fostered an intense local patriotism and considered themselves superior in blood and ability to those sent from Mexico in official capacities. In the north they were the Castros, the Vallejos, the Alvarados, the Estudillos, and the Estradas; while in the southern districts they were the Picos, the Argüellos, the Carrillos, and the Bandinis. All of these young men were imbued with the then popular ideas of French republicanism as interpreted in Mexico, all were inclined to look with envious eyes on the temporalities of the missions, and all were anxious to advance their personal fortunes.

A fifth cause of many of California's troubles in this period was the intense rivalry and sectional jealousy that grew and rankled between the *sureños* and the *norteños*—the south and the north. On the few occasions in which the two sections agreed, harmony among the Californians was soon destroyed by sectional bickerings; if one section sponsored or approved an idea or movement, the other was certain to oppose.

Chapter ii.

Don Agustin Vicente Zamorano's Antecedents.

DON Agustin V. Zamorano was distinctly the product of his heredity and the environment of his youth. Born into a line that had occupied positions of public trust and responsibility for generations, reared by a father who spent a lifetime in the colonial service of the Spanish Crown, and spending his youth in Guanajuato, the very center of the events connected with the struggle for Mexican independence, he was a conservative but not a Tory, a liberal but not a radical. He stood for progress, but respected the weight of authority. He was a republican, but a lover of Spanish institutions. He loved peace because he knew how terrible war could be.

I. Don Gonzalo Zamorano y González.

On the 4th of January in the year 1741, the pastor of the parish church of *Santa María de Castillo*, in the Town of Muriel, within the jurisdiction of the City of Arévalo, Bishopric of Ávila, in Old Castile, Spain, wrote on page 209 of his baptismal register that he had on that day,

> solemnly baptised and anointed with the holy oils a boy named Gonzalo, the legitimate son of Francisco Zamorano and Juaquína González, his legal wife, citizens of this town, the father being a native of the Town of Orcajo de las Torres and the mother a native of the Town of Rasueros, both in this Bishopric of Ávila. The child's godparents were Don Francisco de Mier, proper priest of the Town of Las Oncaladas, and Doña Theresa González, blood aunt of the baptised on the maternal side. I made known the spiritual kinship to the godparents. The baptised one was born on the twenty-second day of December, seventeen hundred and forty. So that it may be of record, I sign this.
>
> Don Juan Portero.[1]

---

[1] *Gonzalo Zamorano, Doc.*, MS., No. 12 is a certified copy of this entry.

Zamorano's Antecedents

As both the Zamorano and González families claimed descent from those hardy Goths who had found refuge in the mountains of Burgos during the spoilation of Spain by the Moors, this boy had the good fortune to be born into an ancient and honorable family of Old Castile. Both families were known as Old Christians. His father and grandfather had been familiars in the Holy Office of the Inquisition, officers in the Brotherhood of the Most Holy, *alcaldes* and *corregidores* of the towns of their residence.[2]

Don Francisco Zamorano, uncle of the boy Gonzalo's father, after long service as major in His Majesty's Royal Guards, had been appointed, in 1698, Deputy Captain General by Land and Sea of the Province of Chili, in New Spain.[3] Don Alonzo Jimenez Zamorano, the boy's own uncle, served, by royal appointment, for thirty-five years as spiritual administrator of the Royal Hospital of the Immaculate Conception in Madrigal de las Torres. This institution prospered exceedingly under his direction and *El Santisimo Christo de las Injurias*, venerated in its Royal Chapel, was known far and wide for its many miraculous cures.[4]

Gonzalo reached maturity in the midst of that renaissance Spain experienced during the reign of Carlos III, a period, in all her history since the sixteenth century, least wounding to Spanish pride. It was an era of splendid achievement and in the field of her vast and far flung colonial empire, talent and energy abounded. The year 1773 found Don Gonzalo Zamorano at the Court of the King, in Madrid, seeking an appointment in His Majesty's colonial service. On June 4, 1774, Don Juan Felix de Rujula, chronicler and king-at-arms to the Court of Spain, issued to Don Gonzalo a *Certificacio de Armas*,[5] which confirmed his rights to the arms of the Zamorano and González families, certified to the antiquity and legitimacy of his lineage, and

[2] *Ibid.*, Nos. 4 to 11, inclusive, are transcripts of petitions, warrants, summons, and testimony before local magistrates in the District of Arévalo, Bishopric of Avila, Old Castile, in connection with a judicial inquiry into the lineage and antecedents of Don Gonzalo Zamorano.
[3] *Ibid.*, No. 11 includes a certified copy of this appointment, dated July 8, 1698.
[4] *Ibid.*, Nos. 1 to 3, inclusive, are statements made before notaries regarding the services of Don Alonzo Jimenez Zamorano.
[5] *Certificacio de Armas de D. Gonzalo Zamorano y González*, MS., Madrid, June 4, 1774, in the possession of Mr. George Henry Dalton, of Tucson, Arizona.

stated, with proper circumlocution, that he was an Old Christian, "clean of the blood of Moors, Jews, and the newly converted to our Holy Catholic Faith." Whereupon, Don Gonzalo received an appointment to a junior position in the *Contaduria General de Exercito y Real Hacienda*—the office of the comptroller general of the army and Royal Treasury, in the Island of Cuba, at Havana, with a salary of forty *pesos* per month.[6] He probably reached Havana early in the year 1775.

On August 30, 1780, Don Gonzalo was made paymaster and finance officer of an expedition under Don Bernardo de Gálvez against Pensacola, in Florida, then held by the British. This expedition was part of Spain's contribution to the cause of the English colonies in America, then in revolt against their mother country. Pensacola was taken and Don Gonzalo returned to Havana in June 1781, and reverted to his place in the office of the comptroller general.[7]

Under the terms of the Treaty of Paris, signed September 3, 1783, Louisiana and West Florida were retained by Spain and East Florida ceded to her by Great Britain. These new territories fell to the jurisdiction of the *Capitancia General* of Cuba and Don Vicente Manuel de Zéspedes was appointed governor of East Florida. Don Gonzalo Zamorano y González was appointed *ministro contador tesorero y comisario de guerra de la plaza de San Agustin de la Florida*, or auditor, treasurer, and quartermaster, at the capital of the province, with an annual salary of twelve hundred *pesos*.[8]

Before leaving for his new post, Don Gonzalo was married, on May 6, 1784, in the Cathedral Church of the Immaculate Conception, Havana, to Doña Francisca Sales del Corral, a native of Havana and the daughter of Captain Don Felix del Corral, of the Royal Navy, and his wife, Doña Juana de Dios Garcia Menocal.[9] The groom was in his forty-third year and the bride in her seventeenth.

Don Gonzalo and his bride reached St. Augustine, with Governor

---

[6] *Gonzalo Zamorano, Doc.*, MS., No. 15 is a certified copy of a statement, dated at Havana, March 28, 1810, by Don Juan José de la Hoz, comptroller general of the Island of Cuba, regarding the service of Don Gonzalo Zamorano.   [7] *Idem.*   [8] *Idem.*
[9] *Ibid.*, No. 19 is a copy of Entry No. 431, page 147 and over, 7th Book of Register of Spanish Marriages in the Cathedral of the Immaculate Conception, Havana, Cuba, certified by Don Francisco Font, Sexton of the Cathedral.

Zéspedes, in June 1784.[10] It is recorded that, on July 17, he purchased a slave from John Allen, a British subject who was leaving because of the change in flags.[11] At that time the population of East Florida, aside from Indians, did not exceed fifteen hundred people. Many of these were negro slaves and most of the remaining were British, Greek and Maiorcan.[12]

The *padron*, or census, of St. Augustine made in 1793 lists Zamorano and his family as living in the house occupied by the Royal Treasury at the corner of the Plaza and San Carlos street. By that year, his marriage had been blessed with four children, three daughters and one son.[13] The house at the corner of the Plaza and San Carlos, now Charlotte, street was built by the English, prior to 1784, and was still standing in 1821 when Florida was purchased by the United States. With the American occupation, this building became known as the "Custom House" and continued to be used for governmental purposes for many years. It was razed in 1871 and a hotel built on the site.[14]

It was probably in this house that Don Gonzalo's seventh child, a son, was born on May 5, 1798. Three days later he was carried to the new church on the opposite side of the Plaza where, with Doña Rosa de la Luz as his godmother, he was baptised by the assistant pastor, Father Don Miguel O'Reilly, and given the name of Agustin Juan Vicente.[15] The church in which the ceremony took place is the present Roman Catholic Cathedral of St. Augustine. It was begun in 1791 and completed and dedicated in 1797. Its construction was paid for

[10] Brevard, *History of Florida*, I, 247.
[11] *Escrituras, 1784-1787*, MS., Folio 2v, in Spanish East Florida Archives, Manuscript Division, Library of Congress. The *Escrituras* for the years 1784 to 1808, inclusive, record many transactions to which Don Gonzalo Zamorano was a party.
[12] Whitaker, *The Spanish-American Frontier*, 21.
[13] *Padron de San Agustin de la Florida, 1793*, MS., in Spanish East Florida Archives, Manuscript Division, Library of Congress.
[14] Map of St. Augustine prepared in 1788 by Don Mariano de la Rocque, in Department of Interior, Washington, General Land Office, Town Site Map Room, Volume 7. Also, letter of December 4, 1933, from Emily L. Wilson, Historian, Historical Society of St. Augustine. I am indebted to Miss Wilson for many courtesies.
[15] Entry No. 443, Page 209, Book II of Register of White Baptisms, Cathedral of St. Augustine, Florida. I am indebted to the Reverend J. Nunan, D.D. and Reverend J. H. O'Keeffe, of the Cathedral staff, for data from their old register.

largely by governmental funds supplied through Don Gonzalo's office. The first building forms the nave of today's church and the original facade, Moorish in design, still stands.[16] It is the church in the left background in the accompanying illustration of the Plaza of St. Augustine. The house in which Don Gonzalo Zamorano is believed to have lived is that with the dormer windows seen through the trees to the right of the obelisk.[17]

In 1809 or 1810, after twenty-five years of service at St. Augustine, Don Gonzalo Zamorano received a promotion in the form of the appointment as *ministro contador de la tesoreria foranea* at Acapulco, a seaport on the west coast of Mexico,[18] and moved his family there by way of Havana, Vera Cruz, and Mexico.

II. Guanajuato.

The territory included within the boundaries of the Province of Guanajuato, in New Spain, was first visited by Spaniards in the days of the Conquest. Soon after, its silver mines were discovered and a small fort was established near the site of the present city of Guanajuato in about 1560. Because of the richness of the mines, a town soon sprang up about the fort. In 1679, the King of Spain granted it the title of *villa* under the name of *Santa Fé de Guanajuato*. In 1741, the town was raised to the dignity of a city and granted a coat of arms.[19] In 1786, with the city as its capital, the province was organized as the *Intendencia de Guanajuato* and became one of the wealthiest and most important in all New Spain. In the early years of the nineteenth century, there were nearly two thousand mines in the province and many thousand people were employed in these mines and the mills for the recovery of the metal. Also, the agricultural and dairying industries of the province were thriving. Its capital was a city of nearly seventy-five thousand inhabitants. But the Province of Guanajuato was to cradle the Mexican Revolution and its capital to suffer most cruelly in loss of life and ruin of prosperity.

---

[16] *Sketch of the Historical Cathedral of St. Augustine*, a folder available at the Cathedral.
[17] This illustration is reproduced from the frontispiece of Fairbanks, *The History and Antiquities of the City of St. Augustine, Florida*.
[18] *Gonzalo Zamorano, Doc.*, MS., No. 14.   [19] Bancroft, *History of Mexico*, IV, 130-3.

Plaza of St. Augustine, Florida

In the town of Dolores, eleven leagues from the provincial capital, on September 16, 1810, Fr. Miguel Hidalgo y Costilla raised his famous call, *El Grito de Dolores,* "*Viva Nuestra Señora de Guadalupe! Viva la independencia!*" This battle cry, invoking the patron saint of the Indians, made its appeal to the racial and class hatreds of the oppressed and soon a rabble numbering many thousands had flocked to Hidalgo's standard. After occupying the towns of San Miguel and Celaya, the next move of the insurgents was against the capital, Guanajuato. There the *Intendant* gathered the Spanish population and such forces as he had at his command, together with the public treasury, into the public granary, a great, two story, stone building called the "Alhóndiga de Granaditas," as famous in Mexican history as the Bastile in that of France. Here a determined stand was made on September 28, but the unceasing tides of infuriated Indians rolled against it and finally over it at an enormous cost in flesh and blood. The Spaniards were butchered and the city sacked and fired in a holocaust of fury that lasted for hours.

As Guanajuato was the first city of importance to fall before the revolutionists, it was also the first to feel the mailed force of the royalist arms. General Calleja retook the city on November 25 and there followed reprisals for the events of September and a second baptism in blood and fire.[20] Stern measures and prompt action soon broke the rebellion. Its leaders were captured and shot. The heads of Hidalgo and his three chief lieutenants were hung in iron cages from the corners of the Alhóndiga de Granaditas in Guanajuato as grim warnings to rebels of their just reward at the hands of Spain. There remained but small and scattered guerilla bands to carry on the fight for independence.

In the reorganization of the provincial government that followed, there were many vacancies, because of deaths, to be filled. One of the most important of these was that of *ministro de Real Hacienda tesorero de la caxas principales,* or provincial treasurer. To this office, Don Gonzalo Zamorano received a provisional appointment, on March 18, 1811, from Don Francisco Xavier Venegas, Viceroy of New Spain.[21] This appointment was confirmed, in Cadiz, by the Re-

---

[20] *Ibid.,* IV, 133-57; 216-28. Also, Priestley, *History of Mexico,* 206-22.
[21] *Gonzalo Zamorano, Doc.,* MS., No. 14 is the original of this appointment.

gency in the name of Fernando VII, on July 25, 1811, with an annual salary of three thousand *pesos*.[22]

But the Guanajuato to which Don Gonzalo removed his family, in his son Agustin Vicente's fourteenth year, was not the prosperous city described above. War had left the unhappy city with less than a tenth of her previous population, the head of Hidalgo still hung in its cage, grass was growing in her unfrequented streets, and abandoned houses could be had rent free. Nevertheless, the rich natural resources of the province and the difficulties of the immediate future made the office of provincial treasurer an important one and the appointment was a distinct compliment to the ability and loyalty of Don Gonzalo; he was at the height of his career. He continued to fill this office until 1820, in which year his successor was installed.[23] Whether he gave up his office, in his eightieth year, because of death or because of retirement, I have been unable to learn.

The crushing defeat given Hidalgo and his followers did not entirely extinguish the flame of independence. Through the following ten years, under varying vicissitudes, there was always some one to raise anew the banner of the Virgin of Guadalupe as it appeared to fall from the hand of her latest devotee. *El Grito de Dolores*, to the confusion of the occupant of the viceregal office, continued to be raised, first in one corner and then in another of the land. Early in the year 1821, as the last feeble resistance of the insurgents seemed about to be stamped out, the cause of independence received a new impetus and burst upon the royal government with such force that Mexico became a free nation. From a series of sporadic and short-lived eruptions of the oppressed masses, the Revolution took on new color and strength from the adherence and support of persons of position and power who previously had been active in its suppression.

On February 24, 1821, Agustin de Iturbide, the commander of a royalist army, issued with Vicente Guerrero, an insurgent guerilla

---

[22] *Ibid.*, No. 16 is the original of this appointment.

[23] Zuñiga y Ontiveros, *Calendario Manual y Guia de Forasteros En Mexico*, an annual publication, lists Don Gonzalo Zamorano as *contador* of the *Caxa Principal de la Intendencia y provincia de Guanajuato* for the years 1811 to 1813, inclusive; and as *tesorero* for the years 1814 to 1819, inclusive. Don Antonio Vallejo is listed as holding the latter office in 1820.

chief he had been sent to suppress, the *Plan de Iguala*, which provided a basis, under the three guarantees of the Catholic religion, absolute independence and racial equality, on which New Spain could unite to throw off the Spanish yoke.

The cause of this Plan was greatly furthered by the almost immediate adherence of Anastacio Bustamante and the addition of his troops to the *Trigarante* forces. Bustamante had been in command of the royal troops in the province of Guanajuato with the rank of colonel. Educated as a Doctor of Medicine, he had early taken to a military career and had risen rapidly in rank. Iturbide soon made him a general. He was a person of fine presence, cultivated, and a lover of civilization. It appears that he had been, in Guanajuato, a close friend of Don Gonzalo Zamorano and was well acquainted with the latter's family. He continued to occupy a prominent place in Mexican history as we shall later see. From Iguala, Iturbide advanced his forces toward Guanajuato where he arrived about the middle of April and was received amidst the plaudits of the people. From this point he planned his march southward against the capital, Mexico, with Bustamante in command of one column of his forces.

By the time of these events, Agustin Juan Vicente Zamorano was a young man. With his close friend and constant companion, Don Romualdo Pacheco, a native of Guanajuato, he heard the *Plan de Iguala* read in the Plaza, watched the arrival of Iturbide and his welcome at the hands of his father's friend, Colonel Bustamante. Although both of these young men were of Spanish blood, they were natives of America and were not long in deciding to join the forces of independence. On May 1, 1821, Bustamante gave a commission as cadet to the son of his old friend in the Treasury and assigned him to the regiment known as the 6th Regular Battalion.[24] A few days later, on May 4, he also commissioned as cadet, Don Romualdo Pacheco.[25]

Soon after, these young men were in the field with Bustamante's army, taking part in the skirmishes on the hills of San Antonio and San Miguel, in the vicinity of Tepotzotlan, in July 1821, and in the

[24] Zamorano, *Hojas de Servicio*, in *Dept. St. Pap., Ben., Mil.*, MS., LXXVII, 2.
[25] Pacheco, *Hojas de Servicio*, in *Ibid.*, LXIX, 6.

hard fought battle at Atzcapotzalco, on August 19. On September 27, they marched into the capital city, Mexico, as part of the *Ejército Trigarante* behind Iturbide on his black charger, as the latter was acclaimed by the people as *El Libertador*.[26]

III. To California.

Unfortunately, it is not possible to follow closely the movements of these young friends during the next four years. Don Agustin, after but five months and twenty-four days service as a cadet, was promoted to ensign on October 25, 1821.[27] Don Romualdo, however, did not fare so well and it was not until after he had served a year, six months and three days as a cadet that he was transferred to the newly organized Engineer's Corps and brevetted ensign on November 7, 1822. He was not confirmed in this grade until January 21, 1825.[28] Being assigned to different organizations was probably considered a serious inconvenience by the two friends. By some maneuver, possibly through his friend General Bustamante, Don Agustin, while retaining his place in the 6th Regular Battalion, managed to have himself assigned temporarily to the Engineer's Corps on April 12, 1824.[29] Such was the situation of these young men when, on or about February 1, 1825, Lieutenant Colonel of Engineers Don José María de Echeandia was appointed governor of the Californias. That officer is said to have been the superintendent of an academy for military engineers and it may have been at this school that he became acquainted with Don Agustin V. Zamorano and Don Romualdo Pacheco.[30]

Under the Mexican Constitution of 1824, the government of each of the territories was divided between two officers, each, in theory, independent of the other. The military command rested in the *comandante general*, or general commandant, while civil authority was vested in a *gefe politico*, literally "political chief," which we shall translate as civil governor. In the distant and more sparsely settled

---

[26] *Ibid.*, LXXVII, 2.   [27] *Idem*.   [28] *Ibid.*, LXIX, 6.   [29] *Ibid.*, LXXVII, 2.
[30] Ord, *Ocurrencias en California*, MS., 42-3; del Valle, *Lo Pasado de California*, MS., 1; Vallejo, *Historia de California*, MS., II, 161, says that Echeandia educated Zamorano and admitted him to the academy for engineers.

territories, such as the Californias, most of the country came under the jurisdiction of the military as few places had been erected into *pueblos*, or towns, and given civil rights. In Alta California, in 1825, there were but two *pueblos—San José de Guadalupe* and *Nuestra Señora la Reina de Los Angeles*. Consequently, it was deemed advisable to fill the two offices with one person. Such was Señor Echeandia's appointment in both the Californias. As he was the first governor to be sent from Mexico under the new regime, it was also thought advisable that he should be accompanied by several junior officers and by additions to the provincial military forces. Soon after Echeandia received his appointment, Don Agustin V. Zamorano was appointed executive secretary of both the military and civil offices and Lieutenant of Engineers Don José María Padrés was appointed adjutant inspector of troops. These appointments were made by the central government and were not personal appointments of Echeandia's, though undoubtedly made with his approval.[31]

Leaving his family in the capital,[32] Echeandia, accompanied by Zamorano, Pacheco and Padrés, set out for Acapulco, where he arrived about March 14.[33] At that seaport, he was joined by Lieutenant of Artillery Don Miguel González, with a platoon of artillerymen,[34] and Ensign Don Rodrigo del Pliego,[35] an officer with an unsavory record but recently reinstated after having been retired for cause. On March 20, 1825, these all embarked on the national corvette of war *Morelos* for San Blas, where they arrived about April 1.[36] Here delays occurred concerning a vessel in which to proceed to Baja California,[37] and Echeandia, with his escort, removed to Tepic, where he found the climate more agreeable to his health.[38] While waiting there for arrangements to be completed, Echeandia attempted to resign his appointment to the Californias and asked instead for the general command of the Engineer's Corps.[39] For this he was rebuked and ordered to proceed at the earliest opportunity.[40]

On May 18, Ensign Don Romualdo Pacheco was appointed aide-de-camp to the general commandant.[41]

[31] In so far as Zamorano was concerned see *Sup. Govt. St. Pap.*, MS., XIX, 41; *Dept. Rec.*, MS., IV, 122. [32] *Dept. Rec.*, MS., II, 25. [33] *Idem.* [34] *Ibid.*, V, 103.
[35] *Ibid.*, II, 25. [36] *Idem.* and *ibid.*, V, 103. [37] *Ibid.*, II, 26. [38] *Idem.* [39] *Idem.*
[40] *Sup. Govt. St. Pap.*, MS., III, 3. [41] *Dept. St. Pap., Ben., Mil.*, MS., LXIX, 6.

On June 12, in company with those named and Ensign Don José María Ramírez, a cavalry officer, Ensign Don Juan José Rocha, who was under sentence of banishment for two years, Ensign Don Patricio Estrada, who commanded a detachment of infantry, and nine Dominican friars, Echeandia sailed from San Blas in the ship *Nieves* for Loreto, in Baja California, which they reached ten days later.[42]

In Loreto, Echeandia busied himself with reorganizing the local government, establishing the territorial deputation, and issuing, on August 19, 1825, a *reglamento* concerning the missions.[43] With these matters disposed of, he left the adjutant inspector, Lieutenant Don José María Padrés, in Loreto as his deputy[44] and started northward overland to Alta California, arriving, as we have seen, at San Diego about October 16, in an exhausted physical condition.

As he was governor of both the Californias and as he feared the effect on his health of the slightly more rigorous climate of Monterey, the recognized provincial capital, Echeandia decided to fix his headquarters at San Diego. That point was conveniently located near the boundary between the two Territories and the excellent harbor and the nearby road overland from the Californias to Sonora afforded a choice of means of communication with Mexico.[45] Some, however, have said that his decision was influenced chiefly by the presence of a certain lady.[46] On October 18, Echeandia wrote to Acting Governor Argüello to come to San Diego for the ceremony of turning over his office. On Argüello's arrival, in November, he was formally installed in office as general commandant and civil governor of Alta California.[47]

Also in the year 1825, the Territory of Alta California received a new treasurer or finance officer. He was Don José María Herrera, who came as *comisario subalterno de hacienda* and was subordinate to the *comisario general de occidente* at Arizpe, in Sonora, and therefore largely independent of the governor in financial and accounting

---

[42] *Dept. Rec.*, MS., II, 27; V, 103.

[43] Bancroft, *North Mexican States and Texas*, 709-10. [44] *Idem.*

[45] Hittell, *op. cit.*, II, 84; Bancroft, *History of California*, III, 10.

[46] Vallejo, José de Jesús, *Reminiscencias Históricas*, MS., 87-9; "Duhaut-Cilly's Account of California in 1827-28," in *Quarterly* of California Historical Society, September, 1929, Vol. III, 218.   [47] Bancroft, *op. cit.*, III, 9.

matters. Herrera sailed from Acapulco in March with Echeandia in the *Morelos* and, after the stop at San Blas, came direct to Monterey in the same vessel, where he arrived July 27 and assumed the duties of his office on August 3. He brought with him a shipment of goods and supplies valued at $22,379 and silver coin to the amount of $22,000.[48]

On the *Morelos* at this time came also Ensign Don José Perez del Campo, in command of a small squad of infantry acting as guards for a group of eighteen convicts.[49] Among the latter was Joaquín Solis, a criminal of notorious reputation, who was soon to assume the leadership of California's first rebellion.

All of these new arrivals, including the new governor and treasurer, were, with the sole exceptions of Zamorano and Pacheco, Mexicans of a class by no means particularly desirable as citizens. Officers, soldiers and convicts, they differed only in the degree of their rascality; they came as carpet-baggers, permeated with the spirit of unrest then spreading so rapidly over all Mexico, and controlled only by their personal ambitions.

[48] *Ibid.*, III, 14.   [49] *Ibid.*, III, 15.

Chapter iii.

Echeandia's Administration, 1825 to 1830.

THE six years during which Echeandia governed the Territory of Alta California was a significant period for the reason that in those years the first fruits were seen of the influences that caused civil strife to become endemic in the years preceding the American occupation. It is difficult to pass fairly on his merits and demerits as governor. There can be but little doubt that he was representative of Mexican republicans of the time. He came with instructions to examine the affairs of the missions, to discover the attitude of the missionaries toward the new Mexican government, and to make recommendations leading to the secularization of the missions. His position was made increasingly difficult by the vacillation of the central government and by the lack of financial support which forced him to exact contributions from the missions.

On the other hand, he lacked tact and energy and strength of principles for emergencies. He was ineffective to the extreme in the administration of justice and the enforcement of military discipline. He could not resist the blandishments of the *hijos del pais*. The anti-mission party came into being under his rule and in the end he was their tool. Don Mariano G. Vallejo and Don Juan B. Alvarado, who were of this faction, in their manuscript histories, praise him and extoll his virtues in extravagant terms. Alfred Robinson, who was certainly a more unbiased observer, called him,

> The scourge of California, and instigator of vice, who sowed seeds of dishonor not to be extirpated while a mission remains to be robbed.[1]

Duhaut-Cilly, master of the French merchantman, the *Héros*, on the coast in 1827-28, described him as follows:

---
[1] Robinson, *Life in California*, 141.

Don José María Echeandia was simply colonel of artillery [sic]; but as he held the title and authority of commandant general, civil and military chief of the two Californias *(comandante general, jefe politico y militar de ambas Californias)*, he was given that of general in the country; and in addressing him, that of Your Lordship *(Usia)*. He enjoyed the most extensive power, and he frequently made ill use of it. The frame of mind in which he found California was well adapted to give him ideas of despotism which he had not, perhaps, brought from Mexico. . . .

We can understand that, with such people, it would have been difficult not to yield to the sweet attraction of power. Of what use could be the assemblies held every year, under the denomination of provincial assemblies *(ayuntamientos de provincia)*? Every member, to the number of twenty, was elected under the influence of authority; and they assembled only to applaud every opinion of the civil and military chief, of which the larger number were against the interest of California. I have sometimes been present, in making claims, at these sessions, and I knew the manner of action. The general made a proposition which he frequently supported with the most specious motive. If some one tried to take the floor, he cut him short by taking it again himself, and he was verbose. If, at the moment of voting, he saw the slightest hesitation in any member of the council, a threatening look fixed this irresolution; and the vote in the negative, metamorphosed at the instant, became a vote of adherence. For prestige only, one or two of his confidants provided the comedy of an opposition agreed upon, which, after some arguments very easy to destroy, always left him the honor of the victory.[2]

I. San Diego.

The San Diego at which Echeandia made his headquarters consisted only of the *presidio*, which was a collection of dark, one story, adobe buildings, in poor repair, located on the slope of a barren hill. The commandant was Captain Ruiz. The other officers of the presidial company were Lieutenant Don José María Estudillo, then absent in Monterey, and Ensign Don Santiago Argüello, a younger brother of the former acting governor. Also at San Diego at this time was Captain Don Pablo de la Portilla, who was in command of a company of cavalry from Mazatlan then split up between the var-

---

[2] "Duhaut-Cilly's Account of California in 1827-28," in *Quarterly* of California Historical Society, June, 1929, Vol. III, 161.

ious *presidios* and mission guards.³ A battery, *castillo*, was maintained at Point Guijarros near the mouth of the harbor with a guard of from sixteen to twenty men which was relieved from the *presidio*.

The families of the officers and men, and such civilians as were present, lived within the confines of the *presidio*. At the foot of the hill, below the *presidio*, they had their gardens.⁴ Mission San Diego, some four or five miles north on the river, was the nearest neighbor of any kind.

On November 19, 1825, about a month after their arrival, Ensign Pacheco, with a small detachment of soldiers, was sent on an expedition to the Colorado River to survey, and if possible improve upon, the overland route to Sonora. During that winter and the following spring he made two more trips into the same country.⁵

Ensign Zamorano found his time occupied with the duties of his office. The records are filled with many small incidents in which he played a part and with territorial papers bearing his endorsements. In April 1826, he defended and secured the acquittal, before a court martial, of a soldier who had shot a civilian while on sentry duty.⁶ On April 28, 1826, he acted as secretary at a conference between the governor and the friars of the southern missions on the subject of the refusal by the missionaries to take the oath of allegiance to the Constitution of 1824.⁷

On his return from the Colorado River, in the spring of 1826, Ensign Pacheco was given the additional duty of assistant to the secretary.⁸ The two friends were together and remained so until Don Cupid came between them.

Although San Diego in 1826 was a very small community there was no other in the Californias that could approach it in either the number of beautiful *señoritas* at the marriageable age or the brilliancy of their smiles. It was but a question of time before the young officers who came with the governor should succumb to their charms. The first to do so was Ensign Don Romualdo Pacheco. On August 4, 1826, with Don Agustin and Don Santiago Argüello as witnesses,

---

³ Bancroft, *op. cit.*, II, 539.   ⁴ Hayes, *Emigrant Notes*, MS., 479.
⁵ *Dept. St. Pap., Ben., Mil.*, MS., LXIX, 6.   ⁶ *Ibid.*, LIX, 5-7.
⁷ *Dept. St. Pap.*, MS., I, 128-30.   ⁸ *Dept. St. Pap., Ben., Mil.*, MS., LXIX, 6.

he was married to Doña Ramona Carrillo at Mission San Diego by Fr. Vicente Pascual Oliva, O.F.M.[9] The bride was the beautiful and vivacious daughter of Don Joaquín Carrillo, a retired soldier of the San Diego Company.

Early in the following spring, the governor, having called the territorial *diputacion* to assemble in Monterey in June, decided to go to Monterey as soon as possible. This sudden decision filled Ensign Zamorano with dismay; he himself was planning to be married soon. The thought of going to Monterey without his bride, to return he knew not when, was not pleasing to contemplate. He hastened to Fray Vicente and asked him to perform the marriage ceremony at once. To this the venerable father demurred, pointing out that the bans had not been posted and that he had no authority to perform the ceremony otherwise without a dispensation from the *padre presidente*. To this Don Agustin impatiently replied that there was not time in which to publish the bans and wait the usual period nor was there time to apply to the *padre presidente*, as the governor planned to leave within eight days. He was very anxious to take his bride with him as there was no way to tell when the governor would return to San Diego, and surely, in the circumstances, the father president would approve. Fray Vicente was a sincere friend of Don Agustin's and earnestly desired to find some way in which he could comply with the young man's wishes. He told his friend that he would see the governor and find out what could be done.

Echeandia confirmed Zamorano's description of the situation, certified that Don Agustin was unmarried, gave his consent and urged the friar to perform the wedding ceremony. Troubled, but believing he was doing the right thing, the father called the people to mass on February 15, 1827 and, with Don Romualdo and the governor as witnesses, married Don Agustin and Doña María Luisa Argüello.[10] As soon as the wedding party had left Mission San Diego, Fray Vicente went to his study, wrote to Father President Duran, at Mission Santa Barbara, told him what he had just done and submitted himself to whatever penance the *padre presidente* saw fit to impose.[11] There is no record that Fray Vicente was censured.

[9] Entry 1609, *First Book of Marriages*, MS., Mission San Diego.   [10] *Ibid.*, Entry 1633.
[11] Fr. Oliva to Fr. President Duran, San Diego, February 14, 1827, MS., in Mission Santa

There is an old and oft repeated legend in California that Zamorano and Pacheco were married to these daughters of the country on the same day and at a double ceremony.[12] *Casa de Carrillo*, the home of Doña Ramona's father, stands today in San Diego and is pointed out as the scene of this double wedding. Unfortunately for this romantic tradition, the marriage register of Mission San Diego is still preserved; all the documentary evidence proves that it has no basis in fact.

Don Agustin was twenty-eight years of age at the time of his marriage; his bride lacked three weeks of being fifteen. Doña Luisa, as she was known, was already famous for a brilliant smile and uncommon vivacity. As the daughter of Don Santiago Argüello and his wife, Doña María del Pilar Ortega, she was a prize to set aflutter the heart of any dashing *caballero*.

Don Santiago Argüello was born at Monterey on July 27, 1792.[13] He entered the military service in 1805 as a cadet in the San Francisco Company, of which *presidio* his father was then commandant. In the following year, 1806, he was transferred to the *presidio* at Santa Barbara. His father, Captain José Darío Argüello, came to California in 1781 and was the founder of the Argüello family in California. He served as acting governor from July, 1814, to October, 1815, when he was appointed governor of Baja California, serving as such until 1822. For many years, Don José was the most prominent, influential and respected man in California.

Don Luis Antonio Argüello, who was acting governor at the time of Echeandia's arrival, was a son of Don José and therefore a brother of Don Santiago. Their sister, Doña María de la Concepcion Marcela

---

Barbara Archives, Document No. 937; summarized in Bancroft's *Santa Barbara Archives*, MS., XII, 342. There is a conflict of dates in Fray Vicente's letter but the entry in the *Book of Marriages* is clear and definite and, as it is the official record, must be accepted. Cf. Engelhardt, *San Diego Mission*, 288.

[12] This romantic legend, often repeated in newspaper and magazine articles, is probably based on Hittell, *op. cit.*, II, 89, which was in turn based on a. manuscript supplied by Don Juan B. Alvarado. Hittell, however, does not say that Zamorano and Pacheco were married at a double wedding. His statement is, "As both intended to accompany the governor to Monterey and desired to take their wives with them, the weddings were celebrated previous to their departure." This is correct insofar as Zamorano is concerned but not in regard to Pacheco.

[13] Entry 1805, *First Book of Baptisms*, San Carlos Church, Monterey. I am indebted to the Reverend P. Gerald Gay, pastor of San Carlos Church, for information from the old registers of that parish.

Argüello, was the famous Chonita whose romance with Rezánof we have noticed. At the time of Don Agustin's marriage to her niece, Doña Concepcion was with her parents in Guadalajara.

In Santa Barbara, while serving there as cadet, Don Santiago met Doña María del Pilar Ortega, daughter of Don José María Ortega, of Rancho del Refugio, on the Santa Barbara Channel, and the son of Sergeant José Francisco Ortega, who came to California with Portolá and Serra and was the discoverer of the Golden Gate. They were married, at Mission Santa Barbara, on May 30, 1810.[14] On March 5, 1812, their daughter, María Luisa Joana Josepha de la Luz, was born. She was baptised two days later in the Mission by Fr. Luis Gil y Taboada, O.F.M., with her grandparents, Don José Darío Argüello and his wife, Doña María Ignacia Moraga, as godparents.[15]

In 1817, Don Santiago Argüello was promoted to ensign in the San Francisco Company but was sent, instead, to the *presidio* at San Diego, where he was serving, with the same rank, at the time of Echeandía's arrival in October 1825. He did not become a lieutenant until several months after the marriage of his daughter.

II. Santa Barbara.

The governor's plans to leave San Diego at once did not materialize. District electors, one from each of the four *presidios* and two *pueblos*, were to meet in San Diego and elect a deputy to the national congress and the full membership of the territorial legislature, which was to assemble in Monterey in June. Because of delays, the first meeting of the electors was not held until February 16. Zamorano was the elector from San Diego and at their first meeting he was chosen as their secretary. On February 18, Captain Don José Antonio de la Guerra y Noriega, commandant of the *presidio* at Santa Barbara, was elected as deputy to the national congress. On the following day, seven members, and three alternates, of the territorial *diputacion* were elected. Their labors completed, the electors adjourned.[16]

[14] *Santa Barbara Libros de Mision*, Bancroft Library.
[15] Entry 398, *First Book of Baptisms of Mission Santa Barbara*, Our Lady of Sorrows Church, Santa Barbara. I am indebted to the Reverend Felix A. Rossetti, S.J., for information from the old registers of Mission Santa Barbara.
[16] *Miscellany—Actas de Elecciones*, MS., 1-4; *De la Guerra, Doc.*, MS., VII, 155.

However, the governor and his party did not leave San Diego until March 18.[17] Because of the presence of the two young brides, their departure was made a gala occasion and half of the population, dressed in their most brilliant attire and mounted on splendid horses, accompanied them for a considerable distance; some, it is said, going all the way to Monterey.[18] The long journey of nearly five hundred miles was enlivened with *meriendas*, and dances, and barbecues, and feats of horsemanship, and every other festive antic with which the lighthearted Californians were accustomed to amuse themselves. After a stop of several days at Mission San Gabriel,[19] the party reached Santa Barbara in the afternoon of April 5, where the governor and his entourage became the guests of the commandant, Captain de la Guerra y Noriega.

Lying in the roadstead off Santa Barbara at the time was the French merchantman, the *Héros*, and her master, Duhaut-Cilly, describes the town and the reception given the governor on his arrival.

> I landed . . . and went to see the commandant, Don José Noriega. He dwelt in the presidio, while waiting for the completion of quite a fine house he was having built without, and for which I was bringing him some beams I had taken aboard at Monterey. In Don José we found a well-informed and estimable man, surrounded by a large and charming family, from whom we had a gracious and hearty reception. His large fortune and fine character were the cause of his enjoying a great influence in the country; and although he was a Spaniard, he had just been nominated delegate to the Mexican congress.
>
> The Santa Barbara presidio, like that at Monterey, is a square enclosure surrounded with one-storied houses and dependencies; near the northwest corner is a building, distinguished somewhat from the others, and surrounded by a balcony: this is the commandant's dwelling. At the opposite corner, turned toward the shore road, appears what the Californian engineers intended to be a bastion; but one would have to be gifted with great good nature to say they have succeeded. The presidio is built upon a plain lying between two small glens where flow two little streams. Around the fortress are grouped, without order, sixty or eighty houses, inhabited by the *gente de razon* and the Indians working

---

[17] *Dept. Rec.*, MS., V, 33.   [18] Hittell, *op. cit.*, II, 89.
[19] *Dept. Rec.* MS., V, 33. The governor and party was at Mission San Gabriel on March 25 and March 27.

as servants to these rational people. Each of these dwellings has a little garden surrounded with palisades.

. . . .

While we were transacting our business with the padres of the missions of Santa Barbara, Purísima and Santa Inés, it was learned that the general had just arrived at Mission Buenaventura, distant seven or eight leagues from Santa Barbara. At once all was in an uproar at the presidio, and a cavalry escort was sent to meet him . . .
Early on the 5th, we learned that the commandant general was on the way; and at noon, we began to make out, far off on the beach which the road from San Buenaventura follows, the large cavalcade accompanying him. An hour later, he entered the presidio to the sound of a salute of seven shots from a field gun, and the same number I had fired from the ship, in conformity to Don José Noriega's invitation. I went immediately to pay him my customary visit, and I easily gained permission to unload at San Diego the merchandise I wished to leave there before returning to Mazatlan.[20]

The stop at Santa Barbara must have been a pleasant one as it was prolonged for nearly a month. The governor and his party did not proceed on their way until after May 1 and reached Monterey about May 15.[21]

III. Monterey.

As Monterey was later to become the home of Don Agustin and his bride and as it was there that he set up the first printing press on the western coast of North America, let us attempt to discover something of the appearance of the town at this time.

Duhaut-Cilly, whose description of Santa Barbara and of the arrival there of Echeandia and his entourage has just been quoted, had come to Santa Barbara direct from Monterey and his description of the latter place is a contemporary one of the town as it first appeared before the eyes of Don Agustin, the only difference being that he approached it from the land. Duhaut-Cilly's description reads,

> One should not expect to see a considerable city on arriving here; such an idea might deceive anyone who thought so as to the true anchorage. The first buildings perceived on rounding Point Pinos are those of the presidio, forming a square of two hundred metres on each side, and

---

[20] Duhaut-Cilly, *op. cit.*, 157-8.   [21] *Dept. Rec.*, MS., V, 44.

which, having only a ground floor, look like mere long warehouses, roofed with tiles. To the right of the presidio, on a little green field, are then seen, scattered here and there, about forty quite agreeably appearing houses, also roofed with tiles and painted white on the outside. These, with as many thatched huts, compose the whole of the capital of Upper California.

Monterey has, however, greatly increased since 1794, when Vancouver anchored here on his return from the northwest coast of America: then there was only the presidio; all of the houses existing today, the larger number of which belong to foreigners, have been built since the independence of Mexico.

Beyond these dwellings rises a line of rounded hills, of charming appearance, where one may admire a picturesque medley of various kinds of trees, among which the firs and oaks always dominate the rest.

Landing is easily accomplished near a small guardhouse, in the innermost part of the creek. A stream, with but little water, flows through a small glen, to the left of the old fort. This spot is quite useful for replenishing water vessels: it would be an excellent watering-place were the spring a little more abundant; but it nearly always suffices for the needs of one or two ships.[22]

Alfred Robinson, who also approached Monterey from the sea about two years later, in February 1829, describes the town as follows,

On our left was the "Presidio," with its chapel dome and towering flagstaff, in conspicuous elevation. On the right, upon a rising ground, was the "Castillo," or fort, surmounted by some ten or a dozen cannon. The intervening space between these points was enlivened by the hundred scattered dwellings that form the town; and here and there groups of cattle grazing.[23]

In *Two Years before the Mast*, Richard Henry Dana, the Harvard College student who went to sea to give his eyes a chance to recover from a recent illness, describes Monterey as it appeared to him from the deck of the brig *Pilgrim* in January 1835. At that time, Monterey was the home of Don Agustin and his family but Dana makes no reference to him that I have been able to identify. Dana writes,

---

[22] Duhaut-Cilly, *op. cit.*, 154-5.
[23] Robinson, *op. cit.*, 10-11. I am indebted to Mr. A. Porter Robinson, of San Francisco, for the use of the drawing of Monterey in 1829.

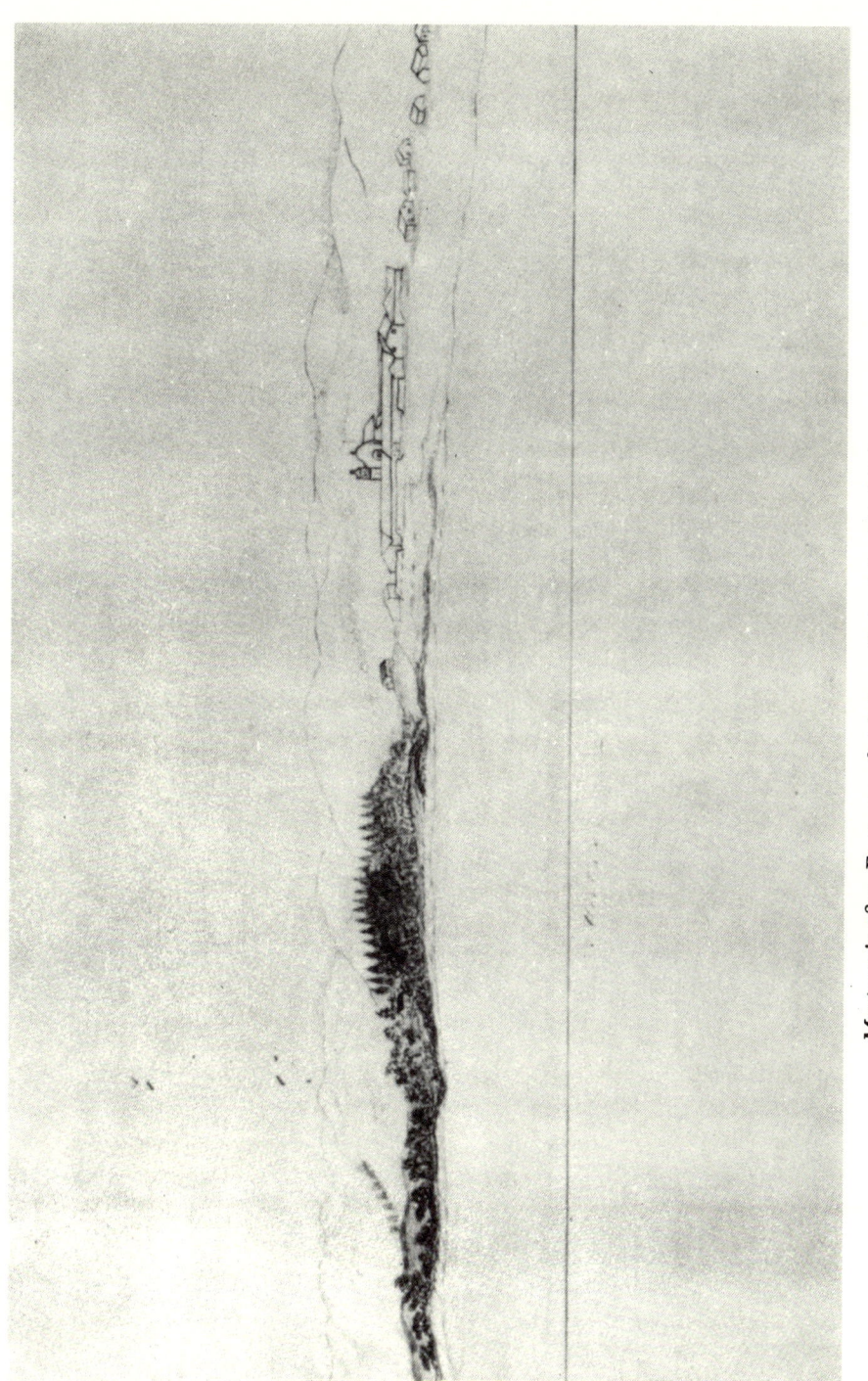

Monterey in 1829. From an unfinished pencil sketch by Alfred Robinson

Echeandia's Administration 31

The bay of Monterey is wide at the entrance, being about twenty-four miles between the two points, Año Nuevo at the north, and Pinos at the south, but narrows gradually as you approach the town, which is situated in a bend or large cove, at the southeastern extremity, and from the points about eighteen miles, which is the whole depth of the bay. The shores are extremely well wooded (the pine abounding upon them), and as it was now the rainy season, everything was green as nature could make it,—the grass, the leaves, and all; the birds were singing in the woods, and great numbers of wild fowl were flying over our heads. Here we could lie safe from the southeasters. We came to anchor within two cable lengths of the shore, and the town lay directly before us, making a very pretty appearance; its houses being of whitewashed adobe, which gives a much better effect than those of Santa Barbara, which are mostly left of a mud color. The red tiles, too, on the roofs, contrasted well with the white sides, and with the extreme greenness of the lawn upon which the houses—about a hundred in number—were dotted, here and there, irregularly. There are in this place, and in every other town which I saw in California, no streets nor fences (except that here and there a small patch might be fenced in for a garden), so that the houses are placed at random upon the green. This, as they are of one story, and of the cottage form, gives them a pretty effect when seen from a little distance.

It was a fine Saturday afternoon that we came to anchor, the sun about an hour high, and everything looking pleasantly. The Mexican flag flying from the little square Presidio, and the drums and trumpets of the soldiers, who were out on parade, sounded over the water, and gave life to the scene. Every one was delighted with the appearance of things. We felt as though we had got into a Christian (which in the sailor's vocabulary means civilized) country.[24]

Zamorano was commandant of the *presidio* at Monterey in 1835 and was, no doubt, on the parade ground on the afternoon Dana describes and probably watched the *Pilgrim* come to anchor. I continue Dana's description,

Monterey, as far as my observation goes, is decidedly the pleasantest and most civilized-looking place in California. In the center of it is an open square, surrounded by four lines of one-story buildings, with half a dozen cannon in the centre; some mounted, and others not. This is the presidio, or fort.... The houses here, as everywhere else in California, are of one story, built of *adobes*, that is, clay made into large bricks,

[24] Dana, *Two Years before the Mast*, 86-7.

about a foot and a half square, and three or four inches thick, and hardened in the sun. These are joined together by a cement of the same material, and the whole are of a common dirt-color. The floors are generally of earth, the windows grated and without glass; and the doors, which are seldom shut, open directly into the common room, there being no entries. Some of the more wealthy inhabitants have glass to their windows and board floors; and in Monterey nearly all the houses are whitewashed on the outside. The better houses, too, have red tiles upon the roofs. The common ones have two or three rooms which open into each other, and are furnished with a bed or two, a few chairs and tables, a looking-glass, a crucifix, and small daubs of paintings enclosed in glass, representing some miracle or martyrdom. They have no chimneys or fireplaces in the houses, the climate being such as to make a fire unnecessary; and all their cooking is done in a small kitchen, separated from the house. The Indians, as I have said before, do all the hard work, two or three being attached to the better houses; and the poorest persons are able to keep one, at least, for they have only to feed them, and give them a small piece of coarse cloth and a belt for the men, and a coarse gown, without shoes or stockings, for the women.[25]

Dana appears to have enjoyed thoroughly his time in Monterey and devotes considerable space to this visit there. Later, in December of the same year, he returned, this time as a member of the crew of the ship *Alert*. Of that visit, he writes,

It was ten o'clock on Tuesday morning when we came to anchor. Monterey looked just as it did when I saw it last, which was eleven months before, in the brig Pilgrim. The pretty lawn on which it stands, as green as sun and rain could make it; the pine wood on the south, the small river on the north side, the adobe houses, with their white walls and red-tiled roofs, dotted on the green; the low, white *presidio*, with its soiled tri-colored flag flying, and the discordant din of drums and trumpets of the noon parade—all brought up the scene we had witnessed here with so much pleasure nearly a year before, when coming from a long voyage, and from our unprepossessing reception at Santa Barbara. It seemed almost like coming to a home.[26]

This, however, is enough of Monterey as a town; let us return to May 1827, and the arrival there of the governor accompanied by Don Agustin and his bride, Doña Luisa.

[25] *Ibid.*, 98-100.   [26] *Ibid.*, 291.

During the next few months, while the governor was busy with the sessions of the territorial legislature, Don Agustin was engaged, in addition to his secretarial duties, in an investigation of the affairs and conduct of office of Don José María Herrera, the *comisario subalterno*. It was inevitable that the governor should soon clash with this officer who was largely independent of his authority. Theoretically, the national treasury should have paid in full the territorial expenses and received the net proceeds of the territorial revenues. Actually, there were never funds forthcoming from the national treasury and the Territory was left to pay its way out of revenues that were always inadequate.

Under these circumstances, it is not surprising that the governor was soon complaining about the manner in which financial matters were administered. In the quarrel that followed, Echeandia was joined by the *habilitados*, or paymasters, of the *presidios*. Herrera's coming had curtailed their previous responsibilities and they resented the supervision his office attempted to maintain over presidial accounts. Furthermore, they could never understand why funds were always insufficient to meet their payrolls in full. To make matters worse, Herrera was a stranger and a Mexican.

There appears to have been no genuine evidence that the financial officer did not conduct his affairs in a proper manner and his official acts were approved by his superiors. Nevertheless, on April 5, 1827, while at Santa Barbara, the governor instructed Don Agustin to make a complete, but secret, investigation into Herrera's conduct of his office. This inquiry was begun by holding hearings and taking evidence in Santa Barbara. The proceedings were continued in Monterey and depositions were taken in Los Angeles. When it is remembered that these proceedings were conducted in secret, that all of the witnesses called were enemies of the accused, and that Herrera himself was not called upon for a defense, little value can be attached to Don Agustin's report as a judicial document. This report was dated July 31, and was probably as near to what the governor wanted as the investigator could bring himself to stretch the meager facts at his command. As we read it today, it was not in fact very damaging. Don Agustin's conclusion was that there could be no doubt that

Herrera had used part of the governmental funds brought by him in 1825 in private commercial speculation, in violation of the law, but that there was no evidence that he had not restored these funds or that his accounts were not then in proper order.[27]

Don Agustin appears to have had no further part, beyond routine duty, in this quarrel. With the aid of Don Juan Bandini, a deputy in the territorial *diputacion*, Echeandia made life so miserable for Herrera that the latter, in September, resigned his office, leaving the administration of financial affairs wholly in the hands of the governor, and demanded his passport to Mazatlan, which Echeandia refused him. There the matter rested, while Echeandia continued to blame Herrera for all the Territory's financial ills, past, present, and prospective.[28]

Another matter which engaged the governor's attention at Monterey was the disciplining of Don Miguel González. That artillery officer had come as a lieutenant with Echeandia in 1825. Soon after arrival, he had received his promotion to the rank of captain. On being ordered to the *presidio* at Monterey, in 1826, he displaced Lieutenant Don Mariano Estrada in the command of that post because of his senior rank. This action, together with a surly disposition, soon made him very unpopular with the native Californian officers. In this quarrel, Echeandia opposed Captain González, prompted, probably, by the fact that Don Miguel was the friend and father-in-law of *Comisario Subalterno* Don José María Herrera. To restore peace in the *presidio* at Monterey, the governor relieved Captain González of that command, ordering that officer to accompany him to Santa Barbara, and made his aide, Ensign Pacheco, acting commandant.[29]

With the sessions of the territorial legislature adjourned and Herrera removed from his office, Echeandia was ready to return to San Diego. Once more the governor's movements were to present a problem to Ensign Zamorano; his wife, Doña Luisa, was *encinte* and daily expecting her confinement. An urgent appeal to a friendly priest could

---

[27] *Dept. St. Pap., Ben., Mil.*, MS., LXI, 11-14; LXXIII, 62-80.
[28] Bancroft, *op. cit.*, III, 59-64.
[29] *Ibid.*, III, 39-40; *Dept. Rec.*, MS., V, 92-3, 108-11.

be of no avail in this situation and there was nothing for the governor of the Territory to do but wait. On November 23, 1827, a daughter was born. Two days later, in San Carlos Church, the chapel of the *presidio*, she was baptised by Fr. Ramon Abella, O.F.M., and given the name of María Dolores Francisca. Her godparents were Lieutenant Don Mariano Estrada and his wife, Doña Ysabella Argüello.[30]

Leaving his wife and child with the Estradas, with whom he and Doña Luisa had become close friends, Don Agustin left Monterey with the governor, a week later, on December 1. That night the party stopped at Mission Soledad. The night of December 3 they spent at Mission San Miguel, that of the 6th at Mission San Luis Obispo.[31] By December 14, they were in Santa Barbara and on that day Don Agustin assigned twenty-five *pesos* per month from his pay to his wife, to be paid her by the paymaster at Monterey.[32]

The governor and his party remained at Santa Barbara until the end of March 1828, when they proceeded to San Diego, where they arrived about April 10.[33] Before they left Santa Barbara, Don Agustin's family had joined him. As we have seen, Don Romualdo Pacheco remained at Monterey as acting commandant of that post; these two friends were never to be together again.

It appears that Don Agustin had attempted to resign his secretarial office, although no record of his petition in the matter has been found. Since it has not been located, we cannot learn his reason for such a request. While he was at Santa Barbara, orders came from the central government in Mexico that Ensign Zamorano continue to discharge the duties of secretary of the Californias.[34]

IV. The Ship *Franklin*.

The Mexican laws of the period regulating maritime commerce were very stringent. Goods could be imported at certain ports only, and tariffs were extremely high. In California, the authorities attempted to maintain some semblance of enforcing these laws. Their efforts were not always pleasing to the traders and resulted in extensive

---

[30] Entry 3525, *Second Book of Baptisms*, San Carlos Church, Monterey.
[31] *Dept. Rec.* MS., V, 115-16. [32] *Idem.* [33] *Ibid.*, VI, 197-8. [34] *Ibid.*, IV, 122.

smuggling. This practice was safe enough so long as the offenders were not deliberately betrayed or did not flaunt their transgressions before the officers.

In June 1828, the American ship *Franklin*, Captain John Bradshaw, was in San Diego harbor. She had been granted all possible privileges and her supercargo permitted to travel by land from mission to mission as he solicited business. One day Captain Bradshaw was called before the governor and accused of smuggling on the Baja California coast, of illegally transfering the cargo of another vessel to his own, of having touched at Santa Catalina in defiance of specific orders to the contrary, and of having failed to show his manifests. Echeandia ordered Ensign Zamorano to make a full investigation into these charges[35] and instructed Captain Bradshaw to bring his officers and crew before Don Agustin for questioning.[36] He also ordered the cargo of the *Franklin* to be deposited in a warehouse on shore pending the inquiry, as security for any duties that might be found due.

Captain Bradshaw and his supercargo, Rufus Perkins, appeared to acquiesce in these commands and, accompanied by a guard of soldiers started to go aboard their vessel to make the necessary arrangements to obey them. At the beach, they managed to elude their escort and, once in their cutter, laughed at the soldiers.[37] On regaining their ship, they shifted her position to an anchorage near the mouth of the harbor. A few days later, on the morning of June 16, Captain Bradshaw cut his anchor cable and made a run for the open sea. To get out of the harbor he had to run the gauntlet of the guns of the battery on Point Guijarros, whose garrison had prepared against such an emergency. Forty cannon shots were fired at the *Franklin* at close range without stopping her, as she passed out to sea with her officers and men shouting their derision.[38] Whereupon, Don Agustin closed his *expediente* covering the case.

[35] *Ibid.*, VI, 56.   [36] *Ibid.*, VI, 61.
[37] Echeandia to Zamorano, San Diego, July 12, 1828, in *Dept. Rec.*, MS., VI, 66.
[38] Echeandia to Secretary of War and Marine, San Diego, July 17, 1828, *ibid.*, VI, 32; Echeandia to Zamorano, San Diego, July 23, 1828, *ibid.*, VI, 72; *cf.* Bancroft, *op. cit.*, III, 132-4.

V. San Diego Again.

A new set of district electors assembled at San Diego in October 1828. Their purpose was to elect a new deputy to the national congress and four new members, with three alternates, to the territorial legislature. Don Agustin was again an elector and was again made their secretary. The meetings were attended by one elector each from the two *pueblos* of San José and Los Angeles and the *presidios* of Monterey, Santa Barbara and San Diego; the elector from San Francisco arrived too late. On October 5, Lieutenant Don José Joaquín Maitorena, of Santa Barbara, was chosen as the deputy to the national congress, with Don Santiago Argüello, now a lieutenant, as alternate. On the following day, the members and alternates of the legislature were elected.[39] Don Agustin was probably surprised to see that he received one vote for the place of seventh deputy.

Following the election of Lieutenant Maitorena, who had been acting as commandant of the *presidio* at Santa Barbara during the absence in Mexico of Captain Don José Antonio de la Guerra y Noriega, the incumbent deputy, Ensign Don Romualdo Pacheco was transferred to that post as acting commandant, on December 31, 1828, from Monterey.[40]

In June 1828, the governor received an inquiry from the Secretary of War and Marine regarding the reported marriages of Ensigns Zamorano, Pacheco, Ramírez, and Rocha with daughters of the country. Ensign Don José María Ramírez had married Doña Dolores Palomares, while Ensign Don Juan José Rocha had married Doña Elena Dominguez. On July 1, Echeandia advised the Secretary that these officers had married with his permission.[41] These marriages, however, were contrary to military regulations which forbade the marriage of junior officers without their having first obtained the permission of the War Department and demonstrated their ability to provide for their wives; Echeandia had exceeded his authority in per-

[39] *Miscellany-Actas de Elecciones*, MS., 6-8; *Dept. Rec.*, MS., VI, 107-8.
[40] *Dept. St. Pap., Ben., Mil.*, MS., LXIX, 6-8.
[41] Echeandia to Secretary of War and Marine, San Diego, July 1, 1828, in *Dept. Rec.*, MS., VI, 30.

mitting them. As a consequence, on March 13, 1829, on instructions from the Secretary, Echeandia found himself required to write to Ensigns Zamorano, Pacheco, Ramírez and Rocha that, by order of the President of the Republic, he imposed on them a month's arrest for having married *hijas del pais* without the formalities required by regulations and that they must present certificates of the baptism of themselves and wives and request from the War Department revalidation of the permission he had given them to marry.[42] The records do not indicate that this arrest was other than nominal or that any of these officers was suspended from active duty.

On March 24, 1829, the general commandant transmitted to Ensign Zamorano his promotion as lieutenant of the Third Company of the 6th Regular Battalion. This commission was dated November 21, 1828, giving Don Agustin seven years and twenty-six days service in the grade of ensign.[43]

Don Agustin's second child, a son, was born at San Diego on April 29, 1829. He was carried on the same day to Mission San Diego, where, with his mother's parents, Lieutenant Don Santiago Argüello and his wife, Doña María del Pilar Ortega, as godparents, he was baptised by Father Oliva and named Luis Agustin Marcelino.[44]

The removal of Echeandia as general commandant and civil governor of the Californias had been contemplated for some time by the central government but the turn of events prevented this step being taken. The Secretary of War and Marine, on July 17, 1828, wrote Echeandia, directing him to turn over his offices to Adjutant Inspector Don José María Padrés and to present himself at the capital. But before Padrés, then acting as Echeandia's deputy in Baja California, could sail for Alta California political disturbances in Mexico prevented further action being taken. On June 1, 1829, however, Echeandia was relieved of the duties of general commandant of Baja California and that office transferred to the general commandant of

---

[42] Echeandia to Zamorano, San Diego, March 13, 1829, *ibid.*, VII, 108.

[43] Echeandia to Zamorano, San Diego, March 24, 1829, *ibid.*, VIII, 105; *Dept. St. Pap., Ben., Mil.*, MS., LXXVII, 2.

[44] *Book of Baptisms*, Mission San Diego. I am indebted to Mr. Thomas W. Temple, of San Gabriel, for information from the old registers of Mission San Diego and for many other courtesies.

Sonora.[45] He continued to hold the office of civil governor of both the Californias.

VI. The Solis Revolt.

Late in November of the same year, 1829, the governor learned that mutiny had broken out among the troops stationed at the Monterey *presidio* and, under the leadership of Joaquín Solis, had spread and was amounting to rebellion.[46] There can be little question that this outbreak was the direct result of the destitution prevailing among the soldiers because of the non-receipt of pay and rations. Many Californians in their written memoirs composed many years later and some historians have placed the blame for this outbreak on Don José María Herrera, the former *comisario;* all these however were the partisans of Echeandia. It is a natural thing for irregularly paid, half-starved, ill-clothed, discontented soldiers to mutiny. Also quite naturally, they blamed the general commandant for most of their ills, although that officer, as a matter of fact, was helpless in the situation.

On the night of the 12th of November, 1829, the soldiers at Monterey took possession of the *presidio* and, after kicking in the doors of the rooms of Ensign Don Mariano G. Vallejo, the acting commandant, and Ensign Don Juan José Rocha, threw them, together with Manuel Jimenio Casarin, the acting *comisario*, and Sergeant Andrés Cervantes, into the post *calabozo*.[47] For a leader they called Joaquín Solis, a convict serving a sentence of exile, from his nearby *rancho* and he assumed the position and title of general commandant. A *pronunciamiento* was needed and this was graciously supplied by Herrera, who was probably glad to be able to help along any movement that would embarass his arch-enemy, Echeandia. This manifesto was made to embody the grievances of both the troops and Herrera and was, at once, sent to the *pueblos* and other *presidios*. All went well and every one seemed in sympathy. Solis made a trip to San Juan Bautista, San José, Santa Clara and San Francisco, receiving in each place assurance of support. Returning to Monterey, he learned

---

[45] *Dept. St. Pap., Ben.,* Mil., MS., LXIX, 2.

[46] *Cf.* Bancroft, *op. cit.,* III, 68-86, and Hittell, *op. cit.,* II, 107-14 for details concerning the Solis revolt.

[47] Vallejo, *op. cit.,* II, 83-96, gives a detailed account of this affair.

that Echeandia was on his way north. Whereupon, late in December, he started south to Santa Barbara with a force of over one hundred men.

Echeandia, in the meantime, on November 25, issued a circular letter to the officers and inhabitants of the Territory, revealing the news of the revolt, and calling on the adherents of Solis to lay down their arms.[48] Two days later, he reported the situation to the War Department, stating he believed Herrera was the real instigator and dealing at length with the difficulties of his position and urging the need of proper support from Mexico.[49] On December 1, accompanied by Lieutenant Zamorano, Echeandia set out for Santa Barbara where he arrived on the 15th, after having stopped at Los Angeles long enough to issue a call for a meeting of the territorial *diputacion* and to arrange for reenforcements to follow.

At Santa Barbara, on the night of December 3, a number of the troops of that *presidio* imprisoned Lieutenant Pacheco, the acting commandant, and Lieutenant Don Rodrigo del Pliego, the second in command. However, Don Romualdo's influence over his garrison was such that he was soon released and all the soldiers returned to their duties except six who had been the leaders in the local mutiny and who thought it best to leave for Monterey.[50]

On Echeandia's arrival everything was done to put Santa Barbara in the best possible state for defense. Reenforcements of men and supplies were received from Los Angeles and the missions and an advance guard under Lieutenant Pacheco was stationed at a point about three miles north of Mission Santa Barbara. But Echeandia's timidity and lack of decision in the face of an emergency brought all these preparations to naught; at the first appearance of the enemy all took refuge within the *presidio*.

Solis, with his force, appeared before Santa Barbara on January 13, 1830. For two days the two generals commandant faced each other. A few shots were exchanged that did no harm. Echeandia was beside himself with fright, to the great disgust of Lieutenants Zamorano and Pacheco. Suddenly, it was all over; the rebel forces disap-

[48] *Dept. Rec.*, MS., VII, 257.
[49] Echeandia to Secretary of War and Marine, San Diego, November 18, 1829, in *St. Pap., Sac.*, MS., X, 53-5.   [50] *Dept. St. Pap., Ben., Mil.*, MS., LXXII, 65-7.

peared. Their leader was a man of no ability and with no control over his men. His force possessed no element of coherence; all was well only so long as things went as it wished. At the first serious resistance, however, it fell apart of its own weight. During the night of the 15th, Solis spiked his guns and fled to the north. His force quickly disintegrated and, singly and in groups, soon took advantage of Echeandia's renewed offers of pardon.

Dr. Stephen Anderson, supercargo of the ship *Funchal,* then lying in the roadstead off Santa Barbara, described the situation to Captain John R. Cooper, of Monterey, in a letter dated January 24,

> I suppose you are anxious to hear how we get on in this quarter but as the vaquero that carries this is on the point of starting, I have only time to say that you would have laughed if you had been here when the gentlemen from your quarter made their appearance. Almost all the people moved into the Presidio & about 30 women went on board the Funchal, bag and baggage. The two parties were in sight of each other for nearly two days & exchanged shots but at such a distance that there was no chance of my assistance being required; about thirty have passed over to this side. The General appears perplexed to know what to do with them; he appears as much frightened as ever. In the Purisima there are a considerable force which I understand proceeds for your quarter but God only knows when.[51]

With the disappearance of the foe, Echeandia's calm and will to rule returned. He immediately despatched Don Romualdo, with a body of troops, to Monterey to assume command and then called all the surrendered soldiers of the revolt before a board composed of himself, Don Agustin and Ensign Don Domingo Carrillo, for questioning. Before Lieutenant Pacheco reached Monterey that place had been recaptured by loyal persons, largely with the aid of the foreign residents. A party sent out at their direction had captured Solis. Immediately on arrival, Don Romualdo, undoubtedly following the governor's instructions, placed Herrera under arrest in his own house.

Next followed the formal investigation of the whole affair and the trial of the imprisoned leaders. In this, Echeandia saw an opportunity to remove from the Territory a number of men against whom he was bitter. To give greater plausibility in the eyes of the central government to the steps he planned to take, the character of the revolt was

[51] Anderson to Cooper, Santa Barbara, January 24, 1830, MS., in *Vallejo, Doc.,* XXX, 7.

changed from that of an uprising of hungry and poorly cared for soldiers against their local commander to that of a planned revolt in favor of Spain. It is needless for us to go into all the testimony or the flimsiness of the reasons given for the steps that were taken; they were typical of Echeandian logic. On March 9, a court martial sitting at Santa Barbara and composed of Echeandia, Juan José Rocha, Domingo Carrillo, Juan María Ibarra, Miguel G. Lobato, Mariano G. Vallejo and Agustin V. Zamorano, all officers and all undoubtedly intimidated in the manner described by Duhaut-Cilly, obeyed the instructions of the general commandant and, with one dissenting vote, sentenced Fr. Luis Martínez, O.F.M., missionary at Mission San Luis Obispo, to exile from the Territory, on the pretext that he had rendered aid to the troops of Solis. On March 20, Father Martínez sailed from Santa Barbara on board the English brig *Thomas Nowlan*, bound for Callao, and from thence to Spain.[52] In this manner, Echeandia disposed of the most outspoken and independent of the missionary friars. On May 9, 1830, the American bark *Volunteer* sailed from Monterey for San Blas with Herrera confined in a pen built for that purpose on her deck and Joaquín Solis and thirteen others in chains in her hold.

California's first revolution was over and Echeandia was more solidly entrenched than ever in his office. If he thought of it at all, he was probably a little grateful to the Monterey troopers who had started the ill-fated insurrection. He was in complete and unquestioned control of the entire Territory and he was prepared to enjoy the sweet taste of undisputed authority.

VII. Don José María Padrés.

Shortly after the close of these events, there appeared in Alta California for the first time one, whom we have mentioned before, whose

---

[52] Bancroft, *op. cit.*, III, 98-100; Engelhardt, *Missions and Missionaries of California*, III, 301-2. It appears that Zamorano was designated as the prosecutor of Fr. Martínez but excused himself from that unpleasant task. Zamorano to Echeandia, Santa Barbara, January 30, 1830, in *Dept. St. Pap., Ben., Mil.*, MS., LXXII, 84. Vallejo, *op. cit.*, II, 96-7, says the court martial that tried the military prisoners was composed of Zamorano, Pacheco, Rocha, Ramírez, Domingo Carrillo, del Campo, and himself, with Zamorano as president.

extremely radical views were to find a fertile field among the younger native Californians and whose greater abilities were to make something of a dupe of Echeandia. This person was Don José María Padrés. As we have seen, he left Mexico in 1825 with Echeandia and had remained at Loreto as deputy governor of Baja California. On the failure of his appointment as governor of Alta California in 1829, he had reverted to his old position of adjutant inspector of troops. In the meantime, he had been promoted to the rank of lieutenant colonel. In line with his duties, he arrived at San Diego on the frigate *Leonore* on July 21, 1830. The following day he wrote Echeandia of his arrival and that, for reasons of health, he was continuing his journey overland.[53] Padrés was a man of pleasing and magnetic personality. Of the same radical republican views, in the Mexican sense of the term, as Echeandia, he greatly exceeded that officer in ability, intelligence, and energy. He soon made friends with the younger native sons of California. His brilliancy impressed them greatly and it was from him that they acquired the ideals and philosophies that later controlled their actions.

VIII. Monterey Again.

Near the end of March 1830, Echeandia and his company continued from Santa Barbara to Monterey. For the next seven years, Monterey was to be the permanent home of Don Agustin and his family. The prospect of being able to settle in one place for an indefinite period must have been pleasing to Doña Luisa; for three years she had followed her husband up and down the Territory.

The command of the *presidio* at Monterey had been vacant for several years; Estrada, González, Pacheco, and Vallejo had acted temporarily in that capacity but no permanent appointment had been made. On August 31, 1830, the governor wrote to the Secretary of War and Marine that this position should be filled and that

> it being necessary to provide it with a person of good conduct, valor and attention to duty, I propose to Your Excellency as the first choice, Citizen Agustin V. Zamorano, Lieutenant of the Third Company of the

---

[53] Padrés to Echeandia, San Diego, July 22, 1830, in *Sup. Govt. St. Pap.*, MS., VI, 9.

6th Regular Battalion, assigned to the Engineers, who had nine years, three months of actual service up to the end of July last—seven years and twenty-six days as ensign and the remainder in his present rank, and who took part in the campaign of the seige of Mexico, and also in the seige of Tepotzotlan, and in the battle of Atzcapotzalco.

As the second and third choices, he proposed Ensign Gervacio Argüello and Lieutenant Rodrigo del Pliego, respectively.

All the three proposed candidates are worthy of being considered but especially Citizen Agustin V. Zamorano, recommended as first choice, because of his rank, training, and capacity and because, also, of the fact that he has served with honesty, continued zeal, and ability for nearly five years as secretary of this *Comandancia General* and, in addition, without any reward or recompense whatsoever, as secretary of the civil government.[54]

District electors again assembled, at Monterey, on October 1, 1830, to elect a new member to the national congress and three new members of the territorial legislature. Don Agustin was not one of the electors this time. After attending mass, the electors met on the 2nd and chose Don Carlos Antonio Carrillo as national deputy. In the election of alternate deputy, Don Agustin received two votes but his brother-in-law, Don Juan Bandini, received three and was declared elected.[55] I have been unable to learn whether Don Agustin sought this office or if the two votes he received were purely complimentary.

[54] Echeandia to Secretary of War and Marine, Monterey, August 31, 1830, in *St. Pap., Sac.*, MS., X, 68.
[55] *Miscellany-Actas de Elecciones*, MS., 9-11; *Bancroft, Doc.*, MS., I, 57.

Chapter iv.

VICTORIA AS GOVERNOR, JANUARY TO DECEMBER 1831.

MEANWHILE, in Mexico, General Anastacio Bustamante, the friend of Don Gonzalo Zamorano and one time commander of the garrison at Guanajuato, became, in January 1830, the President of the Republic. As he was a conservative and a lover of Spanish institutions, Bustamante's elevation was widely regarded as a respite from the extreme ideas that had prevailed generally in the years immediately preceding.

The new President, on March 8, completed the separation of the governments of the Californias by appointing Lieutenant Colonel Don Manuel Victoria as general commandant and civil governor of Alta California and Captain Don Mariano Monterde as civil governor of Baja California. Don Lucas Alamán, Secretary of Relations, and Secretary of War and Marine Facio each wrote to Don José María de Echeandia to that effect and instructed him to turn over his offices to the new appointees and proceed to Mexico.[1]

The new governor of Alta California had been serving since 1825 as *comandante principal* of Baja California, with headquarters at Loreto. He had, therefore, prior to the time the military command of that territory was detached from that of Alta California, in 1829, been subject to Echeandia's orders. Before going to Loreto, Victoria had been commandant at Acapulco, of which place he is said to have been a native. He was a brusque and energetic soldier who had won his rank by personal bravery in the war of independence.[2]

Setting out from Loreto overland, Victoria reached San Diego in November 1830, where he expected to find Echeandia waiting for

---

[1] Alamán to Echeandia, Mexico, March 11, 1830, in *Sup. Govt. St. Pap.*, MS., VI, 7; Facio to Echeandia, Mexico, March 8, 1830, *Ibid.*, VI, 6.

[2] Bancroft, *op. cit.*, III, 181.

him. The latter, however, was not there and wrote from Monterey, on November 22, that it seemed better to await his arrival at that place.³ On receipt of this advice, Victoria started north. On the way he received a second letter from Echeandia, written December 10, which stated the latter would meet him at Santa Barbara.⁴ Stopping at the various towns and missions as he traveled north, in order to acquaint himself with conditions, Victoria reached Santa Barbara on December 31. There he found neither Echeandia nor further word from him.

Alfred Robinson says of the new governor,

> Señor Victoria was a tall, lean, half Indian kind of person, with sufficient resolution and courage to constitute him, in his own opinion, a legion amongst this unsophisticated race of Californians. He came unattended, and required no ceremonious receptions.⁵

With the new governor at Santa Barbara awaiting the arrival there of Echeandia, let us turn back to Monterey to discover the cause of the latter's delay.

I. Echeandia's Secularization Decree of January 6, 1831.

At Monterey the denouement of Don José María Padrés' well-laid plans was being prepared. That officer had wasted very little of the six months that he had spent in the Territory. H. H. Bancroft, the historian, says that,

> There was now a popular feeling in favor of the proposed changes [*the immediate secularization of the missions*] far in advance of Echeandia's personal views, and largely due to the influence of José María Padrés, the newly arrived ayudante inspector. Padrés was a man of considerable ability, personally magnetic, and moreover a most radical republican. He soon became a leading spirit among the young Californians just becoming prominent in public life, intensified their nascent republicanism, taught them to theorize eloquently on the rights of man, the wrongs of the neophytes and the tyranny of the missionaries; and if he also held up before the eyes of the Carrillos, Osios, Vallejos, Picos, Alvarados, Bandinis, and others, bright visions of rich estates to be ad-

---

³ *Dept. Rec.*, MS., VIII, 124.   ⁴ *Ibid.*, VIII, 130.   ⁵ Robinson, *op. cit.*, 98.

ministered by them or their friends, their young enthusiasm should by no means be termed hypocrisy or a desire for plunder.⁶

One hesitates to challenge the considered conclusions of the great historian of California but there is very little evidence indeed that there was any popular feeling in California, outside of the little group composed of Echeandia, Padrés and those *hijos del pais* named by Bancroft, for the immediate secularization of the missions. Also, the acts of those same sons of the country in later years, when they were in complete control and undertook the secularization they professed to yearn for, indicate that "hypocrisy and a desire for plunder" is, perhaps, a more accurate description of their motives than any interest in "the rights of man, the wrongs of the neophytes and the tyranny of the missionaries."

The missions were never intended to be permanent institutions but only temporary schools to train savage Indians for Christian citizenship. The missionary fathers, so far as I am aware, never denied this theory. But their protests that their wards were not fitted to become citizens were waved aside by the advocates of immediate secularization as a worldly reluctance on the part of the friars to give up their control of the temporalities and estates the labors of the neophytes had created. On this point, Bancroft, who, in spite of his protestations to the contrary, was never able to disregard completely the bias instilled in him by those Californians who supplied him with so much of his documentary material on the period and who were of the group he names as so strongly influenced by Padrés, says,

> If the Indians were not fit for citizenship, neither were they being fitted therefore.⁷

Granting that, which was the result not of the mission system, which had proven so successful elsewhere, but of the low caliber of the Californian Indian, the care and control of the Indians remained a great problem to which the missions were supplying an almost perfect answer. That this was true is stated by Echeandia himself in his

⁶ Bancroft, *op. cit.*, III, 184. For an expression of Padrés' extreme ideas, see his report to the central government while waiting, in 1829, for a vessel to take him to Alta California as governor, Padrés to Secretary of Relations, Tepic, March 20, 1829, MS., in XXIV, *Missions*, Archivo General y Publico, Mexico. ⁷ Bancroft, *op. cit.*, III, 101.

reply to an order from the central government to enforce the law of December 20, 1827, which provided for the expulsion of all Spaniards from Mexican soil. In Alta California, this would have meant the banishment of nearly all the missionary fathers. Echeandia, writing in answer to the Secretary of Relations, on June 30, 1829, said,

> There are twenty-one missions, but only three Mexican friars: the others are Spaniards, who by their industry have placed the missions in a state of actual wealth. If unhappily the missions should be deprived of these Fathers, we should see the population in a lamentable condition for want of subsistence. The neophytes would give themselves to idleness and pillage and other disorders which would ruin the missions, and they would resume the savage life from which the greater number or nearly all have come; then, after they have settled down in the mountains, all agricultural and mechanical industry would cease, and the rest of the inhabitants and troops would perish.[8]

This was a frank admission that all others within the Territory were living by the labors of the neophytes and missionaries and without them would be unable to provide for themselves. It is hard, if not impossible, to escape the conclusion that the advocates of immediate secularization were prompted by the very motive which they so vehemently ascribed to the patient padres—they wished to control and administer the great estates and wealth of the missions.

At the July 1830, session of the territorial legislature, Echeandia presented a complete plan for the secularization of the missions. After some slight modification, this plan was accepted by that body and forwarded, on September 7, to the central government for approval.[9] This was the situation when the news reached California of the change to a conservative administration in Mexico and of the appointment of a new governor for the Territory.

During the months of December 1830 and January 1831, the executive secretary of the Territory, Zamorano, was absent from the capital on a trip to the southern part of the Territory. The reason for or the exact extent and duration of this trip, I have been unable to discover. In his absence, the work of the secretarial office was carried

---

[8] Echeandia to Secretary of Relations, San Diego, June 30, 1829, in *Dept. Rec.*, MS., VII, 155.   [9] Bancroft, *op. cit.*, III, 106-7.

on by Padrés, who, by his office and rank, was second in the military command. The situation presented an opportunity that Padrés was not slow to grasp.

Fearing for the success of his intrigues under a new governor appointed by an administration that was known to look with disfavor on immediate secularization, Padrés sought to accomplish his end by making secularization an accomplished fact before Victoria assumed office. As Victoria's arrival drew near and no word came from Mexico as to the approval of the plan submitted in September, Padrés induced Echeandia, probably without great difficulty, to attempt immediate secularization by a *golpe de estado*. On January 6, 1831, Echeandia issued a decree which provided for the immediate secularization of all the missions and took certain steps to place it into effect before turning over his office to his successor.

This decree, in addition to being signed by the governor, was signed also, as was required by law, by Padrés, *"Por ausencia del Scrio"*—"In the absence of the secretary."[10] Knowing the consistent conservatism of Zamorano's official conduct and his restraining influence, up until this time, on Echeandia, I venture the assertion that this decree would not have been issued had the secretary of the Territory been present in Monterey in January 1831. This decree is of peculiar significance in California's history for two reasons, first, it, in a large measure, brought on the revolution of 1831 and 1832, which was the first of a series that afflicted Alta California under Mexican rule, and, second, by its issuance the anti-mission faction threw down the gauge of battle and the struggle over the wealth of the missions did not end until the missions were plundered to their ruin and the Indian neophytes turned out to shift for themselves.

Echeandia's decree provided that Missions San Carlos de Borromeo and San Gabriel were to be organized into *pueblos*, or towns, at once, with similar steps to be taken at the other missions as rapidly as commissioners, to be appointed for that purpose, could carry out their duties. He appointed Padrés as *comisionado* of Mission San Carlos and sent Don José Castro to Mission San Luis Obispo and Don Juan

---

[10] *Bancroft, Doc.*, MS., I, 60, is an original of this decree. A translation in summary in Bancroft, *op. cit.*, III, 302-3.

Bautista Alvarado to Mission San Miguel. On January 10, he wrote to Zamorano regarding the distribution of ground and materials at San Gabriel.[11] This letter probably enclosed a copy of the decree of January 6. If so, it was the only copy that succeeded in passing the new governor at Santa Barbara. Although I know of no documentary evidence existing today that points one way or the other, I believe it is safe to say that the contents of this letter were a complete surprise to Don Agustin. His reaction, undoubtedly, can be read in the prompt protest made by Don Santiago Argüello. Don Agustin was probably in San Diego when Echeandia's letter reached him and he may have helped his father-in-law draft his protest. Don Santiago, as the commander of the San Diego Company, wrote, on January 21, that, even with the supplies furnished by Mission San Gabriel, his garrison suffered from a shortage of foodstuffs for which reason it was impossible to maintain the efficiency of the troops at the expected level and that without the assistance of this mission his soldiers would be in complete indigence.[12]

After this review of the events transpiring in Monterey, let us return to the new governor waiting in Santa Barbara.

II. Victoria's Rule.

Echeandia's decree of January 6, 1831, did not reach Santa Barbara until several days after that date. There it was brought to the attention of the waiting governor designate, Don Manuel Victoria. That officer, soldier-like, went into action at once. He intercepted the mail carrying copies of the decree to points south, issued orders countermanding it, wrote a sharp note to Echeandia on January 14,[13] and, on January 19, sent a long report to the Secretary of Relations, in Mexico, to which he attached copies of the decree.[14] In this report he

[11] Echeandia to Zamorano, Monterey, January 10, 1831, in *Dept. Rec.*, MS., IX, 78.
[12] Santiago Argüello to Echeandia, San Diego, January 21, 1831, in *Dept. St. Pap.*, MS., III, 1-3.
[13] Victoria to Echeandia, Santa Barbara, January 14, 1831, in *St. Pap., Mis. and Colon.*, MS., II, 35-6.
[14] Victoria to Secretary of Relations, Santa Barbara, January 19, 1831, in *Sup. Govt. St. Pap.*, MS., VIII, 8-10.

related events since his departure from Loreto and placed the blame for Echeandia's ill-advised action on José María Padrés, whom he had known in Baja California. He then set out for Monterey, where he arrived on January 29. Before the *ayuntamiento* of the town, assembled for that purpose, on January 31, he took the required oath and formally assumed office.[15] His first official act was the issuance of a short proclamation on February 1. In this, he expressed his hope for the cordial support of the people and stated,

> The laws must be executed, the government obeyed, and our institutions respected.[16]

These events, all beyond his control, destroyed completely Victoria's chances for a successful and harmonious administration; from the day he assumed office there were numerous and powerful forces aligned against him. In his official conduct he made no effort to appease these elements and they were soon involved in plots against him.

In sharp contrast to Echeandia, Victoria was a man of energy and resolution. He was a strict disciplinarian. He enforced the general regulations in the military and executed promptly the findings and sentences of the civil courts, refusing to exercise executive clemency. His political enemies enlarged upon his acts of simple but strict justice as against the lackadaisical, do-nothing habits of Echeandia and made Victoria appear as a tyrant, a despot, and an ogre, who delighted in floggings and executions.

Don José María Padrés, after the defeat of his project for immediate secularization, retired to San Francisco where he continued his plotting. His activities came to Victoria's attention, who banished him from the Territory and shipped him to San Blas. Victoria also sent into exile Don José Antonio Carrillo, of Santa Barbara, and Don Abel Stearns, an American and a naturalized Mexican citizen, living at Los Angeles. These banishments were made with as much legal propriety and with much greater cause than Echeandia's like exiling of Don José María Herrera and Fr. Luis Martínez, but, unlike those

---

[15] Bancroft, *op. cit.*, III, 182.
[16] Victoria, Proclamation of February 1, 1831, copy in *Dep. St. Pap., San José*, MS., IV, 102.

friendless persons, the objects of Victoria's wrath were friends of the native Californians.

However, the act of Victoria's that gave his enemies their greatest political capital was his refusal to call the territorial deputation into session. That body, which in the ordinary course of events would have assembled on March 1, consisted at that time of Don Pio Pico, senior member and president, of San Diego, Don Mariano Guadalupe Vallejo, of San Francisco, Don Antonio María Osío, of Monterey, Don José Joaquín Ortega, of Santa Barbara, Don Santiago Argüello, of San Diego, and Don José Tiburcio Castro, of Monterey, with Don Juan Bautista Alvarado, also of Monterey, as secretary. Victoria knew that many of these men had been under the influence of Padrés and had been party to Echeandia's scheme for immediate secularization. He supposed, and with reason, that sessions of the deputation would be devoted largely to measures designed to embarrass him. He reported the situation to the central government in Mexico and asked for instructions. Meanwhile, he turned a deaf ear to all pleas and petitions that the legislature be convened.

On July 30, the deputies Vallejo, Osío, Ortega and Castro petitioned Victoria that the deputation be assembled,[17] but he made no reply. They repeated their petition on September 11 and closed by saying,

> Having received no answer to our first letter, we beg you a second time, but should Your Excellency not see fit to issue the call we shall then consider it within our rights to take such action as may be within our power.[18]

Not waiting for a reply, which they probably realized would not be made, the same four men sent a long letter, under date of September 18, 1831, from San Francisco to the Secretary of War and Marine.[19]

In answer to these activities, Victoria issued a proclamation on September 21, in which he stated his position in a straightforward manner, that he had reported the matter to Mexico and awaited instructions, reminded good citizens that the way to happiness and pros-

[17] Alluded to in *Legislative Record*, MS., I, 305-9. [18] *Vallejo, Doc.*, I, 237.
[19] *Ibid.*, 238.

perity lay in obedience to the law, and closed, after alluding to the criminal motives and seditious plans of his opponents, by saying,

> I make this address to you in order to prevent the seduction that personal interests disguised in the habiliments of philanthropy, which they desecrate, may attempt.[20]

To this proclamation, Don Juan Bandini, substitute congressman from California and Zamorano's brother-in-law, made a long and verbose reply, dated at San Diego, October 10, 1831.[21] Don Pio Pico, senior member of the *diputacion*, five days later, also from San Diego, issued a bombastic statement that ran to six pages.[22] On November 7, from San Francisco, Vallejo, Osío, Ortega and Castro sent another memorial to Mexico, to the Secretary of Relations; with this they enclosed a copy of Victoria's proclamation and their answer to it.[23] Many of the malcontents in the meantime drifted to San Diego. For this there were two reasons—that place was the farthest removed from the residence of Victoria, whom they all feared if they did not respect, and Echeandia, the former governor, although under orders to proceed to Mexico, tarried there and gave ear to their grievances. José Antonio Carrillo and Abel Stearns slipped across the frontier of Baja California and joined the others.

Victoria was aware of these events but they do not appear to have concerned him greatly. While he was hated by those who have been named, his rule appears to have been welcomed by the more stable and conservative elements of the community. To the missionaries, he came as a great relief; they were left alone and agitation among their neophytes ceased. The merchants and traders were pleased, as business could be carried on in peace and security. The *rancheros* found themselves benefited by the same conditions. These improvements in

---

[20] Victoria, *Manifiesto a los Habitantes de California*, Monterey, September 21, 1831, MS., in *Vallejo, Doc.*, I, 245; also *Legajo* 52-6-6-6.

[21] Bandini, *Contestación a la Alocución del Gefe Politico D. Manuel Victoria*, San Diego, October 10, 1831, MS., in *Vallejo, Doc.*, I, 238.

[22] Pico, Pio, *Protesta al Manifiesto de Don Manuel Victoria*, San Diego, October 15, 1831, MS., in *Pio Pico, Doc.*, 4; also *Legajo* 52-6-6-7.

[23] Vallejo, Ortega, Osío and Castro to Secretary of Relations, San Francisco, November 7, 1831, MS., in *Vallejo, Doc.*, I, 241.

the general state of the Territory were not, however, the objects sought by the plotters in San Diego and they continued to wax eloquent on their lack of representation, the illegal banishment of prominent citizens, and the tyranny of the missionaries.

Of their schemings, Victoria was aware through reports sent him by Captain Don Pablo de la Portilla, who was at the San Diego *presidio*. He concluded, in November, that it was time to act and determined to nip, while in the bud, what appeared to be an incipient insurrection. In a short report to the Secretary of War and Marine, dated November 21, 1831, he reported the situation at San Diego and stated he intended to set out for that place on the next day with the object of restoring the peace.[24] On November 22, leaving Zamorano in command at Monterey, Victoria started for Santa Barbara accompanied by Lieutenant Don Rodrigo del Pliego and fourteen mounted soldiers.

III. The Plan of San Diego.

Affairs at San Diego, as Victoria suspected, were rapidly approaching a climax. The ostensible leader there was Don Juan Bandini, but the real instigators were the two exiles, Don José Antonio Carrillo and Don Abel Stearns. These three were supported wholeheartedly in their intrigues by Don Pio Pico.

Don José Joaquín Ortega, one of the deputies who, with Vallejo, Osío and Castro, had been actively petitioning for the assembly of the deputation, heard, in San Francisco, the rumor that Victoria was leaving soon for the south to punish those guilty of plotting against him. Ortega left at once for San Diego, where he arrived about the middle of November and spread the report that Victoria was on the way and meant, on arrival, to hang Pico and Bandini.[25] This was the spark needed to set afire the tinder of revolt.

Pico and Carrillo went to San Diego from the former's Rancho Jamul and there, with Bandini, decided upon immediate insurrection as the only means of thwarting Victoria's plans. Together, the three

---

[24] Victoria to Secretary of War and Marine, Monterey, November 21, 1831, MS., in *Legajo* 52-6-6-7.

[25] Pico, Pio, *Narración Histórica*, MS., 24-30; Bandini, Juan, *Historia de Alta California*, MS., 73-5; Osío, *Historia de California*, MS., 173-189.

Victoria as Governor

drew up a formal *pronunciamiento*, which they signed on November 29. That evening, with a few companions, they went to the *presidio*, where, doubtless by previous arrangement, the form of a surprise was gone through and the entire garrison, officers and men, placed under arrest. These, however, soon gave their adherence and the officers together with the former governor, Echeandia, signed the Plan on the morning of December 1.

The Plan of San Diego is a long and verbose document.[26] It is much too diffuse to give here even in summary, but in order that the reader may know something of Californian loquacity at its worst—or best, I quote the first paragraph and the paragraphs that state definitely the objects of this revolt:

> *To Mexican citizens residing in the upper territory of the Californias.*
>
> If the enterprise we undertake were intended to violate the provisions of the laws, if our acts in venturing to oppose the scandalous acts of the actual governor, Don Manuel Victoria, were guided by aims unworthy of patriotic sentiments, then should we not only fear but know the fatal results to which we must be condemned. Such, however, not being the case, we, guided in the path of justice, animated by love of our soil, duly respecting the laws dictated by our supreme legislature, and enthusiastic for their support, find ourselves obliged, on account of the criminal abuse noted in the said chief, to adopt the measures here made known. We know that we proceed, not against the supreme government or its magistrates, but, as we are deeply convinced, against an individual who violates the fundamental bases of our system, or in truth against a tyrant who has hypocritically deceived the supreme powers so as to reach the rank to which, without deserving it, he has been raised. The Supreme Being, master of our hearts, knows the pure sentiments with which we set out: love of country, respect for the laws, to obey them and make them obeyed, to banish the abuses which with accelerated steps the actual ruler is committing against the liberal system. Such are the objects which we call pure sentiments and in accordance with public right . . .
>
> For all these reasons, and with all obedience and subjection to the laws, we have proposed:
>
> 1st. To suspend the exercise of Don Manuel Victoria in all that relates

---

[26] *Pronunciamiento de San Diego contra el Gefe Politico y Comandante General de California, Don Manuel Victoria, en 29 de Noviembre y 1 de Diciembre de 1831*, MS., in *Vallejo, Doc.*, I, 283 a copy certified by Echeandia, San Luis Rey, January 5, 1832. In *Pio Pico, Doc.*, 7, a contemporary, but uncertified, copy. In *Legajo* 52-6-6-6. Bancroft, *op. cit.*, III, 202-4, translates in full.

to the command which he at present holds in this Territory as general commandant and civil governor, for infraction and conspiracy against our sacred institutions, as we shall show by legal proofs.

2nd. That when, at a fitting time, the *excelentísima diputacion territorial* shall have met, the military and political commands shall fall to distinct persons as the laws of both jurisdictions provide, until the supreme resolution.

These two objects, so just for the reasons given, are those which demand attention from the true patriot. Then let the rights of the citizen be born anew; let liberty spring from the ashes of oppression, and perish the despotism that has suffocated our security.

. . . .

Thus we sign it, and we hope for indulgence in consideration of our rights and justice.

Presidio of San Diego, November 29, 1831.

Pio Pico
Juan Bandini
José Antonio Carrillo

The supplemental statement to the Plan, signed on December 1 by all the officers at the *presidio* of San Diego, read,

We, Captain Pablo de la Portilla, [*and all the names signed at the end*], acquainted with the preceding plan signed by [*names as above, with titles*], according to which the people of this place surprised the garrison of this post on the night of November 29, consider it founded on our natural right, since it is known to us in all evidence that the civil governor and general commandant of the Territory, Don Manuel Victoria, has infringed our federal constitution and laws in that part relating to individual security and popular representation; and we find ourselves not in a position to be heard with the promptness our rights demand by the supreme powers of the nation, which might order the suspension which is effected in the plan if they could see and prove the accusations which give rise to so many complaints. But at the same time, in order to secure in the enterprise the best order, and a path which may not lead us away from the only objects proposed, we choose and proclaim Lieutenant Colonel of Engineers, Citizen José María de Echeandia, to re-assume the command, political and military, of the Territory, which this very year he gave up to the said Señor Victoria—this until the supreme government may resolve after the proper correspondence, or until, the deputation being assembled, distinct persons may in legal form take charge of the two commands. And the said chief having appeared at our invitation, and being informed on the subject, decided to serve in both capacities as stated, protesting however, that he does it solely in support of public liberty according to the system which he has sworn, cooperation for the best order, and submission to the supreme powers of the nation. Thus, all being said publicly, and the proclamation in favor of Señor Echeandia being general, he began immediately to discharge the duties of the command. And in token thereof we sign together with said chief—both the promoters of the plan who signed it and we who have seconded it—today between 11 and 12 o'clock, on December 1, 1831.

        JOSÉ MARÍA DE ECHEANDIA   SANTIAGO ARGÜELLO
        PIO PICO   JOSÉ MARÍA RAMÍREZ
        JUAN BANDINI   IGNACIO DEL VALLE
        JOSÉ ANTONIO CARRILLO   JUAN JOSÉ ROCHA
        PABLO DE LA PORTILLA   ANDRÉS CERVANTES

This insurrection was not a mutiny of ill-treated and half-starved soldiers as was the Solis revolt of 1829; it was a revolt on the part of men of position and responsibility. In order that we may appreciate the audacity of this seditious proposal to depose the duly constituted governor of the Territory, let us consider, in the order in which they signed the statement of December 1, who they were.

The first signer was Don José María de Echeandia, lieutenant colonel in the Mexican army, former governor of the Territory and, at the time, under orders from the central government to report in person at the capital of the nation.

The second signer and one of the original promoters of the Plan was Don Pio Pico, senior member and presiding officer of the territorial legislature.

The third was Don Juan Bandini, substitute member of the national congress, assistant treasurer of the Territory, and brother-in-law of Zamorano.

The fourth was Don José Antonio Carrillo, a former member of the legislature, brother-in-law of Don Pio Pico, and under exile from the Territory by orders of Governor Victoria.

The fifth signer was Don Pablo de la Portilla, captain in the Mexican army and senior office of that rank in the Territory, commandant of the *presidio* at San Diego, and the officer who had kept Governor Victoria informed as to the activities of the insurgents.

The sixth was Don Santiago Argüello, captain in the Mexican army, commander of the San Diego presidial company, member of the deputation, and father-in-law of Bandini and Zamorano.

The next three signers, Don José María Ramírez, Don Ignacio del Valle and Don Juan José Rocha, were junior army officers.

The last, Andrés Cervantes, was a sergeant of the San Diego Company.

Of the total of ten signers of the Plan, one was a former governor, two were members of the territorial legislature—one being the senior member and presiding officer of that body, one was a civil officer of the Territory, and seven were army officers. Of the latter, little can be said in defense of their position, which would have been perilous under a strong government; they were guilty of insubordination, insurrection and treason and, therefore, subject to trial by court martial and, if found guilty, to execution.

Echeandia's first act on assuming the leadership of the insurrection was to send Captain Portilla with some fifty men to Los Angeles to obtain the support of that town. On December 4, he wrote a report to the President of the Republic in which he reviewed recent events, excused the revolt by placing all blame on Victoria, and stated that he had accepted the leadership only to preserve public order.[27] This finished, Captain Argüello was left in command at San Diego while he, Pico and Bandini prepared to follow Portilla.

That officer and his little army reached Los Angeles in the evening of December 4, where they seem to have been welcomed. They learned that Governor Victoria was approaching from the north and was only a few miles away. There was great activity in the little *pueblo* that night as preparations were made for defense and men recruited for Portilla's army. While these preparations are going on, let us return to the governor.

IV. The Battle at Cahuenga Pass and Its Results.

Victoria's movements after he despatched his report of November 21 to the Secretary of War and Marine, the battle at Cahuenga Pass, the

---

[27] Echeandia to Bustamante, San Diego, December 4, 1831, MS., in *Legajo* 52-6-6-6.

killing of Don Romualdo Pacheco, the apparently fatal wounding of Victoria himself, and his surrender to Echeandia and Portilla, are best told in his own words, which I quote from the report he sent to the central government on his arrival at San Blas, en route to Mexico. It is written in the simple and straightforward language in which all his official communications that have been preserved were composed. This report is supported by all the documentary evidence of which I am aware and I know of no reason to doubt its accuracy. It is addressed to the Secretary of War and Marine.[28]

Most Excellent Sir,

My last report to the Supreme Authority was from Monterey and gave notice of my departure for San Diego, which took place on November 22 last, in company with Lieutenant Don Rodrigo del Pliego and fourteen troopers. At Santa Barbara, I was joined by Captain Don Romualdo Pacheco and nine other soldiers, after considerable persuasion from Captain de la Guerra, making a total of twenty-three men. With that force, I continued my march intending, because of the information I had, to obstruct the progress of the revolution which I heard, while on the way, had broken out at the *presidio* at San Diego under the leadership of the insurgents Lieutenant Colonel Echeandia, Treasurer Juan Bandini, José Antonio Carrillo, and the foreigner Abel Stearns. Their infamy was supported by the officers of the garrison, Captains Don Pablo de la Portilla and Don Santiago Argüello, Ensigns Don Juan Rocha, Don Ignacio del Valle and he of the same rank under arrest, Don José María Ramírez. I am certain that the troops showed considerable opposition to the uprising; but the bad example set by the officers and the insidious deceit of the leaders made them succumb. Of the officers mentioned none was more guilty than Captain Portilla, of the active company from Mazatlan, in whose charge I had placed the command of the *presidio*, with effective and oft-repeated orders to maintain the public tranquility and the safety of the post. He made me trust in his obedience by the reports that he sent me with the deceit revealed later by his fateful actions. This same person then proceeded to the town of Los Angeles to agitate it to revolt, taking with him a force composed chiefly of civilians, among whom were several that, because of their pernicious vices, I had deported from other places to live in that neighborhood as a means of punishment, as well as other prisoners, whom they set free, so I am told, for that purpose.

---

[28] Victoria to Secretary of War and Marine, San Blas, February 5, 1832, MS., in *Legajo* 52-6-6-7.

The small force that I took from Monterey was composed mainly of soldiers sick, as also was I, with chills and fever due to colds, with which sickness all my garrison was prostrated at that time. In this condition, it was impossible for me to make the journey of one hundred and forty leagues in less time and I arrived, on December 4, at Mission San Fernando, seven leagues from the town of Los Angeles. While there, I had news during the night of the arrival there of Portilla with his lot of rebels and, in consequence, I set out in haste the next morning for said town, meeting on the way two armed civilians, who came with the double object of delivering a note to me and of seducing my troops, which they tried to do. I reprimanded them mildly for their audacity, disarmed them, and made them return with my answer. In the above message, Captain Portilla informed me that he was at the head of a number of men in revolt, that they denied me their allegiance, were proceeding against my authority, and that all of that neighborhood had joined him. I answered that my presence was due to that very occurrence, and that I advised him to lay down his arms, as I would hold him responsible for the misfortunes that might arise from his actions on my arrival. Notwithstanding this, I met him, at the outskirts of the town, with his mob in possession of a hilltop, arms in hand, in hostile array, waiting to receive me. Their number must have been, with perhaps a little difference, about the same as that, according to his note, he had brought from San Diego. A fact that proves that until then he had not had the following which Portilla claimed in his letter above. I went as near them as I could in order that they might hear me, calling to them repeatedly so as to check them and so that, in any event, they might not fire; calling to Captain Portilla at the same time in order to awaken in him sentiments of honor and to see if persuasion might not avoid conflict. He made an attempt to descend but it seems that they threatened him should he leave them. Whereupon, they answered me with the utmost insolence that I could attack them if I wished. In the face of that and their firing two shots at me at the same time, I charged them with two officers and eighteen men. I dislodged them from their vantage point and set them in shameful, disordered flight. In the encounter, we had the fatal misfortune of a corporal and two soldiers wounded, the very honorable and commendable Captain Don Romualdo Pacheco killed by a shot in the back, and I mortally wounded in the same cowardly manner. Among the various wounds that I received was a very serious lance wound in the right side which pierced my chest, and by which terrible blow I was unhorsed. The traitor who wounded me, due to the vigor of my own defense, died on the spot, paying for his crime with his life; and that seems to have been the only loss on the part of the insurgents. The rout having been accomplished, I gathered my small force and inspected them, scarcely able to articulate complete words. Finding myself in a condition of complete incapacity, I did not consider it an opportune time to enter the town, where I would of necessity have to address the citizens and exert myself. I believed my death to be very near and certain, and in such a situation it seemed to me more judicious to set out for Mission San Gabriel which I did, passing through the outskirts of the town in an orderly manner. I was sure to find in the hospitality of the Reverend Father Minister of that mission, Fray José Sánchez, the aid I so much needed. And, in fact, there is no doubt that my life in the flesh was saved by the singular efficacy and attention of that venerable friar. That night part of my force fled, frightened perhaps by the death of their captain and my dying condition, and only eleven soldiers remained, models of faithfulness and constancy. Later on, Portilla addressed a message to me inviting me to surrender the command, in which knowledge, I told Lieutenant Don Rodrigo del Pliego to answer him saying that I was dying and to leave me in peace. Satisfied that he would find no opposition, he soon arrived with part of his mob, and the following day, Echeandia, whose cowardice and little honesty does not allow him to expose himself to danger, arrived with the rest.

He wished to see me and, followed by Captain Portilla, entered my chamber of pain with the sort of shame and humility that crime begets. He spoke a lot of nonsense, trying to persuade me that he had no part in the events and that he feared me when I should recover. In his general conversation he again broached the subject of the resignation of the command, and several other absurd proposals. I gave him to understand that I would never do aught, under any human consideration, that would stain my honor; that I was about to die and, because I was in such a condition, I surrendered myself as a prisoner, offering to remain neutral regarding his insurrection. Even in this manner, I could not get him to leave me in the quietude I so needed. After a few days they returned to the town, leaving a considerable guard at the mission, the command of which alternated most of the time between Lieutenant Don Leonardo Barroso, sent to that territory probably because of his many offenses, and the criminal ensign, Don José María Ramírez, a very proper subject for Echeandia's confidences. They were set to watch me and so an opportunity for revenge presented itself, because I had ordered the former to San Diego for the purpose of returning him to San Blas on account of his scandalous conduct and the dangerousness of his impudent ideas, and the latter I had under arrest, by superior orders, until the end of his trial and I had reprimanded him for a breach of military discipline.

In the town, they continued their efforts to make the revolt general, sending messengers to all parts, and Echeandia, more particularly than the rest, took upon himself the contemptible task of impressing upon each and every person the most horrible picture of me in order to exalt himself, taking advantage of every falsehood of which he is capable to deceive the unsophisticated. However, I am sure they found a bad reception at the *presidio* of Santa Barbara, due to the good conduct of Ensign Don Anastacio Carrillo, who is very different in character to his brother Don Antonio of the same rank and company, and at Monterey, because of the two officers whom I left there, Don Agustin Zamorano and Don Juan María Ibarra, the first, my secretary, captain of the presidial company, who remained in command of the post, and the second, lieutenant of the Mazatlan Company. The above opinion and the common displeasure no doubt is the reason why, without the slightest charity or consideration, with my wounds still open, and incapable of traveling in view of my weakness caused by the torment of the pain I suffered, they set me on the road. With haste and a shameful display of a guard headed by Barroso, they carried me more than forty leagues to San Diego, where I was placed on board the North American frigate, *Pocahontas*, chartered for fifteen hundred *pesos*, to take me to the first mainland port. The great suffering which I had endured up to that time lessened considerably after my arrival aboard the ship.

The next few pages of Victoria's report we shall omit. I end his statement by quoting his last paragraph.

The deceased Captain Don Romualdo Pacheco has left a helpless widow and two small sons. I call attention to the sad condition of his family, which is worthy by all rights of the full bounty of the Supreme Government, because of the sacrifice of that officer, in whose misfortune the Nation lost a young military adviser and the unfortunate lady the most loving husband and honorable father of his family.

God and Liberty, San Blas, February 5, 1832.

MANUEL VICTORIA.

That the forces of the insurrection were decisively and completely defeated on December 5, there is not the slightest doubt. Had the second officer with Governor Victoria, Lieutenant Don Rodrigo del Pliego, been an energetic and effective soldier, subsequent events would have been different. The only duty that officer saw, however, was the care of the person of his commander and when Victoria collapsed at Mission San Gabriel the government of the Territory was without representation south of Santa Barbara. For as long a period as two or three days, an energetic and resolute officer, had one been present, could have saved the situation; but there was none. That this was true is well brought out by Don Antonio María Osío, a member of the deputation who was completely in sympathy with the Plan of San Diego although not a signer of that document, in his *Historia de California*. Don Antonio does not allow his sympathies to blind him to the ridiculousness of the situation that followed the charge of Victoria, Pacheco, Pliego and their eighteen men. I quote his description of the rout that followed.

> Don José Antonio Carrillo and Don Pablo de la Portilla on seeing Pacheco fall dead and Ávila likewise immediately after . . . realized that their *pronunciamiento* was no longer a matter of words alone, easy to make and put into writing, and so cowardly fled, leaving as master of the battlefield the wounded Victoria, who desired more to confess than to fight. Notwithstanding their behavior so lacking in spirit, they excused themselves with boastings and it must be admitted that although they had wasted many words since the beginning of the revolt, they still had twice as many in reserve; for all their bragging, they never did explain why they, along with two hundred others, left Ávila and Talamantes, who were the two that put up a fight and who distinguished themselves as brave men, alone to their fate. Their arrogance did not permit them to confess their rout, as was frankly done by the thirty Mazatlan soldiers, who had revolted, by Ensign Don Ignacio del Valle and Don Andrés Pico. The first said that they fled because they were obeying their captain's orders. The second did likewise on seeing his superior and subordinates disbanding, and he found it necessary to run five leagues without stopping to rest his horse until he reached Rancho Los Nietos, in order to stop those who might arrive, so that he could infuse new spirit into them and return them to the fray. And the last, because he did not wish to be left behind; and believing that there would be no safety for him in the town, passed through the whole length of it, spurring his horse to its utmost speed, until he arrived at a lane formed by some vineyards. There he hid his horse in one of them and concealed himself under a thick, wide-spreading vine, remaining there until hunger forced him to come out, little by little, to learn the results of the encounter with General Commandant Victoria.[29]

[29] Osío, *op. cit.*, 187-8.

On learning definitely that Victoria was wounded seriously and expected momentarily to die, the brave leaders of the insurrectionists recovered, in part, their former boldness. We have already read Victoria's description of the interview Echeandia and Portilla had with him at Mission San Gabriel; this interview took place on December 9, 1831. Having seen for himself Victoria's complete incapacity for further effort and having that officer's word not to interfere again with the plans of the rebels but to return to Mexico as soon as his wounds would permit, Echeandia's self-assurance returned and he was consumed with a desire to rule again the Territory of Alta California.

On the same day, December 9, Echeandia issued a circular letter to the commandants of all the *presidios* and the *ayuntamientos*, or town councils, of all the *pueblos*. In this, after stating that the revolt had occurred on November 29 at San Diego and the immediate causes thereof, he said:

> Having accomplished the things here stated, they called me to place myself again at the head and by resuming the offices of civil governor and general commandant, which I had surrendered to Señor Victoria, regulate their operations in such a manner as not to stray from their purpose. I accepted, agreeing to defend the public liberties, always subject to the supreme authority, until such time as the Most Excellent Deputation assembled and, proceeding in the best legal manner, appointed the persons who are to take charge, one of the civil office and the other of the military command.
>
> At this stage of affairs, Captain Don Pablo de la Portilla set out at the head of some soldiers and civilians for the Town of Los Angeles, with the object of aiding that citizenry who clamored to be delivered from oppression and permitted to enjoy the liberty granted by the laws. On the 5th of the present month they pronounced, with their *ayuntamiento*, for the said Plan, promising gladly to sacrifice their lives and property in its support.
>
> This promise they kept and are keeping, for on that same day, the 5th, Señor Victoria, whom we supposed in Monterey, presented himself in the vicinity of the town, and without accepting any arrangement or even discussion, opened fire, thinking to subject them; but in vain, because, anxious for their liberty, they gave themselves up to death, and succeeded in putting Victoria on the brink of death, since seriously wounded he retired with his troops to this mission of San Gabriel where

he is now in bed receiving the attention of a doctor. All the troops that followed him have now joined our forces; only two individuals, who are attached to the said gentleman for private reasons, have not done so.

At the close of yesterday, I came here with Captain Portilla and today, on approaching Señor Victoria, he asked me to permit him, in the event of his recovery, to embark for the interior of our Republic and stated on his word of honor that he will not attempt to mix in current political affairs in the meantime.

I have reported to you substantially what has transpired in the southern part of this Territory from the 29th of last month up to the present. By it you will be at once convinced that due either to the physical inability of Señor Victoria or to the decision he has made, he has ceased to exist in so far as the offices of civil governor and general commandant are concerned. Therefore, according to the dictates of the civil and military laws, we are faced with the necessity of determining who shall provisionally assume the political and who the military office, thus assuring the internal peace and integrity of the Nation and leaving me free to continue on my way to report before the supreme authorities.

It is hereby made known that on this date I have convoked the deputies of the Most Excellent Deputation in order that, when assembled, they may study the affairs that are within their competence. Meanwhile, I await their decision in regard to the revolt, a copy of whose plan I attach for your better understanding. . . .

God and Liberty, Mission San Gabriel, December 9, 1831.

JOSÉ MARÍA DE ECHEANDIA[30]

The absurdity of the tone of Echeandia's letter is readily apparent when contrasted with the statements of Victoria and Osío.

The leaders of the insurrection thought it best that Victoria, so greatly did they fear him, be moved out of the Territory as promptly as possible. Without consideration or mercy, he was taken from Mission San Gabriel on about December 20[31] and, although his wounds were still open and he was tortured by pain, carried as rapidly as possible some one hundred and twenty-five miles to San Diego, where he arrived on December 27. He was at once placed on board the American ship *Pocahontas.*[32] A contract had been made with her

---

[30] Écheandia, Circular Letter, San Gabriel, December 9, 1831, MS., in *Vallejo, Doc.,* I, 245; also *ibid.,* XXX, 276.

[31] Echeandia, Circular Letter, Los Angeles, December 21, 1831, MS., *ibid.,* I, 251.

[32] Echeandia to Commandant of San Francisco, San Juan Capistrano, December 29, 1831, MS., *ibid.,* I, 254.

master, Captain John Bradshaw, and supercargo, Captain Thomas Shaw, by Don Juan Bandini for the transportation of Victoria to Mazatlan for the sum of sixteen hundred *pesos* in silver.[33] Captain Bradshaw was the same officer who had defied the authorities in 1827 and sailed his ship, the *Franklin*, out to sea through the barrage laid down by the *castillo* at the mouth of San Diego harbor. On December 31, Victoria, from on board the *Pocahontas*, wrote to Captain José Antonio de la Guerra y Noriega, at Santa Barbara, that his wounds were healing rapidly and but for his grief at the fate of his *compadre* Pacheco and the bereavement of the widow he would be a happy man.[34] The vessel sailed on January 17, 1832, with Victoria, Lieutenant Rodrigo del Pliego, Fr. Antonio Peyri, O.F.M., of Mission San Luis Rey, two servants and a few neophyte boys as passengers.[35]

Such was the situation in Alta California early in the month of December 1831; by a curious turn of fate the success of the Plan of San Diego appeared to be complete. And so it has been reported by every general historian of California, without, I believe, exception. Actually, however, it had been accepted in but two places—San Diego and Los Angeles—and much remained to be done before, except in the minds of the noisy minority who sponsored it, it could properly be called even a partial success.

V. Don Romualdo Pacheco.

At this point, let us turn aside in our narrative to conclude the history of Don Romualdo Pacheco, who was perhaps the closest friend that Don Agustin V. Zamorano ever had.

As we have seen, Don Romualdo and his bride left San Diego in March 1827, and arrived at Monterey in May, together with Don Agustin and Doña Luisa and the others of Governor Echeandia's party. At Monterey, on November 12, 1827, their first child, a son, was born. He was baptised in the chapel of the *presidio*, San Carlos

---

[33] One of the originals of this contract in *Juan Bandini, Doc.*, I, 18; a copy in *Legislative Record*, MS., I, 297. The amount was reduced one hundred *pesos* by del Pliego paying for his own passage.
[34] Victoria to de la Guerra y Noriega, San Diego, December 31, 1831, MS., in *Bancroft, Doc.*, IV, 925; copy in *De la Guerra, Doc.*, MS., IV, 180. [35] Bancroft, *op. cit.*, III, 210.

Church, on the following day, ten days before the birth of Doña Luisa's first child, and given the name of Mariano Martin by Fr. Ramon Abella.[36] His godparents were Ensign Don Juan José Rocha and his wife, Doña Elena Dominguez.

When Governor Echeandia, accompanied by Don Agustin, left Monterey, on December 1, 1827, to return to San Diego, Don Romualdo remained as acting commandant of the *presidio*. During the following spring, in April 1828, he led an exploring party across the Golden Gate into the country north of San Francisco Bay, going as far as the Russian settlements.[37] He continued in command at Monterey until December 31, 1828, when he was transferred to Santa Barbara to relieve Lieutenant Don José Joaquín Maitorena as commandant of that post because of the latter's election as deputy to the national congress. Don Romualdo was acting commandant at Santa Barbara at the time of his death.

In October 1828, Captain Don Luis Antonio Argüello retired from the command of the *presidio* at San Francisco because of ill health. That command then fell temporarily on Lieutenant Don Ignacio Martínez, an officer with a long record of many years' service. Echeandia, on August 30, 1829, recommended to the War Department that Martínez be made captain of the Santa Barbara Company and that Pacheco be made captain of that at San Francisco. He made this recommendation because San Francisco was an advanced frontier post and needed to be under the command of a young, healthy, experienced officer of proven courage, such as Pacheco.[38] To this recommendation was attached a copy of Don Romualdo's service record. This showed that in eight years, two months, and twenty-seven days actual service to July 31, 1829, he had spent enough time in the field to be entitled to an allowance of four years, ten months, and two days additional service for campaign duty.[39]

Echeandia, on September 5, 1829, forwarded to Don Romualdo his promotion to lieutenant of engineers.[40] This letter of transmittal,

[36] Entry 3523, *Second Book of Baptisms*, San Carlos Church, Monterey.
[37] Pacheco, *Hojas de Servicio*, in *Dept. St. Pap., Ben., Mil.*, MS., LXIX, 6-8.
[38] Echeandia to Secretary of War and Marine, San Diego, August 30, 1829, in *Dept. Rec.*, MS., VII, 36.   [39] *Dept. St. Pap., Ben., Mil.*, MS., LXIX, 6-8.
[40] Echeandia to Pacheco, San Diego, September 5, 1829, in *Dept. Rec.*, MS., VII, 222.

as transcribed by Bancroft's assistants, does not give the date of his commission as lieutenant. On October 1, 1831, Governor Victoria advised Don Romualdo of his promotion to captain of the San Francisco Company.[41] Again, I do not know the date of his commission.

At Santa Barbara, on October 31, 1831, Doña Ramona's second child, also a son, was born. He was baptised in the mission there and named Romualdo.[42]

Before leaving Santa Barbara with Governor Victoria on the campaign that was to end his career, Don Romualdo called on Captain Don José Antonio de la Guerra y Noriega to bespeak his care of his wife and family.[43] Captain de la Guerra proved true to his word and acted as the protector of Doña Ramona and her two children until she remarried.

Doña Ramona's second husband was Captain John Wilson, who was born at Dundee, Scotland, in 1798.[44] They were married by Father Narciso Duran at Mission Santa Barbara on November 9, 1835.[45] One of the spectators at their wedding was Richard Henry Dana, Jr.[46] Captain Wilson was a very prominent figure in maritime circles of the period as master of the English brig *Ayacucho*, regarded as the fastest sailor on the coast. Dana mentions him and his ship many times in *Two Years before the Mast* and pays many compliments to his seamanship, especially to his bringing Dana's ship, the *Pilgrim*, to her berth in San Diego harbor after she had drifted successively into the *Lagoda* and the *Loriette*. Four children were born to Doña Ramona and Captain Wilson; their names were María Ygnacia, Ramonsita, Juanita, and John, Jr.

Captain Wilson continued to follow the sea until after the American occupation of California, when he retired to Rancho de los Osos. His remaining years were spent as a *ranchero* in which business he prospered exceedingly. He died at San Luis Obispo on October 13, 1861.[44]

[41] Victoria, Circular to *presidios*, Monterey, October 1, 1831, *ibid.*, IX, 47.
[42] Barrows, "Romualdo Pacheco," in *Dictionary of American Biography*, Vol., XIV, 124.
[43] Ord, *op. cit.*, 48.   [44] Wilson monument in the Catholic Cemetery, San Luis Obispo.
[45] Entry 211, page 14, Book I, *Register of Marriages*, at Our Lady of Sorrows Church, Santa Barbara.
[46] Dana, *op. cit.*, 473. Dana erroneously states the year of their marriage as 1836.

Doña Ramona lived for many years after her husband's death. She was a kindly, charitable and pious woman and her generosity, supported by her great wealth, was boundless. She died, while on a visit to San Francisco, on December 16, 1886, sixty years after her marriage to Don Romualdo Pacheco.[47]

Her eldest son, Mariano, is said to have been educated at Lima, in Peru. He was a member of the California legislature in 1853. He died at his home on the Piedra Blanca Rancho, now part of the William R. Hearst estate at San Simeon, on January 27, 1865.[48]

The second son achieved a long and brilliant career. At an early age he was sent by his stepfather to the Hawaiian Islands, where he attended a school, at Honolulu, conducted by Andrew Johnstone, a friend of Captain Wilson and also a native of Dundee. At the age of fifteen Romualdo, Jr., was back in California, serving as supercargo on vessels in which Captain Wilson was interested. He is said to have been in command of a ship in 1846 when the American forces occupied Alta California.

He was elected to the California legislature on the eve of his twenty-first birthday and served in both houses of that body. He also served as superior court judge of his county, as brigadier general of the state militia, and, in 1863, was appointed state treasurer by Governor Stanford to fill a vacancy. He was later elected to that office. In 1871, he was elected lieutenant governor of the State and, on Governor Booth's election to the United States Senate, became governor in January, 1875. He served two terms in Congress. President Harrison, in October 1890, named him minister plenipotentiary to the Central American Republics, where his background and training enabled him to render distinguished service. He died at Oakland on January 23, 1899.[42] Romualdo Pacheco, Jr., achieved greater distinction than any other native Californian of his generation. His public record was an excellent one and was marked for its intelligence, probity, and independence.

---

[47] Statement of her granddaughter, Mrs. María Ygnacia Roberson, of San Francisco.
[48] Sacramento *Daily Union*, February 9, 1865 (2-1).

Chapter V.

Zamorano and the Plan of San Diego, December 1831 and January 1832.

As has been stated, Don Agustin V. Zamorano, the executive secretary of the Territory of Alta California, was absent from Monterey, the territorial capital, when, on January 6, 1831, Echeandia issued his secularization decree. The probability of his being present in San Diego when Don Santiago Argüello wrote his protest on January 21 against the immediate secularization of Mission San Gabriel has been pointed out. It is possible that Don Agustin, on his way south, met the new governor as the latter traveled north to Santa Barbara. His presence, as secretary of the territorial government, would be required in Monterey during the impending change of governors and he undoubtedly returned as quickly as possible after the object of his trip was accomplished. Whether he had returned to Monterey by January 31, the date on which Victoria assumed his office, I have been unable to discover, but if not we can safely assume that he arrived there very soon thereafter.

In March, the new governor made a visit to the town of San José and the *presidio* at San Francisco.[1] In June, he made a short, hurried trip to Santa Barbara, Los Angeles, and Mission San Gabriel.[2] It is probable that Don Agustin accompanied him on both these excursions.

Señor Victoria and Don Agustin appear to have worked together harmoniously. This was not surprising as the two men had many

---

[1] Vallejo, *op. cit.*, II, 139, speaks of the visit to San Francisco. *Dept. Rec.*, MS., 6 and 7, are letters of Victoria's dated San Francisco, March 30, and San Jose, March 27, respectively.

[2] *Dept. Rec.*, MS., IX, 27, is a letter from Victoria to Santiago Argüello, written at San Gabriel, June 17.

characteristics in common. As the years had past, Don Agustin had found it increasingly difficult to follow Echeandia in his many extreme ideas and the coming of Don José María Padrés had dispelled the last of the illusions which he, as an enthusiastic young ensign, had held regarding him. Victoria's energy and resolution, his efforts to improve both the conditions and standards of the presidial companies, his enforcement of the regulations, his meticulous handling of official business, his attitude toward the missions, his lack of personal vanity, all won Don Agustin's instant approval. He served Victoria to the best of his abilities and became his steadfast friend.

Late in September 1831, the results of Echeandia's recommendations to the War Department regarding the appointment of permanent commanders of the presidial companies, made in August 1830, reached Monterey. Don Agustin's commission as captain of the Monterey company of regular cavalry was forwarded to him by Governor Victoria on October 1, 1831.[3] This commission was dated March 23, 1831, giving Don Agustin two years, four months and two days service as a lieutenant. On the same date, the governor, by circular letter, advised the *presidios* of the promotions just made. These included, in addition to Don Agustin's commission, the appointment of Don Romualdo Pacheco as captain of the San Francisco Company and Don Santiago Argüello as captain of the San Diego Company.[4] Don Romualdo, as we have seen, never assumed his duties at San Francisco.

I. Zamorano Rejects the Plan of San Diego.

Echeandia's circular letter of December 9, 1831, written at Mission San Gabriel after his interview with the wounded Victoria, which has been quoted, reached Monterey on December 16. With its arrival, Don Agustin was subjected to a test of character such as comes to few men. An insurrection, led by the officer who had been his commander for eight years and to whom he owed, in large part, his ad-

[3] Victoria to Zamorano, Monterey, October 1, 1831, *ibid.*, IX, 48; Zamorano, *Hojas de Servicio*, in *Dept. St. Pap., Ben.*, Mil., MS., LXXVII, 2.
[4] Victoria, Circular to the four *presidios*, Monterey, October 1, 1831, in *Dept. Rec.*, MS., IX, 47.

vancement, by his wife's father, by his brother-in-law, and by others who were his friends, had deposed and seriously wounded his commanding officer, Victoria. His closest and dearest friend, Don Romualdo Pacheco, had died, as an officer and gentleman, in Victoria's defense. This insurrection appeared to be a popular one and would, no doubt, be joined by Ensign Don Mariano G. Vallejo, acting commandant at San Francisco, and Ensign Don Domingo Carrillo, Pacheco's second in command at Santa Barbara, since the first was a member of the deputation and the later a brother of one of the authors of the Plan of San Diego. He only stood between the rebels and complete success. As the sole remaining officer of the executive branch of the territorial government, as the senior military officer who had taken no part in the revolt, as the commandant of the *presidio* at the capital of the Territory, and in receipt of an invitation to cast his lot and influence with the insurrection, what position would he take?

To his very great credit, the situation does not seem to have presented a problem; his reaction was prompt and such as would be expected from a military officer possessed of character and honor. He called Lieutenant Don Juan María Ibarra, the only other officer present, to his quarters and, after discussing the situation far into the night, they prepared the following statement, which I quote in full, in reply to Echeandia's letter.

> At the Port of Monterey, on the sixteenth day of December in the year 1831: The post commandant, Captain of Cavalry, Citizen Agustin V. Zamorano, and the Lieutenant from Mazatlan, Citizen Juan María Ibarra, the only officers present at this garrison, meeting to discuss the circumstances at present confronting the Territory:
> The first stated he had positive information that General Commandant Don Manuel Victoria had suffered defeat and been seriously wounded in an engagement, on the 5th instant, with the San Diego troops and citizens of Los Angeles, who had refused him their allegiance for the various reasons set forth in a circular letter, dated the 9th of this month, issued by Señor Don José María de Echeandia; that according to this, the latter had been called upon to govern until such time as the Most Excellent Deputation shall name the persons that will assume the political and military commands; that the said Señor Victoria, on the 7th of

this month, had written that he was leaving for the interior of the Republic[5], which is now confirmed by the same circular which adds that this gentleman has agreed not to interfere in present affairs; that the remaining officers of greater seniority, on whom the command of the Territory in his absence should properly fall, have decided to join the insurrection; that quite probably the garrison at San Francisco is of the same opinion as that at San Diego, since its commander as a member of the deputation had demanded the convocation of that body and also because he had recently been called to a meeting of the deputation; that the citizens of Monterey were certain to rise in favor of the revolt and they would be joined by a large number of convicts now at liberty, who would welcome disorder as a cover for pillaging; that, having attempted to organize the foreign residents before in anticipation of such a contingency, he had been informed that they would not take a stand against the legitimate authority or side against the popular will.

Therefore, having considered the entire situation and taken into account that the forces available at their disposal are less than twenty-five men of all arms, and consequently no resistance could be made against the combined citizens and forces of the north and south, that resistance would only serve to increase the general spirit of discontent, that blood would necessarily be spilled and irreparable misfortunes follow, and both being convinced that it was prudent to prevent the shedding of Mexican blood, so valuable and desirable in these places for the preservation of the national integrity, they decided that they, for the present, would offer no resistance whatever since they considered it rash, that they would only preserve the public peace, safeguard the lives and properties of all and that they would so answer the aforesaid circular in order that the leaders, on their part, might appoint the persons who would assume the responsibilities of this post, and would ask for their respective passports to the interior of the Republic, as well as for others who might request it, and that arrangements be made for their transportation; also, that they be accorded proper consideration during their stay in the Territory and that those who should insult or injure them because of their views be punished.

---

[5] I am unable to say what letter of Victoria's, written on the 7th, is referred to. It would appear that Victoria was in no condition to write a letter on the 7th and very improbable that he should write that he intended to leave the Territory before his interview with Echeandia on December 9. It is possible that Victoria wrote to Don Agustin on the 9th, after his talk with Echeandia, and advised what had taken place. If so, the date is an error and should have been given as the 9th. In any event, Victoria gave no instructions or advice as to the course Don Agustin should follow in the immediate future.

All having been considered thoroughly, it was decided to forward the above, which we sign on the stated day, month and year.

Agustin V. Zamorano
Juan María Ibarra[6]

The following day Don Agustin forwarded this statement to Echeandia under cover of a short note which read,

Comandancia Militar de Monterey.

I have before me your circular letter of the 9th instant, which informs me of the political events that have occurred in the southern part of the Territory from the 29th of November last to date. Since these events have resulted in the departure of the general commandant, Don Manuel Victoria, who has left for the interior, and there is no one left to whom I can legally give my allegiance and considering other circumstances no less cogent, I have determined to remain at this post only to preserve the public peace and to prevent bloodshed, which I would regret exceedingly to see happen.

In the meantime, pending the arrival here of the person you may designate to assume the responsibilities of this post, my only request is that you be pleased to send me my passport so that I may retire with my family to the interior of the Republic. Also, that you provide passports for Lieutenant Don Juan María Ibarra, a sergeant, a corporal, and three soldiers of the active company from Mazatlan, and also for a sergeant, a drummer, a corporal, and eight soldiers of the regular artillery detachment, all of whom have begged that these be granted to them.

I trust that Your Worship will have the kindness to order that arrangements for our passage be made so that we may take our departure on the first vessel that may sail for the San Blas coast, and that, during our stay in this country, we be shown all due consideration, our properties respected and that punishment be meted out to whomsoever may address any insulting expression to us because of our resolution.

The troop of my company has requested that it be granted that they not be obliged to do service of any kind until such time as the central government of the Union shall determine on a course of action in the matter.

God and Liberty, Monterey, December 17, 1831.

Agustin V. Zamorano

To the General Commandant, Don José María de Echeandia, San Gabriel.[7]

---

[6] Zamorano and Ibarra to Echeandia, Monterey, December 16, 1831, MS., in *Legajo* 52-6-6-10, No. 2.

[7] Zamorano to Echeandia, Monterey, December 17, 1831, MS., in *Legajo* 52-6-6-10, No. 3. This and the preceding letter show that Zamorano did not, as **has been stated**

It was soon apparent that Don Agustin and Lieutenant Ibarra had analyzed the situation correctly. Before the month of December was over the Plan of San Diego had been approved and signed by at least one official in every *pueblo* and *presidio* from Los Angeles north.[8] The first was the *presidio* of San Francisco, where the officers of that post, led by Ensign Vallejo, signed the Plan on December 19. It was signed by a member or two of the *ayuntamientos* of San José on the 22nd, of Monterey on the 26th, and of Santa Barbara on January 1.

Ensign Don Mariano G. Vallejo left San Francisco at once to join the deputation in the south and reached Monterey about December 26. Knowing that Vallejo enthusiastically approved the Plan, Don Agustin advised him of his decision not to partake in its support and that he had requested his passport from the leaders of the insurrection. He also suggested that, in order to relieve him of embarrassment in the situation, Vallejo should assume temporarily the command of the *presidio* at Monterey until Echeandia could make his wishes in the matter known. Vallejo, anxious to join the deputation, declined.[9]

On December 21, from Los Angeles, Echeandia sent out another circular letter to the Territory.[10] In this, after stating that Victoria was on his way to embark, he announced that he would see that the new political and military heads entered into their offices legally until such time as the general sentiment assured the domestic peace and the central government had acted in the matter. He then quoted from

by many historians, accept the Plan of San Diego at first. His addressing Echeandia as "General Commandant" was an act of courtesy and did not imply recognition as such.

[8] Bancroft, *op. cit.*, III, 212, for details.

[9] Vallejo, *op. cit.*, II, 152-3, claims to have started south with a force before he knew of the battle of December 5, in response to a letter from Don José Antonio Carrillo. He says that on reaching Monterey, ". . . the persons there disaffected with the government of Señor Victoria joined my small force. When Zamorano heard that the populace of the Capital made cause with me, he spontaneously surrendered the post to me without firing a shot; a behavior that ill became the conduct which in all cases should be observed by a punctilious officer. I incorporated into my force the few soldiers who had been at Zamorano's orders and started my march in pursuit of Victoria." All of which is not true, as his letters of the period and other contemporary documents amply demonstrate. His aspersions on the conduct of Zamorano do not conceal the fact that Vallejo himself was engaged in the most unpardonable crime a military officer can commit—armed insurrection against his commanding officer.

[10] Echeandia, Circular Letter, Los Angeles, December 21, 1831, MS., in *Vallejo, Doc.*, I, 251, and *Legajo* 52-6-6-10, No. 4.

the national decree of May 6, 1822, which provided for succession to a temporarily vacant office. In accordance with this decree the senior member of the deputation should act as civil governor and the senior military officer should assume the duties of general commandant. He asked that all officers make their opinions in the matter known to him promptly in order that the new leaders could be installed soon and he be relieved of his temporary command so that he might proceed on his way to Mexico as his orders required.

This circular appears to have reached Monterey on December 28. On that day, Vallejo forwarded a copy to Ensign Sánchez at San Francisco, urged him to send his opinion by special messenger and stated that all was peaceful in the south.[11]

On the day following, December 29, Don Agustin wrote to Echeandia,

Comandancia Militar de Monterey.

> Your Worship's circular of the 21st instant, which you were pleased to send me, informs me that the problem of the succession to the political and military commands of the Territory has arisen from the present circumstances, and you have been pleased to ask me for my opinion in the matter so that you may make it known to the Most Excellent Territorial Deputation, for the purpose Your Worship has stated. In my letter of the 17th of this month, which I had the honor of sending Your Worship in answer to your circular of the 9th, I duly stated some of my ideas in the matter. I believe I can now add a little in regard to the military succession, on which I have a right to speak, but I shall withhold my opinion respecting the civil office because I do not wish to expose myself to error. I shall not take it on myself to pass judgment either for or against the actions of Señor Don Manuel Victoria during the time he, as general commandant and civil governor, governed this Territory since that is the privilege of the supreme government of the Union; likewise, neither shall I submit a judgment on the motives that prompted some to deny him their allegiance. But I shall make a brief statement of the opinion that compelled me to take the position I made known to Your Worship in my letter mentioned above.
>
> It is undeniable that the central government has the power to place in the discharge of these offices whatever person may suit its high pleasure; likewise, it is also true that the inhabitants of the Territory are not empowered to deny that person their obedience, except in the event

---

[11] Vallejo to José Sánchez, Monterey, December 28, 1831, MS., in *Vallejo, Doc.*, I, 253.

he may be judged a traitor to the country, since it is obvious that whoever might deny obedience to the ruler sent by the central government disobeys that same government which the former represents. Therefore, because of the weight of the above principle, the obedience denied Señor Victoria by the insurrection of the District of San Diego cannot, I believe, meet with the approval of the supreme authority.

Because the senior officers in my service have decided to support the rebellion referred to, because Señor Victoria is incapacitated to govern the Territory, having been placed in that condition, so I understand, by force, and because I have received no order from him as to whom I shall recognize as my superior (no doubt because he finds himself in the condition Your Worship describes in the said circular letter of the 9th), it is clear that I, having no desire to join in the San Diego uprising because of my regard for the honor of my military profession and having taken, I repeat, the stand that I have already stated, must consider myself as subject directly to the central government only. For that reason and in order that I may present myself before it to answer any charges which it may see fit to make against me as a result of my actions during the days of this month due to the present events, I have asked Your Worship for my passport.

For these reasons and because the officers and troops of this garrison are of the same opinion, I shall refrain from further consideration of the matter prior to the decision mentioned by Your Worship in your cited circular, which I now answer.

God and Liberty, Monterey, December 29, 1831.

AGUSTIN V. ZAMORANO

General Commandant Don José María de Echeandia.[12]

It would seem that Don Agustin's straight thinking and his logical, forceful exposition of his stand was unanswerable. These qualities, however, were lost on Echeandia. It was beyond his comprehension how any officer in California, especially one who had served for so many years under his immediate command, could fail to throw his wholehearted support to the Plan of San Diego. Only by such an hallucination can we explain Echeandia's failure to accede immediately to Don Agustin's polite but firm request for a passport for himself and family and for permission to leave the Territory. On the same day that Don Agustin was answering his circular letter of De-

[12] Zamorano to Echeandia, Monterey, December 29, 1831, MS., in *Legajo* 52-6-6-10, No. 5.

cember 21, Echeandia wrote his reply to the former's statement of December 16 and letter of December 17. Echeandia's letter has not been discovered but, judging from Don Agustin's reply, it must have been similar in content to a letter Echeandia wrote to Ensign Don José Sánchez on January 5, which I summarize.[13] In this, Echeandia made a long argument supporting the legality of the Plan of San Diego and again made his oft-repeated declaration that he was lending his services as a private citizen, awaiting the decision of the central government. In his argument, he stated that Alta California was organized like the rest of the Nation under the Constitution of 1824, which stated that the territories should be subject to two constitutions, the federal one and a local one. That while the former made no provision for the suspension of a governor from office, a special constitution drawn up for California had been introduced for consideration in the Chamber of Deputies on January 7, 1828, which provided that the Territory had the right, in a situation like the present, to bring action against the governor through its legislature and to suspend him from office. Therefore, if the governor, as in the present case, subjected the Territory to despotic rule without representation and denied individual security, its inhabitants, in their extreme desperation, could not be expected to wait six months or more for relief from the central government but had a natural right to act; that Victoria had abused his powers and the people had acted in self-defense only, with no other thought than the preservation of the Constitution.

Echeandia's failure to comprehend Don Agustin's position and his impatience at the latter's delay in giving his support to the Plan of San Diego is apparent in a short personal letter which he attached to his longer official one; he thought a personal appeal was all that was needed to gain Don Agustin's adherence. This letter has been preserved:

Don Agustin—
Señor Victoria, during his governorship here, attacked popular representation and individual security and, therefore, having no immediate hope of redress and pressed to the last extremity, the inhabitants declared themselves in favor of the following Plan:
[*Quotes the Plan of November 29.*]

[13] Echeandia to Sánchez, San Luis Rey, January 5, 1832, MS., in *Vallejo, Doc.*, I, 284.

Now if it [*the deputation*] is not permitted to function, its natural rights are suspended. What other legal recourse was left, except to rebel?

In the rebellion, I have had no part; but once it was done and I was called to organize and stabilize it, I had, by all rights, to accept.

Now at the present time there is no longer room for doubt that you must cooperate in maintaining the peace in which we find ourselves. The central government already knows what has happened and will not delay more than two months in ordering what it may see fit.

I am, as ever, yours,

San Juan Capistrano, December 29, 1831.

JOSÉ MARÍA DE ECHEANDIA

Captain Don Agustin V. Zamorano.[14]

On the same day also, Echeandia issued a third, short circular letter to the Territory. In this he stated that Señor Victoria had embarked on the 27th and that the deputation was expected to convene on a date between January 1 and 4.[15]

These three letters of Echeandia's reached Don Agustin on January 6 and he replied in a personal letter dated the day following. In this he again completely refuted Echeandia's arguments. From his extreme politeness, it is evident that he was concerned over the latter's persistent refusal to see the justice of the position he had taken and to grant him the passport he had requested.

Señor Don José María de Echeandia
My esteemed Chief and Sir:

Yesterday, I received your favor dated at San Juan Capistrano, December 29 last, in which you were pleased to give me the facts on which those in San Diego support themselves in removing Señor Victoria from both of his offices. Since you have had this confidential goodness allow me to give you my opinions.

The prospectus or outline of the special law for the internal government of this Territory, which was read in the Chamber of Deputies on January 7, 1828, and in which is set forth the right of this country, through its deputation, to suspend the civil governor from office should

---

[14] Echeandia to Zamorano, San Juan Capistrano, December 29, 1831, MS., in *Legajo* 52-6-6-10, No. 6.

[15] Echeandia to Commandant of San Francisco, San Juan Capistrano, December 29, 1831, MS., in *Vallejo, Doc.*, I, 254.

he abuse his powers, does not have the force of law for the reason that it had one reading only before that body, which was given the proposed law by the special committee that introduced it. In order that it become law, it is necessary that it receive the approval of both houses and the sanction of the chief executive. Since this has not been accomplished in the four years since the bill was first read, it is certain that it can be of no effect whatsoever as law.

Furthermore, I assume that the first part of Article I, paragraph 3, of the decree of the Cortes dated June 23, 1813, dealing with instructions for *ayuntamientos*, deputations, and civil governors, is still in force. This, in reference to the last named officer, says in conclusion, "And likewise, as he shall be responsible for the abuses of his authority so shall he also be faithfully respected and obeyed by all." From this, I infer that civil governors are subject before the central government to answer charges that may be brought against them before that superior authority by complainants or by those who may have observed infractions or abuse of the authority of the office entrusted to them, but they are never to be divested of the respect and obedience imposed on all of us by the law.

As I understand the abuses attributed to Don Manuel Victoria as civil governor began at the time he assumed command of this Territory, I believe that from then to date those who have observed them or those who have been injured by them, one and the other, have had ample time in which to have filed charges against him, before the central government, in the way they might have found most convenient, with the object of bringing him to order according to the laws. If they have done so, then why have they not waited for the results? If they have not done so, is it just that the complainants shall take on themselves the righting of their wrongs? Are they not trespassing on the authority of the central government and the very laws that furnish us with the legal means to make representations against our superiors? For these reasons, the recourse to insurrection against Señor Victoria is, in my opinion, too hasty and will never be approved by the central government.

If the contrary were true, such recourses to violence, because of our distance from the source of authority, would become incessant and the result would be that whoever considered himself wronged would take similar means to remove the civil governor from office. It is a means which the spirit of the laws prohibits because of the fatal consequences for the territories that result, since necessarily nothing results from such movements but the paralyzing of all business that enriches and improves them and the shedding of blood which, from all points of view, must be prevented.

Whatever person is appointed by the deputation to exercise the authority of civil governor in the absence of Señor Victoria, I hold him to be legally incompetent to act, assuming that he also has taken part in the uprising; as also is whoever is appointed to the military command, not only because it is not in its power to make such an appointment but because whoever may be eligible is also one of the rebels supporting insurrection. Consequently, as an officer, I find no one whom I can legally obey and for that reason I have asked you for my passport. I consider myself subject directly to the central government. In the meanwhile, from the time I am relieved at this post until I shall have taken my departure from the Territory, I shall try to preserve its peace and good order, as I have already informed you in my official letters.

I thoroughly appreciate that you have not been connected with the revolt, but I would have been much more pleased if you had been able to find some way of excusing yourself from the call that was made on you to regulate and organize it, because, in my opinion, you should have considered yourself *en route* under superior orders, which, in the present circumstances, you should have obeyed at all costs.

I trust that you may be in good health and wish that you make use of the affection of your servant who attentively kisses your hand.

Monterey, January 7, 1832.

AGUSTIN V. ZAMORANO[16]

The logic of Don Agustin's answer to Echeandia's arguments was unanswerable and demonstrated that the latter's principles were not only fallacious but dishonest. His courteous pointing out of the true path of duty was not taken kindly and thereafter Echeandia's letters show a bitterness and condescension which was only a shield against reasoning he could not refute. Echeandia chose to ignore the receipt of Don Agustin's letter of December 29 and his reply to it referred only to the letter of December 17.

Gobierno Provisional Politico y Militar de la Alta California.

I respect your conduct and the opinion outlined in your official letter of December 17 last (which was in answer to mine of the 9th of the same month). Also, I received quite some time ago the statement by Lieutenant Juan María Ibarra for the sergeants and other soldiers, which you mention therein.

---

[16] Zamorano to Echeandia, Monterey, January 7, 1832, MS., in *Legajo* 52-6-6-10, No. 7.

You and Citizen Lieutenant Ibarra must remember very well that, during my former term as governor, Solis revolted and tried to depose me from office (notwithstanding the lack of decorations [*condecoraciones*], education or distinguished political conduct on the part of the insurgents). I at once saw that their plan was examined by a council and that two points should be decided frankly: first, whether it could be considered legal, or in any way reasonable; second, whether any one should be named as my successor. It was decided, by an unanimous vote, that their plan was not a reasonable one and that I should continue in my offices, taking public opinion into account. That affair supports my contention that I do not act in anger now and that, by the same token, my actions agree with the rights I know the people possess.

Well now, let us consider—by what right do you, and the honest soldiers who follow you, propose some to leave the country and the others not to continue in the service? Perhaps it is assumed that the rebels and their followers wish to belong to another nation, or to support some other system of government—it can be nothing less than that. By the living God! I accepted the unfortunate offices to which I was called only to see if, by some way, anarchy might not be avoided and our sacred foundations upheld! If Señor Victoria had been unable to govern because of death, or natural sickness, or of suspension according to law, as is well known to everybody, would we rise one against the other, or would we dismember ourselves, dismissing the local authorities? Of course not! We are at present in the last situation, with this difference only—that all have not been able to recognize at once the public right. For the future we should devote our united services to the country. If all those soldiers are in their right minds and could see the peace and order with which our laws continue to be respected, is it to be expected that they would look with horror on their compatriots, relatives and friends who have tried to conserve unblemished the constitutional liberty to which they are pledged and to which we are all bound by the same oath?

In spite of what I have said, I shall not fail to expedite the return of the artillerymen, who must go because they have completed the time for which they enlisted or for other just reasons, neither will I oppose the departure of the soldiers of the Mazatlan company. But I shall appreciate it, as is just, if the necessary steps to that end be taken without hatreds, as though nothing had happened to Señor Victoria. Finally, with respect to the troops of your company, I expect that, because of conviction and reason, they will return to their usual duties and that you

The Plan of San Diego

yourself will take the steps your prudence dictates as most suitable. God and Liberty, Mission San Luis Rey, January 8, 1832.

José María de Echeandia

The Military Commander of the Presidio at Monterey, Captain C. Agustin V. Zamorano.[17]

During the time these letters were being exchanged between Don Agustin and Señor Echeandia, other events were transpiring in the south and in the north.

II. Echeandia Intimidates the Legislature.

A few days after Echeandia wrote his letter of January 8, 1832, to Captain Zamorano, he prepared a report to the President of the Republic, which he forwarded, under date of January 15, 1832, from San Diego. In this he reported events that had transpired since his report of December 4, that Victoria had embarked, that the territorial legislature had begun its sessions at Los Angeles on the 10th, and that the Territory found itself at peace. He closed by saying that he was about to lay down the provisional authority under which he had been acting.[18] On the second day following, January 17, he addressed another circular letter to the Territory. In this he advised the inhabitants that Victoria had sailed on the *Pocahontas* on that date and that the deputation had begun its sessions on the 10th in Los Angeles and that as soon as it had completed the case against Victoria it would turn its attention to appointing a successor in the political office and that he would advise the public of whatever action was taken.[19]

Until this time, Echeandia had remained faithful to the stated objects of the insurrection, as set forth in the Plan of San Diego, and had been trying to win the good graces of the people of the Territory by fair promises. He had repeatedly, as we have seen in his correspondence with Don Agustin, carefully justified his course of action

---

[17] Echeandia to Zamorano, San Luis Rey, January 8, 1832, MS., *ibid.*, No. 1.

[18] Echeandia to President of Mexico, San Diego, January 15, 1832, MS., in *Legajo* 52-6-6-7.

[19] Echeandia, Circular Letter, San Diego, January 17, 1832, MS., in *Dept. St. Pap.*, III, 21; in *Legajo* 52-6-6-10, No. 2. Quoted in full in Echeandia to Pio Pico, same date, in *Legajo* 52-6-6-7, No. 1.

and stated his desire to leave Alta California as soon as peace and order were reestablished. Back of all this, however, he fully expected that the deputation would invite him to serve as acting governor. Of this he was so certain that he neglected to take part in its proceedings.

The territorial legislature met in extraordinary session at Los Angeles on the morning of January 10. The deputies present were Don Pío Pico, Don Mariano G. Vallejo, Don Antonio María Osío, Don José Joaquín Ortega, Don Santiago Argüello and Don Tomás Yorba, an alternate, with Don Juan B. Alvarado as secretary. Don Pío Pico, as senior member, assumed the chair. Its first business was to suspend Victoria from office and to appoint a committee to prepare the case against him to be sent to the central government. These matters disposed of, it turned its attention to the question of naming a successor to Victoria.

In this, their action was based on the national law of May 6, 1822, which stated that in the absence of the civil governor the senior member of the deputation should assume the office. That procedure also was specified in Echeandía's summons of December 9, in which he had asked the deputation to name the two persons who would fill the offices of civil governor and general commandant. After making certain this law was still in force, the members, on January 11, by unanimous vote elected Don Pío Pico to the office of civil governor ad interim and their secretary was instructed to notify the provisional governor, Echeandía, so that he might proclaim their action to the Territory. It was then voted to request Echeandía to call a meeting of the military officers serving in the Territory so that they might name the person to act as general commandant in accordance with their regulations. In the meantime, they had requested Echeandía to be present at their meetings.[20]

Copies of the minutes of their sessions on January 10 and 11, together with their request that he attend their meetings, were sent to Echeandía at San Diego on the 12th. These reached him as he was completing his report of the 15th to the President of the Republic, which was despatched on the *Pocahontas*, sailing on the 17th. He

[20] Minutes of sessions of deputation at Los Angeles, January 10-11, 1832, in *Legislative Record*, MS., I, 173-83; also in *Legajo* 52-6-6-7.

attached these minutes to his report without reading them and on the same day wrote to Los Angeles asking that other copies be supplied him.[21] On the 18th, he advised the deputies that his military duties had made it impossible for him to attend their sessions but that he would make known his ideas on the matters before them in the near future.[22]

New copies of their minutes were sent to Echeandia and their meetings were suspended until they should hear from him. Having received no word from him, the deputies became impatient and assembled again on January 26. Deciding there was no reason to wait longer, they inducted Pico into office as civil governor on the next day. Copies of their minutes for the 26th and 27th were then sent to Echeandia.[23]

When Echeandia received the new copies of the deputation's minutes and saw that they had ignored him entirely in their selection of a civil ruler and had already elected Don Pio Pico, he was completely dumbfounded. His wrath became terrible. Forgetting all the high ideals he had been preaching and all the fine promises he had been making, forgetting for the time being the recalcitrance of Captain Zamorano, he started angrily to Los Angeles to impose his will on the helpless legislature. Reaching Los Angeles on January 31, he at once wrote Pico the first of a series of letters in which he criticised every action the deputation had taken. He claimed that body had taken up the matter of a successor to Victoria too hastily, that it had insulted him by insinuating that he was resisting giving up his provisional authority, that Pico was incompetent to perform the duties of civil governor, and made many other insolent and, in large part, unfounded complaints.[24]

It is not necessary that we here go into the details of the quarrel that followed. In the end, Echeandia completely cowed the legisla-

---

[21] Echeandia to Pio Pico, San Diego, January 17, 1832, MS., in *Legajo* 52-6-6-7, No. 1.
[22] Echeandia to Pio Pico, San Diego, January 18, 1832, MS., *ibid*.
[23] Minutes of deputation, January 26-7, 1832, MS., in *Legislative Record*, I, 186-9; also in *Legajo* 52-6-6-7. Alvarado to Echeandia, Los Angeles, January 28, 1832, forwarding copies of minutes, MS., *ibid*.
[24] Echeandia to Pico, Los Angeles, January 31, 1832, MS. Also, the same, February 1 and February 3, MS. The first two in *Dept. St. Pap.*, III, 27-38, and all three in *Legajo* 52-6-6-7.

ture. That body adjourned its meetings on February 17 and Pico refused to make further claim to the office of civil governor until his honor was vindicated and the legislature free to carry out its duties.[25] Pico's sole claim for recognition as having been governor at this time is that he was recognized as such for twenty days by the five other members of the deputation. On the 24th of February, the members of the deputation forwarded a long and strong case against Echeandia to the central government, together with a statement of their own efforts in the interests of the country.[26]

In this manner, Echeandia removed the territorial legislature as a factor in the insurrection of 1831-32. His actions were treacherous, contemptible, and deliberately contrary to every provision of the Plan under which the insurrectionists were supposed to be operating. On the other hand, the conduct of Pico and his associates was, on the whole, moderate and dignified.[27] As a finale to this episode, Echeandia sent out another circular letter to the Territory on February 25. To this he attached copies of the minutes of the deputation's session of February 12, his letter of February 16 to the deputies, and their reply to him of the same date. At the risk of redundancy, I quote this in full in order that the reader may see the mental state to which Echeandia had by this time been reduced.

Gobierno Provisional Politico y Militar de la Alta California.

> In this circular letter I make clear the illegality of the procedure under which the deputation has proceeded to place its senior member, Citizen Pio Pico, in the office of civil governor as well as my reasons for refusing him recognition as such and state that should the necessity arise of either acting by force against the decision of that body or of giving up the civil command, I would do the latter. From the beginning, I have believed that if I continued to act in that office, the deputies, already irritated (excepting Citizen Tomás Yorba, who took no part in the appointment and who has been of a contrary opinion), would broadcast against me all sorts of incriminations from which new uprisings might result. Unfortunately, not even the offer I made to surrender the civil office

---

[25] Minutes of deputation, February 16-17, 1832, in *Legislative Record*, MS., I, 202-11.
[26] This was prepared by M. G. Vallejo and Santiago Argüello, *ibid.*, 253-68.
[27] For detailed discussion of these events, see Bancroft, *op. cit.*, III, 216-20, and Tays, *Revolutionary California*, MS., Chapter VIII.

has served to stop the great affronts which the deputation has heaped on me. In an effort to preserve the peace and harmony in which the Territory finds itself, I make public here the three following documents and in regard to each the brief comments time will permit me.

In Document No. 1, we have the only minutes in which are set forth all the bases and formalities on which the deputation supports itself in deciding that its member, Citizen Pio Pico, should, according to the best legal form, assume the civil office.[28] In Document No. 2, we have my letter of the 16th of the current month, which I sent to the deputation notifying it that I was surrendering the civil command and, at the same time, that I was making public its last communication to me in which it required me to place in possession the officer it had named to succeed me and excusing myself from that function because I considered his appointment illegal in view of the observations I had made in the matter.[29] To this document, I shall now add the following: That, even though the decree of May 6, 1822, were held to be in good standing in this Territory, as Deputy Citizen Pio Pico had promoted the rebellion, albeit a just one, it sufficed to deprive him of his eligibility, at least while the usual inquiries were being made into the affair. Also, the vote should have been made in secret so as to avoid the embarrassments that arise in such matters. Furthermore, the rules for the internal regulation of that body in its discussions and resolutions were not observed. Finally, as it is required that the two interested members, Citizen Pio Pico and his brother-in-law Citizen Don Joaquín Ortega, absent themselves from the voting (according to what is set down here and in the cited Document No. 2), there remained but three voting deputies and consequently there was no deputation to decide on such an appointment, because by the mandate of the order of May 4, 1814, and the decree of September 16, 1823, at least four deputies are required to constitute the deputation.

In Document No. 3, we have the communication by which the deputation answerd mine, Document No. 2, and in it are seen the ungoverned and immoderate expressions which are commonly those of one possessed by a furious passion.[30] The impartial public will know from the events of the past wherein the right lies, permitting me to say that the members of the deputation, confused by their own conceit, precipitated themselves from one error to another until they dissolved that body under the pretext that they lacked liberty of action. Their

---

[28] Minutes of deputation, February 12-13, 1832, in *Legislative Record*, MS., I, 197-202.
[29] Echeandia to Pico, Los Angeles, February 16, 1832, MS., in *Dept. St. Pap.*, III, 42, and in *Legajo* 52-6-6-7, No. 13.
[30] Pico to Echeandia, Los Angeles, February 16, 1832, MS., in *Legajo* 52-6-6-7, No. 14.

very act denies that statement. All the people in general are witness that they have held their sessions almost by themselves, when and where they have found it convenient and that their peaceful daily and nightly assembly in one place or another has been interfered with by no one. The *ayuntamiento* and the populace of this place in their entirety, on Sunday, the 19th of this month, confirmed their action in not recognizing the Citizen Pio Pico as civil governor, in spite of the exhortations made to the gathering by certain members of the deputation. Such is the conception they have formed of the miscarriage of this affair.

With this statement on record and sensitive to my sacred obligations to the inhabitants of all the Territory, I now again try to surrender the civil office, with the single reservation that it go to whom it belongs in the best legal form.

For this purpose and so that the military command may not suffer any aberration and that civil affairs, which are now paralyzed, may take their course, I now propose, with the honor and good faith that has always characterised me, what, in my judgment, I believe to be legally suited to the present circumstances, namely: That the senior captain, Citizen Pablo de la Portilla, shall assume both commands, or, if opinion is divided because he may be considered as among those who promoted the rebellion, that Captain Citizen Agustin V. Zamorano shall assume both offices, since he was in no way concerned with said Plan and, moreover, has rendered distinguished service in the conduct of governmental affairs in that he has served for more than six years in the satisfactory performance of the duties of both secretaryships.

To carry out this transfer, I await only the acceptance of either one of the two candidates named and the prior approval of all the officers of the four presidial departments, who, in addition to the two candidates proposed, may take under consideration the officer of equal rank, Citizen Santiago Argüello, stating the qualifications which they attribute to him in giving preference. All with the understanding that in event of any delay, I shall deliver the office in the order stated to him who accepts it.

The presidial commanders, the Reverend Father Missionaries, either because of its relation to their privileges or because of its relation to their charges, and the *alcaldes* of the towns, will please answer this in a precise and definite manner so that the captain receiving the command, knowing the public opinion, may act as is fitting.

God and Liberty, Los Angeles, February 25, 1832.

JOSÉ MARÍA DE ECHEANDIA

By chain from the Town of Los Angeles to Mission San Gabriel and the rest of the missions from that of San Buenaventura south to the presidio of San Diego.[81]

---

[81] Echeandia, Circular Letter, Los Angeles, February 25, 1832, MS., *ibid.*, No. 12.

Having issued this highly legal defense of illegality, Señor Echeandia, with his feathers badly ruffled, retired to San Diego to await the replies. Let us now turn our attention to affairs in the territorial capital, Monterey, where an answer was being prepared that caused Echeandia once again to reverse himself completely.

Chapter vi.

Zamorano as Acting Governor, February 1832 to January 1833.

IN their discussion, on the evening of December 16, 1831, of the situation that confronted the Territory, Captain Zamorano and Lieutenant Ibarra had not doubted for an instant that it was their duty to resist and, if possible, to suppress the revolt that had broken out on November 29 at San Diego. They resolved to offer no resistance, for the present at least, because they thought it futile with the limited resources at their command. Don Agustin has often been criticised for not having gone to the aid of Governor Victoria. He did not learn of the engagement at Cahuenga Pass, nearly four hundred miles from Monterey, until eleven days after it had taken place, by which time Victoria had surrendered to Portilla and Echeandia. Therefore, any attempt to go to his rescue would have been foolhardy in the extreme.

It will be recalled that Zamorano and Ibarra expected the revolt to prove popular throughout the Territory. For that reason, they felt there were but two courses open to them—to join the insurrection or to ask for their passports and permission to leave the Territory. For the first two or three weeks, their analysis of the situation appeared to be correct; the Plan of San Diego was accepted noisily by a few public officers in each of the *pueblos* and *presidios*. It was not long, however, before the calmer and more stable elements of the community began to express themselves.

Captain Zamorano, in full possession of the machinery of the territorial government at the capital of the Territory, continued to carry on the routine work of the established government, holding for future decision all matters that required the approval of the governor or that laid beyond his competence as executive secretary. As those who did not approve of the revolt or of the Plan of San Diego desired to make their opposition known, it was the natural and proper thing for them to turn to him, as the remaining officer of the executive branch of the government and ask what that government intended to do.

I. The Monterey Council of February 1, 1832.

None of the letters, unfortunately, that came to Captain Zamorano at this time have been preserved and there is no way by which we can inform ourselves as to the extent of the reaction against the Plan of San Diego. He later said, as we shall see, that he had received many letters from Santa Barbara, San José and San Francisco.

The earliest movement against the Plan of which we have definite knowledge today was among the foreigners who lived at Monterey. These men, many of whom were naturalized Mexican citizens, constituted a large part of the population of the capital and controlled nearly all the business done there. In the past, very few of them had taken any part in political affairs. Although they had taken no formal stand in Victoria's behalf during the past year, they had approved of his strict preservation of order and administration of justice, which had permitted them to carry on their business operations in peace and security. These men had complained continually among themselves during Echeandia's term as governor of the lack of security in their operations and did not now look forward with pleasure to the return of such conditions. They knew nothing, and cared less, about Victoria's sins against the spirit of Mexican institutions. Therefore they feared the revolt that had broken out in the south would prove injurious to their business prospects. Under the leadership of William E. P. Hartnell, an Englishman and a naturalized Mexican citizen, whose firm of McCulloch, Hartnell & Company had carried on an extensive trade with the missions but who at this time was operating as a *ranchero*, the foreign residents of Monterey lost little time in making their opinions known.

There is no evidence that Captain Zamorano at any time failed to realize, or denied, that it was his duty to maintain the duly constituted government of the Territory until a new governor should be appointed. At first he took no positive steps to do this because of his opinion that it would be impossible in the face of popular approval of the revolt and that any attempt to do so would only complicate the situation and add to the general discontent. He was slow to change his opinion and almost six weeks passed before he took any steps in that direction. The continued receipt of protests against the hasty action of some of the public officers in signing the Plan finally led him to the conclusion that there was sufficient popular support to maintain and preserve the territorial government and that it was his duty, as the executive secretary and the senior military officer present, to attempt it. Having reached this decision and determined to act, he, nevertheless, proceeded with caution and some hesitation until he was certain both as to what could be expected of him and as to the resources available.

The first step taken by Captain Zamorano was to call a meeting in the *presidio*, on January 24, 1832, of the foreign residents. To them he described the situation in the Territory and stated that he intended, if support was at hand, to maintain the territorial government. However, the first problem was to provide for the preservation of order in and the protection of the capital, Monterey. As he was well acquainted with all the persons present, many of whom were his close friends, there was, no doubt, a very thorough discussion of the circumstances that faced the Territory. While we have no record of what was said at this meeting, it must have been the general sentiment that the government should be supported as those present agreed to form a military company that would take over the protection of Monterey and thus relieve the troops under Captain Zamorano's command of that duty, if he, in return, would agree not to call on that company for service outside the town. This condition was accepted.

This company was organized at the same meeting and William E. P. Hartnell chosen as its commander. Juan B. Bonifacio, an Italian and a naturalized Mexican citizen, formerly in the employ of McCulloch, Hartnell & Company, was elected as second in command, with Luis Vignes, a Frenchman, as his substitute in case of his dis-

As Acting Governor 93

ability. Members of the company were to be paid at the rate of four *reales* per day for the time they saw actual service. The following were present at this meeting and signed the roll of the *compañia extranjera*:

Agustin V. Zamorano	Juan B. Bonifacio	J. L. Vignes
William E. Hartnell	Timothy Murphy	D. Douglas
Thomas Coulter	William Taylor	Nathan Spear
Juan B. Leandry	James Watson	Santiago McKinley
George Kinlock	John Rainsford	Estévan Munrás
J. B. R. Cooper	John Gorman	José Iglesias
José Amesti	Charles Roe	Walter Duckworth
Luis Pombert	Henry Bee	Thomas Raymore
Samuel Mead	R. S. Barker	John Roach
William McCarty	Edward Watson	Thomas Doak
John Thompson	John Miles	David Littlejohn
James Cook	Joseph Dixon	William Garner
William Johnson	John Roper	Pierre J. Chevrette
William Gralbatch	Guy F. Fling	Charles R. Smith
Juan D. Bravo	John Burns	William Webb
Daniel Ferguson[1]		

With the protection of Monterey provided for but still a little hesitant as to just what further steps he should take, Captain Zamorano called a council of war which met in the *presidio* at Monterey on February 1, 1832. This meeting was attended, in addition to Don Agustin, by Don Rafael Gómez, the *asesor* or legal advisor of the Territory, Don José Joaquín Gómez, acting *comisario* at Monterey, Don Salvador Espinosa, the *alcalde* of the town, Lieutenant Don Juan María Ibarra, William E. P. Hartnell and Juan B. Bonifacio, of the *compañia extranjera*, Don Juan Malarin, merchant, sea captain, honorary lieutenant in the Mexican navy and close friend of Zamo-

[1] *Compañia Extrangera de Monterey, su organización*, Monterey, January 24, 1832, MS., in *Legajo* 52-6-6-10, No. 10. A contemporary, uncertified copy in *Vallejo, Doc.*, I, 285. The original orderly book of this company of volunteers, entitled, *Cuaderno de Ordenes de la Compañia Extrangera de Monterey en 1832. Por su Capitan y Comandante Wm. E. P. Hartnell*, is preserved in the Bancroft Library. The entries in this book show that Monterey was patrolled every night by members of the company from February 9 to April 9 and that, on April 10, the company was thanked for its services by the commandant (Zamorano) and advised that its services, barring an unforeseen emergency, would no longer be needed. The last entry in this record, dated April 12, indicates that Hartnell, because of some misunderstanding between the *alcalde* of the town and Bonifacio in which the commandant agreed with the *alcalde*, resigned his command.

rano, Brevet Lieutenant Don Francisco Pacheco, and Sergeant of Artillery, José María Medrano.

As will be noticed at once, this was not a gathering of officials and therefore, as a council, could have no official standing. Such a status was never claimed for it. It was simply a gathering of men who represented the varied elements of the community and who came at Don Agustin's call to discuss the situation and to give him the benefit of their counsel and advice. As their number included the chief legal officer of the Territory, the local representative of the treasury department, the chief officer of the town government, the military officers present, the officers of the Company of Foreigners, and a prominent merchant, it was the strongest and most influential group of men available. They were responsible persons and not politicians and revolutionists; their standing is indicative of Captain Zamorano's earnest desire for the best advice possible. Many authorities have made the statement that this council met to do the bidding of Captain Zamorano. It would seem, however, that the character and standing of the personnel of this group were sufficient answer to any such aspersion. There is no reason to doubt that the conclusions they reached were the considered judgment of the men present.

Before this gathering, Captain Zamorano laid all the information that had come to him, discussed the resources available and asked advice as to his duty in the situation and as to how far he could be expected to go in attempting to perform that duty. The results of the deliberations of this council were carefully stated in a set of minutes and resolutions which were signed by all those present. As Captain Zamorano's subsequent actions were regulated by the policies set forth in these resolutions, I quote this document in full.

> At the *Presidio* of Monterey on the first of February, eighteen hundred and thirty-two, the military commander of this post, Citizen Agustin V. Zamorano, summoned the following gentlemen: Attorney Citizen Rafael Gómez, *asesor* of the Territory, Citizen José Joaquín Gómez, acting *comisario* of the local sub-treasury, Citizen Salvador Espinosa, constitutional *alcalde* of the neighborhood, Mr. William E. P. Hartnell and Don Juan Bautista Bonifacio, as being in command of the Company of Foreigners, Citizen Juan María Malarin, second lieutenant in the national navy, Citizen Francisco Pacheco, retired ensign in the army,

and José María Medrano, second sergeant and acting commander of the artillery detachment.

These having assembled in the office of the secretary of the *comandancia general*, the military commander advised them that he was reliably informed that in the region from the *presidio* of Santa Barbara to that of San Francisco, which includes the greater part of the Territory of Alta California, the inhabitants were not accepting the Plan which had been promulgated following the revolt that broke out in San Diego on November 29 last, proposing the removal of Señor Lieutenant Colonel Don Manuel Victoria from the civil and military commands, and the assembling of the Most Excellent Territorial Deputation so that it might appoint the persons who should substitute in each command for Victoria. This was evidenced by letters which bore on the matter and which he had in his hands from Santa Barbara, the town of San José de Guadalupe, and the *presidio* of San Francisco, and by reports which had been made confidentially to him. In view of these circumstances, he thought it advisable to call the present gathering so as to discuss with it the following questions:

1. Should the acts of the Most Excellent Territorial Deputation which may emanate from the sessions which its members have been holding in the Town of Los Angeles be held as legal or illegal?

2. In the event of the latter and assuming that Señor Victoria, who was exercising them, is known definitely to have sailed from the Port of San Diego for that of San Blas on the 17th of January last, upon which one, or ones, should the *accidental* civil and military commands fall?

3. Would it be proper to send troops to the aid of Santa Barbara, as that place has requested, and if so, what instructions should the commander of that force observe?

4. Assuming that *comisario subalterno* Don Juan Bandini is one of the principals in the revolt, should his subordinate officer at this place, Citizen José Joaquín Gómez, obey his orders and if not, how shall they deal with each other?

After discussing at length the four questions submitted and considering the opinions of each person present, the following resolutions were agreed on by an unanimous vote:

1. That they considered as null and illegal all the acts that might emanate from the present sessions of the Most Excellent Territorial Deputation, for the reason that it has been convened by an unlawful authority, existing only by means of the present revolt which has trespassed criminally against the representative of the central government in the person of Señor Victoria. Therefore, no obedience or respect was

due to the appointees of the said deputation, it having no power in the matter since the decree of the Cortes of June 23, 1813, which is still in force in our Republic, provides that only the central executive has the power to appoint civil governors.

2. That the office of civil governor should not fall to any person whatsoever until the central government of the Union shall appoint one. As it is hoped to have a decision in this matter within a short time, it is believed that such particular cases as may arise in this office will be of so little importance that their decision can be delayed for three or four months; in the meanwhile the *alcaldes* of the towns and their citizens should be able to carry on for themselves the necessary policing and governing of their towns, with the approval of the *ayuntamientos* to which they belong. In regard to the *comandancia general*, it shall be assumed *accidentale* by the officer of highest rank and seniority who shall have taken no part in favor of the aforesaid Plan. Having looked for these qualities in the officers stationed at Santa Barbara, Monterey and San Francisco, it was agreed that Captain Citizen Agustin V. Zamorano, the only one of his rank, should take charge *accidentale* of the *comandancia general* until the central government has acted, on the theory that it fell to him by regulations to succeed Señor Victoria since the other two officers of the same rank and greater seniority, Don Pablo de la Portilla and Don Santiago Argüello, are implicated in the revolt.

3. That in view of the anxiety of the honorable officers and residents of Santa Barbara to uphold the legitimate authority in that place and in order to avoid a catastrophe there, it is agreed that the largest number of troops that can be spared from this garrison should be sent there as reenforcements. This should also serve as a barrier to control the insurgents of the San Diego Plan and the commander who shall occupy the post of Santa Barbara should be cautioned to use all means possible to preserve the peace and security of that place and not attempt operations against the opposing party unless they attack, in which event he shall defend the place with the gallantry and military conduct demanded of him by the glory of Mexican arms, and in the last extreme, if circumstances permit, he shall advance to the Port of San Diego and capture the principal instigators of the revolt and place them at the disposition of the acting general commandant, who will be guided by circumstances until a decision is reached by a council called to consider the case. That the general commandant shall, at some convenient time, forward a copy of these proceedings to the principal person in authority in the forces of the opposing party with a sharp official note demanding, in the name of the supreme government, for the first and last time, that he place himself, and cause all who follow him in arms to place themselves, at

the disposal of the said acting general commandant, who shall suspend them all from the duties of their offices, as also all other governmental employees and civilians who may have taken part in the said revolt, until the decision of the central government is received, treating each with the consideration due to their stations. In the event they refuse to lay down their arms, they shall be warned not to advance beyond the limits of the territory they now occupy, and that if they do they will be repelled by force and shall be responsible before the central government for all misfortunes that may originate therefrom.

4. Assuming that the *comisario subalterno*, Don Juan Bandini, is one of the leaders of the revolt and that he has taken an active part in it, his orders shall not be obeyed by his subordinate at this port, Citizen José Joaquín Gómez, who shall deal directly with the Quartermaster General of the West.

Additional:

5. On the assumption that the garrison at San Francisco has proclaimed itself in favor of the legitimate authority and holds as prisoner Ensign Don José Sánchez, who commanded it and who favored the said Plan, it is directed that the retired lieutenant, Citizen Ignacio Martínez, shall take charge of the command of that post, leaving, for the present, to the discretion of the acting general commandant the measures he may consider necessary for the safety of the person of the said ensign, with the understanding that he shall be treated with the moderation and consideration due him, under whatever restrictions that may seem proper.

6. That the acting general commandant shall opportunely report to the central government, enclosing a copy of these proceedings as well as of all correspondence that he has had relative to this matter, calling the special attention of the supreme authority to the service by which the foreign gentlemen resident in this place have made themselves creditors of its gratitude in cooperating to sustain the legitimate authority sent by the central government, and enclosing a list of the names of all of them, as also a list of the honorable officers and citizens who have shown the best behavior in these circumstances.

The six preceding resolutions having been approved these minutes were ordered drawn up, and were then signed on this same day, month, and year.

    Agustin V. Zamorano José Joaquín Gómez
    Francisco Pacheco   William E. P. Hartnell
    Salvador Espinosa   Juan Malarin
    Juan Bautista Bonifacio Lic. Rafael Gómez
    José María Medrano   Juan María Ibarra[2]

---

[2] Proceedings of Council of War, Monterey, February 1, 1832, MS. Certified copy in *Vallejo, Doc.,* I, 288; another *ibid.,* I, 286; partial transcript in *Bandini, Doc.,* 28; also in *Legajo* 52-6-6-7, No. 10.

For his decision to preserve the legitimately established government of the Territory, Captain Zamorano, strange as it may seem, has been universally condemned and execrated. By this action, as we shall see, he blocked the plans and ambitions of Echeandia and the supporters of the San Diego revolt and so incurred, as had Victoria before him, the undying enmity of those young native Californians who had become inoculated with the extreme philosophies of Don José María Padrés. Vallejo, Alvarado, Pico, his brother-in-law Bandini, and, to a lesser degree, Osío, in their histories and memoirs dictated many years later for H. H. Bancroft, have difficulty in finding words with which to express their dislike for him and their contempt for his, to them, anti-liberal, reactionary, ultra-conservative actions and principles. They accuse him of having been dishonest, treacherous, ambitious for personal ends, insincere, and of hating the Californians.

Following these sources, American historians of California have found few kind words for him. So eminent an authority as H. H. Bancroft, displaying the bias of which I have spoken, wrote:

> While Echeandia was thus occupied with a revolutionary movement against his own friends in the south [*i.e. the intimidation of the legislature*], another Mexican officer was engaged in developing revolutionary schemes, equally selfish and ambitious, but far less treacherous, in the north. Captain Agustin V. Zamorano and others pronounced at Monterey against the Plan of San Diego, and all who had favored that movement. Zamorano had been Victoria's secretary and friend, but so far as can be known had taken no part in the troubles of 1831, had made no effort to defend his unpopular master in his time of need, but had perhaps promised neutrality. Now that Victoria was out of the country, aware that the popular feeling in favor of Echeandia was by no means so strong as had been that against Victoria, knowing that current disputes must be settled eventually in Mexico rather than in California, and being moreover free from all charges of complicity in the late revolt, the ambitious captain shrewdly saw his opportunity to gain favor with the national authorities, as well as temporary prominence in territorial affairs, and he acted accordingly.[3]

This, as any one who has read the documents quoted here will agree, is not only unjust to Captain Zamorano but is not true. These

---
[3] Bancroft, *op. cit.*, III, 220.

documents, whose existence in the general archives of the Mexican War Department was but recently discovered, clear him of all the charges of duplicity and insincerity that have been brought against him. From the moment he first heard of the Plan of San Diego he refused to give it his approval and consistently remained loyal to the central government. His decision to maintain and preserve the established territorial government was reached slowly and cautiously, after he had been convinced that it was his plain duty to do so and that the San Diego revolt did not meet with the approval of the majority of the inhabitants of the Territory. There's nothing on which to base any doubt as to his sincerity and there is nothing to substantiate the charge that he was scheming for his own advancement. His conduct was honorable, above-board, and consistent throughout. His critics may, perhaps, be pardoned for their lack of understanding, as it is unusual, I admit, to find a Mexican officer of that time possessed of sufficient character to remain true to his principles under such circumstances. However, there were a few such men in California—unfortunately for the Territory their number was very small—and the most outstanding of these was Don Agustin V. Zamorano.

Mexican practice of the time used distinct terms to indicate the quality of the authority by which the holder of a public office exercised his power. If one held an office as the regularly constituted appointee, he held title to his office *proprietario;* if his appointment was temporary or ad interim, his title was *interino;* if he held no appointment and his authority grew out of the circumstances and he acted provisionally, his title was *provisional;* if he acted by reason of being the only officer present and only until such time as an ad interim or permanent appointment was made, his authority was described as *accidental.* Echeandia styled himself, in accordance with the Plan of San Diego, *provisional.* The deputation elected Don Pio Pico as civil governor *interino.* Captain Zamorano, on the advice of his council, as the senior officer present, assumed the title of *Comandante General accidental,* which we shall translate as acting general commandant. He never, also in line with the advice of the council, made any pretensions to the civil governorship—that office was vacant. He continued to perform only such civil functions as were considered immediately imperative and probably justified himself in doing so by the fact that he was still the executive secretary of the civil government, although I know of no statement to that effect on his part.

Captain Zamorano's first act as general commandant was to transmit by circular letter copies of the resolutions adopted by the council of February 1. This letter, which I quote, was a very modest one and did not proclaim him as acting general commandant. That was left to the resolutions.

CIRCULAR.

I have the honor of enclosing herewith for your information and such action as seems necessary, the resolutions adopted by the Council held at this Port on the first day of this month on the circumstances in which the Territory of Alta California finds itself today.

God and Liberty, Monterey, February 2, 1832.

AGUSTIN V. ZAMORANO[4]

In the evening of February 5, word reached Monterey that Ensign Don Domingo Carrillo, who had assumed the command of the *presidio* at Santa Barbara after the death of Captain Pacheco and who sympathized with the Plan of San Diego, had been removed from that command by his brother, Ensign Don Anastacio Carrillo, and that the officers and men of that garrison had repudiated the rebellion and were loyal to the *autoridad legítima*. This change had taken place before the receipt there of news of the council of February 1 and was extremely encouraging. This development in the situation was broadcast to the Territory, without particular comment, by Captain Zamorano in another circular letter dated February 6.[5]

On February 12, Lieutenant Ibarra, in conformity with the resolution of the council of February 1, left Monterey for Santa Barbara with a force of about one hundred men.[6] He carried with him a pack-

---

[4] Zamorano, Circular Letter to *alcaldes* of San José, Branciforte, and San Francisco, Monterey, February 2, 1832, MS. To San José, in *Vallejo, Doc.*, I, 289; to Branciforte and San Francisco, *ibid.*, I, 290.

[5] Zamorano, Circular Letter to *alcaldes* of San José, Branciforte, and San Francisco, Monterey, February 6, 1832, MS., *ibid.*, I, 290.

[6] Bancroft, *op. cit.*, III, 224, says that Ibarra left Monterey "about February 9th." However, Zamorano's letter to Echeandia is dated the 12th and Ibarra later said that it was

age addressed to Echeandia which contained the following letter from the acting general commandant.

Comandancia General accidental de la Alta California.

Time has unrolled to public view the history of Alta California that has run its course since the 29th of November of last year to this date and the most recent events, of which you must know, have caused me to change from my first resolution and will also make you realize that you have been deceived by a few into believing that the majority of the people between Santa Barbara and San Francisco were accepting the pronouncement of San Diego.

To what has happened in this place, I have been an eyewitness and concerning Santa Barbara, San José de Guadalupe, Branciforte and San Francisco, their actions in favor of the legitimate authority justify my statement more eloquently than I can. By this evidence it is not difficult to see that the general opinion of the Territory is not in sympathy with said Plan and that it has wished only, by moderation, to avoid the bloodshed which might have happened from the start and which will happen if you ignore the justice with which, in general, all the inhabitants are resolved to recognize no other authority than the legitimate one.

Therefore, I, who, in company with the others, seek only the most effective means of remedying the situation, require of you, in the name of the supreme government, for the first and last time, that, having perused a copy of the resolutions which I now forward to you, you shall comply with them and obey them in every way that may concern you, because if you do not do so you shall be held responsible before the central government for all the ills that may result from extreme measures.

If you, and all who follow you, take care to avoid the misfortunes that may arise, I doubt not that the clemency of the central government may be obtained. On this supposition, I expect that you will not fail to reply that you are acting in conformity with what is expected of you

handed to him on that date. Osío, *Historia de California*, MS., 192-5, says that Zamorano recruited a force of about one hundred convicts, assassins, and thieves, which he gave the high sounding name of "Division of the Supreme Government" and despatched to Santa Barbara; and that these "knights of the road" so completely plundered the first *rancho* they come to, leaving only "such superfluous things as the tiles of the roof and the stones of the foundation" that Zamorano had to recall them and, in their place, sent Lieutenant Ibarra with a hundred men of different character. This is an example of the attempts by the Californians to slander Zamorano. Hittell, *op. cit.*, II, 150, repeats the story and it can be found in nearly every history of California. It is obvious from the correspondence here quoted that it has no foundation in fact.

and which, for the sake of the general peace of the Territory, is your duty.

God and Liberty, Monterey, February 12, 1832.

AGUSTIN V. ZAMORANO

Sr. General Commandant Don José María de Echeandia
Los Angeles.[7]

Lieutenant Ibarra reached Santa Barbara about February 23, and on that date forwarded the above letter, with the following note.

Comandancia Militar de Santa Barbara.

I forward to you the attached package which Captain Agustin Vicente Zamorano, acting general commandant of Alta California, placed in my hands on the 12th instant, so that in case some one arrived at Santa Barbara I might forward it to you.

God and Liberty, February 23, 1832.

JUAN MARÍA IBARRA

Sr. General Commandant Don José María de Echeandia.[8]

II. Echeandia Refuses to Recognize Zamorano.

Lieutenant Ibarra's note to Echeandia, forwarding Captain Zamorano's letter of February 12 demanding that Echeandia recognize him as acting general commandant, was written two days before that officer, on February 25, issued his circular letter in which he offered that office to either Captain Portilla or Captain Zamorano, depending on which officer claimed it first.

The messenger carrying Ibarra's and Zamorano's letters reached Los Angeles after Echeandia had departed, with, as we have said, his feathers badly ruffled from his encounter with the deputation, for San Diego. Setting out to overtake him, the messenger caught up with him on March 2 at Mission San Luis Rey. Echeandia read Zamorano's letter, read the resolutions adopted by the council of February 1, placed them in his pocket and proceeded on his way to San Diego

---

[7] Zamorano to Echeandia, Monterey, February 12, 1832, MS. Certified copy in *Vallejo, Doc.*, I, 296; also in *Legajo* 52-6-6-7, No. 17.

[8] Ibarra to Echeandia, Santa Barbara, February 23, 1832, MS., in *Legajo* 52-6-6-3, No. 17.

without saying a word. Let us not suppose, however, that he intended, for even a few seconds, to make good on the offer contained in his letter of February 25. He intended to keep his provisional authority and cared not how many reversals of position it cost him.

On March 5, from San Diego, Echeandia wrote to Don Pio Pico, advising him of the proceedings in Monterey and proposed a meeting of the deputation for consultation and offered to attend.[9] But ten days before, in Los Angeles, he had villified Pico, declared him incompetent to serve as civil governor, refused to recognize him as such, insulted the deputation, and offered to give up his provisional command to Captain Zamorano if that officer should claim it. Now in receipt of Zamorano's demand that he be recognized as general commandant, Echeandia turned back to the legislature he had declared to be illegal. It is impossible to explain his actions. It is not enough to say he wished to govern Alta California again and cared not from whence came his support.

Not waiting for a reply to his letter to Pico, Echeandia called a council of war of his followers on March 7 in San Diego. This council was attended by himself, Captains Don Pablo de la Portilla, Don Santiago Argüello and Don Leonardo Diaz Barroso, Lieutenant Don Juan José Rocha, Ensigns Don José María Ramírez, Don Mariano G. Vallejo, Don Juan Salazar, and Don Ignacio del Valle, and Sergeant of Artillery Andrés Cervantes. Seven of this group had signed the Plan of San Diego on December 1, 1831, and two were members of the deputation, still resentful, especially Argüello, of the insults Echeandia had heaped on that body.

To this council, Echeandia read Captain Zamorano's letter and the resolutions adopted by the council in Monterey and followed them with a discussion of their contents that was replete with Echeandian distorted reasoning. He insisted the Monterey council was unknown among their institutions, was illegal, was unnecessary, that it discussed issues already settled by Zamorano who was subject to his authority as provisional general commandant, that it was not a council of war because it included persons not of the military, and that

---

[9] Echeandia to Pico, San Diego, March 5, 1832, summarized in *Dept. St. Pap.*, MS., III, 44.

Zamorano was not entitled to the command unless competent authority disqualified the two senior captains (meaning Portilla and Argüello), or unless they resigned it. He then proceeded to disqualify individual members of the Monterey council—*Asesor* Gómez because he had been a friend of Victoria's, *Comisario* Gómez because there were irregularities in his accounts, the *alcalde* of Monterey because he acted independently of and not with his *ayuntamiento*, and finally the meeting had included two foreigners who were ineligible to take part in governmental affairs. He continued that Zamorano had not given a detailed statement of his opinion, as he had been asked, and that the circular of the 25th was proof that he had consistently desired to surrender his commands to the persons with the best legal claims to them.

Echeandia was shocked that the Monterey council had not recognized that the central government had entrusted both himself and Victoria with the civil office under a law that forbade its separation from the military command and claimed it should remain with the provisional general commandant (*i.e.* himself) until the matter was decided. He pointed out that the council had appropriated the legislative authority of the deputation in declaring the civil office to be vacant and directing the *ayuntamientos* to govern as they chose.

Continuing, he declared the council lacking in competence to decide the military succession, as it had no jurisdiction in the matter since it was not a true council of war because its number of officers was too small and because it had not asked the opinions of the other officers in the Territory. The council, he claimed, had no authority to order troops from Monterey to Santa Barbara. Furthermore, Captain Zamorano had been remiss in his military and social duties in calling the meeting. If all of Zamorano's claims were true, he should have used his powers in the defense of Victoria instead of asking Echeandia for his passport. He then called on Zamorano to admit that there had been a general uprising against Victoria and that he had placed himself under the authority of the chief of the insurrection. As Echeandia had done his utmost to persuade him not to abandon his post and had repeatedly asked his opinion on the succession, Zamorano had no cause for damaging his honor as a soldier by starting an uprising against patriotic officers and municipal authorities. Finally, the council lacked authority to declare the sub-treasury vacant and that *Comisario* Gómez had abused his office in a scandalous manner.

He closed by placing three questions before the meeting:

First, should the Monterey council be held as legal or illegal?

Second, should the military command fall on Captain Zamorano in case Captains Portilla and Argüello waived their rights and providing he gave his oath in writing and solemn assurance that he would not proceed in any way against the supporters of the Plan of San Diego?

Third, if the northern party failed to accept the second above and reenforced Santa Barbara and took other hostile steps, should they consider themselves as attacked and free to defend themselves with all the resources available?

Whereupon, the meeting adjourned for the day.[10]

It is evident that every charge Echeandia brought against the council that had advised Captain Zamorano applied with equal if not greater force against the one he had called. Echeandia's address to the San Diego council was merely a mass of half-truths and contradictions in which he twisted the meanings of statements and laws to give a high sounding justification to fit his particular purpose with a fine disregard for the facts.

On the same day, March 7, Echeandia acknowledged Ibarra's note of February 23. It was obviously intended for Captain Zamorano and Ibarra promptly forwarded it to Monterey. In this letter, with complete duplicity, he gave no indication of the meeting of the council of war which he had called in San Diego.

Comandancia General provisional de la Alta California.

At nightfall on the 2nd instant, at Mission San Luis Rey, I received your official note which was included with the copy of the minutes drawn up at Monterey on the 1st of February last.

In order to give it a fitting answer, it is necessary that the body of officers assembled in council of war, the Most Excellent Deputation, and the *ayuntamiento* of the Town of Los Angeles, as well as the Reverend

[10] Proceedings of Council of War, San Diego, March 7, 1832, MS., in *Legajo* 52-6-6-7, No. 18.

Father Missionaries of this Department, shall be informed on the subject and give their opinions. As for myself, by official letter of February 25 just past, which I circulated from the *presidio* of Santa Barbara south, as well as by my note of the 29th of the same month, which I sent from Mission San Juan Capistrano to the headquarters of the same *presidio*, I have already determined, as you must have seen, to surrender the military command to whomsoever it belongs by regulations, since I have no rights to it as the central government has relieved me of my duties in this country. Thus under the circumstances, the provisions of the succession to the military command, pointed out in my two circulars cited, have agreed with the ideas of the officers who have recognized me provisionally. The agreement so suddenly made at Monterey alone is in opposition. As for the violence and dishonor done our esteemed military privileges by supposing that as rebels we are suspended from our duties, it would be more just to proceed with charges under our inflexible constitutional provisions, which we are pledged to claim and uphold. It would appear that if your side will refrain from committing the violence charged against those of this party, and will not advance into this Department, remaining at the *presidio* of Santa Barbara, until we reach a mutual understanding, everything will end without bloodshed and disorder, which once started would be hard to remedy.

JOSÉ MARÍA DE ECHEANDIA

To Lieutenant Juan María Ibarra
Military Commander of Santa Barbara.[11]

The San Diego council of war convened again on the following day, March 8. At this meeting, Don Juan Bandini, the *comisario subalterno*, was admitted to its membership, whereupon he made a speech regarding the delinquencies of *Comisario* Gómez and announced that he had attempted to substitute Don Antonio María Osío in that office but Gómez had refused to surrender it. The meeting then decided to take an open vote on the questions placed before it on the preceding day. A negative vote was cast on all questions; that is, the Monterey council was declared illegal and Zamorano was not to be recognized. Echeandia then stated that in view of the vote cast on the first two questions he had submitted, it was unnecessary to vote on the third. He advised that he wished to surrender his command and to appoint Captain Portilla as his successor. Discussion of

[11] Echeandia to Ibarra, San Diego, March 7, 1832, MS., in *Legajo* 52-6-6-10, No. 20.

this new problem was deferred until another meeting and the council adjourned.[12]

Again, after the adjournment of his council, Echeandia wrote to Lieutenant Ibarra at Santa Barbara and again he gave no hint as to what was taking place in San Diego.

Comandancia General provisional de la Alta California.

Señor Don Juan María Ibarra:
Unfortunately, the council of Monterey seeks to jeopardize the safety of the officers, *ayuntamientos*, deputation, and all the rest of the private individuals when it intimates surrender and imprisonment to them.

You will recognize that we have, along with the best of them, great patriotism and honor and cannot be indifferent to the degradation with which we are threatened; it would be better to lose our lives than to live in disgrace.

Therefore, I expect that you will agree in good faith not to advance beyond the *presidio* of Santa Barbara, or to give orders for it, because the instant you do so all the good order and harmony with which it is hoped this affair can be concluded will be lost and we shall be enmeshed in disasters.

Your council has considered our Plan as criminal but the truth is that this matter concerns the general congress of the Union, because I am well informed on our rights and liberties.

I am your respectful servant and esteem you.

José María de Echeandía

P.S. Within two or three days, I shall send Zamorano the answer about our new agreement.[13]

It is obvious that Echeandia's two letters to Lieutenant Ibarra were an attempt to commit Ibarra not to advance beyond Santa Barbara and a play for time in which to recruit his own forces.

The San Diego council resumed its sessions on March 13 and after a long discussion on the question as to who should succeed Echeandia, Ensign Don Mariano G. Vallejo moved that as it seemed best that Echeandia should continue in his provisional commands until the entire Territory was again at peace, he should do so. It was finally agreed

---

[12] Proceedings of Council of War, San Diego, March 8, 1832, MS., in *Legajo* 52-6-6-7, No. 19.
[13] Echeandia to Ibarra, San Diego, March 8, 1832, MS., in *Legajo* 52-6-6-10, No. 20.

that Echeandia should continue until the central government had reached its decision. This was exactly what he wanted, so Echeandia thanked his followers for the honor they did him and accepted the offices, again expressing the desire to relinquish them as soon as circumstances would permit. The council then adjourned.[14]

Confirmed in his provisional offices by his own adherents, Echeandia was now free to devote his attention to the efforts of Captain Zamorano, who had been recognized as the legitimate acting general commandant in three of the four presidial districts.

III. The Negotiations Between the Rival Claimants.

On March 11, Captain Zamorano sent a proclamation to the *pueblo* of Los Angeles in an effort to bring that town under the legitimate authority.

> *Comandancia General accidental de la Alta California.*
>
> *Proclamation to the Citizens of the Town of Los Angeles:*
> Until the first of February, I was a spectator only of the criminal movement to depose Señor Victoria from the civil and military commands with which he had been invested by the supreme government of Mexico and I entered into correspondence with Señor Echeandia (the commander set up by the rebels of San Diego) only to refute the arguments by which he tried to win my adherence. On that date I became convinced that the majority of the people of the Territory were friendly to its old government although Señor Victoria had departed. In the circumstances I thought it my duty to call a council of war. Among the decisions reached, the principal ones were: that in Señor Victoria's absence the military command fell to me as the senior officer present who had taken no part in the rebellion; that the civil and military commanders that may be designated by the Most Excellent Deputation should not be recognized and that, since this had been illegally convened, all its acts were tainted with nullity; and finally that, without provoking hostilities, peace should be restored by force. As is well known, my actions have been consistent with the above. I have the satisfaction of believing that if your town has not disapproved of the rebellion by spontaneous action, it will do so as soon as possible.

[14] Proceedings of Council of War, San Diego, March 13, 1832, MS., in *Legajo* 52-6-6-7 No. 20.

Townsmen: The time that has elapsed since the unfortunate fifth of December last, the steps taken by the Most Excellent Deputation, its odious altercations with Señor Echeandia, and the other details of which you have full knowledge and which I omit in order not to appear diffuse, are sufficient to bring disillusionment. Demonstrate that you see the situation in its true light by giving the Territory proof of your submission to the legitimate authorities. This your fellow-citizen expects of you.

God and Liberty, Monterey, March 11, 1832.

AGUSTIN V. ZAMORANO[15]

Captain Zamorano's appeal was well received by the *Angelinos* and the *alcalde* of that place, Don Manuel Dominguez, called the *ayuntamiento*, or town council, to order in an open meeting on March 22, 1832. Zamorano's proclamation was read to the public and discussed fully. The people and the town fathers enthusiastically voted to support the legitimate government and the *alcalde* so wrote to Monterey on the same day.[16] On learning of this action, Lieutenant Ibarra moved immediately from Santa Barbara with a part of his forces and camped in the *pueblo* of the Queen of the Angels.

This undoubtedly was very pleasing news to Don Agustin but had he known the fickle nature of the *ayuntamiento* of the town and that this was but one in a series of political gymnastics he would have instead despaired.

In the meantime, Echeandia was making every effort to gather an armed force. The population of the District of San Diego was sparse and his only hope to obtain one of any strength was to recruit it from the neophytes of the missions. On March 18, he, with Portilla, Barroso, Rocha and Ramírez, established himself at Mission San Luis Rey. There he sent out short notes to the Indian *alcaldes* and majordomos asking that they send him men "to help me defend our constitutional liberty."[17] The Indian neophytes of the missions had never before taken part in the affairs of the *gente de razon* in Alta Cali-

[15] Zamorano, Proclamation to the citizens of the Town of Los Angeles, Monterey, March 11, 1832, MS., in *Legajo* 52-6-6-10, No. 18.

[16] Dominguez to Zamorano, Los Angeles, March 22, 1832, MS., *ibid.*, No. 19; also in *Los Angeles Archives*, IV, 59-60.

[17] Echeandia to Selidonio, *alcalde* of Mission San Juan Capistrano, San Luis Rey, March 19, 1832, MS., in *Legajo* 52-6-6-10, No. 21.

fornia. It was a dangerous thing to remove them from their accustomed restraints and to arm them. This, however, did not deter Echeandia in his desperation. Fr. José María Zalvidea, the missionary father at Mission San Luis Rey, was so concerned with these activities that, on March 21, he sent a letter to the other missionaries, telling them of what was being attempted and that, although Echeandia was not having the success he had expected, he thought the information should be passed on to Don Juan María Ibarra and Don Agustin Zamorano.[18] The missionaries at Mission Santa Barbara brought Father Zalvidea's letter to the attention of Lieutenant Ibarra and that officer at once sent a copy of it to Captain Zamorano.[19]

Twenty-two days after the receipt of Captain Zamorano's letter of February 12 demanding that he be recognized as acting general commandant, Echeandia, in the midst of his warlike preparations among the Indians at Mission San Luis Rey, got around to answering it. In his reply he gave no indication of the activities he was engaged in but, on the contrary, made a proposal of peace.

Comandancia General provisional de la Alta California.
In your official note of February 12, with which you enclose a copy of the resolutions adopted on the first of the same month by the council you called, you advise me that recent events, of which I must be aware, have caused you to change from your first decision and that the same events should convince me that I have been deceived in believing there was acceptance of the Plan of San Diego from Santa Barbara to San Francisco; that you had been an eyewitness of what had happened in Monterey and as to Santa Barbara, San José de Guadalupe, Branciforte and San Francisco, their recent acts in favor of the legitimate authority proved it. From these events, you conclude that the prevailing opinion of the Territory is not in sympathy with the said pronouncement, that bloodshed is certain if I ignore the justice with which practically the entire population are resolved not to recognize any other authority than the legitimate one; and finally, since you are that legitimate authority, you call on me in the name of the Supreme Government, for the first and last time, to comply with and cause to be complied with the decisions reached by the council in so far as they apply to me. That is to

---

[18] Zalvidea, Fr. José María, Circular to missions, San Luis Rey, March 21, 1832, MS., *idem.*
[19] Ibarra to Zamorano, Santa Barbara, March 24, 1832, MS., *idem.*

say, that I, and all those who follow me, should surrender our arms and await the disposition of the central government, or, more properly speaking, of you and your council, for which submission we shall undoubtedly become the creditors of the clemency of the central government.

How monstrous! Let us adhere to the facts. Recent events have changed your decision—rather, is it not just the contrary, these events happened because you had changed? Who called the council? Who composed it of those persons in complete agreement with your ideas? Who proposed the questions on which decisions were reached? And finally, who promoted the revolt of the troops at Santa Barbara and who recruited the Company of Foreigners?

So I have been deceived? Yes! but only by you, who have failed in your military duties and social obligations. Having gained your end, you impose your will on all places from San Francisco to Santa Barbara and cut off all communication between the latter place and this southern department, thus preventing the truth from being known in the north.

By these recent events, which are the outcome of your operations subsequent to the departure of Señor Victoria, you come to the conclusion that during the time that gentleman was in authority there was no popular inclination to deny him obedience, as is stated in the Plan? How ridiculous! During the forty-two days that Señor Victoria remained in the Territory after his deposition, all remained at peace and in harmonious relations with me; after that officer had left the country, you threw it into a state of revolt in order that you might gain his place.

If you did not make any complaints while Victoria remained, in order to avoid bloodshed, why are you now so indifferent to the consequences in your effort to exalt yourself to the military command held by that officer and which you had already recognized in me? It is easily seen that this change has come from the influence that has been gained over you by the *asesor*, the *comisario* and some of the missionary fathers, all of whom think only of their private interests, and the last have the double object of perpetuating the despotic institutions which tyrannize over the unhappy natives and of maintaining those ecclesiastics in places of power to lend the better service to the government of Spain.

Perhaps these truths, after you have meditated on them in solitude and without passion, may induce you to act with that sincerity with which you have impressed me in other times. Then you will realize that the steps which you have taken to acquire the military command are illegal and that you are lacking in authority and competence to judge as criminal the proceedings that led to the deposing of Señor Victoria and to order the surrender and arrest of myself, the officers, and the other authorities and the remaining multitude that have adhered to the Plan. Nor can you be recognized as having the power to offer, in the case of a positive crime, a pardon in the name of the central government—that even itself is powerless to do.

As you can see from what I have said and from the copies which I enclose of the minutes of the council of war held on the 7th, 8th, and 13th of this month at the *presidio* of San Diego, the council which you called at Monterey on February 1 has been held to be illegal and null and all its acts as without force or public benefit; you are not recognized as general commandant since the two senior captains, Portilla and Argüello, do not waive their priority, and the subordinate officers refuse to obey you, because of the distrust you have inspired by your bad faith and reactionary ideas. They have pledged me to continue in the military command. I am willing, for the sake of the peace of the Territory, to suspend my campaign against you and those of your party, until the decision of the central government is received, on the following conditions:

1. That you allow the customary freedom of traffic and intercourse between all the inhabitants of the Territory, so that the affairs of the people may not be harmed.

2. That you withdraw the troops which I understand you are assembling for Lieutenant Citizen Juan María Ibarra from the *presidio* of Santa Barbara, so that he shall be left with only the troops of his company and those of the regular garrison of that *presidio*, in order that I may abstain from gathering alarming resources, thus quieting public fears.

3. That you allow the free exercise of their particular duties to the deputation, the *ayuntamientos*, the sub-treasurer, Ensigns Carrillo and Sánchez, and all other private citizens who perhaps are under arrest for their adherence to the Plan of San Diego.

4. That, because of the problems that might arise to delay our agreement, you allow the deputation and the *ayuntamientos* of Monterey, San José and Los Angeles to act freely in all things pertaining to the civil government, in order that those civil authorities may settle their troubles as they may deem best.

5. That, if you insist on continuing to govern as military commander from Santa Barbara north, you take the oath in the form prescribed by Article 163 of our Federal Constitution, with expressed assurance of complying immediately with the four preceding conditions and remaining at peace and in touch with me or my successor in the command of this department; all to continue in effect until we know the decision of the central government, and without prejudice to the charges that may

be made against you and those of your party in the accusations which will be presented by me or my party in due time and form.

Finally, I am informed that Lieutenant Ibarra has written flattering promises to the *ayuntamiento* of the Town of Los Angeles, so that it will recognize you and that the lieutenant may have unobstructed passage to San Diego. I assure you that this department has been aroused with the greatest enthusiasm to the protection of its liberty and distrusts your conduct; if you do not answer promptly and in agreement with me, I shall hasten my operations to the point of turning into reality the bloodshed of which you speak—and you shall be held responsible before God and the world for whatever disasters that may result from the warfare you have so unjustly and unnecessarily provoked and sought.

God and Liberty, Mission San Luis Rey, March 24, 1832.

JOSÉ MARÍA DE ECHEANDIA

To Captain Citizen Agustin V. Zamorano,
Commander of the party opposing those
who have declared for constitutional liberty.[20]

As Echeandia was about to despatch this letter, word reached him that Lieutenant Ibarra had not only occupied Los Angeles but had advanced to Mission San Gabriel and was then in possession of that mission. This news so excited him that he hurriedly wrote a short note to Captain Zamorano to send with this letter. In this, anger caused him to forget all those little courtesies that officers of that time and place were so fond of observing in their intercourse with each other.

San Luis Rey, March 24, 1832

Don Agustin:

I had just written the attached official letter when I heard that Ibarra is now at San Gabriel.

Never did I imagine that you would act with such villainy, forgetting even that honor which officers show to each other. Ibarra has preferred to associate himself with persons of low rank rather than with me and his captain and comrades.

Finally, you are responsible to God and the Nation for the disorders which California shall experience very shortly and perhaps you shall be the first one to be enveloped by the confusion.

---

[20] Echeandia to Zamorano, San Luis Rey, March 24, 1832, MS., in *Legajo* 52-6-6-7, No. 21; also, quoted in full in Echeandia to Pico, San Luis Rey, March 25, 1832, MS., in *Vallejo, Doc.*, I, 303. Bancroft, *op. cit.*, III, 225, and 226, note 9, erroneously gives the date of Echeandia's letter to Zamorano as March 14 and to Pico as March 15.

Where is that pretended eagerness for your departure in order to avoid outrages? Now we know just how much you desired it by your willingness to act.

I am truly a Mexican and a liberal and I know how to submit to my fate, be it what it may.

José María de Echeandia

To Don Agustin V. Zamorano[21]

Echeandia's injured tone is amusing but nothing more; he would have appeared more convincing if he had addressed Captain Zamorano as one villain to another. At the very moment that he was protesting that officer's warlike attitude, he was rushing the drilling and arming of his Indians, both mission neophytes and savages, as quickly as he could. Father Zalvidea, then at Mission San Juan Capistrano, became so alarmed over the effect of these preparations on the Indians of his district that he, on March 23, 1832, protested to Echeandia.[22] That officer answered promptly, throwing all blame on Zamorano and saying he was making every effort to avoid such a situation but without success.[23] This letter was written on the same day, March 24, that he wrote Captain Zamorano.

A few days later, Father Zalvidea attached Echeandia's reply to a circular letter which he sent from Mission San Gabriel, under date of March 29, to all the missions north to Mission San José. This letter read:

> Considering it essential that the opportunely peaceful inclination in which Señor Echeandia finds himself should come to Your Reverences' knowledge and also that of Don Juan M. Ibarra and Don Agustin Zamorano, I make known the very rational and Christian reply that comes from the mission named on March 28, 1832.
>
> Look carefully over the attached from Señor Echeandia. *Qui legit, intelliga.* [He who reads may understand.][24]

There can be little doubt that the shrewd old missionary, who had had many contacts with Echeandia before, was not taken in by his

---

[21] Echeandia to Zamorano, San Luis Rey, March 24, 1832, MS., in *Legajo* 52-6-6-10, No. 23.

[22] Zalvidea to Echeandia, San Juan Capistrano, March 23, 1832, MS., *ibid.*, No. 25.

[23] Echeandia to Zalvidea, San Luis Rey, March 24, 1832, MS., *idem*.

[24] Zalvidea, Circular to other missions, San Gabriel, March 29, 1832, MS., *idem*.

protestations of peace and was asking his colleagues to read between the lines.

Captain Zamorano, in Monterey, well pleased with the progress that Lieutenant Ibarra had made in Los Angeles and knowing of Echeandía's activities among the Indians through the reports that reached him, worked feverishly to raise as large a force as possible to take south in Ibarra's support. He called on all the *presidios* and towns in the three northern districts to supply him with all the armed and mounted men possible, urging haste as by operating swiftly he hoped for "the best results in securing the peace of the Territory."[25] In the midst of these preparations, on April 1, Echeandía's letter of March 24, in reply to his of February 12, reached Monterey. Captain Zamorano replied on the same day.

Comandancia General accidental de la Alta California.

Today I received your official letter dated at San Luis Rey on March 24 last and I shall answer it from Santa Barbara for which place I shall set out as soon as possible so as to facilitate speedy communication between us. From Santa Barbara, I shall address you again and shall treat the subject as is fitting.

In the meanwhile, if you wish to avoid bloodshed, you will suspend all armed movements. For my own part, I shall give the necessary orders to all the frontier posts in the Santa Barbara jurisdiction to make a like suspension.

God and Liberty, Monterey, April 1, 1832.

AGUSTIN V. ZAMORANO

To Lieutenant Colonel Citizen José María de Echeandía, Commander of those who oppose the legitimately constituted authority.[26]

Echeandía, however, did not wait for a reply from Captain Zamorano before moving north. If he had been truly sincere in his offer of peace, he would have waited a reasonable time for a reply. Some time before, he had ordered Captain Barroso to occupy Paso de Bartolo, on the San Gabriel River, with a force that consisted chiefly of

---

[25] Zamorano to *alcalde* of San José, Monterey, March 30, 1832, in *San José Archives*, MS., II, 60-1.
[26] Zamorano to Echeandía, Monterey, April 1, 1832, MS., in *Legajo* 52-6-6-10, No. 24.

Indians. It was this movement that had led Lieutenant Ibarra to occupy Mission San Gabriel. Captain Zamorano's letter of April 1 found Echeandia en route to Los Angeles. Seeking every possible advantage, he at once wrote to Lieutenant Ibarra.

> *Comandancia General provisional de la Alta California.*
>
> Captain Citizen Agustin V. Zamorano, commander-in-chief of your party, tells me in an official letter of the 1st of this month what I copy to the letter:
> [*Quotes Zamorano's letter of April 1 in full.*]
> Therefore, I expect that you will retire at once from the Town of Los Angeles to the *presidio* of Santa Barbara, without delaying on the way; with the understanding that if you do not do so, I shall assume that you act on your own initiative or that you have secret orders contrary to the ones whcih your commander has sent to me. In that case, we of this party shall have no responsibility whatever if, at the cost of whatever sacrifice necessary, we oblige you by force to make your retirement to Santa Barbara, from which place you overstepped, offending at the same time the rights of the people, for which action I protest henceforth before the supreme authorities of our Nation.
> God and Liberty, on the march to the Town of Los Angeles, April 7, 1832.
>
> José María de Echeandia
>
> Lt. C. Juan María Ibarra,
> Commander of the advance guard of the anti-liberal party, wherever he may be.[27]

Lieutenant Ibarra was in Los Angeles at the invitation of the citizens of that town and as he was receiving his orders from Captain Zamorano, Echeandia's letter did not frighten him in the least; he merely forwarded it to Don Agustin.

Captain Zamorano left Monterey with a force of men about April 7; he was at Mission San Antonio on April 8.[28] On the way south, he received the letter Echeandia had sent to Ibarra on the 7th, and stopped long enough to write a reply.

[27] Echeandia to Ibarra, On the march to Los Angeles, April 7, 1832, MS., *ibid.*, No. 26.
[28] Zamorano to Domingo Carrillo, San Antonio, April 8, 1832, in *De la Guerra, Doc.*, MS., 152.

Comandancia General accidental de la Alta California.

I have just received the official note you addressed to Lieutenant Juan María Ibarra, dated on the march to the Town of Los Angeles on the 7th instant, in which you tell him to retire from that town to Santa Barbara without delay on the way, and in forwarding it the said lieutenant tells me that without my orders he will be unable to do so and that he has so answered you.

When I addressed the official letter to you which you copied in your cited letter, I believed that your forces would not go beyond San Juan Capistrano, where your advance guard was to be found under the command of Captain Barroso, and likewise I supposed that you were waiting my reply to your official note of March 24 last. Subsequently, I have learned that you have made the Father Missionary of San Juan Capistrano, Fr. José María Zalvidea, a go-between to urge Ibarra to withdraw his troops to Santa Barbara and in the meantime, arousing, so I am informed, the Indians of those missions and the neighboring pagans, you have continued to advance your forces all the way to Rancho Caguenga and later encamping at Paso de Bartolo.

Ibarra was on his way to occupy Mission San Fernando, but, before receiving your last communication cited above, I had ordered him to occupy the Town of Los Angeles because it had spontaneously declared in favor of the legitimate authorities and I considered it as belonging to the jurisdiction of Santa Barbara. But hearing that Captain Barroso was at Caguenga waiting to attack him, Ibarra changed his route. It was not strange that he should find that officer there when there has been lacking, on your part, a disposition to make an agreement that would avoid bloodshed and the former had no instructions to suspend his march on Los Angeles. It was up to you, according to your own official letter, to act prudently and to stop your advance by notifying the captain, until you received my decision. You should have reckoned the time it would take for my answer to reach you, judging by the distance to the place where I was.

Unfortunately, I see on the one hand that you promote the bloodshed which on the other you try to prevent, but notwithstanding that I cannot view it with indifference, I find myself still in the necessity of attaining the latter. In that case, if your pretensions are equal to mine, be convinced at once that I have a legitimate right to occupy the town, because it declared in our favor. In order to avoid bloodshed, it is impossible for the forces of either party to remain in that vicinity. Until the points mentioned in your letter of March 24 are agreed upon, it seems that you should place your forces at San Juan Capistrano, with San Gabriel remaining a neutral point, with the understanding that neither party shall advance to it except under great necessity. Until, as I have said, we come to some agreement that may assure the general peace of the Territory, which will come from the letter which I shall send you from Santa Barbara, where I shall arrive soon and proceed at once to my labors for the public good.

God and Liberty, on the way to Santa Barbara, April 12, 1832.

AGUSTIN V. ZAMORANO

Lieutenant Colonel Don José María de Echeandia,
Commander of the party opposing the legitimate authority,
wherever he may be.[29]

This letter gave ample explanation for all the movements made by the forces of the northern party and it would appear that Echeandia could find no possible objection to Don Agustin's peaceful proposals. Nevertheless, he was not satisfied and on April 16 replied in a note that was more belligerent than intelligent.

Comandancia General provisional de la Alta California.

By your official note of the 1st instant, in answer to mine of the 24th just past, you give me no assurance whatever of an early negotiation in conformity with my note just cited, and on the other hand, I presume that you are trying to unite with Lieutenant Ibarra and then, depending on your total force and the information you may get about mine, you will carry out your aims or accept my proposals. On this supposition and taking into account that you, with your flimsy idea that assumes that Los Angeles belongs to you, advanced your troops to this side of the *presidio* of Santa Barbara, you failed once again in the good faith which you promised.

In regard to what was decided at that clandestine meeting or council which you have recognized as legal and sufficiently authorized to decide on the destinies of the inhabitants of Alta California, I will say nothing more than what I told Lieutenant Ibarra in my official letter of the 7th instant, and that is that you confine your forces in total to the *presidio* at Santa Barbara and give me a prompt reply in agreement, sufficiently guaranteed, so that the Territory may be pacified and await calmly the supreme decision that will furnish the remedy for so many abuses.

---

[29] Zamorano to Echeandia, On the way to Santa Barbara, April 12, 1832, MS., in *Legajo* 52-6-6-10, No. 27.

By what has been said, I answer also your note of the 12th instant, giving notice that in the spontaneous recognition by the Town of Los Angeles there are great mistakes, falsehoods, and intrigues which, in case of necessity, I shall point out elsewhere, together with the other points that you touch on.

God and Liberty, Mission San Gabriel, April 16, 1832.

José María de Echeandía

Captain C. Agustin V. Zamorano[30]

Before Captain Zamorano reached Santa Barbara, Lieutenant Ibarra had withdrawn all his forces from Los Angeles and San Gabriel to Mission San Fernando. In this he had been prompted by the increasing hordes of Indians being gathered at Paso de Bartolo.[31] He did not care to risk an encounter with Captain Barroso with the limited resources then at his command. Thereupon Mission San Gabriel was occupied by Echeandía's forces. The Town of Los Angeles, favoring first one side and then the other, became a bone of contention between the two forces and neither cared to precipitate matters by boldly occupying it. Thus matters stood.

Captain Zamorano, on arrival at Santa Barbara, found his forces well entrenched in the territory from Mission San Fernando north and as this was all that he had originally planned to hold and as there seemed to be prospects of an early peace with Echeandía, in spite of that officer's newly assumed belligerent tone, he saw no reason to create new problems unless forced to do so. He was sincerely desirous of a peaceful arrangement as soon as possible in order that the Territory might resume the normal tenor of its ways. There were no subsequent movements of troops of any consequence.

[30] Echeandía to Zamorano, San Gabriel, April 16, 1832, MS., *ibid.*, No. 28.

[31] Osío, *op. cit.*, 196, says that Echeandía entered Los Angeles with one thousand mounted Indians, most of whom were dismissed with presents on reaching San Gabriel. Vallejo, *op. cit.*, II, 165, says that at Paso de Bartolo, ". . . Echeandía's forces numbered 1,500 Indians, of which 1,000 were mounted on good horses and 500 were on foot, belonging to the Cahuillas and Gileñas tribes. The mounted Indians were cowboys from Missions San Diego, San Luis Rey, Capistrano and San Gabriel. The Indians had joined him because Echeandía had tried to free them from mission bondage. There were also 80 white men, who helped in commanding the Indians, teaching them military evolutions, and had charge of the two field pieces that Echeandía had brought with him."

From Santa Barbara, on April 21, Captain Zamorano sent to Echeandia a reply to the latter's letter of March 24. In this he had made certain proposals for a truce between them.

Comandancia General accidental de la Alta California.

As I promised on the first of this month, I now answer your letter of March 24 last and I shall limit myself to the pertinent parts of its contents.

In the first condition imposed, you propose that I leave in their customary freedom the traffic and movements of all the inhabitants so that the affairs of society may not be injured.

What makes you think that I have interrupted that freedom? If the affairs of society find themselves paralyzed, perhaps it may not be because of me as neither I nor those under my command have imposed any restraints. All business people have traveled and are traveling without molestation in any way. Have vessels that arrived in Monterey, and other parts of the coast, been prohibited, in accordance with practices established during preceding administrations, from entering San Diego to pursue their trade? No. Have those who, in the management of their businesses, carry on their affairs by land been denied passports? No. Then why try to impose a condition for which, on your part, no reason exists?

In your second requirement, you propose that I should withhold the force that I am gathering for Lieutenant Ibarra and that he shall remain in possession of this post with only the troops of his company and those of the regular Santa Barbara Company, so that you may also stop increasing your resources and thus allow public disorder to cease. That is to say, I shall weaken my forces that have checked you in your advance and have secured a temporary peace while you double yours and attack me at your pleasure. One would have to be very deficient in military knowledge to accept such a proposition in good faith, especially when it is recorded by your own writings that you have strained your resources to the utmost to increase your forces and that you have aroused the neophytes of the missions in your department with flattering and misleading promises, enticing them from their customary labors, and doing likewise at some of the pagan *rancherias*, in order to expose them to death in the first blow of the attack, or to make it appear, as you have attempted to do, that your department has spontaneously risen against us. A gross exaggeration! The neophytes of your department would, I am sure, never have risen if they had not been incited to do so by you; for which act you alone shall be held responsible.

In your third stipulation, you ask that I leave the deputation, the *ayuntamientos*, the sub-treasurer, Ensigns Carrillo and Sánchez, and other private persons whom perhaps I may have under arrest for their adherence to the Plan of San Diego, in the free exercise of their duties. It is obvious that I cannot allow the acts of the deputation to be recognized in the northern departments of the Territory since that body was illegally convened. The *ayuntamientos* in the north are in the free exercise of their authority and their deliberations are not interfered with, and I assume the same situation prevails in the Town of Los Angeles. In regard to the sub-treasurer, it is clear that, as he has been implicated in the Plan, he has lost his right to function in his office and as a result can ill pretend that the treasury employees in the territory that has repudiated that Plan should obey his instructions. Ensign Don Domingo Carrillo, whom I suppose may be he to whom you refer, finds himself, at this time, it is true, under arrest but that is only until certain points regarding his public conduct are cleared up, at his request, for his vindication. In regard to Ensign Sánchez, he has never been and is not now under arrest, although the minutes drawn up on February 1 last say so. The news that caused the insertion of the additional resolution five having proven false that article remained without force. Subsequently Sánchez, having declared himself for the legitimate authority, has, by my orders, continued in command of the Port of San Francisco, which was left in his charge by Ensign Vallejo. There are a few individuals among us who are known definitely to adhere to the Plan of San Diego but, notwithstanding, there has been no intention of placing them under arrest. On the contrary, they have been told that we do not intend to harm them in any way because, so long as they do not assume a hostile attitude, we know how to respect the opinions of others.

In your fourth condition, you propose that, until our temporary scheme is brought to a close, I shall allow the deputation and the *ayuntamientos* of Monterey, San José de Guadalupe and Los Angeles to act freely in matters that pertain to the civil command. As regards the first body, it is obvious that, since it assembled in your department, I have interfered in no way with its relations to the civil officer who presides over it and it has acted as it has seen fit. The *ayuntamientos* of Monterey and San José de Guadalupe, not having recognized the civil governor designated by the deputation, are proceeding as was planned. These bodies, up to the present, have solved their problems within themselves without difficulty. That of the Town of Los Angeles finds itself divided into two factions because of the divergent opinions of its members in the present circumstances and, I am informed, the *alcalde* and other members of that body find themselves driven from its midst by threats made against them by members of your party. I understand they will not rejoin that body until the present troubles in the country come to a complete end.

You propose in your fifth and last stipulation that, if I insist on continuing in the military command from Santa Barbara to San Francisco, I should give the oath in due form as provided in Article 163 of our Federal Constitution, with the further agreement that I will conform to the four stipulations preceding and keep the peace and maintain harmonious relations with you and whomsoever may succeed you in the general command of the southern department, all until the decision of the central government is received, and without prejudice to the charges that may result against me and those under my command from the accusations which you and those of your party intend to present in due form. No one knows better than yourself, and also others among those who follow you, that I am, and have always been, very far from seeking and aspiring to offices that I do not deserve. To corroborate this statement, I wish to remind you of the fact which you will remember although it may seem foreign to the present subject, that, at the time of my promotion to the captaincy of Monterey which I now hold, I made the double objection that I did not aspire to even the lowest of military commands and should be free of all responsibilities other than those connected with the office I was holding so that I might remain close to the general commandant of the Territory and make my residence in whatever place he might be located. Now, however, having been informed by the council of February 1 that the regulations require that I assume the temporary military command in the absence of Señor Victoria (that, if I did not, I became subject to the severe censure of the central government) I do so and find it to be my duty to insist on it, in spite of my natural repugnance to the idea and those who wish to believe to the contrary can believe whatever they may desire. I assure you on the word of a gentleman that if there had been present another officer of higher rank or greater seniority than mine to whom the command could have legally fallen, the greatest joy would have been mine.

Returning to the subject, I understand that you are agreed that I shall continue to govern from Santa Barbara north, provided I take the oath required in the mentioned article of our Federal Constitution and agree to fulfill the other conditions. The oath is just and I would not hesitate to take it provided there was someone before whom I could legally do so. I gather from the context of your official note that this oath should be taken in due form before you. To this I object as you are not a legitimately constituted military authority in the Territory.

Since you have been relieved of that duty by the central government, as you have stated, and since I have never recognized you as such, long before the council of February 1, after you announced that you were assuming the responsibility of regulating and controlling the insurrection to depose Señor Victoria, you can ill pretend that I should take the oath before you. Assuming that it was necessary, the taking of the oath before some one without the authority to receive it would be sufficient to render it absolutely void. And what connection is there between the taking of the oath and the four conditions that makes the taking of the former an acceptance of the latter?

As for the friendly and harmonious relations that you insist I must maintain with you and with whomsoever may succeed you in the command of your department, I wish to say that you have but to review our past correspondence and you will see that I have always treated you with consideration, showing you a deference which does not legitimately belong to you, that I have always written with calmness and courtesy. A like regard you have not seen fit to show me, as in some of your letters you have addressed me respectfully while in others you have abused me in the basest manner, as best suited your purpose. That, for the present, I let pass. When you and those who follow you make the charges which you tell me will be prepared against me and those I command, then shall the motives of each of us be weighed in the balance of Justice and punishment administered to the one who shall deserve it; the outcome of that decision will not remain long in doubt.

In conclusion, I assume that you are agreeable to bringing the disorders in the Territory to an end by allowing it to remain divided under two military commands, which conforms in part with the intent of the resolutions of February 1, and that you decline to lay down your arms as you were requested. Our purpose at all times has been to restore, by every possible means, the public peace and tranquility without bloodshed (except in the unexpected event of our forces being attacked by those opposed). However, you do not impose any restrictions whatever on yourself in the stipulations which you proposed and pretend I of necessity must accept. If you are sincere in your protestations of anxiety to preserve the public peace, you will agree to the following articles.

1. That until the central government shall decide on the legality of the Plan of San Diego to depose Señor Victoria from both commands, or there arrives in the country with the proper credentials the person whom the central government shall appoint, or may have appointed, to govern the Territory, you shall cease all military operations and withdraw your forces to Mission San Juan Capistrano so as to prevent their coming in close contact with mine.

2. That, for the sake of the peace of the Territory, it shall remain divided into two parts, one under your command or that of whoever may succeed you and the other under mine, it being understood that the part governed by you shall comprise the territory from San Gabriel to San Diego and that from San Fernando north shall be my responsibility, leaving the Town of Los Angeles to its own wishes in order that it may join which ever side may please it best.

3. That, since the territorial deputation is convened illegally and the northern *ayuntamientos* do not recognize its acts, for that reason and so that its name may not become an object of ridicule, it shall abstain from sending them instructions.

4. That, for the same reasons and also because it is known that the person to whom the appointment has fallen was implicated in the recent uprising and has forfeited his rights thereto under the law of May 6, 1822, and is very far from able to maintain his position in the present circumstances, neither shall the civil governor appointed by the Most Excellent Deputation have relations with the northern *ayuntamientos*. Also, for the same reasons, he shall have relations with the *ayuntamiento* of the Town of Los Angeles only in the event it adheres to your department.

5. That trade, travel, and the interests of society shall continue as they have to date without being interrupted by either party, excepting only the movements of those persons who may have taken an active part in the present disturbances, because of the mutual distrust the opposing parties have shown toward each other, with the understanding that any person included in this restriction who may break it shall be subject to immediate arrest.

6. That, in conformity with the resolutions of February 1, the subtreasurer shall have jurisdiction over treasury affairs only in the territory under your command.

7. That, for no political reason or on any other account, shall the neophytes of the missions, and least of all the pagan inhabitants of the *rancherias*, take an active part in our dissensions or internal differences; that you shall disarm them and order them to return to their homes and resume their tasks, without prejudice to the charges that may be placed against you because of the fatal consequences of great magnitude which may result from the bad example you have set by this action.

8. That, until the arrival of the new governor in the Territory, the Most Excellent Deputation shall refrain from making any changes in the missions.

9. That the troops of both parties shall not pass beyond their respective boundaries, with the understanding that which ever party does so

will be engaged by the opposing force and shall be responsible for all misfortunes that may arise therefrom.

10. That these articles shall remain in force until the arrival of the new governor, who shall be free, within his authority, to act as he deems best.

The above articles manifest the good intentions of our party to preserve the general peace of the Territory. In case you do not accept and observe them and you should abuse the frankness with which you have been treated or attempt, in the future, to go beyond the limits that have been marked out for you, yours shall be the responsibility for the misfortunes that may result as well as for those that have already resulted from your instigations and the encouragement given by your support. I expect that you, on considering the matter carefully, will give me a prompt reply in order that I may circulate it in the northern portion of the Territory and restore the peace which the unfortunate insurrection at San Diego destroyed.

God and Liberty, Santa Barbara, April 21, 1832.

AGUSTIN V. ZAMORANO

Lieutenant Colonel Don José María de Echeandía,
Wherever he may be.[32]

The above letter reached Echeandia on April 23 at San Gabriel. He had made so many protestations of peace that it would appear he was now cornered. The terms suggested by Captain Zamorano were simple, fair and honorable. If he was sincere he could not avoid accepting them. But lacking the candor to admit that he had been bluffing in his expressed desire to reach an agreement, Echeandia tried to becloud the issues between them by raising minor objections and seeking to change the context of most of the articles and thereby to gain the advantage. He replied on April 24.

Comandancia General provisional de la Alta California.

In reply to your official letter of the 21st instant, which I received yesterday afternoon, while your introduction to the terms of agreement proposed do not satisfy all of the points which it tries to refute, I shall nevertheless limit myself to the essentials of our compact so that public peace may soon return and we may attain complete tranquility. It is worthy of note that five hundred armed men were under my command

---

[32] Zamorano to Echeandia, Santa Barbara, April 21, 1832, MS., in *Legajo* 52-6-6-10, No. 29.

at this place until the morning of the 17th, when Lieutenant Ibarra, already in dispute with his soldiers, retired for your place with his troops and today the numbers of my force passes six hundred men. However, not desiring to drench the countryside in blood, then or now, and believing our agreement accomplished (by the above letter), I began at once to retire several detachments of my force and to calm their warlike spirits.

I am going to condense my terms and yours in the manner that appears most obvious to me, which is as follows:

1. That, until the arrival in the Territory of the governor appointed by the central government or of special orders from that superior authority in favor of some person living within the country, the Territory shall remain, with respect to the military command, divided into two parts, one under your control from Mission San Fernando to the north and the other under my command from San Gabriel to the south; you are not to advance bodies of troops farther south than Mission San Buenaventura, or I farther north than that of San Juan Capistrano, except for the ordinary guards in each of the missions beyond those points, which shall number not more than five to seven soldiers.

2. That in the event of disturbances in our respective departments, mutual notice and help shall be given if the internal state of our departments will permit it.

3. That the officers who expressed their adherence to the Plan of San Diego shall be free to come to live in this southern part, that the soldiers of the Mazatlan Company shall be free to join their commander here, and, likewise, that the artillerymen in this department be permitted to join the chief of their service in the north. Also, that individuals of civil status shall be free to reside in the department of their choice.

4. That neither of us shall have other military relations with the Town of Los Angeles than those formerly maintained by the two military commanders of Santa Barbara and San Diego.

5. That should any armed force pass the prescribed limits without previous agreement, it may be attacked by the offended party without incurring any responsibility, and any other breach shall give cause for official complaint which shall be answered satisfactorily at the earliest convenience.

6. That the contents of the regular mails of the 7th and 22nd of each month shall be treated with the good faith demanded by that service.

7. That without other delay than that due to the distance between us you shall sign this agreement and return the duplicate, which I enclose for that purpose, along with the special oath mentioned in Article 163 of our Constitution, taken under the formalities you may find most fitting to the circumstances.

Furthermore, I find it necessary to protest to the central government against your actions, because of the manner in which you have encouraged the embezzlement of the Treasury by depriving the sub-treasurer of jurisdiction over his subordinate in Monterey and, also, because of the embarrassment you have caused the Most Excellent Deputation by obstructing its actions on civil matters that fall within its province.

God and Liberty, Mission San Gabriel, April 24, 1832.

JOSÉ MARÍA DE ECHEANDIA

To Captain C. Agustin V. Zamorano.[33]

It is strange to see Echeandia championing in civil affairs the legislative body he had, in February, branded as illegal and all its acts as null and void. The above letter reached Don Agustin at Santa Barbara at 10:30 p.m. on April 25, which was very fast time for the one hundred and fifteen mile ride. He replied the next day.

Comandancia General accidental de la Alta California.

Last night at half past ten o'clock I received the official letter, in duplicate, that you sent me on the 24th of the present month in reply to mine of the 21st. Having acquainted myself with the new terms you propose, I shall add requirements to some which will greatly clarify them and to others make objections that I believe just, and consider those of which I shall make no mention as being agreed upon. I shall take them in their numerical order.

I infer that the first part of Article 3 applies in spirit to Ensign Don Domingo Carrillo, he being the only one who found himself under simple arrest. Notwithstanding that some steps had been taken toward the defense he claimed, as was indicated in my last letter, he was advised this morning that he was at liberty and free to decide frankly if he wished to adhere to the Plan of San Diego. To this end, I read to him the article in question and he promptly replied that it did not apply to him and that he did not belong to that party, pointing out that his signature did not appear on the said Plan nor did he approve of it and other measures advanced by you. As regards the second part of the article, it is impossible at this time to allow the men of the Mazatlan Company to join the commander of their company or the artillerymen the commander of their service for several reasons: one of them being, in regard to the former, that they have pledged themselves not to leave the lieutenant of their company under whose orders they now find themselves

---

[33] Echeandia to Zamorano, San Gabriel, April 24, 1832, MS., *ibid.*, No. 30.

until the central government or the governor whose arrival we expect shall decide what is best. The artillerymen in your department must be in a similar position, with the additional reason for remaining where they are that they are necessary for the servicing of the guns at San Diego or for any other service in which you may employ them. Furthermore, in the present circumstances, it would not be wise for the Mazatlan troops to go to your department and for the artillerymen to do the reverse because there would most certainly arise arguments between them and their comrades or others concerning their personal opinions, which while originating in fun might end in disasters that would not be easy to remedy. Now that we are determined to avoid unpleasantries, let us take no chances on provoking new ones.

Concerning Article 6, the regular mail will leave in the north on the 7th of each month, as was done before the pronouncement at San Diego, and it appears best that it leave San Diego on the 22nd of each month.

Because of these changes in some of the articles, I return to you the duplicate without the signature you asked; this letter can serve the same purpose.

Concerning the oath provided in Article 163 of our Federal Constitution, I have already sufficiently stated my point of view; I now add that since the temporary command that has fallen to me is a purely military one and as I gave the proper oath at the time of my original appointment, I consider this unnecessary. However, in order not to appear obstinate on this particular issue, I shall take the matter under advisement at once to see if there is in this northern part of the Territory some one before whom I can legally take it.

I am quite agreeable to the protest that you propose to make against me before the supreme authority on the points you state and it will not be allowed to interfere with the complaints which I shall make.

If you take it upon yourself to open the mail sent by the central government to the Territory, yours shall be the responsibility as also for the non-observance in this northern part of the Territory of such new laws and instructions that may have been delayed or in the future may be delayed in the post office at San Diego.

I believe that sufficient has been said for us to agree on all points and I only wait your reply, acknowledging your agreement, before issuing the necessary instructions and placing our conclusions in the knowledge of the public for the general good.

God and Liberty, Santa Barbara, April 26, 1832.

AGUSTIN V. ZAMORANO

Señor Lieutenant Colonel D. José María de Echeandia.[34]

[34] Zamorano to Echeandia, Santa Barbara, April 26, 1832, MS., *ibid.*, No. 31.

Before this letter could reach Mission San Gabriel, Echeandía had set out on his return to San Diego. He replied, on May 3, from Mission San Luis Rey. While he agreed with all that Don Agustín had said, he could not resist making a few suggestions.

Comandancia General provisional de la Alta California.

I am informed of the contents of your official letter of April 26 last, to which I reply as follows:

With reference to the second paragraph of your letter, it is proper to remark that because of the general way in which Article 2 speaks of disturbances, it is to be understood that it refers to occurrences that might take place against the national integrity, its federal form of government, distinction of classes, etc., etc. Likewise, when in this article it says, "and help shall be given," it is to be supposed that it shall be that which may seem convenient to the commander of the department in disorder; therefore, if on giving notice of his circumstances, or subsequently, he does not ask for assistance, it is to be inferred that he does not need it and therefore none shall be given him. It seems that all can be remedied by stating the article in these terms:

Article 2. That in case of disorder in our respective departments, we shall give each other immediate notice, stating when and how we believe it convenient to receive such aid as is needed which shall be supplied if the internal state of our departments permit it.

With reference to the third paragraph, which deals with Article 3, I must reply that if one or several officers have given you to understand that they were not adherents of the Plan of San Diego, I have been informed to the contrary and that is why I held them in respect. However, be that as it may, it appears that this article does not bother us in that connection and leaves the conduct of each of us free. If the Mazatlán soldiers under you are resolved to recognize you only, being free to act as they choose will not cause them to act differently. However, if some should come to join the troops here, they would not be jeered at, because the fact of their coming would demonstrate their agreement with us. The artillerymen, as I have said, are free to remain here or to join their commander, but if that does not seem right they may remain here.

Concerning your fourth paragraph regarding the mail, if your side does not find it possible to have two mails each month, I agree to but one, which shall leave Monterey on the 7th and San Diego on the 22nd.

With regard to the fifth paragraph, in which you give your reasons for considering the oath as unnecessary, I say that it is imperative—that the law requires it of all public officers without exception.

As regards the seventh paragraph concerning the opening of correspondence from the central government, it is worthy of note that up to the present I have received none nor do I know of any that has come to the post office at San Diego. However, if any should come, we shall act with due delicacy and consideration.

In conclusion and in reference to your eighth and last paragraph and the remarks you make, it would seem that everything is settled from my viewpoint, and I shall make public immediately those articles on which we are in complete agreement, mentioning those that remain pending until your decision and leaving until then their further treatment.

God and Liberty, Mission San Luis Rey, May 3, 1832.

José María de Echeandia

*To Captain Citizen Agustin V. Zamorano,
Santa Barbara.*[35]

With Echeandia's latest counter-proposals and his statement that all appeared to be in agreement between them at hand, Captain Zamorano took the entire correspondence that had passed between them and drew up a new set of twelve articles. In these he was very careful to include only those items on which there had been specific agreement and to state them in a manner that would leave no ground for objection by Echeandia. This done, he felt that a definite truce had been arranged and that he could announce to the Territory that peace once more prevailed.

On May 8, he enclosed these articles in a letter to Echeandia for his final approval. This letter he closed by saying,

> I believe that these articles as stated give the true spirit of our negotiations and I assume them to be agreed upon and now devote my attention to giving them to the public, which is anxious to learn the result, in proper form. For my own part, I have nothing to say in regard to the last point raised by your last official letter concerning the treatment of what is still pending between us. As this has no bearing on the matters in hand, it seems better not to discuss it and so avoid new differences.

God and Liberty, Santa Barbara, May 8, 1832.

Agustin V. Zamorano

Sr. Lieutenant Colonel Don José María de Echeandia.[36]

---

[35] Echeandia to Zamorano, San Luis Rey, May 3, 1832, MS., *ibid.*, No. 32.
[36] Zamorano to Echeandia, Santa Barbara, May 8, 1832, MS., *ibid.*, No. 33.

So certain was Captain Zamorano that his peace terms would be accepted that he did not wait for Echeandia's ratification before issuing, on the following day, May 9, a proclamation to the inhabitants of his section of the Territory, quoting in full the terms of the agreement and requesting that all observe them.

The Citizen Agustin V. Zamorano to the Inhabitants from Santa Barbara to San Francisco.

Fellow Citizens and Friends:
From the instant in which, because of the absence of Lieutenant Colonel Citizen Manuel Victoria, I took charge of the military command of the greater portion of this Territory I have overlooked no means by which the order and peace of the country might be restored, although agitation has been incessant since the pronouncement at the *presidio* of San Diego. I now have the satisfaction of informing you that at last these have been secured through the means of just and reasonable agreements without the necessity of shedding a single drop of Mexican blood by either side. The conditions mutually agreed on by Lieutenant Colonel Citizen José María de Echeandia and myself, I hasten to bring to your knowledge in the following manner:

Articles of the agreed conditions.

1. That until the arrival in the Territory of the governor, or governors, appointed by the central government, or express orders from the supreme authority in favor of any person residing within the Territory, the military command shall remain divided into two parts—one, from San Gabriel south, being under the orders of Lieutenant Colonel Don José María de Echeandia, and the other, from San Fernando north, under the orders of Captain Don Agustin V. Zamorano. The latter is not to advance any military force south of San Buenaventura and the former north of San Juan Capistrano, excepting only the ordinary guards of five to seven men in those missions beyond the border lines.

2. That the Most Excellent Deputation shall abstain from sending instructions to the *ayuntamientos* located in the northern division. The same is understood in regard to the civil governor whom that body has appointed, or may appoint.

3. That trade, travel, and social relations shall not be interfered with by either of the contracting parties.

4. That the Most Excellent Deputation shall undertake no innovations in the missions of the District of San Diego.

5. That in case of disturbances of any sort, either party shall give the

other immediate notice, requesting aid if needed which shall be given, internal conditions of his division permitting.

6. That neither party shall have any other relations with the Town of Los Angeles than the military ones heretofore existing between that town and the presidial commanders at Santa Barbara and San Diego.

7. That any armed advance, without preliminary agreement, beyond the prescribed limits is to be repelled without any responsibility being incurred by the offended party; other breaches that may be committed shall be the subject of official representations which are to be answered satisfactorily and promptly.

8. That the usual mail shall leave Monterey for San Diego on the 7th of each month, and from the latter to the former on the 22nd.

9. That in opening official despatches from the central government great delicacy is to be used, with responsibility in the matter resting on the commander of the southern department of the Territory.

10. That civilians who have taken no part in the contentions shall be free to live wherever they please; others shall stay where they are.

11. That the neophytes of the missions, and their pagan neighbors, for reasons of prudence and recognized good, are to take no part in our internal differences but shall be returned unarmed to their respective missions and *rancherias* and permitted to engage in their usual occupations.

12. That, for the sake of peace and the saving of Mexican blood, these articles shall remain in force until the person appointed by the central government as chief of the territorial government shall have been recognized.

These, my Fellow Citizens, are the results of the journey that brought me to this place. I congratulate myself and you, as well as the brave and judicious ones who made it possible, on thus reestablishing peace and order. You can now, without fear, return to your every day tasks and labors, depending on the assurance of your fellow citizen and friend.

AGUSTIN V. ZAMORANO

Santa Barbara, May 9, 1832.[87]

This proclamation was transmitted on the same day to the commandants of the *presidios* in the north. It was read as part of the orders of the day in the *presidio* at Santa Barbara on May 10, at Mon-

---

[87] Zamorano, Proclamation to the inhabitants from Santa Barbara to San Francisco, Santa Barbara, May 9, 1832, MS., in San José Spanish Archives, City Hall, San José, II, 694-7, and copied in *San José Archives*, II, 89-93. Also, in *Vallejo, Doc.* I, 309; translated in summary, Bancroft, *op. cit.*, III, 228.

As Acting Governor 133

terey on May 13, and at San Francisco on May 17.[38] With peace restored and the government of the Territory preserved and recognized in three of the four presidial districts, Captain Zamorano returned to Monterey. He had been able to carry out all the plans and policies agreed upon at the council of February 1. He was probably well pleased with the situation and looked forward to the arrival of the new governor and the time he could give up the office he had so reluctantly assumed and return to his normal duties.

IV. Zamorano as Governor.

As might have been expected from his past performances, Echeandia, on the receipt of Captain Zamorano's letter of May 8 enclosing the redrawn set of articles of agreement between them, did not reply that he accepted them and that all was settled between them. In this connection, the statement by Don Lucas Alamán, Secretary of Relations in the central government at Mexico, in a letter dated May 17, 1832, to the Secretary of War and Marine concerning the situation in Alta California, is very much to the point. After stating that the responsibility for the rebellion should be definitely fixed, he said,

 . . . it is exceedingly important to the peace of Alta California that Lieutenant Colonel Don José María de Echeandia shall leave its territory at once.[39]

Had Echeandia known that the central administration considered him such a menace to the peace of the Territory, he would have hastened to accept Don Agustin's latest proposal. Instead, believing himself to be in the good graces of the supreme authorities, he proceeded to raise new objections. He claimed, on May 22, 1832, that they had reached an agreement on three articles only, namely the first, fifth and eighth, and that the others were still open because there was need of further discussion on them to avoid new ruptures. He promised to take the subject up again at an early date.[40]

---

[38] Zamorano to commandants of Santa Barbara, Monterey, and San Francisco, Santa Barbara, May 9, 1832, MS., in *Vallejo, Doc.*, I, 308.
[39] Alamán to Secretary of War and Marine, Mexico, May 17, 1832, MS., in *Legajo* 52-6-6-10.   [40] Echeandia to Zamorano, San Diego, May 22, 1832, MS., *ibid.*, No. 34.

This he did in a letter dated May 28. In it, he objected to the manner in which Don Agustin had stated the restriction on relations with the Town of Los Angeles, that he had forbidden not only military relations but also civil. He then went into a long dissertation as to why he considered himself invested with civil authority over the entire Territory. In the midst of this letter he was perturbed by news of an armed disturbance in Los Angeles and called on Don Agustin for an explanation.[41]

This letter reached Monterey on June 5 and Captain Zamorano replied on the same date that the incident in Los Angeles was due to an indiscretion on the part of the *alcalde* of that place and he presumed that Echeandia was completely informed in regard to it by that time,[42] that it called for no action on Echeandia's part with the risk of disturbing anew the peace of the Territory, and that he was waiting for the continuation of the discussion of the matters between them.[43]

Taking advantage of a ship about to sail, Don Agustin sent a short report to the central government on June 6, 1832. This was his first letter to Mexico after the outbreak of the insurrection on November 29.

Comandancia General accidental de la Alta California.

> As I wish to take advantage of the departure of a vessel, lack of time does not permit me to give Your Excellency a duly detailed account of all the events of the rebellion that broke out at the Port of San Diego on November 29 of last year with the object of deposing Señor Don Manuel Victoria from both commands and I shall limit myself to making known to Your Excellency the state in which the Territory finds itself today.
>
> It is divided into two military commands, the Department of San Diego, which is under the orders of Lieutenant Colonel Don José María de Echeandia, and from San Fernando north, which is under mine. The Town of Los Angeles remains neutral territory. By this means, I have secured the peace and tranquility of the country, which awaits the decision of the central government. The opposition has not ceased their

---

[41] Echeandia to Zamorano, San Diego, May 28, 1832, MS., *ibid.*, No. 35.
[42] For details of this movement, led by Antonio Avila, a convict, see Tays, *op. cit.*
[43] Zamorano to Echeandia, Monterey, June 5, 1832, MS., in *Legajo* 52-6-6-10, No. 36.

instruction of the neophytes of the missions of the Department of San Diego, whom they have excited, in the use of arms. This is an evil which I consider great, not only for the present but for the future as it will be the source of truly harmful results.

If the Most Excellent Vice-President does not decide, with the promptness the present state of affairs demands, to send a commander to govern this country, together with troops, munitions, arms, and funds the integrity and safety of the Territory is in imminent danger from dissensions that may arise because of new pretensions by the opposition; of these I have already received some indications.

All of which I have the honor to make known to Your Excellency for your information and guidance.

God and Liberty, Monterey, June 6, 1832.

AGUSTIN V. ZAMORANO

His Excellency, the Secretary of War and Marine, Mexico."

Echeandia continued the discussion of the terms of the truce in a letter dated June 19, 1832, in which he raised objections to several of the articles. He could not agree to the last part of the first article as it was necessary for him to maintain a larger guard than seven men at Mission San Gabriel because that place was the center of a large traffic between California and New Mexico and Sonora. His other objections were minor and chiefly complaints that Don Agustin had injected new matters which should be the subject of detailed correspondence. His last paragraph read,

> By the national schooner *Joven Victoria*, which anchored in this port on the 10th of this month, came several passengers, among whom was Captain of Artillery Citizen Juan Antonio Muñoz, who comes to take command of his branch of the service, and from whom we learn that Brigadier General Citizen José Figueroa is on his way to assume command of Alta California. Seeing that the governor appointed by the central government draws near, it behooves us to spend more time on the negotiations concerning the new terms that have been proposed between us."

[44] Zamorano to Secretary of War and Marine, Monterey, June 6, 1832, MS., in *Legajo* 52-6-6-7.
[45] Echeandia to Zamorano, San Diego, June 19, 1832, MS., in *Legajo* 52-6-6-10, No. 37.

This letter reached Captain Zamorano at Monterey on July 7 and he replied at once in a note that was a model of brevity.

> *Comandancia General accidental de la Alta California.*
> I have received your official letter of June 19 last.
> Assuming that the information contained in your last paragraph is true, I believe it unnecessary to comment on the other paragraphs which refer to certain articles of the agreement under consideration between us.
> God and Liberty, Monterey, July 7, 1832.
> AGUSTIN V. ZAMORANO
> *To Lieutenant Colonel Don José María de Echeandia,
> San Diego.*[46]

This short note brought to a close the correspondence between these two officers that had begun with Echeandia's circular letter written at Mission San Gabriel on December 9, 1831, after his interview with the wounded Victoria. In these letters, nearly all of which I have quoted in full, we have practically the entire history of the San Diego rebellion of 1831 and 1832. In them also, we have the measure of the character, sincerity, and ability of the two principal actors on that stage. From June 1832, to the following January, all was quiet politically throughout Alta California.

With Echeandia disposed of and the new governor on his way, Don Agustin at once passed the welcomed news to his people. He issued a second proclamation on July 7.

> *The Citizen Agustin V. Zamorano to the Inhabitants from
> Santa Barbara to San Francisco.*
> *Fellow Citizens:*
> Subsequent to my last statement to you in which were set forth the different articles of the conditions agreed upon between Señor Echeandia and myself in order to preserve the peace of the country and to maintain all affairs in their then condition until the decision of the central government should arrive, I received an official communication from the said Echeandia in which he explained that properly speaking we had agreed on but three of the articles and that the others needed

---

[46] Zamorano to Echeandia, Monterey, July 7, 1832, MS., *ibid.*, No. 38.

clarification as to their true significance. At the same time, he informed me that he would send me his opinions regarding the articles which he considered as not agreed upon by special messenger.

In time, I received this last communication. In it he no longer aspired to command the whole of the Territory as general commandant but very much so as civil governor. The thread of his discourse was cut off by the news brought him concerning an armed party that was approaching the Town of Los Angeles from this direction and he offered to continue his remarks later. Meanwhile I awaited those remarks, ready to meet whatever objections that might be raised. Finally, by the last monthly mail, his letter came to my hands. In it, after some explanations, he reports substantially that assuming that Señor Brigadier General Don José Figueroa will arrive soon in this Territory to take command of this office by appointment of the central government, he believed it best that no time be wasted in arguments but that an early agreement be reached on the articles pending before the two parties. With confirmation of the news of the coming of the said brigadier general in other letters, I have no desire to communicate further with Señor Echeandia on this subject.

I now await only the arrival of the said general in person to turn over to him the command which I hold temporarily and place myself immediately under his orders.

In the meantime, as always, I shall use every means at my disposal to preserve the public peace and individual security.

For your part, I beg you to continue to cooperate, as you have in the past, for the advancement of all the sciences and arts in these towns which form an integral part of the confederation of our Mexican Republic. This your fellow citizen and friend expects of you.

AGUSTIN V. ZAMORANO

Monterey, July 7, 1832.[47]

On the same day, in order that he might have complete information at hand and readily available for the new governor, the acting general commandant wrote to all the presidial commanders instructing them to send him a report on the number of effective troops under their command, with their assignments, and on the amount and condition of munitions and armaments in their districts.[48]

---

[47] Zamorano, Proclamation to inhabitants from Santa Barbara to San Francisco, Monterey, July 7, 1832, MS., in *Vallejo, Doc.*, I, 314.
[48] Zamorano to commandant of San Francisco, Monterey, July 7, 1832, MS., *ibid.*, I, 315.

Captain Don Juan Antonio Muñoz, whose arrival on June 10, was reported by Echeandia, was senior in grade to Captain Zamorano. Therefore, Don Agustin wrote to Captain Muñoz, on August 4, that because of his seniority the commandant of the *presidio* at Santa Barbara had been ordered to recognize him as *comandante general accidental* as soon as he arrived at Santa Barbara on his journey to Monterey.[49] To this Captain Muñoz replied, from Santa Barbara on September 4, that he would not assume the office of acting general commandant until after he had assumed the artillery command and not then until he had an opportunity to discuss the political situation in the Territory; furthermore, he thought it probably best that he remain as en route until the arrival of the new governor.[50] On his arrival at Monterey, Captain Muñoz declined to assume the general command temporarily unless Captain Zamorano would first repudiate the agreement reached with Echeandia, saying he wanted no inconvenient restrictions on his efforts to redeem that part of the Territory found under Echeandia's orders. This Don Agustin refused to do, as that meant plunging the country into new disorders. As a consequence, Captain Muñoz did not assume even his artillery command but remained as under travel orders until the new governor arrived.

Although he made no claims to the office of civil governor, which he held to be vacant, Captain Zamorano did perform such civil functions as were made necessary by the exigencies of the situation. Such acts as he did perform affected the Territory in general and as a whole; he never took it upon himself to interfere or to take part in the purely local functions of the *alcaldes* and the *ayuntamientos*. He permitted local elections to be held as usual but refused to allow the meeting of district electors to elect members of the deputation and a successor to the incumbent deputy in the national congress, since there was no civil governor to sign the credentials. Nor would he admit Echeandia's pretentions to that office. He frankly expressed his regrets that the inhabitants were without representation but con-

---

[49] Zamorano to Muñoz, Monterey, August 4, 1832, summarized in *Dept. St. Pap.*, MS., III, 80.

[50] Muñoz to Zamorano, Santa Barbara, September 4, 1832, summarized, *idem.*

sidered it would be a greater loss to permit Echeandia to take part in the election as civil governor.[51]

Every effort was made by Don Agustin to prevent the enforcement of military regulations from lapsing again into the laxity reached during Echeandia's term of office. As had Victoria before him, he passed several cases of a criminal nature to the *asesor* of the Territory for review.[52] In these matters, he appears to have taken a firm but humane position.[53] He allowed some convicts to be farmed out to the custody of the *rancheros* as laborers[54] and sent others to the *presidios* to be used in the repair and maintenance of those posts.[55]

In September and again in December 1832, Captain Zamorano granted a license to Don José Ramon Estrada and Don José Castro to hunt otter out of the Port of San Francisco. It was stipulated that not more than six *cayucos*, or small fishing boats, were to be used, that at least two-thirds of their crews must be natives of the country and that no catches were to be made within the port itself. The commandant of the *presidio* at San Francisco was ordered to watch their operations and, if any of the restrictions were not observed, to report the number of pelts involved to the custom house at Monterey for the collection of duties.[56]

Don José Joaquín Gómez, *sub-comisario* at Monterey, resigned his office in October 1832. It will be recalled that the sponsors of the Plan of San Diego, particularly his superior, Don Juan Bandini, had made many complaints against the alleged irregularities in his conduct of his office. Whether these complaints had any part in the events that led to his resignation, I am unable to say. Don Agustin appointed his close friend, Don José Mariano Estrada, as the successor

---

Zamorano to *alcalde* of Monterey, Monterey, August 4, 1832, in *Monterey Archives*, MS., VII, 38; cf. *ibid.*, VII, 39, 40.

Zamorano, Criminal case of Juan Antonio Arceo, Monterey, February 7, 1832, in *Dept. t. Pap., Ben., Mil.*, MS., LXXIII, 1.

Zamorano, Criminal case of Rafael Garcia, in *De la Guerra, Doc.*, MS., I, 216-18.

Zamorano to commandant of San Francisco, Monterey, November 8, 1832, MS., in *Vallejo, Doc.*, I, 329.

Zamorano to commandant of San Francisco, Monterey, August 1, 1832, MS., *ibid.*, XX, 316.

Zamorano to commandant of San Francisco, Monterey, September 8, 1832, MS., *ibid.*, 323; license to José Castro and José Ramon Estrada, MS., *ibid.*, XXX, 337.

of Gómez in that office.[57] Don Mariano was one of the most highly respected men in northern California and well qualified for the place An attempt was then made to reorganize the Territory's financial affairs and Don Agustin ordered the *habilitados*, or paymasters, of the *presidios* to submit estimates of the monthly salaries and expense of their posts, together with estimates of the assistance that was expected from the missions. Thereafter a more equitable distribution of available funds between the three garrisons under his command was attempted.[58] No funds were allotted to the *presidio* at San Diego As Monterey was the only port of entry, at that time, and possessed the only custom house in Alta California, all maritime customs which constituted the chief source of territorial revenue, were collected there. Therefore, the District of San Diego did not receive any of the territorial receipts during the year 1832 and the officers who had adhered to the Plan of San Diego and those who were employed by Echeandia's provisional government went without their pay.

In an effort to encourage the commerce of the country, Captain Zamorano allowed whaling vessels, after first calling at Monterey, to purchase supplies in Californian ports without incurring any cost other than the payment of anchorage fees.[60]

Several Indian disturbances occurred during the year 1832. These were chiefly in the neighborhood of San José and consisted of raids by the pagan Indians on the missions of San José and Santa Clara Many *ranchos* were raided for their horses and there resulted at one time a scarcity of those animals. There was trouble also with the Indians around Mission San Rafael. The operations against the Indians were carried on under the command of Ensign Don José Sánchez, commandant of the *presidio* at San Francisco, but the maintenance of a supply of men and materials was a problem for the acting general commandant.[61]

[57] Zamorano, Circular announcing appointment of Estrada, Monterey, October 18, 183 MS., *ibid.*, I, 326.
[58] Zamorano to *habilitado* of San Francisco Company, Monterey, October 18, 183 MS., *ibid.*, I, 325.
[59] Echeandia to Secretary of War and Marine, San Diego, January 13, 1833, MS., *Legajo* 52-6-6-7, No. 1.
[60] Zamorano to commandant of San Francisco, Monterey, October 26, 1832, MS., *Vallejo, Doc.*, I, 327.
[61] Zamorano to Sánchez, Santa Barbara, April 19, 1832, MS., *ibid.*, I, 307; and Zamrano to commandant of San Francisco, Monterey, December 9, 1832, MS., *ibid.*, I, 34

On November 16, 1832, after having waited nearly six months for the arrival of the new governor, Captain Zamorano again wrote to the Secretary of War and Marine, in Mexico.

Comandancia General accidental de la Alta California.

Most Excellent Sir:
On June 6 last, taking advantage of an opportunity that presented itself suddenly with the appearance of a vessel, I had the honor of addressing to Your Excellency a brief report on the state in which this Territory found itself at that date and the lamentable results I feared. Since that time we have been waiting the arrival of Brigadier General Don José Figueroa, who, according to reliable reports, has been appointed to the military and political commands of this Territory and who many months ago sailed from Acapulco in the national trading brig *Catalina*. All affairs have remained in a state of expectancy because of this report. However, up to this date, neither the vessel nor the brigadier general has arrived on this coast and, though it is reported that this officer touched at Cape San Lucas on the 5th of September last, more than sufficient time has now elapsed for him to have reached Alta California. For this reason, we fear that he may have been shipwrecked and I cannot do less than call it to Your Excellency's attention.

This supposition, which is based on the long delay, Your Excellency may be assured will have an heartening effect on the San Diego faction, leading them to attempt new disturbances, and the enemies of the Nation will spread the rumor that Mexico is unable to protect and maintain its officers in the Territory, thus strengthening an idea which exists already in the minds of many Californians. The foreigners, especially the North Americans who never lose an opportunity to encroach on our territory, are expecting, I have no doubt, a new pronouncement which will make it easy for them to join the San Diego movement so as to make the Territory independent of Mexico and then take possession of it themselves, an attitude they have held toward all the disturbances that have occurred.

Let us confess the fact that California has been only a source of expense to the Nation, but let us also admit that it is a very valuable part of Mexico, for it is no less than the master key that will safeguard us from the west and which, in time and with its treasures, which are today stolen secretly without molestation by the foreigners, will be a productive and happy state in the Union. Cast the eye thoughtfully over her and one can see every good that may possibly be found. But none of this happiness shall be ours if the national government does not take its development seriously and quickly adopt wise measures to assure the integrity of these offices by sending the officer, troops, arms, munitions, and funds of which I spoke before, the necessity for which makes itself felt with increasing force day by day.

By Exhibit No. 1, which I attach, Your Excellency will see the forces that are stationed at the three posts of San Francisco, Monterey and Santa Barbara, all of which are pledged to good order under my command. However, in the face of necessity this force could never be mobilized as a unit; to do so would mean the abandonment of their posts to the threats of the Indians who only await such an opportunity to attack and destroy with deadly fury the settlements they protect. Furthermore, these troops do not inspire confidence, especially those native to the country, as they have never been under fire and all are on friendly relations or bound by ties of kinship with those of the San Diego faction and also are steeped in the idea of independence. For these serious reasons, I suggest that the central government send as the minimum requirement for safety a force of at least one hundred loyal, well-disciplined and equipped soldiers. If this is not done, any measures taken by whomever is sent to California are doomed to failure and they will share the fate suffered by Señor Victoria on that unlucky fifth of December last. Unrest in this country, whose peace has heretofore been the envy of all others, will not cease until its intentions are realized.

The armament available is insufficient to equip the force that is indicated on the exhibit I have mentioned. Although some expenditures have been made for its repair, it is so old that slight use soon restores it to its former state of worthlessness.

The attached Exhibit No. 2 shows the total amount of ammunition available, the deterioration of which may be easily inferred from the length of time that has passed since it was made and the lack of care it has received from the persons charged with its preservation.

There is also the serious necessity of repairing the mountings of nearly every piece of artillery. For some years past these have not received even the slightest attention. As a consequence, at every post, there are many pieces lying in the dust, rusting, and those that equip the batteries can scarcely be used even for firing salutes. As these are mounted on naval gun carriages and therefore cannot be moved, there is no way to give direction to their fire.

Recently, at great effort and expense, I have been able to procure little lead from which the rifle balls listed on the last exhibit have been made.

Finally, the Indians of the missions in the San Diego district have become so unmanageable, so I am told, that Echeandia has hardly been able to control them and he is constantly threatened by parties of wild Indians who may bring some misfortune at any time. Likewise, the mission Indians about San Francisco Bay are equally aroused. There has been one small revolt which we fortunately managed to control, but the leaders fled and found refuge in the almost impenetrable forests where they maintain themselves, aided and strengthened by pagans. There is another place, called the "Stockade," which they have fortified and where all the neophytes who flee from the villages of San José and Santa Clara assemble and which they make a depot for the stealing of stock, principally horses, of which they have almost cleaned out the neighboring ranches and missions. These places require a strong expedition to destroy them.

All of which I have the honor to bring to Your Excellency's attention for the consideration of the central government.

God and Liberty, Monterey, November 16, 1832.

AGUSTIN V. ZAMORANO

Most Excellent Sir, the Secretary of War and Marine, Mexico.[62]

As we look back today, with our knowledge of subsequent events, we see that Captain Zamorano was gifted with the power of prophecy on the day he wrote this letter.

V. The Arrival of Brigadier General Figueroa.

In Mexico, in the meanwhile, Californian affairs were receiving considerable attention.

The first to report the revolt of November 1831 to Mexico appears to have been Captain William A. Richardson, an Englishman and a naturalized Mexican citizen, then in command of the Mexican schooner *Guadalupe* and remembered today as an early resident of San Francisco. He wrote President Bustamante from Cape San Lucas on December 23, 1831, and reported what little he had heard before sailing from Monterey.[63]

---

[62] Zamorano to Secretary of War and Marine, Monterey, November 16, 1832, MS., in *Legajo* 52-6-6-7. Unfortunately, the exhibits mentioned in this report have not been located.

[63] Richardson to Bustamante, Cape San Lucas, December 23, 1831, MS., in *Legajo* 52-6-6-6.

The second person to report was Captain Henry Virmond, a German and a naturalized Mexican citizen, who, with headquarters at Acapulco, was the owner of a large number of ships and carried on an extensive trade with California and South America. He traveled widely, had an extensive acquaintance and possessed great influence with Mexican officials of all ranks. Captain Virmond wrote from Mazatlan on December 27 and again on December 30 to President Bustamante and passed on the news brought from California by the master of one of his ships.[64]

During the next few weeks several other reports arrived including those, as we have seen, by Echeandia on December 4, 1831, and January 15, 1832, and by Victoria on February 5. By means of these letters and reports the central administration was well informed of all that happened in Alta California. The situation was discussed fully and carefully, and recommendations were made by the several departments interested as to the steps that should be taken. One of the most interesting of these was a memorandum prepared for the President by the Acting Secretary of War and Marine, Don Antonio Campo, which gave a shrewd and brilliant analysis of the situation.[65]

California's representative in the national congress at the time was Don Carlos Antonio Carrillo. He had talked long and eloquently to his colleagues in the congress and to the officers of the administration on the resources of his country and the virtues of his countrymen as law abiding citizens. The news of the revolt against Governor Victoria was a great disappointment to him and he wrote bitterly to Captain Don José Antonio de la Guerra, of Santa Barbara,

> Every hope for a separation of the military and civil commands, for an organic law, for courts, for a proper distribution of lands, have gone to the devil and I am placed in a most awkward position after having sung the praises of the Californians in Congress.

If we are to credit the statements of Don Carlos, the central government determined to punish the rebels severely and he saved the

---

[64] Virmond to Bustamante, Mazatlan, December 27, 1831, MS., in *Legajo* 52-6-6-6; same, December 30, 1831, *idem*.

[65] Campo to Bustamante, Mexico, January 26, 1832, MS., *idem*.

leaders only by the most strenuous efforts, first from death, then from banishment, and finally secured their pardon.[66]

In the month of March 1832, the question of who should be appointed governor of Alta California was receiving serious consideration. It appears that President Bustamante had at one time definitely made his decision to appoint Captain Zamorano to that office. In this he was influenced by his former acquaintance with him and the fact that he had taken no part in the insurrection.

But Congressman Carrillo did not approve of this idea. He had complained bitterly of Zamorano's rapid promotion and had come to feel that Don Agustin was being pushed ahead at the expense of native Californian officers. On March 15, Don Carlos wrote to Captain de la Guerra in desperation,

> Señor Virmond has just been with me on a visit, it being three days since he arrived in this capital from Acapulco. In the long conversation we had concerning the recent events in California, one of the things that he told me was that Zamorano only had not taken part in the dance by the rebels in forming the Plan. Also, that he had that same day informed the President on that particular point, as well as Secretary Alamán, and, in view of it, Bustamante had told him that he was going to appoint Zamorano civil governor of the Territory and that he had approved Bustamante's idea. But it is very likely that this idea may not have come from the President but from Virmond. That is the way everything goes. I already had assumed that when this gentleman arrived he would try to do something in favor of Zamorano, because that is the way they got the captaincies. I believe that he [*Virmond*] did the whole thing himself and so likewise will it be with all subsequent things. Well, in some ways the Señor of Vera Cruz [*Santa Anna?*] speaks very true. Now I shall put a cork in my mouth and I shall not butt in or say anything. Victoria is still to come and so is Father Peyri. What will they say about the miserable Californians—and del Pliego on another hand also?
>
> I have already told you in other letters about the conversation which Bustamante had with me and of the word he sent me by Sánchez Yoalgo, and also the answer that I made. But to tell you the truth, I do not like

---

[66] Carrillo, Carlos Antonio, to J. A. de la Guerra y Noriega. An extremely interesting series of letters, dated November 16, 1831, January 5, 20, March 15, April 14, 21, and May 11, 1832, in *De la Guerra, Doc.*, MS., 223-52.

Zamorano as civil governor and, if it should happen thus, I shall do all I can to see if they will not send someone else from here. But at any event, the office remains in the hands of the military. Please give me your views.

. . . .

After all the talk of Virmond's, I have not wanted to go near the government to hear what they will tell me on the subject although they have already told me much as I have written you in other letters. But one of these days I shall have to go and see what they have to tell me and I shall reprove them about Zamorano if they say anything to me, and with some spirit, too. But Virmond gets away with whatever he wants as you shall see.[67]

I am unable to account for the great interest in Don Agustin V. Zamorano which Don Carlos says Captain Virmond had always displayed. This, however, proved to be one instance in which Captain Virmond did not get what he wanted. Apparently Don Carlos did remove the cork from his mouth and he must also have talked with considerable spirit as Don Agustin did not receive the appointment. I know of no evidence that he ever knew his name was under consideration. As we have seen, his first report to the central authorities was not made until June 6, which was much too late to aid the advancement of his cause. In all probability he never aspired to or thought of himself as a candidate for the office.

The appointment as general commandant and civil governor of Alta California went to Brigadier General Don José Figueroa. This officer had been prominent during the closing years of the Mexican Revolution, had served as general commandant of Sonora from 1824 to 1830 where he had gained some knowledge of Californian affairs, and as vice-governor of the State of Mexico in 1831. As a result, he was a person of prominence with something of a national reputation. Politically he was not in sympathy with Bustamante's administration and it has been suggested that he was exiled by being appointed governor of California.[68]

General Figueroa did not set out immediately on his journey to

---

[67] Carrillo de la Guerra, Mexico, March 15, 1832, *ibid.*, IV, 235. I do not know the letter in which he reported his conversation with the President.
[68] Bancroft, *op. cit.*, III, 234.

Alta California. He lingered in the capital for several weeks, receiving his instructions and studying the reports that had been received. He was provided with a force of about seventy-five men; these, however, were *cholos*, recruited at Acapulco from those newly released from prisons. In June, the general went to Acapulco to superintend the outfitting of his company and, on July 17, sailed from that port in the brig *Catalina*.

It was many weeks, however, before he reached California. It is unnecessary for us here to go into all the trials and troubles the new governor encountered on his way, which included a mutiny among his troops, the seizure by them of his ship, and a long wait for the vessel's return. Finally, he arrived, on January 14, 1833, at Monterey, accompanied by Captain Don Nicolás Gutiérrez, Captain Don Francisco Figueroa, his brother, Lieutenant Don Bernardo Navarrete, Don Rafael Gonzáles, who came to take charge of the custom house, Surgeon Don Manuel Alva, about thirty soldiers, and ten Franciscan friars from the College of Zacatecas who came to relieve and reenforce the missionaries.[69] The next day the party landed and Figueroa at once assumed his office as governor of Alta California.

All the records and correspondence of the period that have been preserved indicate that, both by the authorities in Mexico and by General Figueroa, Captain Zamorano was considered and recognized to be the legitimate acting governor of Alta California. Figueroa's first act on landing was to present a letter to Don Agustin in which he quoted the orders of his appointment as general commandant and inspector of the Territory, asked that they be published in the orders of the day, and expressed the appreciation of himself and the central government of the service rendered by him and the other officers of the military for having "followed the pathway of honor in complete obedience to the military laws that govern us." On the same day, Captain Zamorano wrote all the presidial commanders, quoting the general's letter in full and adding,

> By its orders, I transmit it to you and have the satisfaction of informing you of the happy arrival in this Territory of the same brigadier general and ordering that you shall cause him to be recognized as general com-

[69] For details of Figueroa's trip, *cf.* Tays, *op. cit.*

mandant and inspector of this upper territory in the general orders of the day, observing that the proper demonstrations of joy, in keeping with such an happy event, are made."[70]

Such were the formalities by which Brigadier General Don José Figueroa assumed his office as general commandant.

On the same day, Figueroa sent letters to the various local civil authorities notifying them of his arrival and announcing his appointment. He also issued a printed proclamation which he had brought with him from Mexico.[71] With this was circulated also a small announcement of his arrival which, as we shall later see, was printed locally.

The chief immediate concern of the new governor was Lieutenant Colonel Don José María de Echeandia. On January 14, also, Figueroa wrote to Echeandia, announced his arrival, quoted the orders given him requiring Echeandia to report in person at Mexico as soon as possible, extended amnesty to him and all the officers "who took part in the movements of the year 1831 against the gentleman who was my predecessor" under the law of April 25, 1832, asked that Echeandia and those who followed him recognize him as governor at once, and promised that no action would be taken against any of them.[72]

Echeandia, on January 13, 1832, tired of the long wait for the new governor's arrival and unaware that the *Catalina* with Figueroa aboard was approaching Monterey harbor on that same day, sent a long report to the Secretary of War and Marine. In this he reviewed all that had transpired in Alta California since his letter of January 15, 1832. This report was a most interesting admixture of truth, half-truth, and outright falsehood.

Figueroa's letter reached Echeandia at San Diego on January 28 and that officer replied on the next day that he had ordered Figueroa to be acknowledged as general commandant and civil governor in all the posts and towns within his district. He ignored Figueroa's offer of amnesty and protested his sincere belief that he had served the

---

[70] Zamorano to commandant of San Francisco, Monterey, January 14, 1833, MS., in *Vallejo, Doc.*, II, 1.
[71] Figueroa, Proclamation, *ibid.*, I, 288.
[72] Figueroa to Echeandia, Monterey, January 14, 1833, in *Dept. St. Pap.*, MS., III, 76.

Nation well in the months that had followed the revolt against Victoria, and closed by expressing the hope that he might be of further service to Figueroa.[73] Thereafter several friendly letters were exchanged between them and Echeandia appears to have made a real effort to give the new governor help in gathering information on conditions in the southern missions. Echeandia sailed from San Diego on May 14 for Mexico.[74] He arrived at Guadalajara on June 6 and thereafter very little is known of him.[75] Figueroa reported his departure to the War Department on June 18.[76]

The new governor was under instructions to prepare a report to the federal government covering the events following the revolt against Victoria. For this purpose, Captain Zamorano, who had reverted to his former office of secretary of both the military and civil branches of the territorial government, had copies made of all the correspondence and other documents touching on the events that had occurred since November 29, 1831, and these were placed before the governor. Figueroa acknowledged these papers in the following letter.

Comandancia General de la Alta California.

The collection of copies which you have laid before me, containing an account of the different occurrences during the unsettled state in which this Territory was thrown by the rebellious *junta* of the 29th of November, 1831, at San Diego, has put me in possession of the various particulars worthy of the attention of the supreme government of the Union. Among the most notable of these, I find the documents dated January 24, 1832, in which appears the efforts of the voluntary company of forty-six foreigners residing in the country in taking up arms in favor of the constitutional government and law, to maintain public order in the capital, as well as the legally constituted authorities and to repel the aggressions of the mutineers in the event of an attack. Their noble

---

[73] Echeandia to Figueroa, San Diego, January 29, 1833, MS., in *Legajo* 52-6-6-10, No. 44.

[74] Figueroa to Santiago Argüello, Monterey, June 3, 1833, in *Dept. St. Pap., Ben., Mil.*, MS., LXXIX, 23.

[75] Cuesta, José de la, to Secretary of War and Marine, Guadalajara, June 7, 1833, MS., in *Legajo* 52-6-6-10, No. 36.

[76] Figueroa to Secretary of War and Marine, Monterey, June 18, 1833, MS., *ibid.*, No. 44.

and generous conduct is the highest proof of their patriotism, of their love of order, and their fidelity to the government.

The document dated February 1 of the same year demonstrates the wisdom with which were determined the principles which served as the basis for the firm resolution to resist and bring to order those who had gone astray. Highly praiseworthy, without question, were the motives of the authors of this document, which you have satisfactorily carried out by placing yourself at the head of public affairs and taking over the temporary command, which, by regulations, was yours by right of succession. Highly worthy of recommendation and recompense, in my opinion, were the services rendered by yourself, by the faithful officers, by the citizens of all classes who assisted you, and by the foreigners who willingly lent their aid by taking up arms.

Justice and duty force me to recommend them particularly to the central government of the Union which I shall do, extolling, as I am in duty bound, the merit they have acquired in the defense of the country. In the meantime, in the name of the country and the central government, I extend to you the most distinguished and deserved thanks and request that you will give the same to every person who has taken part in the preservation of order, assuring them how pleasing their conduct has been to me and how much esteem and gratitude I profess towards such honorable patriots. For the reasons given above and because those who went astray have at length returned to their obedience, I have a double reason for congratulating them.

I assume that every citizen will share in the pleasure I feel in having reestablished constitutional order without the necessity of sacrificing any of our compatriots.

We have yet to consolidate peace and union amongst all the elements in the Territory and in this task, as well as in that of the internal and external defense of this part of the Republic, I rely on your assistance and patriotism. I trust that you will use your influence towards bringing about a general pacification.

God and Liberty, Monterey, February 15, 1833.

JOSÉ FIGUEROA

To Captain Don A. V. Zamorano."

Three days later, on February 18, the captain of the Company of Foreigners, William E. P. Hartnell, called all the members of that organization to a meeting at his house and read to them the thanks

---

[77] Figueroa to Zamorano, Monterey, February 15, 1833, MS., in *Vallejo, Doc.*, II, 12. This is an early English translation, apparently made by W. E. P. Hartnell.

of the new governor for the manner in which they had conducted themselves.[78]

On March 26, 1833, General Figueroa made his final report on the revolt against his predecessor, Don Manuel Victoria.

Comandancia General de la Alta California.

Most Excellent Sir:
I have the honor to forward herewith to Your Excellency thirty-eight numbered copies of documents turned over to me by Captain Don Agustin V. Zamorano at the time I took charge of this command in order to acquaint me with the events that took place between the 29th of November, 1831, and the 14th of January last, the date at which I arrived at this Port.

The enclosed transcripts give a complete review of the revolution promoted in this Territory against the Señor General Commandant my predecessor, the consequences that resulted therefrom and the status of affairs in the country until my arrival. I have thought it advisable to forward these documents in order that the superior authorities may be informed of all the details which they contain; furthermore, they show in brief the plans of the faction which deposed Lieutenant Colonel Don Manuel Victoria from office and forced him to return to Mexico after they had seriously wounded him in an encounter.

Having thus disposed of Señor Victoria, the faction placed Lieutenant Colonel Don José María de Echeandia in command and he freely exercised the authority of general commandant and civil governor. However, with the passing of the first surprised impression, the opinion of the saner portions of the Territory became known; they disapproved of the usurpation and dared to oppose it. Captain Don Agustin V. Zamorano, who had taken no part in the revolt, convoked in this capital a council of officers, civil employees of the treasury, and the most respected and important citizens to deliberate and take some action with the object of maintaining the authority of the central government and protecting the public peace against the insidious propaganda of the revolutionists. As Zamorano was the only captain who had not taken part in the revolt, he took temporary charge of the military command, which was his by regulations according to the order of succession, and the other employees and citizens pledged themselves to sustain him and to aid him in preserving the Territory to the orders of the central gov-

[78] Hartnell to Members of Company of Foreigners, Monterey, February 18, 1833, MS., *idem.*

ernment. This is set forth in the proceedings dated February 1, 1832, Document No. 13, and in it are set out the principles that served as a basis for their actions and a plan of operations for subduing the rebels.

In compliance with his duty, Zamorano organized his forces in the best possible manner; he increased them with citizens who volunteered, he prepared a defense for the capital, and, mobilizing the available troops, advanced to meet the rebels. The distance at which he found himself from the seat of government, the lack of orders to guide his actions, and the fear of risking the undertaking to an unfortunate outcome, as well as his scrupulousness and the difficulty of his position, made him proceed with great circumspection and prudence, in the hope of allowing sufficient time to elapse so that he might at least receive orders and instructions from the central government.

Nevertheless, he opened communication with the rebels, suggesting that they lay down their arms and submit to the Government. After several letters and threats, a sort of armistice was agreed on under the terms of which Zamorano retained under his command the major portion of the Territory from the Town of Los Angeles to the Port of San Francisco, and Echeandia, with his followers, was reduced to the District of San Diego under the solemn promise to obey the central government and the officer that it might appoint to this command.

Under the terms of this treaty, hostilities stopped and each maintained a force on guard at the stipulated places. In this manner civil war was avoided and disorders and troubles were controlled to a certain extent. Such was the situation in the Territory when I assumed the command. I believe the measures taken by Zamorano contributed to making the insurgents acknowledge me and consequently to the general pacification which we now enjoy.

For all these reasons, I have believed it but justice to approve the conduct of Captain Zamorano, who, in my judgment, has earned special consideration for the distinguished service he has rendered the Nation in the interests of the people of California, the Constitution and laws, and the honor and dignity of the central government. For this reason, I take satisfaction in recommending him very highly to Your Excellency, requesting that you see fit to make his merit known to the Most Excellent President of the Republic in order that he may receive the thanks and reward His Excellency may see fit to bestow on him and which is his just reward.

Also praiseworthy has been the conduct of the lieutenant of the Mazatlan Company, Don Juan María Ibarra, and the ensign of the presidial company at Santa Barbara, Don Anastacio Carrillo, as these officers by their honesty, fidelity, valor, and constancy have been the firmest

As Acting Governor 153

support to Zamorano in the maintenance of the laws, the public peace, and the government. Their example and their influence over their subordinates have contributed greatly toward maintaining the fidelity of the soldiers in their respective troops. For these reasons, I have the satisfaction of recommending them with equal particularity to the high consideration of His Excellency, the President.

All the officers who have contributed to the upholding of the legitimate authority are worthy of the consideration of His Excellency and I hope Your Excellency will be so kind as to make their good behavior known to him.

The residents of this capital took an active part in maintaining order and kept themselves under arms as long as their services were considered necessary. The same was done by various foreigners, residents in this same capital, who also drew up the proceedings of January 24, 1832, which are attached as Document No. 10, and by which they solemnly pledged themselves to uphold by force of arms the authority of the Government, forming for that purpose a company that was maintained under arms for some days. These individuals are deserving, in my opinion, of the gratitude and consideration of the Government, in whose name I have thanked them. As also are those who took part in the preservation of the public peace, as Your Excellency can see from the document which I enclose as No. 39.

Later I shall recommend to Your Excellency the persons who have especially distinguished themselves by their good services, and I shall inform you of all those who deserve the attention of the Government. I have not the time to address you at greater length in this report as I wish to take advantage of a vessel that is about to sail for Acapulco and my illness has prevented me from doing so before this.

All of which I have the honor to make known to Your Excellency to the end that you may bring it to the superior knowledge of His Excellency, the President, for whatever action he may see fit.

God and Liberty, Monterey, March 26, 1833.

José Figueroa

The Most Excellent Secretary of War and Marine, Mexico.[79]

---

[79] Figueroa to Secretary of War and Marine, Monterey, March 26, 1833, MS., in *Legajo* 52-6-6-10. Transcribed in part in *Dept. St. Pap.*, MS., III, 104, where the date is erroneously given as March 23. This transcription is an example of the advantage taken of Bancroft by some of his native Californian assistants. In this only the first page or two is transcribed and the remainder very briefly summarized, with the result that Bancroft and his senior assistants never saw Figueroa's appraisal of the service rendered by Zamorano. Bancroft, *op. cit.*, III, 243, note 5, refers to this document and says the thirty-eight documents mentioned are not given, which means they did not exist in the territorial archives at the time he was working. They were probably extracted many years before. They were unknown until found in the archives of the War Department in Mexico

Although we have completed our narrative of the revolt that took place in Alta California during the years 1831 and 1832, there remain a few comments that need to be made on the manner in which historians of California have been in the practice of presenting these events. Nearly all who have written of this period have represented the revolution that broke out at San Diego on November 29, 1831, as a success, and have either stated or inferred that Echeandia was governor of California during the year 1832. These conclusions I wish to refute.

It will be recalled that the Plan of San Diego announced as its purpose two objectives: the deposing of Governor Victoria and the temporary filling of the two offices of general commandant and civil governor by distinct persons who were to be selected by the territorial legislature. Only one of these objectives ever came to pass and that through circumstances fortuitous in the extreme; it was Don José María Ávila, piqued at an imagined personal affront, who deposed Victoria on the battlefield and not the *pronunciados* of San Diego. The revolt of November 29 was in fact a complete failure.

If Echeandia's intimidation of the deputation and his usurpation of the command of the rebels is to be considered a counter revolution that relieved of responsibility the other proponents of the Plan of San Diego, the new revolution can be accounted a success against his colleagues only and Echeandia was twice the traitor. Echeandia's efforts can not be credited with success because, as Vallejo says he complained, "Zamorano had him cornered in a very small territory."[80]

When confronted with the question as to who was governor of Alta California in the year 1832, most historians have either named Echeandia, because he claimed to be, or withdrawn into magnificent impartiality and permitted "the reader to decide for himself." By this leave, let us review the situation and attempt a decision.

All admit that Don Pio Pico's claims to be considered as the governor in the year 1832 can be dismissed with their mention; he was recognized as such only by the revolutionary body that named him and by it for a period of approximately three weeks.

Likewise, all admit that Lieutenant Colonel Echeandia maintained

---

[80] Vallejo, *op. cit.*, II, 165.

his authority in the District of San Diego and that Captain Zamorano did the same in the three remaining districts. Echeandia was never, at any time, recognized outside a single district. In that district, he was supported as general commandant by the military officers who followed him and he claimed the civil office because he insisted the two positions, under the law, were inseparable.

Captain Zamorano, on the other hand, was recognized as general commandant in three presidial districts and made no claims to the civil office, which he said was vacant. However, in his normal capacity as secretary of the civil government, he performed such civil functions as could not be deferred. He supported his claim to the office of general commandant with the fact that he was the senior officer present who had not taken a part in the rebellion and the office was his under the rules of succession laid down in the general regulations of the army. In addition, he was the senior remaining officer of the legitimately established territorial government, he was in physical possession of the archives and other physical equipment of that government, the legal adviser of that government told him it was his duty to assume the temporary command, he controlled all the territorial revenues, and he was recognized as the acting governor by Victoria's officially appointed successor. The fact that he did not receive the appointment himself, although considered as Victoria's successor, does not reflect and has no bearing on his claims to having been acting governor.

If we are to be technical in our conclusions, we must find that the office of civil governor was vacant; Echeandia's claims and his performance of a few civil functions in one small sparsely settled district are insufficient to justify the contention he held that office. As regards the office of general commandant, we must find that Captain Zamorano actually held that office but was denied in one district; again Echeandia's claims and maintenance of himself in one district are insufficient to outweigh the other three districts.

If we are not to be so technical in our conclusions but are to consider the term governor in the more general and usual sense as applying to the chief executive officer of the Territory, we are faced with the inescapable necessity of concluding that Captain Zamorano was that officer but was defied in the execution of his duties by a revolutionary chief who succeeded in maintaining himself in one small district. There is no escaping the fact that Don Agustin V. Zamorano was both *de jure* and *de facto* governor of Alta California from February 1, 1832, to January 14, 1833, and that Echeandia was but a revolutionary guerilla chieftain who managed to maintain some semblance of local autonomy in defiance of the government of the Territory.

Chapter vii.

Figueroa, Gutiérrez, Chico, and again Gutiérrez as Governors, January 1833 to November 1836.

WHEN Brigadier General Don José Figueroa assumed office as governor of Alta California, Don Agustin V. Zamorano reverted to his former position as executive secretary of the civil and military governments. This place he continued to fill during the next four years.

General Figueroa served as governor until his death in September 1835, when the office of civil governor fell temporarily to Don José Castro, the senior member of the territorial legislature, and the office of general commandant to Lieutenant Colonel Don Nicolás Gutiérrez, the senior military officer in the Territory. Castro, on January 1, 1836, relinquished his office to Gutiérrez who acted in both capacities until the arrival, in April 1836, of Colonel Don Mariano Chico, who had received the appointment as Figueroa's successor.

After a short but tumultuous rule of three months, Chico voluntarily left the country at the end of July and the office of acting governor again fell to Lieutenant Colonel Gutiérrez. That officer continued to act in that capacity until November 1836, when a revolt, led by Don Juan B. Alvarado and Don José Castro, resulted in his capture and banishment, along with many other Mexican officers, from the Territory.

As we are not faced with the responsibility of giving in full California's history during these years, it is intended to mention only those events in the administration of these officers with which Zamorano was concerned.

1. Brigadier General Don José Figueroa.

General Figueroa is described by H. H. Bancroft in the following terms:

> In person, he was a little below medium height, thick set, with a swarthy complexion, black and abundant hair, scanty beard, piercing eyes, protruding lip, and large prominent teeth. He is believed to have had a large admixture of Indian blood. In manner, he was extremely affable and fascinating, especially in his intercourse with inferiors. His favorite vice was gambling; and though there is some evidence that he had a family in Mexico, he kept a mistress, and left a natural daughter in California. He brought to the country a military reputation, considerable experience, good administrative abilities, and great skill in the arts by which personal popularity was acquired. His term of office in California was brief, and the circumstances of his rule were favorable. His enemies were for the most part men of straw; his partisans were then and later the controlling element of the population. Even the padres were forced by circumstances into a partial and negative support of his policy. Moreover, he did some really good work in organizing territorial and local government, and he made no serious errors. He was liberal in the matter of land grants and in his policy toward foreigners. He antagonized no class, but flattered all. Hence an enviable reputation, for the Californians have nothing but praise for the character and acts of Figueroa. He has been fortunate in his fame. Eulogy has been exaggerated; I think the man's acts and correspondence show traits of character that under less favorable circumstances would have given him a much less favorable record. Nevertheless, he is probably entitled to his position in history as the best Mexican governor ever sent to rule California.[1]

Our historian is none too liberal in his praise. The situation in California in January 1833 was tense and fraught with more dangers than Bancroft admits. Don Agustin's report of November 16, 1832, and many other documents, indicate that the difficulties in the path of the new governor toward a successful and harmonious administration were many. Figueroa must have possessed great ability and tact in addition to a most pleasing personality, as within a few months he

[1] Bancroft, *History of California*, III, 296.

had the machinery of the territorial government functioning normally again and had made all elements in the community not only his friends but his partisans. One of the most zealous of these was Don Agustin; he served the new governor well and devotedly and a warm friendship grew up between the two men.

The months of July to September 1833 were spent by the governor on a tour of the southern part of the Territory on which he was accompanied by Don Agustin. The object of this trip appears to have been the study of conditions in the missions of that section. I am unable to say when the governor's party left Monterey but they were in San Diego on July 24, on which date Figueroa sent an interesting report to the Secretary of Relations in Mexico.[2] They remained at San Diego until August 17 and possibly longer.[3] On September 21 they were in Los Angeles,[4] and they returned to Monterey early in October.

The territorial deputation, to which new members were elected in 1833, met in ordinary session, on May 1, 1834, at Monterey. This session lasted until August and was followed by an extraordinary session that continued from October 17 to November 3, 1834.[5]

It was during these months that the first printing press arrived at Monterey and the first of its products to reach the dimensions of a book was the *Reglamento* adopted by the legislature, at its session on July 31, for the government of its deliberations. The story of the coming of the printing press, however, I leave for the next chapter.

Aside from the activities of the deputation in the first year, the history of Figueroa's administration during the years 1834 and 1835 is largely that of the controversies that arose with the arrival in the Territory of the Híjar and Padrés Colony. The Padrés involved in that grandiose scheme was the same Don José María Padrés whom Governor Victoria had banished from California in 1831. It will be recalled that he left in California an enthusiastic group of young supporters, thoroughly inoculated with his extreme republican ideas

---

[2] Figueroa to Secretary of Relations, San Diego, July 24, 1833, in *Dept. St. Pap., Ben., Mil.*, MS., LXXXVIII, 11.

[3] Zamorano to Figueroa, San Diego, August 17, 1833, in *Dept. St. Pap., Ben., Custom House*, MS., II, 20.   [4] *D. Carrillo, Doc.*, MS., 79.

[5] For summary of activities of the deputation see Bancroft, *op. cit.*, III, 249, note 18.

and plans for the early secularization of the missions. In Mexico, he had found himself out of sympathy with Bustamante's administration and had remained out of politics. In the meantime, he sang the praises of California to his friends and all others who would listen to him; its climate was perfect, it was the promised land, indeed an earthly paradise. It was not long before he was working to interest his acquaintances in that country as a field for colonization. He convinced Don José María Hijar, a wealthy and influential resident of Jalisco, of the practicability of his scheme and together they set about promoting such a colony. They organized the *Compañia Cosmopolitana* whose purpose was to encourage colonization in California and to trade in Californian exports.

In April 1833, General Don Antonio Lopez de Santa Anna was elected President of Mexico with Don Valentin Gómez Farías, a close friend of Padrés, as Vice-President. Soon after, Santa Anna retired to his *hacienda* in Vera Cruz and left the government of the country in the hands of the Vice-President. This was an opportunity that Padrés did not neglect. At about this time, Don Juan Bandini arrived in Mexico as the new congressman from Alta California. As an old friend, he soon heard of Padrés' plans, endorsed them enthusiastically, and became a stockholder and vice-president of his company. Also, at about this time, the report reached Mexico that Governor Figueroa was very ill and desired to be relieved of his office. As Padrés still retained his appointment as adjutant inspector of Alta California and as such was second in authority in the military command of that Territory, that command would fall to him in the event of Figueroa's incapacity—provided he was present to exercise it.

Under these circumstances, rapid progress was made in carrying forward Padrés' plans. On July 15, 1833, Vice-President Gómez Farías appointed Don José María Hijar as civil governor of Alta California. On the following day, he named him director of colonization also and a few days later Padrés was named assistant director. A group of about two hundred and fifty colonists was recruited on the promise of free transportation, free land, and financial assistance through the first year in the new country. These people reached San Blas in July and on August 1, 1834, sailed in two parties, on the brig

Natalia, which had been bought for the purpose, and on the national corvette-of-war *Morelos*, for Alta California. Those interested, who remained behind, secured the passage in congress, on August 17, of a law which provided for the immediate secularization of the Californian missions and, on November 26, the issuance of a decree which provided the measures whereby the colonization and secularization could be carried into effect, and made available the resources of the Pious Fund for financing the colony then bound for California. There appeared to remain no obstacle between the promoters of the *Compañia Cosmopolitana* and success.

The *Natalia*, with Hijar and Bandini aboard, arrived at San Diego on September 1, 1834. The colonists were warmly welcomed by the local residents and started north overland to Monterey, where Hijar arrived on October 14. The *Morelos*, with Padrés aboard, reached Monterey on September 25, where its group of colonists were as warmly welcomed as had been their fellows in San Diego.

On July 25, 1834, President Santa Anna came out of his retirement and resumed control of the federal government. He did not approve of the plans of the promoters of the colony to California or of the privileges granted them. He sent an order to San Blas forbidding the colony to sail but the order arrived there after they had gone. He then sent a special courier overland in all haste to Monterey with orders countermanding Hijar's appointment as civil governor and directing Figueroa to continue in that office. After the quickest trip on record between the national and territorial capitals, the messenger placed his despatches in Figueroa's hand on September 11. On the same day, Figueroa learned of Hijar's arrival at San Diego.

The governor received these messages as he approached Monterey on his return from a trip north of San Francisco Bay. For the past year, he had been making every effort to strengthen the northern frontier against the encroachment of the Russians who had established themselves at Bodega and Fort Ross, and against the Indians who were giving trouble at the missions of San Rafael and San Francisco Solano. In April 1833, he had announced his intention of building a new *presidio* north of the Bay and had sent Ensign Vallejo on a reconnaissance of the country and that officer had reported in an informative document dated May 6, 1833.⁶ Later in the same year, ten families were located at Petaluma and in June 1834, Rancho de Petaluma was granted to Vallejo. On learning of the coming of the colony from Mexico, the governor decided that its settlement in this territory would serve both its and the public interest. Late in August 1834, accompanied by Captain Zamorano and a small force of men, he made a trip north of San Francisco Bay to examine the country for himself. On this trip he visted Fort Ross, which, so far as I know, was the most northerly point reached by Don Agustin during his years in California. In the Santa Rosa Valley, a town, which was to become the place of residence of the colonists and which was named *Santa Anna y Farías* in honor of the President and Vice-President, was laid out by Don Agustin. At a simple ceremony, Figueroa struck the first blow with a pick, gave the place its name, and Vallejo began the erection of a building.⁷ Soon after, the governor and his party recrossed the Golden Gate and reached Monterey on September 12.⁸

In the circumstances, there was nothing Hijar and Padrés could do but accept with the best grace possible the situation created by the President's orders. They fell back on their appointments as director and assistant director of colonization, which were recognized. They then demanded supplies for their colonists and that they be put in possession of the mission properties. The governor laid these matters before the deputation assembled in extraordinary session, where the decision was reached that Hijar could proceed with his plans for colonization but he could not secularize the missions. The situation became complicated and Padrés, falling into his old habits of hatching schemes under cover, attempted to revive the former enthusiasm for secularization among his native Californian friends. They, however, turned a deaf ear to his eloquence; they were interested in no plans that would place Mexican administrators in charge of the mission estates—that, when the time should come, was to be a prerogative they intended to exercise themselves.

⁶ Vallejo to Figueroa, Confidential Report, San Francisco, May 6, 1833, MS., in *Vallejo, Doc.*, II, 140. ⁷ Vallejo, *Historia de California*, MS., II, 10.
⁸ Documentary sources regarding this trip are extremely meager. The governor was still at Monterey on August 21, cf. *Dept. St. Pap.*, MS., III, 172. Figueroa gives the date of their return in his *Manifiesto*, 7.

Padrés' fortunes waned fast and misfortune followed misfortune until Figueroa, disgusted and distrustful of their subversive activities, ordered him and Hijar to be deported. On March 26, 1835, they were conducted on board the bark *Rosa*, then in San Francisco harbor, by Ensign Vallejo. At Santa Barbara, on April 16, they, and others who had been too active in their interests, were transferred to the American brig *Loriot*, with which Figueroa had made a contract for their transportation to San Blas. With the sailing of the *Loriot*, the incidents and controversies connected with the Hijar and Padrés Colony reached their end.[9] The net result of their venture was that over two hundred colonists, most of whom were valuable additions to the population and some of whom achieved considerable prominence later, settled in various parts of the Territory.

Early in March 1835, a revolt had broken out at Los Angeles. On the night of March 6, a group of *vaqueros* from Sonora, led by a cobbler and a cigar-maker, advanced on the town, seized the town hall, broke into it and appropriated a cannon and a small supply of ammunition stored there. Calling the *ayuntamiento* and people to an open meeting, they read a *pronunciamiento* which declared the governor and deputation had disobeyed the central government, and had ruined the missions; they deposed Figueroa from office and named the *alcalde* of Monterey as civil governor and Captain Portilla as general commandant. In addition, various policies which were intended to restore California to the splendor of its former prosperity were advanced.[10] This insurrection proved to be but a flash and collapsed at once for lack of support. The leaders were seized by the local authorities and sent to Lieutenant Colonel Gutiérrez, who was in command of the troops in the south with headquarters at San Gabriel. The news of these events reached the governor on March 13 at Mission San Juan Bautista, where he had gone to investigate a local disturbance. The skilled hand of Padrés was seen behind this episode which was the immediate cause of the governor's instructions that Padrés and Hijar be placed aboard the *Rosa* for deportation.

[9] For detailed history of the Hijar and Padrés Colony, see Bancroft, *op. cit.*, III, Chapters IX and X; also Tays, *Revolutionary California*, MS., Chapter XIII.
[10] Proclamation of Inhabitants of California against Figueroa, Los Angeles, March 7, 1835, in Figueroa, *Manifiesto*, 131-3; and MS. in *Vallejo, Doc.*, III, 15.

Figueroa, accompanied by Captain Zamorano, went south in May to make his own investigation into this abortive plot. I do not know the exact date of either their departure or return. They were at Mission San Gabriel on May 21, on which date the governor wrote Ensign Vallejo in regard to the case against Padrés.[11] They were back in Monterey by June 6, as on that date Don Agustin made a report to the sub-treasury of miscellaneous expenses, amounting to one hundred and ten *pesos*, incurred on the trip.[12]

Governor Figueroa returned from this trip in ill health and the few remaining weeks of life left to him were spent, in large part, in compiling his *Manifiesto de la Republica Mejicana*, which was a history and defense of his policies in connection with the colony and the *Compañia Cosmopolitana* and which remains today the chief source of information regarding that ill-fated venture. In this, he had the help and editorial assistance of Don Agustin, who undertook its printing. The work was on the press at the time of the governor's death.

The illness of the governor rapidly grew worse and by early September he was confined to his bed. He died on September 29, 1835, at 5:45 p.m., of a stroke of apoplexy. At once, as executive secretary of the government, Don Agustin announced his death to all officers.[13] He also wrote personal letters to the most prominent men outside Monterey, urging them to come to the funeral.[14] These letters indicate that Don Agustin felt the governor's death keenly as a great personal loss.

II. Lieutenant Colonel Don Nicolás Gutiérrez.

General Figueroa, on August 29, 1835, very ill and possibly realizing his end was near, asked Don José Castro, as senior member of the deputation, to assume the duties of the civil governorship in an acting

---

[11] Figueroa to Vallejo, San Gabriel, May 21, 1835, MS., in *Vallejo, Doc.*, III, 23.

[12] Zamorano to *comisario*, Monterey, June 6, 1835, MS., in *Dept. St., Pap., Ben., Mil.*, MS., LXXXI, 7.

[13] Zamorano to commandant of San Francisco, Monterey, September 29, 1835, MS., in *Vallejo, Doc.*, III, 75.

[14] Zamorano to Vallejo, Monterey, September 29, 1835, MS., *ibid.*, III, 74.

capacity.[15] Just before his death, the governor designated Castro to succeed him in that office as *jefe politico interino* and Lieutenant Colonel Don Nicolás Gutiérrez, as the senior military officer in the Territory, to follow him as *comandante general interino*. On September 22, he summoned Gutiérrez to the capital from San Gabriel but that officer did not reach Monterey until several days after his death. Gutiérrez had come to California with General Figueroa with the rank of captain, but was promoted in the following year to that of lieutenant colonel. He was a Spaniard by birth and had emigrated as a boy with his parents to Mexico, where he soon after joined the army as a drummer.[16]

On his arrival at Monterey, Don Nicolás called a council of war before which he urged various reasons why he should not assume the military command. He protested his ill health, lack of ability, aversion to taking the place of his deceased friend, and his Spanish birth. The officers present, however, insisted the office was his under the rules of succession prescribed by military regulations and that it was his duty to accept. Reluctantly, he assumed the office of acting general commandant on October 8, 1835.[17]

Don José Castro was not, strictly speaking, the senior member of the deputation; he was third in rank. The first member was absent in Mexico and the second was ill at his home in San Diego. There was some question as to the propriety of Castro becoming acting civil governor but it was soon dismissed and he entered upon his duties.

Don Juan Bautista Alvarado, in his *Historia de California*, says that Zamorano urged General Figueroa to leave both offices to Lieutenant Colonel Gutiérrez and that his motive was his dislike for all the Californians.[18] It is possible that Don Agustin made such a recommendation, although I know of no other evidence on the point, because

---

[15] Figueroa to *alcalde* of Monterey, Monterey, August 29, 1835, in *Dept. St. Pap.*, MS., IV, 48; same, Los Angeles, in *Dept. St. Pap., Angeles*, MS., XI, 37; same, San Diego, in *San Diego Archives*, MS., 50; same to prefect of missions, in *Arch. Arzobispado*, MS., V, pt. II, 11.

[16] *Cf.* Bancroft, *op. cit.*, III, 448, 772 for biographical sketches.

[17] Gutiérrez to Castro, Monterey, October 8, 1835, in *Dept. St. Pap.*, MS., IV, 56; to commandants, in *Dept. St. Pap., Ben., Com. and Treas.*, MS., III, 70; to *ayuntamientos*, in *Dept. St. Pap., San José*, MS., V, 1.

[18] Alvarado, *Historia de California*, MS., III, 42.

there was some question whether the two commands could be legally separated. However, we may be sure that he was not prompted in this advice for the reason charged by Alvarado. Alvarado also says that Castro, in his capacity as civil governor, ordered Don Agustin to prepare plans for taking the waters of the Carmel River to Monterey. If so, it is certain the idea never got beyond the initial stage of discussion.

There was one matter that occupied a considerable part of Captain Zamorano's time and attention during the months of October and November 1835. The cavalry company stationed at the *presidio* of Monterey, of which Don Agustin was commandant, had for some years used two nearby small ranches as pasture land for its horses. The first of these, called El Toro, consisted of about one and a half square leagues of land and was located a little more than four leagues from the *presidio*. The horses in actual use at the post were relieved from a small herd maintained at El Toro under the care of three or four soldiers stationed there for that purpose. The other place, called San Francisquito, consisted of about two square leagues of land and was about seven leagues from the *presidio*. It was normally vacant and was used chiefly during the summer months because it was better supplied with water than El Toro. How long the presidial company had been in the habit of pasturing its horses at these places I cannot say, but Figueroa had approved their use of them and had set them aside as government reservations. Captain Zamorano, in February 1833, had advised the *alcalde* of Monterey that El Toro had been designated for the use of his company and therefore was not within the jurisdiction of the local *ayuntamiento*.[19]

In October 1835, Don José Ramon Estrada induced the *ayuntamiento* to declare Rancho El Toro a part of the communal lands of Monterey and to make him a grant of that property. This grant then passed to the deputation for approval. Don Agustin, quite naturally, went to the defense of what he considered to be the property of his military company. In a long letter to the acting general commandant, dated October 20, he reviewed the history of the company's use of

---

[19] Zamorano to *alcalde* of Monterey, Monterey, February 21, 1833, in *Monterey Archives*, MS., VII, 60.

El Toro and asserted there was no grounds for the claim it was part of Monterey's communal lands as it lay outside the boundaries of those lands. He said the garrison at that time had one hundred and thirty head of horses which had to be kept at some close and convenient place and that there were neither funds nor stable room to keep them in the town. He pointed out there were thousands of square leagues of unclaimed land in the Territory to which Señor Estrada could go and that the military service should not be crippled by depriving it of a convenient and readily accessible place in which to keep its horses.[20]

Unfortunately, the question was one that was outside the jurisdiction of the general commandant. He could only forward Captain Zamorano's protest to the deputation with his endorsement, which he did on the same day.[21] The deputation, on November 7, asked that Captain Zamorano present the documents that would prove his company's rights to and possession of the land in question.[22] Don Agustin, however, fought a losing battle as the grant, although I have not seen the final documents in the case, appears to have been confirmed.

On January 2, 1836, Castro transferred the civil office to Gutiérrez and both issued announcements to that effect which were printed on the press belonging to Don Agustin.[23] These announcements gave as the reason for this transfer the receipt of an order from the central government that the civil and military commands should be held by one person. No particular comment seems to have been made on this transfer of the office by a native Californian to a hated Mexican, although Don Juan Bandini suggests that Castro's real motive was to anticipate the claims of the second senior member of the deputation who was recovering from his illness and whose home was in San Diego.[24]

Lieutenant Colonel Gutiérrez' rule as both civil governor and general commandant lasted from January 2 to May 2, 1836. In that

[20] Zamorano to Gutiérrez, Monterey, October 30, 1835, in *Dept. St. Pap.*, MS., 60.
[21] Gutiérrez to Castro, Monterey, October 30, 1835, *ibid.*, IV, 67.
[22] Castro to Gutiérrez, Monterey, November 7, 1835, *ibid.*, IV, 68.
[23] Copies of these announcements in Bancroft Library.
[24] Bandini, *Historia de California*, MS., 79.

time there occurred but two events that need to be mentioned here.

A national decree, dated May 23, 1835, was published by Governor Gutiérrez on January 4, 1836. This decree elevated the Town of Los Angeles to the dignity of a city, the first in Alta California, and made it the capital of the Territory.[25] This act increased the popularity of Gutiérrez in the south with a like diminution of his standing in the north. An effort was made to put this decree into effect in February but the *Angelinos* of that time, unlike their descendants of today, were so lacking in public spirit that no way could be found to provide a building rent free for governmental use until one could be erected, as the governor required, and the matter was dropped. The Territory remained with two capitals, Los Angeles *de jure* and Monterey *de facto*.

The other event that may be mentioned took place in Mexico. There the centralist party came into power. The governor of Alta California, on January 10, 1836, circulated a letter he had received from the Secretary of Relations, in Mexico, which spoke of the possibility of future changes in the form of government and warned territorial authorities to guard against disorders that might grow out of popular feeling based on vague rumors and played on by seditious leaders.[26]

III. Colonel Don Mariano Chico.

Colonel Don Mariano Chico was appointed to succeed Brigadier General Don José Figueroa as governor of Alta California on December 16, 1835, before, apparently, the news of Figueroa's death reached Mexico.[27] He sailed for his new post on the *Leonor* and landed at Santa Barbara on April 19, 1836.[28] After a stop of a few days in the home of Don Carlos Antonio Carrillo, whom he had known in Mexico, he proceeded to Monterey where he arrived on May 1.[29] He assumed the office of general commandant on the next day[30] and

[25] Gutiérrez to *alcaldes*, Monterey, January 4, 1836, in *Dept. St. Pap., Angeles*, MS., XI, 40, and *Los Angeles Archives*, MS., IV, 183.
[26] Gutiérrez to *alcaldes*, Monterey, January 10, 1836, in *San Diego Archives*, MS., 72.
[27] Bancroft, *op. cit.*, III, 421.
[28] Chico, Report to Secretary of War and Marine, Monterey, July 22, 1836, MS., in *Legajo* 52-8-7-1.   [29] Gómez, R., *Diario*, MS.
[30] Chico to Vallejo, Monterey, May 2, 1836, MS., in *Vallejo, Doc.*, III, 199.

that of civil governor on May 3.[31] Although his coming was unexpected, since notice of his appointment had not arrived, he appears to have been warmly greeted and was welcomed by a hurriedly organized reception which ended in a *fiesta* and ball.[32]

It is very difficult to state exactly the situation that confronted the new governor. There can be little doubt there was a tenseness, a growing sentiment for the old federalism as against the new centralism, a distrust and a suspiciousness toward the new Mexican governor, that is not indicated in the records of the period that have been preserved. Likewise, it is very difficult to say exactly what manner of a man the new governor was. He was not possessed of tact and not blessed with the ability to make friends, qualities which General Figueroa had possessed in such marked measure. He was energetic and resolute. He came accompanied by a beautiful young woman whom he introduced as his niece, Doña Cruz, but who turned out to be his mistress. The Californians, with one accord, in their memoirs and histories, characterize him as a rascal, a tyrant, and a fool.

On the day he took office, Governor Chico issued a proclamation, printed by Don Agustin, in which he announced his arrival and reported the death of President Barragan. However, Don Agustin appears to have been among the first with whom Chico had altercations. The reason for their break I have not learned but within ten days, by May 11, Don Agustin had either resigned or been dismissed from the secretaryship of the civil government; on that date the governor issued another proclamation which, while printed by Don Agustin, was signed as secretary by Lieutenant Don Francisco del Castillo Negrete. Captain Zamorano continued as secretary of the military government but, as we shall see, undoubtedly thought he was serving a mad man.

The new *bases* of centralism were presented to the people by Chico on May 20 for their swearing of allegiance. This he appears to have handled in a skillful manner, as the event, although the Californians claimed to be strong federalists, went off smoothly and with no dis-

[31] Chico and Gutiérrez to *ayuntamientos*, Monterey, May 3, 1836, in *Dept. St. Pap.*, MS., IV, 108.
[32] Chico, Report to Secretary of War and Marine, Monterey, July 22, 1836, MS., in *Legajo* 52-8-7-1, says he arrived at Monterey on May 2 and assumed office on May 3.

turbances. On this day the governor issued another proclamation, also printed by Don Agustin, in which he lauded centralism in an extravagant manner and congratulated the Californians in flattering terms on their glorious future under the new regime.

Under the new system, Alta California became a Department and the legislature became the *junta departamental*. The *junta* met at the governor's call on May 27. At its opening session, Chico delivered an address of considerable length. This oration was also printed by Don Agustin and received a rather large circulation.

The governor, early in June, left Monterey for a trip through the south. He reached Los Angeles on June 15 and left San Gabriel for the north on June 28, arriving in Monterey on July 8. At every place he visited, he created new enemies. His popularity in Monterey had not increased during his absence and he was soon entangled in a purely local matter that engulfed him and caused him to leave, more or less voluntarily, the Department.

This situation grew out of a scandalous love affair between Don José María Castañares, a clerk in the custom house, and Doña Ildefonsa, wife of Don José María Herrera, who had regained his office as *comisario subalterno*. Doña Ana, wife of Castañares and daughter of Don Rafael González, administrator of the customs, had exposed the unfaithful pair in February 1836, whereupon Herrera had sued her for slander. Wasting no sentiment on her husband's shortcomings, Doña Ana, who was a shrewd person, gathered abundant proofs with the result that when the case came to trial in June and Herrera saw her evidence, he asked that the case be dismissed. He then instituted another suit against his wife and Castañares, charging adultery. The pair was arrested; Castañares was confined in the jail and Doña Ildefonsa, according to custom, deposited in the home of a respectable citizen.

Such was the situation of this affair as the governor's birthday, July 26, approached. A company of *maromeros*, or strolling players and acrobats, came to Monterey at this opportune season and the citizens, always ready for a pleasant time, decided to honor the governor with a performance. One of the rooms in the *presidio* was prepared for the occasion and, as was usual on such rare events, everyone within miles was present. As the performance was about to begin, the governor entered, escorting Doña Cruz and her friend, Doña Ildefonsa, whom he had liberated for the evening, and occupied the box of honor. This was more than the socially élite of Monterey could stand. Many of the women arose, gathered up their skirts and swept out of the room in all the haughtiness of their offended dignity. Among them was the wife of Don José Ramon Estrada, the *alcalde* of Monterey. Don Ramon was about to enter the room when he met his wife on her way out. Learning what had taken place, the *alcalde*, who had committed Doña Ildefonsa to confinement and who felt his authority was being usurped by her release, went to the town jail, released Don José María Castañares, took him to the hall, and seated him beside himself. Castañares, always the lover, was soon engaged in a pleasant flirtation with Doña Cruz, the governor's paramour.

It was then the governor's turn to be insulted and he proceeded to fly into a rage. He demanded of Estrada an explanation for Castañares' presence and received the flippant reply that Estrada had invited him. The governor ordered the prisoner back to jail at once, which order the *alcalde* ignored, taking his guest to his own home as sanctuary against Chico's authority. As can be imagined, the entertainment never began and the town was soon in a turmoil of excitement.

It is said that the governor spent a sleepless night in search of ways in which to turn the tables. Very early the next morning, he called Captain Zamorano to his quarters and ordered him to turn out the troops at his command and assemble them in formation, with full equipment, before his quarters at once. When this was done, he gave the company a rigid inspection. With all in order to his satisfaction, he ordered Captain Zamorano to follow him and stalked across the green to the house of *Alcalde* Estrada. There he ordered the troops to load their guns and to deploy about the house. After all was arranged, he ordered Don Agustin to seize any one who should come out. He then, without rapping, threw open the front door of the house and entered. Castañares was led out and escorted back to jail.[20]

Later in the same day, Chico sent the *alcalde* a written order sus-

Osío, *op. cit.*, 267.

pending him from office. Estrada ignored the order. Again the governor ordered Captain Zamorano to call out his company and again paraded to, surrounded, and entered the *alcalde's* house. When Estrada refused, on demand, to surrender the *vara*, or symbolic staff of the *alcalde's* authority, Chico took it from him by force after a considerable struggle. As he was about to leave, Don Mariano Estrada, father of the *alcalde* and close friend of Don Agustin, protested against such unseemly conduct in his home and received a severe reprimand.

The Estradas, father and son, were very popular men and the indignation of the citizens of the capital flamed high at these high handed proceedings. The details of the events of the next two days are too complicated for rehearsal here. The governor was practically besieged in the *presidio* and soon found that the sympathies of its garrison were completely with the people.

On July 30, Governor Chico issued his last order to the military officers in California. He stated he was leaving the Department because of the insurrection and because he lacked the physical force to apply the proper remedy; he was going to Mexico to get the aid necessary to restore order and instructed all to recognize Lieutenant Colonel Gutiérrez, on whom the command fell by regulations.

Chico sailed from Monterey in the evening of July 31, on the *Clementina*. The vessel stopped at Santa Barbara for fresh supplies but the people there would not permit him to land. She stopped at San Pedro and sailed again on August 10.[34]

Before leaving, on July 22, 1836, Governor Chico sent a long and extremely interesting confidential report to the Secretary of War and Marine. Unfortunately, it is much too long to be quoted or even summarized here. In it, one of his chief complaints was the lack of dependable and capable assistants and he made the following comment which, without doubt, applied to Don Agustin V. Zamorano although he is not named.

---

[34] The documentary sources covering Chico's rule are too numerous to cite. The papers covering the *causa célebre* of Castañares and Doña Ildefonsa will be found in *Vallejo Doc.*, I, 257-380. For complete statement of this period based on the most recent research see Tays, *op. cit.*, Chapter XV.

... the moments in which I have to write are so short and such is the scarcity of helping hands to carry on the governmental work, and such the distrust which I feel even of the very secretary of this command, who sold out Señor Victoria, making his measures ineffective and disclosing his resources to the enemies of that time, that it is impossible for me to carry on my duties and at the same time give Your Excellency a detailed account of events. I find it necessary to write even the first draft of official notes of reference in both offices under my charge...[35]

This, as we know, does not agree with Victoria's estimate of the same secretary. We do not have Don Agustin's comments on Governor Chico; they would be interesting reading.

IV. Lieutenant Colonel Gutiérrez Again Acts as Governor.

Lieutenant Colonel Gutiérrez at the time of Chico's departure, on July 31, was in command of the troops in the southern part of the Department and did not reach Monterey to reassume the acting governorship until September 6. During the interim it is probable that Don Agustin carried on the routine work of the departmental government, although it is possible that Captain Muñoz, who arrived at Monterey on August 8 and who was his senior in grade, may have acted after that date. I know of no record, however, of either having exercised any authority.

Some time during the summer of 1836, orders came from Mexico that relieved Captain Zamorano of the command of the *presidio* at Monterey and named him captain of the presidial company at San Diego. These orders were dated, in Mexico, on June 16, 1835, and were signed by President Barragan.[36] I have not been able to learn why such orders were issued or the exact date of their arrival in Monterey. In any event, they do not appear to have changed Don Agustin's status in any way as he continued in command of the company at Monterey and also as secretary of the military government.

The second period in which Lieutenant Colonel Gutiérrez acted as governor of Alta California was very brief, lasting from September to November 4, 1836. On the latter date, he was overwhelmed by

[35] Chico, *op. cit.* [36] *Dept. St. Pap., Ben., Mil.*, MS., LXXIX, 85.

a revolution which became the most important and successful one in all California's history.

Although there were a few minor incidents that disturbed the relations of the acting governor with the departmental *junta*, there was no overt act or unpopular policy that was the immediate cause of this revolution. The Californians, in their memoirs and histories, are much less violent in their denunciations of Gutiérrez than they are of Victoria or Chico. A few make charges against him that are of little importance. Some have no complaints to make of him whatsoever, and some condemn him in general terms as though such was their duty without their knowing why. On its face this revolt appears to have been the rash venture of two rather foolhardy young men. But the success and support they attained so quickly indicate they struck at an opportune time to crystallize the deep-seated aversion for all things Mexican that had been growing slowly but steadily for many years.

In the eleven years that had passed since the arrival, in 1825, of Echeandia, the first Mexican governor, the mass of the Californians had come to feel that Mexican republicanism had brought only evil to the land and the missionaries, looking back regretfully to the old Spanish days, fostered, unconsciously perhaps, the antipathy to all that was Mexican. The sending of incompetent officers and of convicts as soldiers intensified provincial prejudice and the better Californian families came to regard themselves as superior in blood and ability to the Mexicans "from the interior." Mexican revenue laws were unsound and a handicap to California's growing commerce. The foreigners, whose numbers had steadily increased, claimed, with interested motives but sound arguments, that California had received nothing but neglect and ill treatment from Mexico. The result of all this was that when Don Juan Bautista Alvarado and Don José Castro, both young men still in their twenties, appeared at Monterey, in the evening of November 3, 1836, with a hundred armed men at their back and the cry of *"Viva el estado libre y soberano de Alta California"*—"Long live the free and sovereign state of Alta California," on their lips, they struck a responsive chord in the hearts of nearly all the Californians. It was a popular uprising not against individual men but against policies, discrimination, and neglect.

FIGUEROA, GUTIÉRREZ, CHICO

The leader of the movement was Don Juan Bautista Alvarado, then twenty-seven years of age and employed as an inspector in the custom house. Bancroft, the historian, says of him,

> In 1836 Alvarado was a young man of much practical ability, of good character, of tolerably steady habits, though rapidly acquiring too great a fondness for strong drink, and of great popularity and influence with all classes, though he had been one of the first to resent Mexican insults to his countrymen, and had consequently been involved in personal difficulties with Rodrigo del Pliego and others *de la otra banda*. He was perhaps better qualified than any other of the younger Californians to become a popular and successful leader.[37]

After a quarrel with the acting governor, in October, Alvarado left Monterey and, in company with Castro, began active preparations for an uprising. He visited his uncle of about the same age as himself, Don Mariano G. Vallejo, who had recently been promoted to the rank of lieutenant, at the latter's frontier post of Sonoma and tried to enlist his support. Vallejo was sympathetic but refused to give him help. So great, however, was Vallejo's influence and standing with the settlers in the northern territory, that Alvarado, on his return, claimed to have secured Vallejo's support and said that Vallejo was following with a large force.

In the meantime, Castro had succeeded in raising a small revolutionary army among the *rancheros* of the Salinas and Pájaro valleys. A Tennessee hunter that had come from New Mexico three years before, Isaac Graham, by name, who was a crack-shot with the rifle and a reckless fellow that despised all Mexican "varmint," was interested in their cause. Graham recruited about twenty-five men of his own sort who became known as the "American riflemen" and who were by far the strongest part, from a military viewpoint, of the revolutionary army. With about one hundred men and equipped with an old Mexican flag and some fifes and drums found at Mission San Juan Bautista, Alvarado and Castro started for Monterey.

There, by a show of force and methods typical of California's bloodless revolutions, they soon had the governor and all loyal officers besieged in the *presidio*. It was early evident that the governor's situa-

---
[37] Bancroft, *op. cit.*, III, 451.

tion was desperate and he called a council of war on the morning of November 4. This council was attended by Gutiérrez, Captains Portilla, Muñoz, Castillero and Zamorano, Lieutenants Navarrete and Estrada, Ensigns Ramírez and del Valle, Surgeon Don Manuel Alva, the phlebotomist Don Manuel Crespo, the district judge Don Luis del Castillo Negrete, the clerk Don M. M. González, and the schoolmaster Don Mariano Romero. Reports by the officers showed their forces were melting away because of desertions and that the loyal troops were exhausted from lack of sleep. As further resistance was impossible, word was sent to Castro that the post would be abandoned.[38]

On the morning of November 5, the garrison stacked their arms in the artillery barracks and marched out. The revolutionary army, led by a band from the ship *Quixote*, then marched in. In this way, according to the report Gutiérrez later made to Mexico, the government of the Department saved its face; the post was evacuated, not surrendered, and the civil and military commands were suspended and not given up.[39]

On the following day, November 6, Castro sent Gutiérrez the following note,

> In order to safeguard your person, I find myself obliged to ask you to prepare to leave the Territory aboard the English brig *Clementina*, on which you will embark this very day.[40]

Similar notices were sent to many of the other officers.

Gutiérrez and his followers boarded the ship on the afternoon of November 9, and she sailed the following day with about seventy passengers, among whom were Captain Muñoz and Lieutenants Estrada and Navarrete. Captains Portilla, Castillero and Zamorano, and Ensign del Valle were permitted to remain. The latter officers, however, believing the atmosphere of Monterey unhealthful for persons of their positions and loyal affiliations, left immediately for Santa Barbara.

With the fall of the *presidio*, the Californians gave themselves up to a triumphant celebration, in which all but the Mexican officers

---
[38] *Ibid.*, III, 463.
[39] Gutiérrez, Report to Secretary of War and Marine, Cape San Lucas, November 30, 1836, MS., in *Legajo* 52-8-7-1, No. 1.
[40] Castro to Gutiérrez, Monterey, November 6, 1836, MS., in *Legajo* 52-8-7-1.

participated. The revolutionists seized Don Agustin's printing press and with it, on November 6, the legislature printed California's declaration of independence. The country was declared a free and sovereign state and henceforth was to have but a federal union with Mexico. The legislature became the constituent congress of the new state and elected Alvarado as governor and Lieutenant Vallejo as general commandant. The new government was quickly organized and to all appearances was off to a splendid start.

Chapter viii.

THE PRINTING PRESS ARRIVES IN CALIFORNIA.

AS Don Agustin V. Zamorano never returned to Monterey after leaving so hastily early in November 1836, and as the revolutionists appropriated his printing press and it was thereafter operated by others, this would appear to be the proper place to turn back and review the beginnings of printing in California.

Even as the origin of printing in the fifteenth century, and its first use in the new world at Mexico City in the sixteenth, are clouded by obscurity, so the introduction of printing into Alta California is among the forgotten details of a period that seems more than a hundred years removed. No one knows what was the first piece of printing done in California or where, when, and by whom it was executed.

It is generally accepted that Zamorano set up the first printing press in California and on this point there is no occasion for doubt. He, however, did not leave an account of his work with the press or any statement as to how, when, and why the press came. Nor is there the slightest reference to the press in all the papers preserved today that are known to have passed through his hands. With no help available from the man who could speak with the greatest authority, we turn to the comments of his contemporaries and their immediate successors.

I. Contemporary References to the Press.

Unfortunately, the archives of the provincial, territorial, and departmental governments of Alta California are not available. Containing thousands of documents, the archives, which reposed for many years in the office of the United States Surveyor General in San Francisco, were completely destroyed by the fire of April 1906. The archives

The Printing Press

are known to have contained specimens of nearly every piece the press produced. Rufus C. Hopkins, who, for many years, was directly in charge of this great depository of source material for California's history, is credited with the statement that he never saw in any of the documents in the archives a statement regarding the origin of the pioneer press. We can probably assume with safety that the only help we could obtain from that source, were the archives available today, would be the indirect assistance of having many more examples of the products of the press at hand for examination.

Although the archives are gone, there remain in such depositories as the Bancroft Library at the University of California, Berkeley, the Henry E. Huntington Library, San Marino, and the California State Library, Sacramento, several thousand documents of the period. In addition, there are in private hands a few large collections of papers and documents relating to the Mexican period in California's history. In none of these that it has been my privilege to examine has any reference been found to the printing press.

At the Bancroft Library are many manuscript memoirs and histories written for, or dictated to the assistants of, H. H. Bancroft. None of these contain more than a most casual mention of the printing press.

This complete lack of source material regarding the first printing equipment operated in California among the many thousand papers and documents of the period that have been preserved is startling and difficult to explain. The subject that has interested so many people in recent years appears to have been of no interest whatsoever to the men of the time.

The paucity and lack of dependability in secondary sources is no less discomforting. The coming of the press appears to have been very early wrapped in mystery. Various traditions sprang up and these have been passed on year after year although their falseness and improbability can be easily demonstrated.

The earliest mention of the press of which I am aware is that by Eugène Duflot de Mofras in his *Exploration du Territoire d l'Orégon, des Californies, el de la Mer Vermeille*, published in Paris in 1844. Duflot de Mofras was an attaché of the French legation at

Mexico who made a visit of exploration and observation to Alta California in 1841. The results of his studies were published in this book. In speaking of the Hijar and Padrés Colony, this writer says the colony included "several printers who took along a small press— the first press to be brought to California."[1]

The Hijar and Padrés colonists, as we have seen, came in two groups which landed at San Diego on September 1 and at Monterey on September 25, 1834. We shall later see that the press was in operation in July of that year. Therefore it is impossible for Duflot de Mofras' statement to be correct.

The next earliest mention of the press is found in the remarks of the Reverend Walter Colton in connection with the founding of the *Californian* at Monterey in August 1846. This, California's first newspaper, was printed on the first press, which was discovered stored in a room of the government building. In his *Three Years in California*, Colton says that his partner, Robert Semple, "created the materials of our office out of the chaos of a small concern which had been used by a Roman Catholic monk in printing sectarian tracts."[2] This, as the most casual student of the subject knows, had not the slightest foundation in fact.

Colton was apparently under the same impression when he wrote a small notice that appeared in an extra issue of the *Californian* for January 28, 1847. In this he said, "Our type is a Spanish font picked up here in a cloister and has no W's in it as there is none in the Spanish alphabet . . . in the meantime we must use two VV's." Yet the character used for "W" is a capital W and the issue contains several lower case W's. The very printing of his notice disproves the statement it contains. It is annoying that Duflot de Mofras and Colton, with the opportunity at hand to learn the truth, should give us statements that are obviously the products of their imaginations.

With the coming of the Gold Rush more interest was displayed in the pioneer press. As it led the advance of the printed page into the mines by printing the first newspapers to appear at Sacramento,

---

[1] Duflot de Mofras, *Exploration du Territoire de l'Orégon, des Californies, et de la Mer Vermeille, executée pendant les Années 1840, 1841, et 1842*, I, 295.
[2] Colton, *Three Years in California*, 32.

Stockton, Sonora, and Columbia, the editors of the State paid it their respects as the symbol of the progress of their craft. None, however, attempted to learn its true history and all assumed that it must have come from Mexico, although some recognized that it was of American manufacture. This explanation of its origin was repeated many times and came to be accepted for the truth. There are many references to the old press in the newspapers of the early 'fifties but the only variation from the usual story of its history is the following, quoted by the San Francisco *Alta California* for October 20, 1851, from the Sonora *Herald*.

> The Columbia *Star* will make its appearance with one strong recommendation in its favor, namely, that it will be printed on an old Ramage press—the *pioneer* press of California. In what year this press was built, or how it was used prior to its embarkation from New York, tradition doth not inform us; but its career of emigration commenced by a trip from New York to Texas. Thence it traveled through Mexico; thence to Monterey in California, where it was used by the Governors for printing proclamations and other public documents.[3]

This, of course, is merely the product of someone's lively imagination.

We now come to the only serious attempt ever made to give the true history of California's first printing press. This was contained in the introduction of a long article entitled, "The History of California Newspapers," which appeared in the Christmas 1858 issue of the Sacramento *Daily Union*. This article, which is unsigned, was written by Edward C. Kemble. Before quoting Kemble's findings, which I believe to be substantially correct, let us inquire as to who he was and the reasons why his unsigned, undocumented newspaper article merits serious consideration.

Kemble arrived in California, at San Francisco, on July 31, 1846, with Samuel Brannan and his colony of Mormons on the ship *Brooklyn*. Brannan planned to print a newspaper in the new country to which he was bringing his colony and brought with him the complete equipment of a printing office. Kemble, a printer by trade, was engaged to work on the new paper. This paper, the *California Star*,

[3] *Alta California*, October 20, 1851 (2-3).

San Francisco's first, was established in January 1847. At the time of its first appearance, Kemble was absent from San Francisco with Fremont's Battalion. He returned in April and at once took his place on the staff of the paper. A short time after he became the editor. A few months later he purchased the *Star* from Brannan. In the meanwhile, in May 1847, the *Californian* was moved to San Francisco from Monterey. The first rush to the mountains after the discovery of gold suspended both papers and Kemble laid down his editorial pen to go to the mines. He returned to San Francisco in September 1848, purchased the equipment of the *Californian*, combined it with the *Star*, which he already owned, and, on November 18, 1848, began the publication of the *Star and Californian*. In this way Kemble became the owner of both of California's pioneer printing presses.

The *Star and Californian* continued through the remainder of the year and was succeeded, on January 4, 1849, by the *Alta California*, published by Edward Gilbert, Edward C. Kemble and G. C. Hubbard, and edited by Kemble. The *Alta* became the great newspaper of the Gold Rush period and Kemble became California's foremost journalist of the time.

Kemble always displayed a real affection for the pioneer press of the State and the keenest interest in the history of the newspapers and printers of his time. Our greatest source today for information regarding the newspapers and printers of the Gold Rush period is the file of the *Alta California*, whose columns are replete with notices of the births of new papers, the deaths of old ones and the movements of members of the craft.

In 1855, Kemble retired from the *Alta* and returned east. He was back in California within a short time and joined the editorial staff of the Sacramento *Daily Union*. His "History of California Newspapers," in that journal, is not the hurried compilation usually found as newspaper articles. He devoted several months to gathering his material and sent questionnaires to every one in the State who could assist him in his search for information. When it is remembered that his article is a serious study, that he at one time owned and operated the first printing press, and that he was personally acquainted with and a friend of many of the persons who had operated it before him,

THE PRINTING PRESS 183

his statement of the history of the press commands respect and must be accepted unless there is dependable evidence to the contrary. After giving a description of the first printing press to be used in California, Kemble wrote,

This old press came to California about the year 1832. It is believed that it was contracted for in 1829 or '30. It was brought to these shores with a small quantity of old bourgeois type, two meager fonts of shaded title letter, and the necessary fixtures of a fourth rate country printing office, by Thomas Shaw, a Boston merchant. Its degree of completeness may be calculated from the amount paid for it by the contractor at Monterey, which was $460. The person to whom belongs the honor of first introducing printing on the northwest shores of the Pacific is Augustin [sic] V. Zamorano, former Secretary to Governor Echeandria [sic]. This gentleman contracted with Shaw to bring out from Boston a press and type, and the order was filled doubtless from the meanest and cheapest material in the market. We have before us a sample of some of the first printing executed with it. It shows the type to be about worn out, and the press to have given a very uneven impression. It was an actual printing press and fixtures, however, and Zamorano was the first California printer. In 1825, when he came from Mexico as Echeandria's secretary he brought a small seal press and an alphabet sufficient for Government stamp purposes. Its utmost capacity was a hundred words, and we do not hear that it was applied to any other use than for official seals. When the Boston printing press arrived the office was set up at Monterey, and probably one of the first documents printed was a circular issued by Zamorano announcing the establishment of the press and his readiness to serve the public. We are so fortunate as to have one of these cards of the first printer in our possession. It is dated Monterey, 1834, two years after the press arrived. As California was a pretty slow country in those days, the intervening time may have been occupied in setting up the office, perhaps in finding a typesetter, or in instructing some one of the natives in the art, which is more likely. Perhaps, as printers have never been remarkable since the art was invented for a surplus of means, Zamorano may have found some difficulty in raising $460, and it must have been a small fortune in this country, where money was not then actually needed, after it was raised. But whether established earlier or not, the first evidence of its existence and of the readiness of the old press to serve its new and foreign masters is Zamorano's card, which we print, in order that those interested may compare the tariff of prices of the present day with those that existed twenty-four years ago.[4]

[4] [Kemble], "History of California Newspapers," in Sacramento *Daily Union*, December 25, 1858, as reprinted in book form by The Plandome Press, 2.

Kemble then quotes in translation and describes Zamorano's announcement of the establishment of the press. His sentimental attachment to the old press is evident in this brief statement of its history.

With Kemble's statement as a starting point, let us examine all the available sources and attempt to reconstruct this bit of forgotten history. In this we shall find that the products of the press will be our chief source of dependable information. We shall also find that books and broadsides were not the only products of the press and that such ephemeral pieces as letterheads and sealed-paper headings are sources that cannot be overlooked.

II. Printing in Alta California Before June 1834.

One does not proceed far in his search for locally printed items, among the documents and papers of the time that have been preserved, before one is aware that the printing press was far from idle and that there was printing of a sort in Alta California before the press itself arrived. The press, as we shall see, reached Monterey in June 1834 and was in operation by July. In this section, I shall discuss the printing done in California before the arrival of the press. With but two exceptions, so far as I am aware, all of the work done in this early period consisted of letterheads and sealed-paper headings. The existence of these items has but recently been pointed out.[5]

In the accompanying illustration are shown the three earliest forms of printing in California that have been found. These are letterheads and were all printed from wood-blocks. The blocks used in printing the top and center headings were made, obviously, by a person, or persons, possessed of some skill in the cutting of such blocks.

The top heading reads, *Gobierno Superior Polytyco De Ambas Calf^s*. There is a letter, that appears to be in Zamorano's handwriting, on paper with this heading, signed by Echeandia and dated San Diego, October 30, 1826, preserved in the office of the Recorder of Santa Cruz County, Santa Cruz.[6] The letter from which the illustra-

---
[5] Mr. John Howell, of San Francisco, appears to have been the first to call public attention to these items printed in California before the arrival of the press in 1834.
[6] Santa Cruz County Spanish Archives, Recorder's Office, Santa Cruz, 62.

Letterheads printed from wood-blocks, 1826-1829

tion was taken is dated Monterey, September 26, 1827, and is obviously in Zamorano's hand.[7] I have seen a third example of this heading on a letter, which may also be in Zamorano's hand, dated San Diego, June 19, 1829.[8]

The center heading in the illustration reads, *Gobierno Superior Militar y Politico de Ambas Californias*. Of this heading I have seen three specimens. The earliest is on a letter, which appears to have been written by Zamorano, dated San Diego, April 28, 1827.[9] The second earliest specimen, from which the illustration was made, is on a letter, not written by Zamorano, dated San Diego, December 18, 1828.[10] The third specimen of this heading is on a letter, in Zamorano's hand, dated Monterey, March 2, 1829.[11]

The bottom heading of the three reproduced in this illustration appears at the first glance to have been printed from type. A more careful study, however, shows it also to have been printed from a block. This block was cut, I believe, by an amateur block-cutter. The irregularities and crudities of the individual letter forms would indicate that it was not the work of a professional. There are eight cuttings of the letter A in this block and no two are exactly alike. The three C's vary in form. The variations in the three Y's are very evident. In fact, the comparison of any single character with other cuttings of the same letter shows that they vary considerably in detail. It is incredible that a practiced block-cutter would release a block so crudely executed.

Of this heading also, I have seen but three specimens. The earliest is on a letter dated Monterey, November 28, 1827, and is the one reproduced in the illustration.[12] The next earliest is on a letter dated Santa Barbara, December 31, 1827,[13] and the latest on one written at the same place on January 15, 1828.[14] All three of these letters, while signed by Echeandia, are in the handwriting of Zamorano.

On the basis of these three headings, I submit the following hypothesis regarding them. When Don Agustin came in 1825 with

---

[7] *Vallejo, Doc.*, I, 109. [8] In collection of Mr. Edwin Grabhorn, San Francisco.
[9] *Estudillo, Doc.*, 240. [10] *Pio Pico, Doc.*, II, 151.
[11] *Taylor Documents*, Archives of the Archdiocese of San Francisco, V, pt. 1, 305.
[12] *Vallejo, Doc.*, I, 112. [13] *Ibid.*, I, 5. [14] *Ibid.*, I, 118.

Echeandia, who was both civil governor and general commandant of the Californias, he brought with him, as part of the equipment of his secretarial office, the blocks of the top and center headings in the illustration. From these blocks he took impressions as was needed. One of these blocks enabled him to provide stationery for the office of the civil governor. The other block allowed him to provide paper for joint use of both the civil and military offices. These two offices, although held by the same person, were in fact distinct and a need was felt for stationery bearing the name of the military command only. This need Zamorano undertook to fill by cutting with his own hands a block for that purpose. There is, of course, no evidence aside from the three headings illustrated to support this supposition. However, Zamorano's bent toward the graphic arts and his known propensity to dabble in them makes such a conjecture plausible.

Letterheads printed from type were not used in California before the year 1830. From this fact, I believe that Kemble's informant was mistaken when he caused Kemble to write that Zamorano brought with him in 1825 "a small seal press and an alphabet sufficient for Government stamp purposes. Its utmost capacity was a hundred words, and we do not hear that it was applied to any other use than for official seals." It is more probable that Zamorano brought with him from Mexico only the two wood-blocks that have been mentioned and that the equipment of which Kemble speaks was delivered to him in California in 1829 or early in 1830.

It also appears that this equipment consisted of a small font of type and a few ornaments only. The two or three hundred specimens of its products that I have been privileged to examine do not appear to have had the benefit of a press in their production. Their impression, or "presswork," is extremely uneven and varies widely between individual pieces that must have been printed at the same time. I think it probable that there was no press and that they were printed in a manner similar to the way in which a printer of today takes a proof with planer and mallet.

Four letterheads that were printed from type with this equipment are illustrated. The three upper headings in this illustration are the earliest known use of type in California. The earliest use of the top

1830 - Oct. 7
Gefatura Politica
de la alta California.

Nº 7

Comandancia General Ynspector.
de la Alta California.

COMISARIA SUBALTERNA, Y
ADUANA MARITIMA PROVICIO-
NALES DEL PUERTO DE
MONTERREY.

1830 - Aug.ᵗ 25.

Recivi de
la cantidad de

AYUNTAMIENTO
CONSTITUCIONAL
DE
MONTERREY.

N. de Casas   Nombres   Estado, Edad

         Santiago Moreno   Casad. 30.

Letterheads printed from type, 1830

THE PRINTING PRESS 187

heading which reads, *Cefatura Politica | de la alta California*, is on a letter dated Monterey, August 29, 1830.[15] This letter is not in the handwriting of Zamorano but I have seen letters with this heading, dated in the following month, September 1830, that were.

The second heading in this illustration reads, *Comandancia General Ynspector | de la Alta California*. The earliest use of this heading I have found is on a document, which is signed by Zamorano, dated Monterey, September 18, 1830.[16]

It will be noticed that these headings read for Alta California only and not for both the Californias as do the earlier headings which were printed from wood-blocks. As Echeandia was relieved of the military command of Baja California in June 1829, we can assume safely that these headings from type were first used after that date. It follows that this printing equipment was received in California at some time between June 1829, and the dates of these documents.

The third heading shown in this illustration is found on a letter dated Monterey, August 25, 1830.[17] To this letter belongs the distinction of being the earliest dated document known with a heading that was printed from type in California.

The bottom heading in this illustration is shown because of the large ornamental dash it contains.[18] Twelve varieties of letterheads are known to have been printed with this typographical equipment.

Sealed-paper *(papel sellado)* is a means of giving formality and validity to legal documents that is common to the Latin countries. Its use in Spanish America dates from the earliest times. The use of this paper was required for all documents possessing the slightest legal character. It was issued in several varieties and could be obtained at any revenue office. The variety of sheet, and its cost, to be used for a particular transaction was determined by its nature and the amount involved. Such paper was required to be used for wills, depositions, powers of attorney, receipts, deeds, notes, drafts, etc., etc., and even many kinds of commercial transactions. Its use was extensive and its sale the source of considerable revenue to the state.

The national laws regulating the use and issue of sealed-paper

[15] *Ibid.*, I, 216.   [16] San Jose Spanish Archives, City Hall, San Jose, I, 369.
[17] *Vallejo, Doc.*, XXX, 116.   [18] *Ibid.*, XXXI, 76.

specified that it be habilitated for a stated biennium, that it carry an engraving of the national seal, and prescribed the wording to be printed on each class of paper. Such paper for use in California was originally supplied from Mexico and was held for sale at the *Comisaria Subalterna* at Monterey. It was not long before shipments of this paper from Mexico failed to arrive and the *Comisaria* at Monterey was forced to supply its needs locally. Before printing equipment was available, this was done by writing the prescribed formula at the top of blank sheets of paper. These sheets, in California, carried the names of the civil governor and the *comisario subalterno* as signatures to the legally required wording. To each sheet these officers signed their *rúbricas*. When printing became available locally, the headings on the sealed-paper were printed. The quantity of such paper used was considerable and sealed-paper was the chief product of both the printing press and the small equipment in use before its arrival.

The printing equipment we are now discussing produced the first sealed-paper printed in California. The first paper to be printed locally was habilitated for the single year 1831. The reason why none was printed for the year 1830 is not clear. It may have been that it was feared the local printing of such paper would injure its legality and that permission to use the local printing equipment in its production was obtained from Mexico before any was printed. In any event, no sealed-paper was printed during Echeandia's term as governor.

The earliest form of locally printed paper that has been found reads, *Sello Quarto De Officio. | Habilitado provicionalmente por la Comisaria principal de la álta California para el año de 1831. | Victoria. Bandini.* It is found on a document dated Monterey, May 15, 1831.[19] As Victoria assumed office on January 31, 1831, this heading was printed some time between that date and May 15. Sealed-paper was usually habilitated for two years but the first of such headings to be printed in California were for use in one year only, namely, 1831. These headings, therefore, contain the first printed date.

Of such headings, printed with the equipment we are here discussing, I have seen two varieties for the year 1831, three for the

[19] *Ibid.*, XXI, 64.

SELLO TERCERO DOS REALES.

Habilitado provicionalmente por la Comisaria subalterna interina d'el puerto de Monterrey de la Alta California, para los años de mil ochocientos treinta y uno y ochocientos treinta y dos. J. J. Gomez

Rehabilitado por a espresada Oficina para los años de 1833 y 1834.

SELLO QUARTO UNA QUARTILLA.

Habilitado provicionalmente por la Comisaria principal provicional de la Alta California para el año de 1831. Bandini.

Victoria. REVALIDADO por la Administracion de la Aduena Maritima de Monterrey para los años de mil ocho cientos treinta y tres, y mil ocho cientos treinta y cuatro. José Rafael Gonzales.

Figueroa.

Sealed-paper headings, 1831-1834

The Printing Press 189

biennium of 1831-2, two for 1832-3, three for 1833-4, and five for 1834-5. In addition, one variety for 1831 and three for 1831-2 have been found that carry a second printed impression which revalidated them for use in the biennium of 1833-4. Reproductions of two of these sealed-paper headings with the later imprinting are shown in the illustration.[20]

With the exception of a large brace, the last two illustrations show the entire typographic resources of this equipment. It consisted of a font of roman capitals and lower case, three varieties of unit ornaments, a large ornamental dash and a large brace. Some of the sealed headings contain a capital S of the same size and design as the two-line capital R in the heading shown in the illustration. It is possible there was a complete alphabet in this size but no use of any of the other letters than S and R has been found. The type of this equipment belongs in design to the general classification known to printers and typographical students as "old style." It is a sturdy, round face with no hairlines and with heavy serifs. The printing of the pieces produced with this equipment is so wretched that it is difficult to distinguish the details of the type design. The font was possibly of Spanish origin but there is little on which to base a considered opinion as to its source.

Other than letterheads and sealed-paper headings, two items only are known to have been printed with this equipment. The earliest of these was Governor Figueroa's announcement of his arrival, dated January 16, 1833. This was a brief statement set in nine lines of type and printed on a small sheet that was produced to accompany a printed proclamation the new governor brought from Mexico. The existence of but one copy of this famous little broadside is recorded in recent years and that has now disappeared. This piece has heretofore been called the first use of type in California and considered the earliest known specimen of California printing.[21] Although it is impossible for me to state with certainty that this announcement was printed with the equipment we are here discussing, since I have never

---

[20] Upper heading from *Valle, Doc.*, 31, and the lower from *ibid.*, 34.

[21] Bancroft, *History of California*, III, 241; Cowan, *Bibliography of the Spanish Press of California*. Both quote this piece in full and both thought Figueroa brought a small printing outfit with him from Mexico with which this announcement was printed.

seen a copy of it, there appears to be little reason to doubt that it was. We know that printing was done with this font of type both before and after Governor Figueroa's arrival and we can safely assume that it was printed with the same materials. Its text was within the capacity set by Kemble and both Bancroft and Cowan state specifically that it was not printed from the type used later by Zamorano. Neither of these authorities appear to have recognized that the letterheads and sealed-paper headings described above were printed from the same type.

In none of the pieces printed with this equipment which we have yet considered is there any positive evidence, direct or indirect, that they were printed by or at the direction of Zamorano. The only indication that they may have been printed by him is that the letterheads printed from wood-blocks, which were the first things to be printed, and the first letterheads to be printed from type were for the use of the two offices over which he exercised secretarial supervision. In the last piece we have to consider and which may well have been the last work done with this equipment there is more definite, although indirect, evidence that this equipment was either the property of Don Agustin or part of the equipment of his secretarial office.

This piece consists of a printed heading and closing endorsed on a proclamation printed in Mexico. Of this, I have seen three specimens, two dated May 28, 1834, and the third, May 30, 1834. These endorsements, except for the date written in with a pen, are the same on all three pieces. That of May 30, 1834, is reproduced in the illustration.

Obviously these blocks of type were set with the object of using them on several different proclamations. As the font available was not large enough to permit keeping these lines of type standing for any length of time, it is probable they were set for the purpose of endorsing a quantity of proclamations received in one shipment from Mexico, and the type then distributed. Of the many proclamations that must have been so endorsed but the three mentioned are known to exist today.[23] This endorsement was printed from the same materials as were the letterheads and sealed-paper headings shown in the previous illustrations.

[23] This reproduction made through the courtesy of a private owner who desires to remain anonymous.

José Figueroa, General de brigada de la República Mexicana, Comandante general inspector y Gefe Superior Político del Territorio de la Californía.

PRIMERA SECRETARIA DE ESTADO.
DEPARTAMENTO DEL INTERIOR.

Por la Secretaría de Relaciones Interiores se me ha dirigido á superior orden que á continuación se inserta y fue recibida por el último correo llegado del interior.

El Exmo. Sr. Vice-Presidente de los Estados-Unidos Mexicanos se ha servido dirigirme el decreto que sigue —————— y elecciones correspondientes.

Dios y libertad. México Febrero 6 de 1834.

Lombardo.

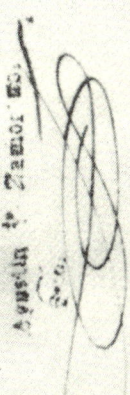

Y para que llegue á noticia de todos y nadie alegue ignorancia, mando se publique por bando en esta Capital, se fije en los lugares públicos acostumbrados y se circule á quienes toque cuidar de su observancia. En Monterrey á 20 de Mayo de 1834.

José Figueroa.

Agustín V. Zamorano.

The Printing Press

Our greatest interest, however, in these printed endorsements arises from the fact that they carry the printed name and the *rúbrica* of Don Agustin V. Zamorano. This piece of printing is clearly the work of the office of the executive secretary of the Territory and gives us reason to believe that this printing equipment was controlled by Zamorano.

The dates of May 28 and May 30 on the three known items bearing this printed endorsement do not necessarily mean they were printed on those dates. But if our conjecture that the scanty resources of this equipment would not permit keeping two such large blocks of type standing is correct, they must have been printed within a few days of the dates they carry. If so, they were among the last products of this equipment. The ship bringing the new press was soon to anchor in Monterey Bay and all printing done after the dates of these pieces was executed with the new equipment.

III. The Ship *Lagoda*.

Late in the month of May 1833, the ship *Lagoda* dropped down the bay of Boston Harbor and stood out to sea, bound for the Sandwich Islands and the coast of California. She was a ship of three hundred and forty tons and carried a crew of about fourteen men before the mast. Her master was Captain John Bradshaw and her supercargo, Captain Thomas Shaw. Although this was the first voyage of the vessel to the Pacific, it was not a new type of venture for her owners. She and her cargo were the joint risk of ten persons, of whom several had shared in previous voyages to the northwest coast of America.

A copy of the invoice of the ship's cargo and outfit was supplied one of her owners, James Hunnewell, and is preserved among the papers of this once prominent New England maritime merchant in the collection known as the Hunnewell Papers at the Harvard College Library.[23] This document, covering seven folio leaves and dated May 20, 1833, is entitled,

> Invoice of Cargo shipped by William Oliver & Osias Goodwin on board the Ship Lagoda, John Bradshaw, master, bound to the Sandwich

[23] I am indebted to Miss Adele Ogden, of Berkeley, for help in tracing the movements of the *Lagoda* and in locating this copy of her invoice.

Islands & Coast of California, consigned to Thomas Shaw, supercargo on board, for sale & returns on account & risk of the owners of the Ship, all of whom are natives of the United States of America.

William Oliver and Osias Goodwin appear to have acted as agents and were, in addition, part owners of the venture.

This invoice shows that the total cost incurred was $51,761.71, with the ship and her outfit accounting for $21,235.72 of the total, leaving $30,525.99 as the value of her cargo. The cargo of the *Lagoda* on this voyage consisted of miscellaneous merchandise and was probably typical of the "Boston ships" then trading on the California coast. It included some fifty odd thousand feet of dry lumber, dry goods, men's and women's clothing, notions, light and heavy hardware, musical instruments, staple groceries, liquors, boots and shoes, saddles (made to pattern), harness, wagons, carts, paints, crockery, tobacco, etc., etc. However, the item of greatest interest on the manifest of her cargo is the following:

1 Case. Printing Press, Type & Apparatus, complete.

The *Lagoda* was taking the first printing press to California.

The master and supercargo of the *Lagoda* were veterans in the California trade and together owned a tenth interest in the present venture. Captain John Bradshaw was first on the Coast in the years 1827 and 1828, as master of the ship *Franklin*. On that voyage he was often in trouble with the Californian authorities because of his smuggling activities and we have seen how he escaped arrest and the threatened confiscation of his cargo at San Diego, in July 1828, by cutting his anchor chain and boldly running the gauntlet of the full fire of the *castillo* at the entrance of the harbor.

Captain Thomas Shaw, the supercargo of the *Lagoda*, first came to California in 1826 as clerk, and later supercargo, on board the *Courier*. He was at San Diego at the time of the arrival there of Jedediah Smith, the first American to lead a party overland to California, and was one of the five Americans who signed a statement, on December 20, 1826, that Smith's papers were in order and his motives doubtless pacific.

Both Bradshaw and Shaw returned to California in 1830 as master

THE PRINTING PRESS 193

and supercargo respectively of the *Pocahontas*. They sailed on their return trip from San Diego, on January 17, 1832, taking as passengers, Governor Manuel Victoria and Padre Antonio Peyri, of Mission San Luis Rey. These passengers were landed at San Blas on February 5, 1832, and the ship proceeded on her way around Cape Horn to Boston. It is entirely possible that Captain Shaw carried with him on this trip the order of Zamorano for a printing press. Kemble, in his article, says the press "came to California about the year 1832. It is believed that it was contracted for in 1829 or '30." His informant, forgetting Shaw's later trip in the *Lagoda*, probably had this trip of Shaw's in mind when he said the press arrived about 1832.

The *Lagoda*, after the voyage around Cape Horn, arrived at Honolulu, in the Sandwich Islands, about October 1, 1833.[24] She sailed again for Monterey, in Alta California, on November 8.[25] At that time, Monterey was the only port of entry in California and the law required all vessels, before entering into trade, to call there and declare their cargos. Presumably the *Lagoda* complied with this requirement but no record of her being at Monterey late in November or early in December 1833 has been found. It is known, however, that she was on the southern coast a short time later.

Her cargo of merchandise was to be traded for hides and, as was the practice with most of the vessels engaged in the trade, she made San Diego the depot for collecting, curing, and storing those she gathered until a full cargo was collected. With San Diego as her base, she made several short trips to San Juan Capistrano, San Pedro, and Santa Barbara. In May 1834, she left San Diego for her first trip to the windward ports of Monterey and San Francisco.[26] She was at Monterey in June and appears then to have delivered the printing press.[27] She was at San Francisco from July 20 to August 16[28] and returned to San Diego on September 25.[29]

The *Lagoda* made another trip to Monterey in the same year. She

[24] Pierce to Hunnewell, Honolulu, October 4, 1833, MS., in Hunnewell, *Papers*, Harvard College Library. [25] Pierce to Hunnewell, Honolulu, December 1, 1833, MS., *ibid*.
[26] Shaw to Hunnewell, San Diego, May 25, 1834, MS., *ibid*.
[27] Shaw, Bill against John R. Cooper, Monterey, June 27, 1834, MS., in *Vallejo, Doc.*, XXXI, 101. [28] *Pinto, Doc.*, I, 28.
[29] McKinley to Stearns, San Diego, September 26, 1834, MS., in Gaffey, *Papers*.

left San Diego in October,[30] and was at San Juan Capistrano on November 3,[31] at Santa Barbara on December 1,[32] and at Monterey on December 10.[33] Soon after the beginning of the year 1835, she returned to the southern coast. She was in San Diego harbor taking on her cargo for the return trip when the brig *Pilgrim*, with Richard Henry Dana aboard as one of her crew, entered that harbor on March 14, 1835, and proceeded to drift, broadside on, into her.[34] Dana describes her then as "a large ship, with top-gallant-masts housed and sails unbent, and looking as rusty and worn as two years' 'hide droghing' could make her."[35] He describes her crew as "a hardy, intelligent set, a little roughened, and their clothes patched and old, from California wear; all able seamen, and between the ages of twenty and thirty-five or forty."[36] In April or May 1835, with a cargo of over thirty thousand hides tightly "sheeved" beneath her decks, the *Lagoda* sailed for home. She reached Boston in October.[37]

Captain John Bradshaw never again returned to California. He died, in May 1880, at his home in Beverly, Massachusetts, at the age of ninety-four.[38] Captain Thomas Shaw made another trip to California in 1839-40 as supercargo of the *Monsoon*. By March 1848, he appears to have deserted the sea as he was then acting as secretary, in Boston, of the Baptist Foreign Missionary Society.[39] He is said to have died in 1866.[40]

The *Lagoda* was built in 1826 by Seth and Samuel Foster at their shipyard at Wanton, on the North River, Plymouth County, Massachusetts, and was owned by them and Thomas Otis, of Scituate. She was 107.5 feet long, with a beam of 26.8 feet, and a depth of 18.3 feet. It was intended that she be named for Lake Ladoga, in Russia, but in making her name-board the consonants were misplaced and

---

[30] Shaw to Stearns, San Diego, October 3, 1834, MS., *ibid.*
[31] Shaw to Stearns, San Juan Capistrano, November 3, 1834, MS., *ibid.*
[32] Shaw to Stearns, Santa Barbara, December 1, 1834, MS., *ibid.*
[33] McKinley to Stearns, Monterey, December 10, 1834, MS., *ibid.*
[34] Dana, *Two Years before the Mast*, 135.   [35] *Idem.*   [36] *Ibid.*, 138.
[37] Hunnewell to Pierce, Charlestown, Mass., November 9, 1835, in Hunnewell, *Papers.*
[38] Bancroft, *op. cit.*, II, 726.
[39] Shaw to Hall J. Kelley, Boston, March 28, 1848, quoted in Kelley, *History of the Settlement of Oregon*, 53.   [40] Bancroft, *op. cit.*, V, 718.

the error was never corrected. Her builders sold her to the persons who sent her on the voyage to California in 1833-4. In 1841, she was sold to Jonathan Bourne, of New Bedford, who, during forty-five years, sent her on twelve whaling voyages to the Pacific, only one of which was not a notable financial success. Her original rig was that of a ship but she was altered into a bark in 1860. She was sold by Bourne, in 1886, to John McCullough, who, in 1887, sold her to William Lewis and others, also of New Bedford, who continued to use her as a whaler. In August 1889, in her sixty-fourth year, and fifty-five years after she had delivered California's first printing press at Monterey, the *Lagoda* put into San Francisco, from the Arctic, with a cargo of bone and oil. She returned to the Arctic soon after. This proved her last visit to California. In the following year, 1890, she reached Yokohama in a badly damaged condition. On being pronounced not worth repairing, after an official survey, she was sold at auction and purchased by the Canadian Pacific Company for use as a coal barge. Her long life of useful service ended in 1899, when she was sold to the Japanese, burned, and broken up at Kanagawa. In a large room in the Bourne Memorial Whaling Museum of the Old Dartmouth Historical Society, New Bedford, there stands today a half-size model of the *Lagoda*, rigged and equipped as a whaler, complete in all detail. This model, which is probably the largest ever constructed of a sailing vessel, measures eighty feet, six inches in length over all and stands fifty feet in height from the water line to the main royal truck. The model and museum building were erected by a daughter of Jonathan Bourne as a memorial to her father."

IV. The Press and Its Equipment.

The earliest evidence of the use of the new printing equipment is a sealed-paper heading which reads, *Sello Cuarto De Oficio.* | *Habilitado provicionalmente por la Administracion de la Aduana maritima de Monterey de la alta California para* | *los años de mil ochocientos treinta y cuatro y mil ochocientos treinta y cinco.* | *Figueroa. A. Ramirez.* There is a document dated July 28, 1834, on paper with

[a] Briggs, *History of Shipbuilding on North River*, 237; Dana, *op. cit.*, 504.

this heading in the Bancroft Library.⁴² Therefore the new equipment was set up and in use by that date at the latest. From the evidence we have examined, we know the press was received and set up some time during the two months between May 28 and July 28, 1834.

The announcement of the opening of a printing office at Monterey was made in a small broadside, which is reproduced in the illustration. At this point let us return to Kemble's statement regarding the press and resume our quotation from it.

> The circular appears on a half sheet, Spanish letter paper, yellowish with age, and is printed with very old bourgeois newspaper type, in which the capitals and small capitals form the only display lines. We translate Zamorano's card almost literally:
> "NOTICE TO THE PUBLIC.
> "At the Printing Office of the citizen Augustin [sic] V. Zamorano & Co, established in this Capital is offered to serve the public with the greatest exactness and care; receiving all kinds of writing under the rules established by the laws for the liberty of the press, subjecting the loose impressions to the following rates, and agreeing at more equitable prices with gentlemen who may wish to establish any periodical.
> "Rates for the Impressions.
> "Congratulation billets, per hundred, three dollars.
> "Invitation notes, and others similar, do. do., five dollars.
> "The eighth of a sheet of paper do. do., seven dollars.
> "The fourth do. do., eight dollars.
> "Half a sheet do. do., ten dollars.
> "One sheet do. do., twenty dollars.
> "The impression of more than 100 copies of said classes, 1 *peso*, 4 *reales*, 6 *granos el ciento*.
> "The impressions made on account of the Government of the Territory shall be taken with consideration for the equity of the prices.
> "The paper shall be paid for separately, according to its just value, or shall be furnished at the pleasure of gentlemen who wish their writings printed.
> "The character of the letter that shall be used is the same as that on which this impression is served.
> "Monterrey, 1834.
> "Imprenta De Zamorano Y Ca."⁴³

Kemble's sentimental attachment to the pioneer printing press o

---
⁴² *Vallejo, Doc.*, XXXI, 110.   ⁴³ Kemble, *op. cit.*, 4.

AVISO AL PUBLICO.

En la imprenta del Ciudadano Agustin V. Zamorano y Compañia establecida en esta Capital, se ofrece servir al público con la mayor puntualidad y esmero, admitiendo toda suerte de escritos, bajo las reglas establecidas por las leyes de libertad de imprenta, sujetandose los impresos sueltos al siguiente ARANCEL y conviniendo a precios mas equitativos con los Sres. que quieran establecer algun periódico.

ARANCEL PARA LAS IMPRESIONES.

Los billetes para dar dias: por la planta y hasta cien ejemplares, pagaran 3 pesos.
Las papeletas de convite y otras semejantes: por la planta y hasta cien ejemplares pagaran 5 pesos.
El octavo de pliego: por la planta y hasta cien ejemplares pagará 7 pesos.
El cuarto de pliego: por la planta y hasta cien ejemplares pagara 8 pesos.
El medio pliego: por la planta y hasta cien ejemplares pagara 10 pesos.
El pliego: por la planta y hasta cien ejemplares pagara 20 pesos.
La impresion de mas de cien ejemplares de las clases espresadas pagará á razon de 1 peso cuatro 6 granos el ciento.
Las impresiones que se hagan por cuenta del Gobierno del Territorio, se tomaran en consideracion para la equidad en los precios.
El papel se pagara por separado segun su justo valor, ó lo daran á su gusto los Sres. que en se les imprima sus escritos.
El caracter de letra de que se hará uso es igual al que ha servido para este impreso.

MONTERREY 1834.
IMPRENTA DE ZAMORANO Y Cª.

The Printing Press 197

California leads him into making some misstatements regarding this announcement, which he considered to be a specimen of the first printing in California. We must take exception to his statement that this circular was printed from "very old bourgeois newspaper type." A careful examination of the reproduction of this broadside will convince the reader that the type from which it was printed was not old and worn, and the trained eye of the printer will discover that it was small pica in size and not bourgeois.

Zamorano's circular announcing the opening of a printing office is also a specimen sheet of the typographical equipment he then possessed. The new type was, in design, of the group termed "modern" by typographical students. It was a highly modeled face with a decided vertical feeling, many hairlines, and long, sharp serifs. Research has proved that it was the Small Pica, No. 1, of the Boston Type and Stereotype Foundry, Boston. A page showing this face and size from the Boston Foundry's *Specimen Book* of 1845 is illustrated. The same letter and size is also shown in their specimen book of 1826.[44]

The shipment of typographic materials to reach Monterey with the press appears to have been limited in extent. With the exception of two or three varieties of small decorative units on small pica bodies and a plentiful supply of dollar marks, the entire resources, typographically, of the office are shown in the announcement. There was available but one size of text letter, with capitals, small capitals, and figures of the same size. There was no italic. And there were no accented letters.

To overcome the lack of the latter, an effort was made to use the accented letters from the old-style font previously in use. Close examination of the circular will show that all the accented letters with the exception of the Spanish "ñ" are wrong font. The "ñ" was made by shaving the top of the type and laying above a comma on its side. This use of the accented letters from the old equipment, with the additional fact that some of the decorative materials used in printing the earlier headings are found on the title-pages of some of the books

---

[44] I am indebted to Mr. D. B. Updike, of Boston, for the loan of his copies of these early specimens of the Boston Type Foundry, and to Mr. H. H. Taylor and Mr. Edwin Grabhorn, both of San Francisco, for checking my typographic researches.

printed with the new equipment, indicates that, by this time at least, Zamorano was the owner of the old material and probably the printer of the sealed-paper headings and letterheads printed with that equipment.

For a description of the press itself, we return to Kemble's statement. In it we have a description written by one who had owned and operated it.

> In the Patent Office at Washington, preserved under a glass case, is an illustrious member of the family of printing presses, from which the newspapers of California are descended. The visitor is shown the old relic as a curious specimen of the art before the Revolution. But that which gives it its chief interest is the fact of its being the press at which that honored representative of "the craft," Benjamin Franklin, worked when a printer. It is probably the oldest printing press in America, though the same style, known as the Ramage press, has continued in use until within ten or fifteen years. The frame, platen, ribs, and part of the bed are of wood, the bed on which the type forms lie is of stone, and the screw, which is the mechanical principle by which the impression is taken, is of iron, and large enough to raise a building, to which the main uprights which support the press are of timber sufficiently thick for sills. This old Franklin machine with its worm-eaten and well worn timbers is an exact counterpart of the press which, also furnished by the city of Boston, executed the first printing on the northwest shores of America; the press which gave to California the first newspaper, and on which was afterwards printed the first journals of the interior and the mines. We know not what relation its origin sustained to the Franklin press at Washington. They were probably never on speaking terms, having flourished at intervals doubtless wide apart. They may have come from separate manufactories. But the date at which our venerable California ancestor arrived on these shores, and the years and hard service which it had evidently seen before it left Boston, justify the presumption that it came into existence not far from the locality and era in which the Franklin press labored. That it was a member of the same extensive family is unquestionable.[45]

V. Zamorano's First Printer.

The announcement of the opening of the printing office at Monterey is signed *Imprenta de Zamorano y Ca.* but this imprint soon became

[45] Kemble, *op. cit.*, 1.

Small Pica, No. 1.

Quousque tandem abutere, Catilina, patientia nostra? quamdiu nos etiam furor iste tuus eludet? quem ad finem sese effrenata jactabit audacia? nihilne te nocturnum præsidium palatii, nihil urbis vigiliæ, nihil timor populi, nihil consensus bonorum omnium, nihil hic munitissimus habendi senatus locus, nihil horum ora vultusque moverunt? patere tua consilia non sentis? constrictam jam omnium horum conscientia teneri conjurationem tuam non vides? quid proxima, quid superiore nocte egeris, ubi fueris, quos convocaveris, quid consilii ceperis, quem nostrum ignorare arbitraris? O tempora, o mores! Senatus hoc intelligit, consul videt: hic tamen vivit. Vivit?

ABCDEFGHIJKLMNOPQRSTUVWXYZ

ABCDEFGHIJKLMNOPQRSTUVWXYZÆŒ

0123456789 0

If there be any among us who would wish to dissolve this Union, or to change its republican form, let them stand undisturbed as monuments of the safety with which error of opinion may be tolerated, where reason is left free to combat it. I know, indeed, that some honest men fear that a republican government cannot be strong; that this government is not strong enough. But would the honest patriot, in the full tide of successful experiment, abandon a government which has so far kept us free and firm, on the theoretic and visionary fear, that

Quousque tandem abutere, Catilina, patientia nostra? quamdiu nos etiam furor iste tuus eludet? quem ad finem sese effrenata jactabit audacia? nihilne te nocturnum præsidium palatii, nihil urbis vigiliæ, nihil timor populi, nihil consensus bonorum omnium, nihil hic munitissimus habendi senatus locus, nihil horum ora vultusque moverunt? patere tua consilia non sentis? constrictam jam omnium horum conscientia teneri conjurationem tuam non vides? quid proxima, quid

ABCDEFGHIJKLMNOPQRSTUVWXY

BOSTON TYPE AND STEREOTYPE FOUNDRY.

Imprenta del C. Agustin V. Zamorano. I am of the opinion the press was the private property of Don Agustin only. While he undoubtedly liked to work with the printing equipment, he was not a printer by trade and there is no indication that he had printing experience before coming to California. He was a person of too many interests and responsibilities and the product of the press was too great for him to have been its operator.

In the period from June 1834 to November 6, 1836, during which Zamorano controlled the operations of the press, it is obvious from the pieces printed, that two different persons were handling the equipment. I have been unable to determine the identity of these men. It appears that they were employes of Don Agustin and probably possessed no proprietary interest in the press.

The first of these men to operate the press was but a fair printer. The type-setting of the pieces printed by him do not display any particular skill or imagination on the part of their compositor and their presswork is, in general, rather poor. This man was prone to over-ink his forms and to neglect his make-ready of the press. The result was that many letters filled with ink and the impression was uneven. His careless work is the reason why many writers, including Kemble, have thought the equipment old and worn.

Ephemeral pieces produced by Zamorano's first printer, who operated the press from July 1834 to the end of the year 1835, are scarce and difficult to find. Seven varieties of sealed-paper, habilitated for the years 1834 and 1835, are known but, curiously, I have never seen any such paper printed for the biennium of 1835 and 1836. Only five varieties of letterheads printed in this period are known. The most unusual piece of work was an invitation to a ball that was given by the governor on November 1, 1834, to welcome the Hijar and Padrés colonists.[46]

The first major piece of printing to follow the circular announcing the opening of the printing office was a small book, the first to be printed in California. Of this little volume, but one copy is known to exist today. It was preserved by Don Agustin Olvera, a brother-

[46] Cowan, *op. cit.*, 13.

in-law of Zamorano.⁴⁷ Its contents are the rules and regulations adopted by the territorial legislature for the government of its organization and deliberations. It consists of sixteen pages that measure 9.7 x 13.0 centimeters, plus a title-page on a separate leaf. The title reads,

> Reglamento Provicional [*capitals*] | Para [*small capitals*] | El Gobierno Interior [*small capitals*] | De La [*small capitals*] | Ecma. Diputacion Territorial [*capitals*] | De La [*small capitals*] | Alta California [*capitals*] | Aprobado por la misma Corporacion en sesion | de 31. de Julio del presente año. [*two lines in capitals and lower case*] | [*ornamental dash, composed of four rule units between two capital V's laid on sides*] | Monterey 1834. [*small capitals*] | [*brace, laid on side*] | Imprenta De A. V. Zamorano Y Ca. [*small capitals*] | [*all within border of composed rule units, with dot corners and a dollar mark in center of top and bottom lines*].

The type in this pamphlet is set solid and a few of the accented letters from the old-style font are used. There is no colophon or imprint other than that on the title-page. The paper used is an antique finish, wove, with no watermark, of American manufacture, and not of the kind usually found in use in Alta California at that time.

This small book was followed from the press by three broadside proclamations by Governor Figueroa. The earliest of these carried the first date, Monterey, August 6, 1834, to be printed with the new equipment. It concerned taxes and public financial matters and was entitled:

> Plan de Propios y Arbitrios para fondos municipales de los Ayuntamientos | del Territorio de la Alta California. | [*two lines in small capitals*].

It consisted of seventy-three lines of type, besides the signatures, of which sixty-four were devoted to the text of twenty-one numbered articles.⁴⁸ There was no imprint.

In this proclamation, no effort was made to use the accented letters of the old-style font as had been done in the previous two pieces.

[47] Now in Bancroft Library. This book is translated in summary in Bancroft, *op. cit.*, III, 252, note 24.
[48] Copy in Bancroft Library. Translated in summary in Bancroft, *op. cit.*, III, 380, note 21.

The old-style font was on a different size of body than the new, which made the use of the two in combination difficult. The old font appears to have been completely discarded after the printing of the *Reglamento* and thereafter the only accented letter used was the Spanish ñ, made by shaving the top of the type and laying a comma above.

The second proclamation, dated August 9, 1834, was Governor Figueroa's,

> Reglamento Provicional [capitals] | Para La Secularisacion De Las Misiones De La Alta California. [small capitals].

These regulations for the secularization and administration of the missions were approved by the deputation in its session of August 2. The text of this proclamation was long and it was printed on three sheets of paper which were then pasted together to form a large broadside measuring 19.0 x 63.5 centimeters.[49] This also carried no imprint.

The third printed proclamation by the governor was that of March 16, 1835. This was an address to the people of the Territory which was issued immediately after Figueroa ordered Ensign Vallejo, at Mission San Francisco Solano, to conduct Hijar and Padrés aboard the *Rosa* for deportation. In this the governor bitterly denounced the leaders of the colonists, congratulated the people that he had been able to save the country, and promised a more complete vindication later of his policies.[50]

This proclamation was printed as a broadside in two columns of thirty-eight lines each, with a vertical rule of composed units between, over a third, short, center column of eight lines. At the bottom, set in capitals, was the imprint, *Imprenta del C. Agustin V. Zamorano*. The press work of this piece, in the copies I have seen, is particularly poor.

The governor's vindication of his policies regarding the activities of Hijar and Padrés took the form of a book. I have already stated

---

[49] Copy in Bancroft Library. Translated in full in Bancroft, *op. cit.*, III, 342, note 4, and in Engelhardt, *Missions and Missionaries of California*, III, 253.

[50] Copy in Bancroft Library.

Don Agustin V. Zamorano

that Governor Figueroa had the editorial assistance of Don Agustin in the preparation of this work and that it was on the press at the time of the governor's death. This volume was the only book of size and importance to be produced in Alta California before the American occupation and was easily the most extensive and the most important product of the press during the time Don Agustin controlled its operation. Its title reads,

> Manifiesto [capitals, letter spaced] | A La [small capitals] | Republica Mejicana [capitals] | Que Hace El General De Brigada [small capitals] | Jose Figueroa, [capitals] | Comandante General Y Gefe Politico [small capitals] | De La [small capitals] | Alta California, [capitals, letter spaced] | Sobre su conducta y la de los Señores | D. Jose Maria de Hijar y D. Jose Maria | Padres, como Directores de Colonizacion | en 1834 y 1835. [four lines in capitals and lower case] | [diamond shaped ornament, composed of nine asterisks] | Monterrey 1835. [capitals] | [line of composed rule units] | Imprenta Del C. Agustin V. Zamorano. [small capitals] | [all within box border of composed rule units, with dot corners].[51]

A perfect copy of this very rare California imprint should collate as follows: two blank leaves; [i], title, as above; [ii], blank; [iii]— [iv], Nota Del Impresor, followed by Erratas; [i] to 183, text; [184], proposed inscriptions on monument to Figueroa; two blank leaves; colored paper covers pasted across spine and flat to outside of front and back blank leaves. An untrimmed copy should measure about 10.4 centimeters in width by 14.6 centimeters in height. It is only fair to say that I have never seen a perfect copy.

In binding, the printed sheets were not folded and gathered as signatures. Each pair of printed leaves was cut from the sheet and folded once, as in a folio volume. A complete copy of this book, therefore, would consist of forty-nine folds of two leaves each. There were no signature marks. In sewing, three holes were stabbed through the thickness of the book in the back margin and the book sewn through those holes. The paper used for the covers was of various colors.

The paper on which this book was printed was an Italian hand-

---

[51] Copies in Bancroft Library; California State Library; Coronel Collection, Los Angeles Museum; and Henry E. Huntington Library. A translation in full was printed at the office of the San Francisco Herald in 1855.

made, with the watermark, "GiorMagnanieF." This paper was in common use in Alta California at the time and was used in several of the products of the press.

The text of this volume is set solid in a measure of seven and a half centimeters, thirty-one lines to the page. There being no chapters, the text is continuous to page 177. The remaining pages of the book were devoted to the resolutions adopted by the territorial legislature following Governor Figueroa's death. Paragraphs are heavily indented and page folios are at top center. There were no accented letters other than the Spanish ñ. The presswork throughout the volume was fair only, although no worse than is usually to be found in books printed by pioneer presses. The forms were not carefully inked and the impression was heavy. The result was a muddy volume of uneven color. No effort was made for register in backing the pages.

The *Nota Del Impresor*, on the third preliminary page, read,

> Se suplica a los Señores lectores se sirvan disimular la falta de acentos que notaran en esta obra, originada par no haber venido aun el surtido completo de letra que se esta esperando: asi mismo se suplica presten su indulgencia por cualquiera otro defecto tipografico que adviertan en la referida obra, teniendo en consideracion que es la primera en su clase que se da a luz en la unica imprenta de esta Alta California.

This may be translated:

> PRINTER'S NOTE.
> Readers are asked to overlook any lack of accented letters they may notice in this original work, since an expected complete stock of type has not arrived; likewise, they are asked to be indulgent toward any other typographical defects they may discover and to remember that this is the first work of its kind to be produced on the only press in Alta California.

There was, however, no reason for the printer to be apologetic concerning his effort, as this book, notwithstanding its defects, was a very real achievement for a pioneer press. California's fine printers of today will never, in the eyes of the collectors of Californiana, produce another volume that will approach this most desirable of all California imprints.

VI. Zamorano's Second Printer.

On January 2, 1836, Don José Castro, who became acting civil governor of Alta California on the death of Governor Figueroa, turned over his office to Lieutenant Colonel Don Nicolás Gutiérrez, the acting general commandant. Each issued a printed proclamation announcing this transfer of the civil authority.[52] With the appearance of these pieces, it becomes apparent that a new hand was operating the press. In all the pieces printed before these proclamations, the type was set solid, the composition was only fair and the presswork generally poor. The texts of these proclamations consisted of only two or three short paragraphs but they were set with skill and imagination, their lines were leaded, they were pleasingly placed on the sheet, and their presswork was much superior to that of any piece printed before them. The products of the press during the period from January 2 to November 4, 1836, are without doubt the work of a skilled printer.

We have noticed that Governor Chico and Don Agustin had little regard for each other. However, Governor Chico provided considerable work for the press during his short stay of three months, and the finest products technically of the press in all its history were the printings of Chico's proclamations and speeches. The first of these was the proclamation of May 3, 1836, to the people of the Territory, issued immediately after the governor assumed office. No copy of this is known to exist today but it has been described as a broadside on blue paper, printed in two columns of forty-eight lines each, with two lines of heading, one of signature, and two of imprint.[53] The imprint read *Imprenta Del C. Agustin V. Zamorano.*

Kemble had a copy of this proclamation before him as he wrote the article from which we have quoted. Of it he says,

> One of the most curious documents preserved of the times in which the old press figured is a proclamation issued by Governor Mariano Chico, who arrived from Mexico in 1836, with titles long enough to confound a courtier of the days of Louis XIV. His first salutation was a model of bombast and self-conceit. It complimented the Californians on their

[52] Copy of each proclamation in Bancroft Library.   [53] Cowan, *op. cit.*, 14.

docility, and spoke of the gratitude they owed him for his sacrifice in leaving his wife and children in Mexico, and consenting to be their governor.[54]

Eight days later, on May 11, Governor Chico again addressed the inhabitants of Alta California by means of a printed proclamation. This dealt with commercial matters. It prohibited selling at retail on board foreign vessels as had long been the custom, required the landing of all cargos at Monterey, and imposed other restrictions that were more in accordance with the Mexican laws on the subject than with previous usage in California.[55] The presswork of this piece of printing was far superior to that of the proclamations printed for Governor Figueroa. It was printed on a blue hand-made paper that appears to have been of English manufacture. It consisted of three lines of heading, forty-six lines of text, and the signatures. There was no imprint.

On May 20, 1836, the oath of allegiance to the *bases* of the new centralist constitution was taken by the people of Monterey and the governor delivered a public address. In this he lauded centralism in extravagant terms, as roundly denounced federalism, and flatteringly congratulated the Californians on their glorious future under the new laws. This address was printed and circulated throughout the Territory. One copy only of this address, *Discurso Pronunciado Por El Sr. Comandante General Y Gefe Politico De La Alta California Coronel D. Mariano Chico. Despues del acto del juramento de las bases constitucionales, el dia 20 de Mayo de 1836*, is known to have been preserved and that is in the Archivo General, Secretaría de Gobernacion, Mexico.[56] My efforts to obtain a reproduction of it have been fruitless. It has been described as a broadside, printed on both sides of the sheet, containing four lines of heading and forty-eight of text on the obverse and seven of text, one of imprint, and a woodcut of a ship on the reverse.[57]

The next piece we have to consider was an address delivered by Governor Chico, on May 27, 1836, before the opening session of the

[54] Kemble, *op. cit.*, 6.
[55] Copy in Bancroft Library. Translated in summary in Bancroft, *op. cit.*, IV, 82.
[56] Bolton, *Guide to . . Archives of Mexico*, 319.   [57] Cowan, *op. cit.*, 15.

territorial legislature. In this he reviewed many matters of public interest. This address, *Discurso Pronunciado Por El Señor Gefe Politico De La Alta California Coronel D. Mariano Chico, al abrir sus sesiones ordinarias la Ecsma. Junta Departamental el 27 de Mayo de 1836,* was printed as a four page leaflet that measured 20.3 x 29.6 centimeters.[58] The first page of this leaflet carried four lines of heading and forty-eight of text; the second page, sixty-six lines of text; the third page, nineteen lines of text, a Bewick-like wood-engraving of four figures under a tree, and one line of imprint. The imprint read, *Imprenta del C. Agustin V. Zamorano.* The fourth page was blank. The upper half of the first page of this leaflet is reproduced in the illustration.[59]

Early in May 1836, the additional typographic equipment mentioned in the *Nota del Impresor* in Governor Figueroa's *Manifiesto* reached Monterey. The first use of the new materials was in Governor Chico's *Discursos* of May 20 and May 27. With its arrival there became available a full range of accented letters, small pica italic, "four lines pica" shaded capitals, "two lines brevier" double shaded capitals, five or six additional varieties of decorative units, a woodcut of the Mexican eagle, and a few wood engravings. All these are shown in the Boston Type and Stereotype Foundry specimen books of 1826 and 1845. The second shipment of typographic materials to reach Monterey must have equaled, if it did not exceed, the first.

The *Discurso* of May 27, 1836, was the highest point in technical excellence reached by California's first press. By every standard that can legitimately be applied this must be credited with being a superior piece of work for a pioneer press. There were many metropolitan printing offices of the time, in both the United States and Mexico, that were not producing better work than this leaflet.

The last proclamation by Governor Chico was issued on July 24, 1836. The news of the defeat and capture in Texas of Santa Anna had just been received in California and this proclamation was the governor's outburst of patriotic indignation. It was a broadside of three lines of heading, twenty-five of text in three paragraphs, one of sig-

[58] Copies in Bancroft Library and Henry E. Huntington Library.
[59] From copy in the collection of Mr. Henry R. Wagner, of San Marino.

DISCURSO

PRONUNCIADO POR EL SEÑOR GEFE POLITICO DE LA ALTA CALIFORNIA

CORONEL D. MARIANO CHICO,

al abrir sus sesiones ordinarias la Ecsma. Junta Departamental el 27 de Mayo de 1836.

Ecsmo. Sr. = Al recibirme del Gobierno de este Departamento, tengo la desgracia de encontrar un inmenso rezago de negocios, que el fallecimiento de mi digno antecesor el General D. Jose Figueroa, y las circunstancias que subsiguieron, y callo por notorias, han aumentado, dando á algunos un carácter de complicacion que hace muy dificil su curso. Y si se agrega á estos accidentes la llegada de los dos posteriores correos de la Capital, abundantisimos en correspondencia, llena de diversos y graves asuntos, originados de los cambios políticos de la administracion, y del sistema que nos regia. V. E. convendrá en que es preciso que me encuentre rodeado de inconvenientes poderosos de que tan solo me pondrá en salvo el tino, discrecion y empeño de esta Junta, si toma en consideracion cuanto voy á esponerle, para consultar las medidas que deban adoptarse, ya trazando el camino que tomen unos, ya enderezando los pasos que hayan dado otros, á los cuales yo he prescripto la via, sin el norte del consejo de V. E. por que no ecsistia reunida á mi ingreso al Gobierno, y era forzoso espedir la marcha de negocios que pedian violenta atencion. El primero de aquellos consistia en los sucesos escandalosos habidos en el pueblo de los Ángeles, donde una reunion tumultuaria de vecinos que se dejaron seducir por cuatro discolos maliciosos, sobreponiendose á la autoridad y á las leyes, y despreciando la sana moral, cometieron el atentado sabido de arrancar de las manos de la justicia á dos miserables reos que ella tenia asegurados para castigar sus crimenes y los hicieron perecer en el patíbulo, negándoles aun los aucsilios espirituales que ecsige la sagrada religion que profesamos. Todos los caracteres que presentaba este suceso eran peligrosos á la sociedad, por que ella no permite mas que á los jueces la aplicacion de los castigos, y de otro modo la balanza del orden perderia su equilibrio. Yo entraba de nuevo á esta magistratura y mis primeros pasos debian ser á la vez prudentes, enérgicos y seguros; se me presentaba la perspectiva de un hecho que llamó la espectacion de todas las clases á observar mi conducta, y debí adoptar resoluciones que no marcasen mi carácter con la nota de frio y apático, mácsime cuando los amotinados no satisfechos con el acto de atrevimiento que ejecutaron, eludieron la averiguacion que justamente dispuso practicar el Teniente Coronel D. Nicolás Gutierrez Gefe politico interino, renovando el escándalo con presentarse al juez de la causa en número imponente para publicarse culpados todos á fin de impedir las providencias que fuera de necesidad tomar sobre los cabecillas: conducta que me obligó á persuadir con pesar, de que no la crápula producida del sentimiento de ver comunmente impunes los delitos mas atroces en este pais por los motivos que alegaron, fué la causa provocadora del hecho; si no que una resolucion meditada por ocultos genios anárquicos para desquiciar al Gobierno, inspiró á los incautos Angelinos la funesta idea de amotinarse con un pretesto aparentemente sano, para traerlos despues á servir á miras siniestras en que mas de una' vez han sido iniciados los directores públicos y secretos de ese motin, dando dias bastante amargos al Departamento, cuya direccion se me confia, y es mi deber cuidar de su sosiego. Yo me puse al alcance de los peligros al pisar la playa del puerto de Sta. Bárbara, é intenté desde allí dirigirme á aquel pueblo con objeto de interponer mi **mediacion** y conseguir que se retragesen á su habitual docilidad los ecsaltados, no entorpeciendo el ejercicio de las leyes; mas algunas personas principales se opusieron á mi designio asegurandome que se ajarian los respetos de la mia, no yendo aun investida con la autoridad del mando; y por otra parte que los motores ocultos del escándalo se prevaldrian de desconocerme para atentar contra mi, como el obstáculo en que se estrellara la realizacion de sus miras verdaderas. Puesto pues en el caso de dictar providencias, y de hacer eficaz su resultado, determiné al momento de arribar á esta capital, que la fuerza militar disponible acudiese al pueblo de los Ángeles en apoyo de aquellas autoridades atropelladas; y aunque procuré aprestar un número respectivamente considerable á las órdenes inmediatas del precitado Sr. Gutierrez, no ha sido por que temiera que una cuarta parte de aquella tropa no fuese sobrada para refrenar á los tumultuarios, si no por que no quise que costase una víctima su redencion, y el modo de lograrlo era mandarles una fuerza tan superior que á primera vista los convenciese de que no podrian ha-

nature, one of date, and one of imprint, which read, *Imprenta Del C. Agustin V. Zamorano*. It also was an excellent example of pioneer printing.

Acting Governor Gutiérrez does not appear to have used the press; at least no printed proclamation was issued by him. There were, however, a few important unofficial pieces printed by Zamorano's second printer. The first was a small catechism, *Catecismo De Ortologia. Dedicado a los Alumnos de la Escuela Normal de Monterrey*. One copy only of this little book has been recorded in recent years and that has now disappeared. It has been described as the first sixteen pages of an incomplete work and measuring 8.3 x 10.3 centimeters. It was dated *Monterrey 1836* and the imprint read *Imprenta Del C. Agustin V. Zamorano*.[60] Don José Mariano Romero, the author or compiler of this book, was a school teacher who came to California in 1834 with the Hijar and Padrés Colony. He established a school of higher education at Monterey which he called a normal school and to the alumni of which this catechism was dedicated. He refused to join the supporters of Alvarado and Castro in the revolution of November 1836 and returned to Mexico on the *Clementina* with Lieutenant Colonel Gutiérrez.

There was also printed during 1836 a small arithmetic. The name of the author is not indicated but its text was probably prepared by Romero. This and the catechism were the first school books known to be printed in California. The single copy of this arithmetic that has been preserved measures 6.9 x 9.4 centimeters and consists of twenty unnumbered pages.[61] Its collation is: [1], title; [2], blank; [3] to [19], text; [20], blank. The title-page reads,

Tablas [*capitals*] | Para Los Niños [*small capitals*] | Que Empiezan A Contar. [*small capitals*] | [*small brace, on side*] | Imprenta De A. Zamorano. [*small capitals.*] | [*all within border composed of dollar marks*].

The binding of this small book was done in the same manner as was that of Governor Figueroa's *Manifiesto*. Each pair of printed leaves was cut from the sheet and folded individually. Five of these folded leaves made the total and were sewn through four holes

[60] Cowan, *op. cit.*, 21.   [61] In Henry E. Huntington Library.

stabbed in the back margin. A paper wrapper was then pasted across the spine to the back margin. The typographical plan of this booklet is pleasantly conceived and quite well executed. It was printed some time before May 1836, as the only accented letter to be found in it is the Spanish ñ, made by laying a comma above the letter.

The contents of this little arithmetic were also printed as a broadside within a border. No copy is known to exist today but it has been described as measuring 30.4 x 45.6 centimeters.[62]

In connection with the celebration of the Mexican national holiday of September 16, the press in 1836 printed a small patriotic poem. The author's name is not indicated. The title was *En Recuerdo Del Glorioso Grito: Dado En El Pueblo De Dolores, En El Año De Mil Ocho Cientos Diez*. The poem consisted of two stanzas of four and six lines, which were printed on a blue paper within a border of unit ornaments around a box of rule units.[63]

After the fall of the *presidio* at Monterey on November 6, 1836, the printing press, by either purchase or confiscation, passed to the new revolutionary government.[64] It was operated by various persons at various times at Monterey and at Sonoma until March 1845. It was then stored in a room of the government building at Monterey, where it was discovered by Robert Semple and used by him and Walter Colton in printing the *Californian*, which first appeared in August 1846. In May 1847, the office of the *Californian* was moved to San Francisco. Kemble, in November 1848, became the owner of the press when he took over the *Californian* and it was used by him in the printing of the *Star and Californian*. In the spring of 1849, he took the press to Sacramento and with it began the publication of the *Placer Times*, the pioneer journal of Sacramento and the interior of the State. The next move was to Stockton, where the first issue of the Stockton *Times* was printed on the press on March 16, 1850. In a few weeks new equipment displaced the old press and it continued on to Sonora, in the southern mines, where on July 4, 1850, the first issue of the Sonora *Herald* appeared. The last move was to Columbia,

[62] Cowan, *op. cit.*, 21.   [63] Copy in Bancroft Library.
[64] Bancroft, *op. cit.*, V, 292, says the press was purchased by the revolutionary government, but cites no authority for the statement.

where, on October 25, 1851, the Columbia *Star* made its appearance. At Columbia, the career of California's pioneer printing press came to its end. For the history of the last days of the press, we turn, as we did for the story of its coming, to Kemble's article in the Sacramento *Daily Union* for December 25, 1858.

... We have reached the last stage of its long life of usefulness, and must deal circumstantially with the events which terminated its career. In October, Dr. Gunn, of the Sonora *Herald*, sold the Ramage press and some of the old type to G. W. Gore, of Columbia, for the purpose of commencing a paper in that town. The material was removed and the publication commenced on the date above given. A balance of three hundred and seventy dollars remained unpaid, however, for which Gunn sued and attached the press and type. It was sold under execution, and bought by some person bidding for Gunn, for three hundred and ten dollars. After the sale, the press was left standing upon the sidewalk, it being difficult to get a cart the same afternoon to remove it to Sonora, which is but a few miles distant. That night the press was removed into the middle of the street and an act of vandal ruffianism committed which will always be a reproach to the town of Columbia. Either led or instigated by Gore, his companions and sympathizers kindled a fire under the aged relic and destroyed in a few moments what, even in barbarian countries, would have been held in veneration a lifetime, if only as an unmeaning curiosity. A greater outrage never desecrated the name of an American town, or disgraced American citizenship, and the only possible palliation that can be suggested is the very meagre one that the incendiaries may not have known the age and historical value of the old press. There were those in Columbia who evidently attached an archeological interest to the first issue of the press in that town, for we read that an ounce was paid for the first copy of the *Star* that was printed. What a misfortune that these could not have interposed to prevent the destroying of a relic whose history would have been more curious than that of any similar article, perhaps, now in existence. As an heirloom of the art on these shores, its value would have been almost priceless. The destruction of the old press took place on the night of the 13th November. The Sonora *Herald* of the following week, commenting on the occurrence, uses the following language:

"We sent, yesterday, for the charred and half-consumed timber which constituted the frame, and brought it to our office, in front of which it is now deposited, for examination by all who feel interested in the relic. It shall be duly labelled and preserved, not only to show what it once was, and in memory of its past services, but also to show to the better members of society, who are fast emigrating to California, how different has been the character of some of the settlers. The appearance of the press alone, as it now stands, forms a chapter in the history of the State; and whenever a State museum may be established, it shall be placed in it."

Unfortunately for the good intentions of the editor, Sonora has been swept five or six times by conflagrations, and as we do not hear that the remains of the press are still preserved, there is every reason to believe the charred timbers of the Columbia incendiarism have not escaped a second burning, and that they have long since mingled their ashes with those of the town whose fortunes they may have helped to originate, in the printing of the first mining newspaper. As for the Columbia *Star*, it only blinked twice, and was then lost in the glare of the heathenish conflagration it had kindled.[65]

[65] Kemble, *op. cit.*, 198-200.

Chapter ix.

ZAMORANO'S REMAINING YEARS IN CALIFORNIA, NOVEMBER 1836 TO THE SPRING OF 1838.

HERETOFORE, it has been possible for us to follow the movements of Don Agustin V. Zamorano, with more or less certainty. From this point we shall find it much more difficult. He was at Santa Barbara on November 28, 1836.[1] Although I know of no conclusive evidence on the question, I am under the impression he left Monterey too hurriedly for Doña Luisa and the children to accompany him. It is probable that he remained at Santa Barbara until his family could join him. From there, they went to San Diego where they found a home with Doña Luisa's father, Captain Don Santiago Argüello.

That officer had retired from active service in 1835 and Don Agustin had been transferred, on paper as we have seen, from the command of the *presidio* at Monterey to that of San Diego. As Don Agustin did not assume his new post in 1835, the temporary command of San Diego fell to Ensign Don Juan Salazar. When, in December 1836, Captain Zamorano arrived at San Diego there was little over which to take command and it does not appear that he ever did so. Most of the garrison of that post was then scattered among the *escoltas* of the missions of the district and the *presidio*, whose buildings were in a sadly dilapidated condition, was occupied by a mere handful of soldiers.

I. San Diego's Opposition to Alvarado.

The first reaction in the south to the news of the Alvarado-Castro

[1] Statement by Zamorano that Ignacio Coronel had remained loyal to the government and had spurned the advances of the rebels, Santa Barbara, November 28, 1836, MS., in *Coronel, Doc.*, 191.

revolt at Monterey in November 1836 was one of surprised timidity. The southerners had not been close witnesses of the caprices of Chico and had not experienced the excitement of personal participation in the recent events at Monterey. Nor had they been moved by the eloquence and personal magnetism of Don Juan Bautista Alvarado. They were stunned by the news of a rebellion in which they could see neither rhyme nor reason.

As the loyal military officers who left Monterey as quickly after the fall of the *presidio* as possible, reached the south the worst fears of the local residents were confirmed. Judge Don Luis del Castillo Negrete, for whose numerous family room could not be found aboard the *Clementina*, traveled by land from Monterey to San Diego, where he embarked for Mexico. During the weeks he remained in the south, he devoted his time with great energy to attacking the leaders of the revolution with arguments that were sound, invectives that caught the popular fancy, and ridicule that hurt. Such efforts were fuel to the flames of sectional prejudice and soon, in the minds of the *sureños*, the revolt was the work of the *norteños* only and would lead to the oppression of the south. An unswerving and wonderful loyalty and patriotism, as the result, swept the southern country. The central government was being defied. The Church was being attacked. Mexicans were being banished and their property and lives endangered. All hurried to express their loyalty and devotion to the Mexican nation and to put themselves right on the record and thereby avert the terrible consequences of the wrath of the central government when it should learn what had happened.

The first news of the events at Monterey appears to have reached the south by way of the Mexican schooner *Leonidas*, which touched at Santa Barbara about November 15. From Santa Barbara the news spread to Los Angeles and San Gabriel. Lieutenant Don Juan José Rocha, in command of the guard at San Gabriel, on November 19 wrote to Ensign Don Juan Salazar, the commandant at San Diego, and gave him the news from the north. Don Santiago Argüello, the *alcalde* of that place, called a special meeting of the *ayuntamiento* on November 22, to which the public was invited. At this meeting, the town fathers and the people voted, after a long discussion, to remain

Remaining Years in California 213

loyal to the central government, that the "national honor and integrity were at stake," and to send Don Juan Bandini and Don Santiago E. Argüello[2] as commissioners to consult with the authorities at Los Angeles and Santa Barbara on the course to be pursued.[3]

These commissioners reached Los Angeles in time to participate in a special meeting of the *ayuntamiento* and people of that city on November 25 and 26. On the first day, a plan under which the Territory was to be saved was accepted. By its terms, the Monterey revolt was repudiated as an act of violence, the other communities were invited to send three delegates each to a conference at Los Angeles which should select a provisional civil governor, the law making Los Angeles the capital was to be enforced, Lieutenant Rocha was to ask the military officers who had not accepted the Monterey rebellion to select an acting general commandant, the plan was not to be put into effect until the cooperation of San Diego and Santa Barbara was assured, and was to be effective until the national laws were restored.[4]

The commissioners from San Diego returned home and, on November 29, prepared a report of what had taken place at Los Angeles. This report, full of loyalty and determination to avenge the insult to the Mexican nation, was presented at a special public meeting of the *ayuntamiento* on the following day. The plan proposed at Los Angeles was approved and the three commissioners required by it were named.[5]

On December 13, 1836, Don Santiago Argüello sent a report on recent events to the Secretary of Relations in Mexico.[6] As this report, which was forwarded by way of the Colorado River and Arizpe, discussed local efforts only in opposition to the Monterey rebellion and showed a lack of exact knowledge as to what had transpired in

---

[2] Don Santiago E. Argüello was a son of Don Santiago Argüello and a brother of Doña Luisa Argüello de Zamorano.

[3] Minutes of *ayuntamiento*, in *San Diego Archives*, MS., 137-8; also in CLXXXII *Justicia*, Archivo General y Publico, Mexico.

[4] Minutes of *ayuntamiento*, in *Los Angeles Archives*, MS., II, 67-8; IV, 200-12; also in CLXXXII *Justicia*, Archivo General y Publico, Mexico.

[5] Minutes of *ayuntamiento*, in *San Diego Archives*, MS., 139-43; also in CLXXXII *Justicia*, Archivo General y Publico, Mexico.

[6] Santiago Argüello to Secretary of Relations, San Diego, December 13, 1836, MS., *ibid*.

the north, I believe we can safely assume that Don Agustin and his family had not reached San Diego by that date.

All appeared favorable to the creation of a provisional government in the south when, on December 10, the Los Angeles *ayuntamiento* received from that of Santa Barbara a refusal to approve the plan formed at Los Angeles. Santa Barbara refused to take part in a sectional conference and proposed that four delegates from each *presidio* and three from each town should meet at Mission Santa Inés to consider the problems of the Territory as a whole and to choose provisional rulers. The *ayuntamiento* of Los Angeles could see nothing desirable in the new proposal and, after voting thanks to San Diego for its support, adjourned, greatly discouraged.[7]

At San Diego, the schooner *Leonidas* was about to sail for Mazatlan, and Don Santiago Argüello, on December 25, took advantage of that opportunity to duplicate his report of December 13 to the Secretary of Relations. In this report, he displayed a knowledge of the details of events at Monterey and I think it probable that Captain Zamorano aided him in its preparation. Therefore, we can conclude, with reasonable safety, that Don Agustin and his family arrived in San Diego sometime between the 13th and 25th of December, 1836. Don Santiago claimed American adventurers had played a large part in the revolt and that its leaders were doing all they could

> to interest these foreigners in their pronouncement, enticing them with promises of religious freedom and by declaring, as they have already done, all those at present resident in the country to be Californian citizens. Furthermore, there is current a very definite rumor that a considerable force will come from the Sandwich Islands and with them some Protestant missionaries to establish new churches. By these means, they seek to interest the adventurers from the north.

As he was about to close this letter, he received advice from Los Angeles of the refusal of Santa Barbara to support the plan sponsored by Los Angeles and San Diego. Argüello reported this action in his letter and expressed his great disappointment that all their labors had been in vain.[8] This letter he entrusted to Judge del Castillo Negrete

[7] Minutes of *ayuntamiento*, in *Los Angeles Archives*, MS., IV., 215-19.
[8] Santiago Argüello to Secretary of Relations, San Diego, December 25, 1836, MS., in CLXXXII *Justicia*, Archivo General y Publico, Mexico.

whom he asked to inform the central government of the patriotic desires and efforts of himself and the people of San Diego in this crisis.[9] The ship sailed on December 29. Such was the situation at the end of December 1836.

With the opening of 1837, new town councils and officers were installed at the different towns. This appears to have instilled courage in the *ayuntamientos* of both Los Angeles and San Diego, as a new plan was proposed at Los Angeles on January 3. Under this proposal, the Monterey plan was not recognized in so far as it related to independence from Mexico, electors were to assemble "in this capital" and choose a new deputation according to law, the *ayuntamiento* of Los Angeles was to be the chief authority until the meeting of the new deputation, and all was to be submitted to the central government for approval.[10] San Diego accepted the new plan with enthusiasm.[11]

In the meantime, the revolutionary governor, Don Juan Bautista Alvarado, after obtaining a grant of extraordinary powers from the "constituent congress," left Monterey late in December 1836, to quiet the *sureños*. Accompanied by a force that consisted of about sixty Californians and twenty-five foreign riflemen under Graham, he arrived at Santa Barbara on January 3, 1837. There he was received and recognized as governor by Captain Don José Antonio de la Guerra y Noriega and Father Narciso Duran, *padre presidente* of the missions. He was also accepted enthusiastically by Don Carlos Antonio Carillo. Alvarado's reception at the hands of these venerable persons immediately removed all doubt as to Santa Barbara's attitude toward the new government.[12]

The complete success of Alvarado at Santa Barbara was known at Los Angeles by January 8. Alarming rumors prevailed that he intended to march south at once and all the people of the southern city were called to arms. The southern missions were called on for supplies and a request was sent to San Diego to send at once an armed body of patriots to assist in repelling the invader.[13] The *ayuntamiento*

[9] *San Diego Archives*, MS., 149.
[10] *Los Angeles Archives*, MS., I, 126-7.
[11] *San Diego Archives*, MS., 151-3.
[12] Bancroft, *History of California*, III, 491-2.
[13] *Los Angeles Archives*, MS., IV, 228-32.

of San Diego, notwithstanding its previous zeal for the legitimate cause, was rather startled at this sudden, concrete demand and, deciding to move slowly and cautiously, asked for more definite advice as to how the requested force was to be used. A satisfactory reply was received a week later and, on about January 18, twenty men under the direction of Don Pio Pico and Don Francisco Alvarado, as commissioners, started north.[14]

The *Angelinos* did not permit the tardiness of San Diego to interfere with their own preparations for defense and by January 16 about two hundred and seventy men were stationed at Mission San Fernando under the command of Lieutenant Rocha.

The next day, a letter from Alvarado, dated at San Buenaventura on the 16th, was read at a meeting of the Los Angeles city council. Alvarado's allusions to his large resources for war dampened considerably the pugnacious attitude of many of the members and, after a long discussion, it was voted to send two commissioners, Don José Sepúlveda and Don Antonio María Osío, to treat with Alvarado and effect a settlement.[15]

After some delays, in the hope the San Diego representatives would arrive, the commissioners met with Alvarado on January 20. Instead of attempting to arrange a treaty, the commissioners showed their instructions, which were meant to be secret, to Alvarado and obtained his penciled notation of approval written on the margin. The commissioners then claimed that a treaty had been signed and that Alvarado should disband his forces and return to Monterey. This Alvarado, of course, refused to admit. He finally brought the discussion to a close by issuing an ultimatum that if Mission San Fernando were not surrendered to him at once, he would take it by force.

Alvarado's order was obeyed; Rocha retired toward the city with his force, protesting bitterly the decision of the commissioners. The revolutionary army took possession of the mission in the afternoon of January 21.

The contingent from San Diego reached Los Angeles on the same day, before the fall of San Fernando was known. They continued on

[14] Minutes of *ayuntamiento*, in San Diego Archives, MS., 155-66.
[15] Minutes of *ayuntamiento*, in Los Angeles Archives, MS., IV, 238-41.

their way to San Fernando and met Rocha's army in full retreat. There followed another scene between the leaders over the failure to resist Alvarado's advance.[16]

The Los Angeles *ayuntamiento* met again on the following day and, after listening to full reports from its commissioners, voted that no treaty had been made, that all arrangements had been made under duress and were void, that Alta California was not a sovereign state, that Alvarado was not its governor, and that Los Angeles remained ready to defend the national integrity to the last extremity.[17] Two days later, Alvarado marched into and camped within the city without the least resistance being offered. Lieutenant Rocha and his troops were returned to their post at San Gabriel and the local volunteers were disbanded.

On January 26, the *ayuntamiento* met in a special meeting that was attended by all its members, the San Diego commissioners, and Alvarado, accompanied by part of his staff. The patriotic resolutions adopted at the meeting of January 22 were ignored by all present. Alvarado presented a new plan which he thought should be acceptable to all. Its chief point was that a new deputation, to be elected at Santa Barbara on February 25, should pass on all that had been done under the Monterey plan, always supporting federalism and insisting on a native governor. This was formally approved by all present and there followed congratulatory speeches, among which those of Don Pío Pico and Don Antonio María Osío were the most enthusiastic.[18]

With all arrangements made and peace secured, Alvarado moved to San Fernando on February 5 and by the 7th was back at Santa Barbara, from where he sent the Monterey soldiers and Graham's riflemen north.

At San Diego, in the meantime, word came on January 31 that the northern leaders had surrendered.[19] When the truth was learned a few days later, the people were filled with dismay and felt their commissioners had betrayed them to Alvarado. The small body of troops and volunteers that had accompanied the commissioners returned bearing rumors that a force was to be sent to San Diego to organize a

[16] *Ibid.*, IV, 242-52.   [17] *Idem.*   [18] *Ibid.*, IV, 254-62.
[19] *San Diego Archives*, MS., 165.

local company in the newly created civil militia of the new state. The future looked dark to the loyal people of San Diego but there was no thought of giving recognition to the revolutionary government.

Fearing they might be persecuted for their continued loyalty to Mexico, many families emigrated across the frontier to Baja California and others deserted the town for nearby *ranchos*. The military company was disbanded and most of its members also went to the border so as to be beyond call. When Ensign Don Eugenio Montenegro, with about fifty men, reached San Diego on March 13, seeking recruits for the civil militia, he found the town practically deserted. The next day he retired to San Gabriel taking with him a small cannon found at the *presidio* and Don Martín Sánchez Cabello, the customs receiver, Don José María Mier y Teran, the *sindico*, and Don Domingo Amao, secretary of the *ayuntamiento*, as prisoners.

Among those who had withdrawn from the town to nearby *ranchos* was Don Santiago Argüello and Captain Don Agustin V. Zamorano. When Ensign Montenegro reached San Diego they were at Argüello's Rancho de San Antonio Abad, which was better known as Rancho de Ti Juan, from a local Indian name. This place, about twenty miles south of San Diego, was then in Alta California. It is now within the boundaries of the Mexican state of Baja California and the city of Tijuana stands today on ground that once was the property of Don Santiago Argüello. From there, on March 15, 1837, Don Santiago reported again to the Secretary of Relations. He told of the events that had occurred since his report of December 25 and of the efforts that San Diego and Los Angeles had made to oppose the Monterey faction. He painted a sad and gloomy picture of the deplorable state of affairs in Alta California and urged that the government send troops to assist the loyal people of the Territory, who could do nothing because of their lack of resources.[20]

Also from Rancho de Ti Juan, Don Agustin, on April 24, 1837, sent a report to the Secretary of War and Marine. As this was his first letter on events in Alta California after the evacuation of the

---

[20] Santiago Argüello to Secretary of Relations, Rancho de San Antonio Abad, March 15, 1837, MS., in *Legajo* 52-6-9-2.

presidio at Monterey on November 6, 1836, I quote this interesting document in full.

Most Excellent Sir:
When the revolution broke out on November 3 of last year, I was at Monterey serving as secretary of the *comandancia general* under the orders of Lieutenant Colonel Don Nicolás Gutiérrez, who was in temporary command of the Territory because of the absence of Colonel Don Mariano Chico, and I had not taken charge of my regular command which is the cavalry company at San Diego and to which place I have now removed.

The revolutionists forced us to capitulate. Because of this misfortune and because I have a large family which I could neither abandon nor transport to the interior of the Republic, I decided to come to this place, where I have greater resources for a livelihood and from where there are more opportunities to communicate to the superior authorities for their high consideration news of the more important events in the Territory relative to the revolution, as I promised Lieutenant Colonel Gutiérrez I would do.

As I presume the Most Excellent President is familiar with the disturbances that have taken place from the time of the early events up to the departure of the national schooner *Leonidas* at the end of December last, I excuse myself from repeating them so as not to burden the attention of Your Excellency. Therefore, I shall limit myself to subsequent events.

The City of Los Angeles and the Town of San Diego, being disposed to resist the rebels from Monterey, placed more than two hundred men under arms. A few days later, Don Juan Bautista Alvarado, who calls himself colonel of the civil militia and governor of the State of Alta California, appeared before Mission San Fernando with sixty men, and, on seeing the forces that were upholding order, asked for a conference. On the field of battle, he agreed, with the second *alcalde* of the City of Los Angeles, Don José Sepúlveda, the customs receiver, Don Antonio María Osío, and the commissioners from the *presidio* of San Diego, Don Pío Pico and Don Joaquín Ortega, to the treaties which were later formally approved and which are on record in the form of an agreement with the *ayuntamiento* of the City of Los Angeles and of which I have the honor to enclose to Your Excellency a copy that happens to have reached my hands. Although this agreement did not meet with the entire approval of both towns, nevertheless, it was believed it should be ratified. However, at the meeting of the territorial deputation at Santa Barbara, this treaty was completely ignored and that body resolved to carry out the decree which turned it into a constituent congress and the Territory of Alta California into a state.

Persecutions have followed the above act and the revolutionists have proceeded to arrest the persons of Lieutenant Don Juan José Rocha, Don Manuel Requena, Don Antonio del Valle and others, who have been taken to Santa Barbara and from where, it is said, they will be transported to Sonoma, the northernmost settlement in the Territory.

It is reported with considerable reliability that at this place of Sonoma, where Mission San Francisco Solano is located, there is being built a fortress under the direction of Lieutenant Don Mariano G. Vallejo (who is at the head of the rebels, with the title of general commandant of the State and the rank of colonel), with the object of providing a place of refuge in the last extremity should the revolutionists find themselves attacked by Mexican forces.

Also, that Alvarado, out of his private funds, has contracted with a trader from the Sandwich Islands for five hundred guns and considerable ammunition in order to arm the civil militia, which was ordered raised by a decree of the state congress. Instructions for the organization and discipline of this militia have been sent repeatedly to this place but they have been ignored. In the other towns it is already organized. The rebels propose, in case of war, to arm some vessels as coast guards to obstruct any expedition the superior authorities may send to this country, and they have ordered the slaughter of over sixty thousand head of cattle from the missions to meet the expense of this and other measures contingent on the war and for the maintenance of their troops and employees, which are composed of their minions and favorites.

In the near future, Vallejo, according to what he has told Alvarado, is coming to San Diego with two hundred men to entrench himself and repel the forces that are expected by way of the Colorado River from Sonora under the command of Lieutenant Colonel Don Juan José Tobar, who, it is said, awaits only the decision of the central government to set out. Would to God it were tomorrow! I have heard it is said among them that in the event the national government, which they believe to be without resources, should decide to send a military force to this country to reduce it to order, an American foreigner Geems [*Graham*] (who calls himself captain of the Company of Riflemen, composed of American adventurers and of whom there is an abundance in the country) has offered, within two months time, to place at the disposal of the Californians from one to two thousand riflemen, whom he would bring from the Columbia River and other places in the Sierra Nevada occupied by the beaver trappers. Although this can be set down as a bold lie, made with the object of giving himself importance, nevertheless, it does not seem proper that I should keep it from the knowledge of the supreme authorities, as experience in Texas has shown us the venality of these American adventurers, who probably wish, in every way they can, to do just as much harm to Mexico in California.

Due to the disorders in the Territory and because he had not the resources to maintain it, the ensign of my company, Don Juan Salazar, disbanded the remaining troops. Recently Ensign Salazar, as commandant of San Diego, received orders from Vallejo to reassemble the company. When he attempted to do so, Corporal Cristóbal Duarte refused to obey him, as did also Bugler Antonio Elizalde and the soldiers Francisco Silva, Santiago Leiba, Joaquín Soto, Ysidoro Alvitre and Alipas Leiba, telling him they did not recognize the order as it came from the rebels. These men having presented themselves at this ranch, I ordered them to go to the frontier of Baja California, where they would be beyond the persecution of the rebels, and there attach themselves to the frontier company and so continue their service, until they should receive new orders, legally given. They complied with my instructions at once.

During the last few days, various persons have emigrated from San Diego, fleeing before a party of some forty or fifty men commanded by Major Don Eugenio Montenegro, who remained at that place only two days, because he found it almost depopulated and without resources. On retiring, he took with him as prisoners the customs receiver, Don Martín Sánchez Cabello, the *sindico*, Don José María Mier y Teran and Don Domingo Amao, secretary of the *ayuntamiento* of San Diego. The first was taken to Santa Barbara but the other two escaped and have crossed the frontier.

All of which I have the honor of bringing to the superior knowledge of Your Excellency so that you may be pleased to transmit it to the Most Excellent President of the Republic, asking at the same time that you receive my protestations of loyalty and profound respect.

God and Liberty, Rancho de Ti Juan, April 24, 1837.

AGUSTIN V. ZAMORANO

Most Excellent Sir,
Secretary of the Department of War and Marine,
Mexico.[21]

[21] Zamorano to Secretary of War and Marine, Rancho de Ti Juan, April 24, 1837, MS., *ibid.*, No. 22.

II. Zamorano Again Serves as Acting Governor.

The next concerted effort to resist the revolutionary government of Alvarado was made by the military officers. Of all such officers in the Territory on November 6, 1836, only Lieutenant Don Mariano G. Vallejo, and those serving under him, recognized Alvarado as governor. The others wandered to various points in the south, chiefly around Los Angeles and San Diego, and awaited an opportunity to strike. In addition, one or two officers who had sailed with Gutiérrez managed to find their way from Cape San Lucas, where they were landed by the *Clementina*, back to the Alta California frontier.

In the spring of 1837, the district of San Diego, in addition to its other troubles, was harassed by outbreaks of the Indians. Because of the disorganized state of the regular San Diego presidial company and the mission guards, the Indians became bold in their operations. Several *ranchos* were raided by them and many outrages were committed.

While on an expedition against the Indians, Don Santiago Argüello, Captain Zamorano, Don Juan Bandini, Ensign Don Nicanor Estrada, Lieutenant Don Aniceto María Xavaleta, and Don Santiago E. Argüello camped, on May 15, at a place they called Campo de la Palma, several miles south of San Diego. They had with them a force of thirty-nine men that included a sergeant and eleven men of the old frontier cavalry company, a bugler, corporal and six soldiers of the San Diego Company, and nineteen volunteers. They had captured Indians, who, on being questioned, said their activities had been instigated by persons connected with the Monterey rebellion.

This was bitter news to Argüello, Bandini and Zamorano. It was enough that men whom they had known for years and claimed as friends should defy the government and set themselves up as the rulers of the Territory. It was the last dreg in their cup of despair to learn that those same men had incited the savages of their district against them. They became convinced there was no limit to the desperate means to which the leaders of the Monterey faction would descend in their efforts to destroy them. As to the truth of this accusation, I am unable to produce any evidence one way or the other. It would appear very unlikely that it was true. Bancroft dismisses it as absurd.[22] Be that as it may, there can be no doubt as to the sincerity of Argüello, Bandini, and Zamorano in believing it to be true and there can be no question concerning the fury of the Indian depredations.

After bitterly discussing the situation in which they found themselves, the men at Campo de la Palma determined to make a stand, on their own initiative, in the name of the central government against the revolutionists. A new plan was drawn up by Bandini and accepted by all those present. This plan was a rather long document, as those produced by Bandini often were, of twenty articles. Its general purport, after a preamble in which the situation in the Territory and the grievances against the Monterey faction were recited, was that the civil and military commands of the Territory were to be invested temporarily in the senior military officer, the country was to be governed under loyal auspices until the national authority was fully restored and those who had sponsored the Monterey rebellion were to be treated as erring brothers to be forgiven.[23] The senior military officer in the Territory was Captain Don Pablo de la Portilla. Until he could be notified of their action and accept the command of their efforts, Don Agustin, as the officer next senior in rank, agreed to act.

After a few days spent in campaigning against the Indians, the party returned to San Diego on May 20 and, on the following day, submitted its plans to the *ayuntamiento* of that place. It was accepted at once by that body.[24] Don Juan Bandini and Don Santiago E. Argüello were then sent as commissioners to present the new plan to Los Angeles and carried as their credentials a letter from Don Agustin written in the name of the *Comandancia General y Gobierno Politico interino de Alta California*.[25]

---

[22] Bancroft, *op. cit.*, III, 614.
[23] Plan of San Diego, Campo de la Palma, May 15, 1837, MS., in *Legajo* 52-6-9-2, No. 1; *Los Angeles Archives*, MS., IV, 434-45; summarized, Bancroft, *op. cit.*, III, 517, note 3.
[24] Zamorano to *Ayuntamiento* of San Diego, San Diego, May 21, 1837, in *San Diego Archives*, MS., 178; *Dept. St. Pap.*, MS., 83-5.
[25] Zamorano to *Ayuntamiento* of Los Angeles, San Diego, May 21, 1837, in *San Diego Archives*, MS., 178; *Dept. St. Pap., Los Angeles*, MS., XI, 83-5.

The commissioners from San Diego, on arrival at Los Angeles, acted in secret for a few days, taking only a few trusted friends into their confidences. As half of the members of the *ayuntamiento* were believed to favor the revolutionary government, it was thought best to capture the guards and guns of the local militia company before appealing to the people. This seizure was effected on the evening of May 26. The following morning the *ayuntamiento* was convened and Bandini presented his plan. After considerable discussion, it was accepted by the majority.[26] A few days later, an urgent call for assistance came from Captain Zamorano. The Indians had defeated a detachment sent against them and every effort was being made to raise a large force to conquer them once and for all. The city council met in a secret session on May 31 and voted to suspend all political and military plans for the present and to send assistance to the southern frontier.[27] Bandini and his party returned at once to San Diego, taking with them the cannon that had been carried off in March.

In the midst of the preparations for the expedition against the Indians, Captain Portilla arrived at San Diego. On June 5, Captain Zamorano turned his provisional command over to him and, on the same day, sent the following report to the Secretary of War and Marine, in Mexico.

Most Excellent Sir:
Various individuals of the Town of San Diego, who have remained faithful to the will of the central government of the Mexican Republic, finding themselves threatened by the insurgents of the north, determined to retire to the mountains and abandon their homes and families, rather than allow themselves to be ruled by that faction.

The unjust persecutions by the rebels and the threats of the neighboring savage Indians, caused a handful of these truly honorable inhabitants to declare in favor of the restoration of the Territory of Alta California to the order and obedience of the national government. In this, they counted on no other resources than their own persons, some old muskets, which with a thousand troubles they repaired, and a few homemade lances. I have the honor to pass to Your Excellency's superior hands a copy of their Plan as Document No. 1.

[26] Bandini to Zamorano, Los Angeles, May 28, 1837, MS., in *Legajo* 52-6-9-2; *Los Angeles Archives*, MS., IV, 434-45.
[27] Minutes of *ayuntamiento*, in *Los Angeles Archives*, MS., IV, 316-18.

The rebels from Monterey have neglected no opportunity to remind us that they prefer to see the ruin of their country than to see it once more dominated by the Mexicans, whom they stupidly call their oppressors. To that end, they aroused the neighboring pagan Indians, sending them against this town, which, with great courage and desperation, has determined to die or conquer those tyrannical usurpers of a power they are unfitted to wield and destroyers of the little wealth and peace that benefited this Territory.

It was not many days before we suffered the effects of a project as horrible as it was fantastic. At the beginning of last month, some pagan *rancherias*, together with a few converted neophytes who lived among us as domestics, plotted an uprising against this *presidio* and the ranches within its jurisdiction. They planned to strike the fatal blow at all places on the same day, in order to kill all the men whom they call white and to carry off all our women to the mountains and there begin a new race. Happily, one of the bands of barbarians got ahead of the day set for the execution of this horrible and bloody plan, and, invading Rancho de Jamul, the property of the *Señores* Pico, and combining with the Indian servants of that establishment, cruelly massacred all the few whites found there. They carried away two daughters of the majordomo and some stock, and set fire to the house and such of its contents as they were unable to remove. This event, which took place before the pronouncement of the Plan of which I speak, forced us to form an expedition against these savage aggressors. They were attacked wherever the roughness of the terrain in the mountains where they fled would permit, and suffered the loss of twenty dead and some wounded while we suffered two slightly wounded. The detachment retired soon after, because it was impossible to drive the enemy from the wilderness before darkness set in.

From the testimony taken from the lookouts of the enemy, who were captured, and the statement made by one of the Indian servants, who was invited to attend the questioning, their criminal plan was luckily discovered. We captured five of those implicated and executed them at once; one of them leaving the statement they had been aroused by the rebels in the north. The day before, another Indian, being drunk, dared to cry publicly, "Long live California the Free!" which is the cry by which the northern revolutionists distinguish themselves. When he was sought for arrest, he had fled among the pagans.

Our expedition returned to the *presidio* of San Diego on May 20 last. The following day, the Plan was made public and the *ayuntamiento* and its people accepted it immediately. By virtue of it, I was entrusted with the political and military commands until Captain Don Pablo de la Portilla, who was absent, should take ad interim charge of them.

It was then decided to send a second expedition to the mountains and, while the operations against the rebellious savages were being carried out, a commission to carry our Plan to the City of Los Angeles so that its *ayuntamiento* might accept and proclaim it. However, as that city was occupied by a guard left there by the northern rebels, the commissioners thought it best to surprise that garrison first and to discharge afterwards the mission with which they were entrusted. The result was a happy one and copies Nos. 2 and 3 will inform Your Excellency in detail of all that took place at that time.

In the meantime, I was awaiting the return of the second expedition to the mountains and the completion of the mounting of a six pound piece. I then planned to march the forces that followed me to the City of Los Angeles, take possession of the town of San Gabriel, establish my general headquarters there and from that point begin my campaign against the rebels in the north. In all this, however, I was frustrated by the receipt of a note from the sergeant in command of the expedition to the mountains, a copy of which I duly enclose for Your Excellency as No. 4. This reverse forced us to change the direction of our thoughts and we dedicated ourselves exclusively to the suppression of the insolent savages, who were inflated over the victory they had gained. I then ordered the commission which I had sent to the City of Los Angeles to return with the piece of artillery it had recaptured. I was in the midst of the preparations for the third expedition against the Indians when Captain Don Pablo de la Portilla arrived to take charge of the command and I at once turned it over to him. That officer is now in charge and is making the necessary preparations to attend to both enemies.

The northern rebels thought the pacification of the Territory complete, as Your Excellency will learn from the printed broadside published by him who calls himself governor of the State, which I also duly attach for Your Excellency as No. 5. In it Your Excellency will find a number of contradictions and see the insolence with which they dare insult the supreme government of the Nation.

The rebels, having received news of the impending arrival of troops sent by the national government, have withdrawn the bulk of their forces to Monterey. In the meantime, they have made a horrible slaughter of cattle, in order to pay, with the hides, for a vessel, which, so it is said, they intend to arm as a coast guard to prevent the landing of the troops sent by the central government.

I urgently beg Your Excellency to interpose your powerful influence to the end that the troops which, according to the unofficial advice we have, are being sent by order of the national government, may arrive in this Territory as soon as possible. The hope of seeing on these shores the gleam of the bayonets which make the valiant Mexican eagle invincible will inspire us to maintain ourselves in our firm resolution for a few months. On the other hand, their delay will encourage the enemy, who possess all the resources we lack, and will confirm their idea that Mexico is too weak to send troops to this distant region of the Republic, and they will continue preparing themselves for an interminable war.

It is my duty to recommend very especially to the consideration of Your Excellency the retired captain, Don Santiago Argüello, who, because of the arrival at this port of a party of rebels from the north, emigrated on March 15 to the frontier of Baja California in company within Ensign Nicanor Estrada and Don Juan Bandini, for the purpose of enlisting men and declaring themselves against the insurgents. They were able to assemble some soldiers from the frontier company, in the absence of the sergeant who commanded them, and others who, like themselves, had emigrated from San Diego. This force Señor Argüello transferred to the Ti Juan Ranch, a property of his, and maintained out of his private purse from that date until May 20 last, when we set out for this point. Also, he provided two thousand rifle balls, a small amount of powder in bulk, which were the only ammunition on which we could count, and the guns that he had provided for the defense of his ranch, which he finally abandoned to the Indians, with its buildings and its planted fields, in order to support our pronouncement. He also offered his personal services in the class of a simple volunteer.

A like sacrifice, and for the same principles, was made by Don Juan Bandini of his ranch named Tecate, where his loss was considerable, and I recommend this good patriot also to Your Excellency.

Also, I recommend to the consideration of Your Excellency Ensign Estrada because of his personal services in the repair of various firearms, which he placed in condition for use, and in the construction of fifty lances, which he made with skill and for which task he transported with considerable difficulty his blacksmith's tools all the way to the frontier.

I have the duty of enclosing for Your Excellency as No. 6 a list of the names of the soldiers and civilians who composed the force supporting our Plan, believing it justly within my duty to recommend them also to Your Excellency's consideration, as I now do, because of the courage these stalwart defenders of the Mexican government possessed, in the midst of the miseries and persecutions they suffered, to proclaim themselves for the order of the Laws against the greater part of the Territory.

All of which I have the honor of reporting to Your Excellency in compliance with my duty, begging you to be so kind as to bring it to the superior knowledge of the Most Excellent President of the Republic for whatever use he may see fit, and that Your Excellency will be pleased to accept the protestations of my high consideration and profound respect.

God and Liberty, Port of San Diego, June 5, 1837.

AGUSTIN V. ZAMORANO

Most Excellent Sir,
Secretary of the Department of War and Marine,
Mexico.[28]

III. The Campaign of 1837.

Just as Captain Zamorano's report, quoted above, gives the history of the San Diego effort, in 1837, to oppose the revolutionary government headed by Don Juan Bautista Alvarado to June 5, the report rendered to the Secretary of War and Marine on September 12, 1837, by Captain Portilla gives the complete story of the campaign that followed. Don Agustin was present with Portilla's forces throughout this campaign.

Most Excellent Sir:

As a result of the pronouncement made by some of the citizens of San Diego, with the object of restoring Alta California to the order of the Laws, I was called on to assume the political and military commands, and, on the fifth of June last, I was placed in ad interim possession of them by Captain Don Agustin V. Zamorano, who was discharging them provisionally until such time as I could present myself.

That officer had organized an expedition to the mountains to pacify the pagan Indians, who were on the warpath, and I ordered his plan to be carried out because I believed it necessary. This expedition had departed, and was in fact four leagues distant from this post, when, on June 12, I received positive information that the rebels from the north had invaded the City of Los Angeles on the tenth of the same month with eighty men and were then marching on San Diego with the intention of reducing it to their will. This advice made it necessary to order the return of the expedition sent to the mountains. In the meantime, some fifty-one rounds of grape and cannon balls for the two pieces of four and six pounds and two thousand or more cartridges for the guns were manufactured as ammunition for the division, composed of seventy men which I commanded in person. We set out, determined to engage the rebels from Monterey wherever we might meet them.

[28] Zamorano to Secretary of War and Marine, San Diego, June 5, 1837, MS., in *Legajo* 52-6-9-2, No. 34.

Remaining Years in California 229

On the same day, the twelfth, we received unofficially a copy of the constitutional laws, which were sent to us from the frontier by the Reverend Father Fr. Felix Caballero. We published them at once and the *ayuntamiento* and citizens of San Diego took the oath to them. In possession of these august laws, we laid aside the Plan proclaimed on May 15 at Campo de la Palma, of which my immediate predecessor has already given Your Excellency an account, and the object of our journey was now to make the northern rebels take the oath, willingly or by force, to these laws. I took for myself only the title of Commander of the Division of Operations of the Supreme Government.

We wrote, on the thirteenth, to Captain Don Andrés Castillero, commandant of the frontier, that, in the event he was free to aid us with the force with which he had arrived there, he should do so, as we were threatened by the northerners and it was imperative that we repel them.

On the same day, the thirteenth, with all in readiness, we began our march, leaving Captain Don Santiago Argüello, retired, to attend to the warring savages. On the fourteenth, we arrived at Mission San Luis Rey.

The fifteenth, we spent at that place in making repairs to the four pounder, as its limber had completely broken down and it was necessary to construct a forked pole for it so that it might be easily drawn by oxen. At this mission, we were joined by Captain Castillero, accompanied by a sergeant and eight dragoons from the frontier, in answer to the assistance we had requested of him. This captain then stated to us verbally that he had received a commission from the central government to mediate the Monterey revolution, but that he had left this document at the frontier with his baggage because of the haste in which he had left to join us. Because of this and my previous knowledge of him, I believed he spoke in good faith and, naturally, I then considered him as invested with the character of an envoy from the superior authorities for the object stated. We agreed that he might discharge his mission within sight of our division.

We went, on the sixteenth, to Mission San Juan Capistrano, where we arrived at eight o'clock at night. There we found Lieutenant Don Andrés Pico and Ensign Don Ignacio Palomares, who had deserted from the division of Don José Castro, with ten men they had gathered. They had taken possession of that place and soon presented themselves before me as having declared in favor of the Constitution and the Government. On the seventeenth, I ordered them to be attached to the company of volunteers and we continued our march to the Santa Ana Ranch.

On the eighteenth, I set out with the division for the City of Los Angeles. At Rancho de los Nietos, we were met by the ensign of the Santa Barbara Company, Don Anastacio Carrillo. He appeared before me and stated that he came as commissioner from Don José Castro, commander of the division of the north, who desired to have an interview with Captain Don Andrés Castillero in the City of Los Angeles so that he might inform him of his good disposition toward the Constitution and his desire that all should end in a reasonable manner. Before giving Ensign Carrillo a reply, I ordered the division to continue to the San Gabriel River, which may have been half a league distant. At Paso de Bartolo, on that river, I ordered a halt to consider Castro's request and so that the men might eat. We had hardly established our camp when we took up our arms because of the warning that the northerners were bearing down to attack us on our right flank, the opposite direction from where we supposed them to be. We prepared to fight them. No action took place, however, as it proved to be Lieutenant Don Juan José Rocha coming to our camp with a few servants from the Alamitos Ranch. Nevertheless, we remained on guard and doubled the number of our pickets. We then held a council of war to consider if Captain Castillero should or should not go to Los Angeles, as Castro desired. It was decided that both divisions should form in line of battle within sight of each other at the distance of a cannon shot apart, that Captain Castillero should grant the interview requested by Castro half way between, and that our opponents should be required to choose, in that interview, between taking the oath to the Constitution, laying down their arms and submitting to the central government or, in the event of refusal, engaging our division in battle. Castro's commissioner left at once and I, with a view to selecting the most suitable place at which to hold the interview, ordered the division to resume the march toward Los Angeles. On the way, we met Don Pio Pico who gave me a message from the commissioner, Carrillo, which said that he had informed Castro of our decision but that the latter was unable to decide the question alone and needed to consult with Don Juan B. Alvarado, to whom he had to show consideration as he considered himself so pledged; therefore, as a prudent man, he found it best to retire toward the north. We continued our march and at six o'clock in the evening came in sight of the capital city and camped on the hills facing it. We then considered sending a party after that of Castro and surprising him that same night by overtaking him at Mission San Fernando, where we supposed he might be. But it was not deemed advisable as we believed our party could not overtake him since we knew he was traveling in great haste to Santa Barbara and had put a lot of ground between us. While it might have been possible to have followed him to that place, doing so would have meant leaving our two field pieces exposed to capture by some of our many enemies living in the City of Los Angeles. For these reasons, it was decided not to follow him. Therefore, we passed the night on the hills.[29]

On the morning of the nineteenth, we entered the City of Los Angeles. I immediately ordered the Illustrious *Ayuntamiento* to assemble and, making the constitutional laws known to it, we proceeded to their publication, which was solemnly done by national edict. They were publicly sworn to by that body, before whom I took the oath at once. It was also taken by the officers and troops of the division, who formed in the principal square, immediately after. When this act, which was solemnized by the ringing of bells and salvos of artillery, was concluded, I ordered the division to march to San Gabriel, a distance of three leagues, where we arrived at three o'clock in the afternoon.

We delayed at this mission through the twentieth and twenty-first. This time was spent in repairing the trailer of the six pounder, some of its tools, and those of the other piece, which had been broken on the march, and in making others that were needed for replacements. All the ammunition for the cannons had to be made over, either because it was badly constructed in the beginning or because it was damaged on the road from not having been packed securely.

On the twenty-second, the division was again put in motion and continued to Mission San Fernando. We went by way of Los Angeles for the purpose of picking up one hundred and fifty *pesos* in silver and one hundred and seventy in goods which the commercial interests of that city furnished as a voluntary loan, as was requested of them, to supply the urgent needs of the troops, and to add to our division the volunteers requested of the first *alcalde*. After we had received a load of rice and the sum of money mentioned and found that the first *alcalde* was unable to assemble the men that had been requested of him, the order was given, at three o'clock in the afternoon, to continue the march.

At sunset, we camped near the Rancho de los Verdugos, and there

---

[29] From his camp at Santa Rita, Castro wrote to the leaders of the Southern army as follows: "*Señores Bandini, Zamorano, Cabello, and Ramírez:* Let the Californians alone and they will come out all right. If you continue among them, you will cause the country's ruin and that of the families and people. If Don Pio Pico, Andrés Pico, or the Argüellos were leading your division everything could be settled. But you are very wicked men, you have no prestige, or a cent of money. Lose all hope that we shall ever be centralists, or that any of you shall ever be governor of this Department. If I say nothing about Don Pablo de la Portilla, it is because he is a very good man. Watch out, for I am not far from you, and if I did not have good intentions it would be a different situation. We shall soon see each other. *José Castro*." In *Legajo* 52-6-9-2, No. 1.

passed the night. Soon after leaving Los Angeles, however, I received word that the requested enlistment of *Angelinos* as volunteers had not been accomplished because of the lack of energy on the part of the first *alcalde* and the influence in that city of those who favored the revolution, which made all endeavor fruitless, but that, nevertheless, if I presented myself in company with Don Pio Pico and Don Antonio María Lugo in that city those gentlemen could levy on all the persons who might be able to go on a campaign as well as on those who might lend weapons and those who might lend horses. Therefore, I returned with those gentlemen and Captain Castillero and that afternoon those who were to render one or the other kind of assistance were selected. They were advised that I would wait for them at San Fernando. Captain Castillero and I then returned to the division, which we found at Los Verdugos.

We continued our march on the twenty-third and took possession of Mission San Fernando. There we stayed through the twenty-fourth and twenty-fifth, in order to repair some of our arms requiring it and to await the force that was being sent from Los Angeles. At this mission, we received the information that Castro, with his division and the forces he had assembled at Santa Barbara, had fortified himself at the place called El Rincon in order to obstruct our passage and waited there to resist us. In the afternoon of the twenty-fifth, Don Antonio María Lugo arrived with twenty-four men he had collected in Los Angeles. The same day the order was given to march on San Buenaventura and take possession of that place.

On the twenty-sixth, in the morning, as the division was about to move against San Buenaventura, I received a letter from the military commander I had left in San Diego stating that place was threatened by the pagans and that many families, from fear of them, were planning to desert the town. I had a private conference with all the officers of the division on the question of which would be the better thing to do—to go to the aid of San Diego or to continue our march on San Buenaventura. The majority of the officers thought we should go to the relief of the Dieguiños, who were defenseless. Therefore, the order was given to suspend the march.

At the angelus on that same evening, the twenty-sixth, Don Carlos Antonio Carrillo, administrator of Mission San Buenaventura, presented himself as an envoy from Don José Castro with a letter for Captain Don Andrés Castillero. In this, Castro stated his inclination to accept the present form of government but that he waited the arrival of the governor, Don Juan B. Alvarado, and the general commandant, Don Mariano G. Vallejo, before doing so and that Carrillo came as his commissioner to make his other sentiments known. In view of this and in order to solve the problem with proper circumspection, I gave orders to call a council of war. It was agreed, when all the officers had assembled, that Carrillo should be admitted to the meeting to state Castro's propositions. When they were heard, it was decided that, since Captain Castillero had repeatedly stated he came on a commission from the national government to settle the Monterey revolution, he might attempt to do so and he was given, on behalf of our division, several reasonable instructions. By this means we hoped to avoid shedding the blood of Mexicans. The details of what took place at this council are given in the minutes, a copy of which I have the honor of placing in Your Excellency's hands as No. 1.

In agreement with the decision of the council, Captain Castillero departed for Santa Barbara before dawn on the twenty-seventh, in company with Don Carlos A. Carrillo. I gave him some instructions, of which I duly enclose a copy as No. 2. While he was absent on this matter, the division occupied itself with making repairs to its unserviceable armament and the troops employed their time in regular drills, especially the volunteers, who had to maneuver as infantry.

Captain Castillero returned on the thirty-first and informed us that on arriving at San Buenaventura he was received by an advance guard of the northern insurgents and conducted to the place known as La Cañada de los Sauzes [the glen of the willows], where he had an interview with the governor, Don Juan B. Alvarado, who had just come down from Monterey with additional troops to reenforce the place El Rincon, which they had fortified. In this interview, Alvarado stated that he and his forces would not take the oath to the constitutional laws so long as our division should insist on compelling them to do so by force, but that they would take it voluntarily and would place themselves at the disposal of the central government. In corroboration of this, Captain Castillero showed us the letter that Alvarado had given him, a copy of which I pass to Your Excellency's superior hands as No. 3. In addition, he told us that Alvarado had given little heed to the instructions I had given him and, furthermore, that Alvarado wished to deal with him only in the matter and not with our division. This can also be inferred from the contents of the cited document No. 3, as in it can be seen the resentment he bears against the *Dieguiños*, who have never accepted his schemes and have been consistently faithful to the central government. And he accuses them of being fratricides! How absurd! If those rebels were so willing to take the oath to the constitutional laws, why did they not do so before our movement started, since they had them in their hands before we did? If our division had not moved with the object of making them take the oath, would the northern revolutionists have declared themselves for these laws? It is evident that they would not have; and it is also obvious that fear of our arms and the force from Mexico, concerning which a rumor that it was soon to occupy Alta California was circulated with great benefit, and nothing else, made them change so promptly from the error into which they fell on November 7, when they proclaimed the unfortunate federal system. If they were so well disposed toward and so much in sympathy with the opinions Señor Castillero stated to them, why then, in their original pronouncement, did they overthrow the basic laws of the present system, which last year were published and sworn to throughout all California? Did those august basic laws indicate they would deprive California of the great advantages it was going to enjoy by being raised to the level of the rest of States, now Departments? Why then did they ignore them and proclaim themselves for federalism? How they have tried to disguise their crimes! If your Excellency will be pleased to make a comparison of the proclamation printed on May 10 last, which was issued by Señor Alvarado and which was sent to Your Excellency by my immediate predecessor, with the original document I enclose as No. 4, Your Excellency will see sentiments that are diametrically opposite, and all from his Worship, the self-styled acting governor, Don Juan B. Alvarado.

I would have made this Señor Governor deal with me, notwithstanding his excuses, but to do that would have meant using force and would not have made him and his followers take the oath to the Laws and we would have lost that victory, which, however much he may wish to deny it, was due to the sight of our forces. For the mere presence of Señor Castillero would have seemed insignificant to him, especially as the latter presented himself without credentials to authenticate his commission. There were also many other considerations, not the least of which was that already mentioned, the threats of the savages against San Diego, to which it was necessary that I attend, and, finally, if hostilities had been started by our division the war would, I am firmly convinced, have lasted interminably. There were also the considerations that we would be stirring up against us the odium of all the patricians [*patricios*] and that the northern revolutionists, already so inclined, might call to their aid the forces of the foreigners, principally those of the North Americans, who would unite with them readily, either because of the warlike moves which the Northern States have been making against Mexico or because of the propensity we hear among them to possess themselves of California. We would be giving them a powerful incentive to attempt what they might, perhaps, accomplish, to the detriment of the national honor, and it might be very difficult and costly to the government afterwards to recover these possessions. Therefore, ignoring the disdain of Señor Governor Alvarado, which I believed was only the child of his resentment, I sent him a note, of which I enclose a copy to Your Excellency as No. 5, and which was delivered by Captain Castillero, who returned to Santa Barbara to conclude his mission. I then ordered the division to leave San Fernando and to establish its general headquarters at Mission San Gabriel. This was done, so as to be within sight of the northerners and to attend to the savage enemies in the south. However, there was disorder in the division that day and each man went off in his own direction. I reached San Gabriel with scarcely forty men. This was caused by Ensign Don Nicanor Estrada, who was the only officer opposed to affairs being settled in a reasonable and amicable manner.

While I was at San Gabriel, Captain Castillero returned from Santa Barbara. He then assured me that Alvarado and his forces had retired from El Rincon and had taken the oath to the Constitution and issued instructions that this be done in the northern towns. He delivered to me the official letter from Alvarado of which I enclose Your Excellency a copy as No. 6. Although I several times requested Captain Castillero to give me in writing the results of the mission with which our division had entrusted him, he never wanted to do so and made only promises. In the end, I never did receive it and for that reason I state that his reports to me were verbal. Finally he sailed for Acapulco in company with Ensign Estrada. They, according to reports, are going as commissioners from Alvarado with letters to the central government.

With the taking of the oath to the Constitution by the north, the reorganization of order and the peace of California has resulted. However, there remained the problem of its chief political authority. Although, by the supreme order of January 21, 1835, that office should fall on the general commandant, which office I believe I should exercise because the succession to the military office belongs to me under the general regulations of the army, I did not wish to contest it with Alvarado, who is the senior member of the Most Excellent Deputation, for the reason that to do so would make it necessary to disturb anew the peace that was beginning to prevail. Furthermore, Alvarado's procedure was consistent with the Constitution, which supercedes the order of January 21, 1835, and I left it to him to discharge until the central government makes its decision and contented myself solely with exercising the general command of the army, to which effect I wrote the letter of which I send Your Excellency a copy as No. 7. In this, it did not seem to me necessary to point out that this office belonged to me but I wanted to have his opinion in order to judge his good or bad intentions after his change in principles. The copy marked No. 8 is his reply and, as a result of it, the lieutenant of the San Francisco Company, Don Mariano G. Vallejo, who holds the office of general commandant in conformity with the resolution of the deputation on November 7 last, sent out to all the officers present in the Territory the circular letter given in copy No. 9, asking them to assemble at Monterey to determine, in a council of war, the person on whom the office of general commandant should rest and to make delivery of it. I have replied to him that there is no necessity for such a council because the general regulations of the army clearly indicate what should be done in this case. Up to the present there has been no action in the matter.

This, Most Excellent Sir, is the state in which the country finds itself today. However, Your Excellency, the permanence of peace cannot be assured for long, because, I believe, from the steps taken to date and the bitterness against the Mexicans to be seen in their writings, they wait only to learn the news of the political state that exists generally throughout the Republic before proceeding in accordance with their own ideas. For this reason, it is my belief that the national government should not neglect this country, which is the master key that guards the western departments, but should arrange to protect it by sending a military chief of good judgment, with a force sufficient to make him respected; because if this is not done, its measures will be without force and the country exposed to total ruin.

All of which I have the honor to advise Your Excellency, asking you to be pleased to bring my exposition before His Excellency, the President of the Republic, for whatever use he may see fit, assuring him at the same time of my protestations of profound respect and high consideration.

God and Liberty, Port of San Diego, September 12, 1837.

PABLO DE LA PORTILLA

Most Excellent Sir,
Secretary of the Department of War and Marine,
Mexico.[30]

There are many bits of internal evidence that this report was either written by Captain Zamorano or that he assisted in its preparation. The first of these is its straightforwardness and explicitness, characteristics not found in most of the documents left by Captain

---
[30] Portilla to Secretary of War and Marine, San Diego, September 12, 1837, MS., in *Legajo* 52-6-9-2, No. 39.

Portilla, who, as an officer, was notorious for his slackness. Another is the many references to and the writer's evident familiarity with Don Agustin's report of June 5, 1837, to the Secretary of War and Marine. A third indication is that Portilla's concluding sentiments are almost identical with those expressed by Don Agustin in his report of November 16, 1832, to the same department. In that report he had written that California was

> . . . no less than the master key that will safeguard us from the west . . . But none of this happiness shall be ours if the national government does not take its development seriously and quickly adopt wise measures to assure the integrity of these offices by sending the officer, troops, arms, munitions, and funds of which I spoke before, the necessity for which makes itself felt with increasing force day by day.

This was a recommendation he made many times and he no doubt felt that recent events had confirmed his earlier judgment.

Alvarado and his followers took the oath to the new constitution at Santa Barbara on July 9, 1837. This step was at once his greatest defeat and his greatest triumph. As an advocate of a free and independent Alta California and of federalism, it was a humiliating retreat. On the other hand, with the Territory restored to its national allegiance, the deputation resumed its former powers and Alvarado, as its senior member, became the legal acting governor, which was a crushing defeat for the *sureños*. Castillero's authority in claiming a commission from the national government and the arguments and inducements he used to convert Alvarado to centralism are mooted questions in California's history. They are of slight interest to us here, however, and we shall not go further into them.

Captain Portilla on July 4, 1837, from Mission San Fernando, sent the southern *ayuntamientos* notice of the results of Castillero's negotiations. From San Diego, on July 8, Don Santiago Argüello replied, complaining bitterly. It was his opinion the rebels should have been forced to negotiate with Captain Portilla and to take the oath before his division. He claimed the victors had been dictated to by the vanquished and feared that a trick had been played and that all his sacrifices would prove to have been in vain.[31] There is no doubt that

[31] Argüello to Portilla, San Diego, July 8, 1837, *ibid*.

many of the *sureños* felt they had been tricked and deceived by their supposed friend, Captain Castillero. That officer's failure to render a report to his supporters was rather shabby treatment after the service they had rendered. If he had presented himself without written credentials and without the support of the southern army, Alvarado, as Portilla said, would have paid him slight attention. There was nothing, however, that the southern patriots could do but nurse their disappointment and wait for whatever the future might bring.

The chief question that remained unanswered was who should fill the office of acting general commandant. Lieutenant Don Mariano G. Vallejo had filled that office under Alvarado's revolutionary government but he was obviously not entitled to it under the constitutional regime then being set up; it belonged, by the general regulations of the army, to the senior officer present in the Territory. That officer was Captain Portilla. In this connection, Alvarado wrote two interesting letters from Santa Barbara to Vallejo. These were personal letters and show Alvarado's skill at playing the game of politics. The letter of July 12, written three days after he had taken the oath to the new constitution, was his first to Vallejo after that event.

Santa Barbara, July 12, 1837.

My dear Uncle:

You must know by now, from the circular I sent north after my last interview with Don Andrés Castillero, of all that has happened with me since I left you. On the ninth, we took the oath to the central constitution, not because there is no longer any other remedy but, on the contrary, because it actually offers us guaranties and gives us advantages which we did not enjoy under the defunct one. Read it and you will see that it is not the flattery of a widower bridegroom.

All is now arranged except concerning the *comandancia general* and I do not know whether it should fall to Don Pablo de la Portilla or to Don José Antonio de la Guerra y Noriega. I should lean by preference in favor of the former and you may give me your opinion in the matter.

Castillero and Don Pio are here, the former is in the best of disposition and is willing to accompany the commission that may go to Mexico. I believe that he may be of some service, not only because he has been an eyewitness of our pronouncement and its consequences but also because of the influence exercised by his brothers in the national government, as at present it is to our advantage to place ourselves under its protection. After that let come what may.

In the meantime, order as you will of your affectionate nephew, who kisses your hand.

JUAN B. ALVARADO[32]

Santa Barbara, July 17, 1837.

My esteemed Uncle:

Yesterday the deputation convened here. I called it so as to begin the organization of a constitutional regime and, also, I found Don Pio in a mood to cooperate with that crowd of hoodlums that continues, gathered in part at San Gabriel, under the command of Portilla, whom the ruffians and drunkards want as general commandant and civil governor (even though the constitution may not appoint him) because he is a great tolerator of mischief, due to his generous heart and that of his director, Zamorano.

Señor Castillero has decided to protect the stability of my government—he even went so far as to point out to me that if it were not for the obstacle presented by the laws the *comandancia* should be left in your hands, because, from what he had seen, he had not found an officer in all that rabble in the south capable of preserving order even in his own home. He has assured me that he is going to make it so known to the government. Therefore, I intend sending him to Mexico in the schooner and he has offered to act as the commissioner who will talk to the government and he will convince it more completely that justice has been on the side of the natives.

Captain Castillero left here yesterday for San Gabriel to withdraw the troops he brought from the frontier, which I asked of him in view of the fact that the Indians are menacing that district and because of the disorders, tolerated by Portilla and Zamorano, committed by the soldiers at San Gabriel, who, without thinking, want to make them the rulers of the country. There are twenty-four mounted soldiers from the frontier, undisciplined and insubordinate. He will soon return here.

Nothing has been said concerning the *comandancia general* because I have not wanted it considered in the deputation. Portilla and Zamorano are wanting it; so it is time that you, acting as such, should make the required invitation to Noriega. The latter has turned into a friend against the former, and, according to what he told me yesterday, he has no confidence in a single officer other than yourself (but he does not expect anything on that account; he has remained very quiet). Your proclaiming, without reservation on your part, of Noriega, who is of our party, will leave Portilla and Zamorano fooled, and give them a good drubbing. I, remaining with the powers of governor, in con-

---

Alvarado to Vallejo, Santa Barbara, July 12, 1837, MS., in *Vallejo, Doc.*, IV, 282.

formity with the constitution, will help a little and then you will have us as victors in everything. These are my opinions and the reasons why I hurry this special message.

Bandini has already retired, quite satisfied that I should hold the reins of government, because Castillero told them that was the law and that they should not deviate the slightest from it. The aspiring leaders of the other side have been left humiliated and the whole division has dispersed except for some hungry colonists and some very poorly armed men from the frontier.

Such is the condition in which things are. I continue in this place with some concern.

The Indians are attacking San Diego. They burned all the nearby ranches and they almost captured the *presidio*.

The commission to Mexico will leave soon and it would be a good thing if you should send a communication to the government.

Yesterday, I received mail from Monterey in which Villa tells me officially that he has been acting with respect to the affair of the *castillo* in accordance with orders that you have given him.

I commend that rascal Peña to you, and also Ramírez and all the rest. Castillero tells me that any troops the government may send will be delayed a long while and that there is time for him to arrive there to prevent any such expedition. It is necessary to move at once so that we may remain well fixed.

The *Padre Presidente* has shown himself as my best friend, and of all the Californians. Some day, I shall have a talk with you on that point, and shall give you proofs of his good behavior. As soon as I send the vessel and can leave these places in order, I shall go north and I wish that you would come south and have an interview with Noriega.

This gentleman, as you know, is an upright officer and will agree with you without argument on the organization of the presidial companies similar to what they used to be, which opinion you have given me on previous occasions. I also think the same.

JUAN B. ALVARADO[33]

Lieutenant Vallejo does not appear to have accepted gracefully Alvarado's suggestion that he relinquish the military command. On August 1, he sent letters to all the military officers. In these he stated that as all the troubles were over he was considering resigning the command to which the legislature had called him. Therefore, he thought it opportune to assemble the officers in a council of war at

---

[33] Alvarado to Vallejo, Santa Barbara, July 17, 1837, MS., *ibid.*, IV, 283.

Monterey on August 31 for the purpose of selecting an acting general commandant and making delivery of that office. If they could not be present, he asked that they advise him of their choice.[34] It was evident that Vallejo had received his training under Echeandia.

Most of the officers in the Territory paid little attention to this summons as they thought the council was unnecessary; the regulations were clear in the matter and the office belonged to the senior officer present—Portilla. The meeting, therefore, was never held, Vallejo's intended resignation was never made, and the military was without a commander.

Captain Zamorano returned to San Diego sometime during the month of August. He had promised the officers of Portilla's division to prepare a complete and detailed report of the division's operations and the negotiations with Alvarado. However, as Captain Castillero, after his successful interview with Alvarado, never saw fit to take his southern colleagues into his confidence and as the negotiations with Alvarado were the most important thing on which to report, Don Agustin's exposition of the southern division's operations was never prepared.[35]

Captain Don Andrés Castillero returned to Santa Barbara from the southern frontier early in August. On the 24th of that month, he and Ensign Don Nicanor Estrada sailed for Mexico as Alvarado's commissioners to the central government. The *comisionados* landed at Acapulco on September 15 and were in the capital city by the end of the month. Meanwhile, in California, all awaited the results of the commissioners' negotiations.

IV. Don Carlos Antonio Carrillo Claims the Governorship.

A month before Alvarado's meeting with Captain Castillero and almost three months before the latter reached the capital of the Mexican Republic, the general government appointed Don Carlos Antonio Carrillo as civil governor of California. This appointment, which was obtained for Don Carlos by his brother, Don José An-

[34] Vallejo to Portilla, Sonoma, August 1, 1837, MS., in *Legajo* 52-6-9-2, No. 9.
[35] Santiago Argüello to Gervasio Argüello, San Diego, November 1, 1837, MS., *ibid.*

tonio Carrillo, who was then member from California of the national congress, carried the power to locate the capital of the Department provisionally wherever circumstances might require.[36]

This news reached Los Angeles on October 20, 1837, on which date a letter from Don Luis del Castillo Negrete, written from Baja California, accompanied by a copy of Carrillo's appointment, was read to the *ayuntamiento*.[37] Ten days later, at Monterey, Alvarado received a letter, written at La Paz on August 20, from Don José Antonio Carrillo, forwarding copies of the appointment. Presumably the original reached Don Carlos at Santa Barbara at about the same time. Alvarado, on October 31, issued a proclamation in which he made known the news he had received unofficially "by yesterday's mail" and said,

All the Department may be assured that I shall deliver the office to the nominee on receiving the slightest intimation from the supreme government.[38]

The *sureños*, although Carrillo had been a partisan of the north during the late troubles, received this announcement with great delight. The *Angelinos*, in their enthusiasm, acknowledged the new governor at once, sent him their congratulations, and paid him the honor of a grand illumination of their city. Don Carlos thanked them for their compliments and promised to make Los Angeles his capital, which was an impolitic commitment to make before he had assumed his office.

The situation created for Alvarado by this appointment was a peculiar and difficult one. He was the leader of a successful revolution who had, in the end, recognized the authority of the general government. After that recognition, he considered himself the legitimate acting governor of the Department. However, the national government had not recognized him. To surrender his office without such recognition would have been to brand himself a revolutionist and to condemn his followers to the same status. It had always been the custom for the incumbent in the office of governor to re-

[36] Peña y Peña to C. A. Carrillo, Mexico, June 6, 1837, MS., in *Carillo (D.), Doc.*, 1; also *Legajo* 52-6-9-2, No. 35; transcribed in *Dept. St. Pap., Angeles*, MS., XI, 92-3.
[37] *Los Angeles Archives*, MS., IV, 326.
[38] *Dept. St. Pap., Angeles*, MS., X, 20; also *San José Archives*, MS., VI, 5.

ceive orders to deliver his office as well as for the nominee to receive orders to assume it. The implication of recognition contained in such an order was of vital importance to Alvarado and his partisans. He determined to await its arrival before relinquishing his office. Furthermore, he did not desire to give up his authority before he had heard of the success or failure of Captain Castillero's mission.[39]

There the matter stood for several weeks, with Don Carlos, who possessed little political skill, claiming the office and Don Juan Bautista, who was a master at the politician's art, refusing to surrender it until he had received instructions to do so from the general government. In all probability no trouble would have come from this anomalous situation if Carrillo and Alvarado had held a conference on the subject, as the latter requested. This Don Carlos, influenced by some of his southern friends, refused, deploring the "frivolous pretexts" causing the delay.[40]

Los Angeles, meanwhile, could wait no longer. The *ayuntamiento* of that place refused to recognize any other authority than Carrillo and invited him to come to that city and set up his government.[41] Before a special session of the *ayuntamiento*, in the morning of December 6, Carrillo took the oath of office as civil governor amid general rejoicing. The new governor delivered an inaugural address and a mass and *te deum* followed at the church.[42] San Diego promptly recognized the new executive on December 10.[43]

Carrillo's brother, Don José Antonio, who had recently returned from Mexico, was then sent to Santa Barbara to obtain the recognition and support of that place. But the *Barbareños* refused him and were a little indignant that one of their own number should make so treacherous a suggestion.[44]

In this way, the division of the Department that had existed at the

---

[39] Bancroft, *op. cit.*, III, 536-8.
[40] Carrillo, C. A., to Alvarado, Santa Barbara, November 14, 1837, MS., in *Vallejo, Doc.*, IV, 345.
[41] *Los Angeles Archives*, MS., IV, 329-30.   [42] Bancroft, *op. cit.*, III, 539-40.
[43] Alvarado, Francisco, to C. A. Carrillo, San Diego, December 10, 1837, in *San Diego Archives*, MS., 189-90.
[44] Alvarado, J. B., to Vallejo, Monterey, December 20, 1837, MS., in *Vallejo, Doc.*, IV, 361.

beginning of the year was reproduced by the end of the year. And thus it continued for the next two months, with Carrillo performing routine duties from his capital at Los Angeles, with many earnest and fiery letters passing between prominent men, and with Alvarado continuing in his adamantine refusal to surrender his office except on direct instructions from the general government. This dilemma fed the passions of sectional prejudices and it was but a question of time before the *sureños* and the *norteños* would again be flying at each other's throats.

There is little question but that the south must bear the responsibility for the campaign of 1838. It is the habit of the general historians to attribute the continued opposition to Alvarado to the old struggles of Los Angeles for the capital and of San Diego for the custom house and to the activities of such civilian politicians as Don Juan Bandini, Don Pio Pico, Don Manuel Requena and Don José Antonio Carrillo. An even more powerful influence was the military officers present in the south. The senior and most prominent of these officers were Captain Portilla, Captain Zamorano and Lieutenant Rocha. These men, sworn to uphold the national government, had been forcibly deprived of their commands by the revolutionists under Alvarado. They had opposed him with every resource available and they felt that their campaign in June 1837 had contributed in large measure to Alvarado's decision to recognize the national government. They had accepted him as the legitimate acting civil governor grudgingly and nursed their resentment at his failure actively to recognize their senior, Captain Portilla, as acting general commandant. They did not recognize the revolutionary general commandant, Lieutenant Vallejo, for whom they felt a supreme contempt for his failure to abide by his oath as an officer and refusal to obey the orders of his seniors. These men cared not where the custom house was located or which city possessed the capital. They did not care if the occupant of the office of civil governor was a native of California or if he came from "the interior of the Republic." But they were greatly concerned as to the reaction of the national government to events in Alta California. They were sworn to uphold that government and, as with all military officers in every country, their advancement and promotion depended on the War Department's view of their records.

Unfortunately for their effectiveness, the senior of the three officers named, Captain Portilla, was the least capable and the least energetic. The campaign of June 1837, as we have seen, was organized by Captain Zamorano and he had supplied Portilla, after that officer assumed the command, with sufficient energy and resolution to cause Alvarado to dub him Portilla's "director." Military etiquette required submission to Portilla's slow and ponderous movements, which were an insurmountable handicap. A combination of three or four effective officers under an energetic senior could have made a great difference in the history of the years 1837 and 1838 in Alta California.

Captain Zamorano was not and never attempted to be a field officer. His work in organizing and supplying the expeditions that opposed Alvarado in 1837 and 1838 was, in view of the resources available, extremely well and effectively done. Those expeditions did not accomplish more because of the lack of effective and energetic leadership in the field. Their opponents, under Don José Castro, enjoyed a field leadership that was far superior. Don Agustin probably wished many times that his old companion in arms, Captain Don Romualdo Pacheco, could return; together they might have accomplished a great deal and historians have had a different story to tell.

Following Alvarado's submission to the general government in July 1837, the military officers in the south considered Captain Portilla to be their commander. Vallejo continued to call himself general commandant and Alvarado to address him as such but he did not attempt to exercise any authority south of Santa Barbara and he would have been denied obedience if he had done so. Portilla, with headquarters at Mission San Gabriel, was at the head of military affairs in the south. He recognized Don Carlos Antonio Carrillo at once on the latter's inauguration and was, in turn, recognized as general commandant. Whereupon, every military officer in the south gave his support and loyalty to Carrillo. This conduct on their part, regardless of what may be said of that of Carrillo and their civilian friends, had every merit of consistency and technical correctness.

The exact beginnings of the military resistance to Alvarado, or rather support of Carrillo, in 1838 are not clear. Late in February, *Alcalde* Estudillo, of San Diego, in compliance with Carrillo's instructions, sent a small force of volunteers under Don Pio Pico and a supply of ammunition to Los Angeles.[45] I believe Captain Zamorano accompanied this party.

By the time the *Dieguiños* reached Los Angeles, or very soon thereafter, Captain Portilla moved his troops to that city from Mission San Gabriel. In a few days it was determined to send an expedition to occupy Mission San Buenaventura. The fact that Don Carlos Antonio Carrillo was the administrator of that mission may have had some bearing on that decision. The command of this expedition was entrusted to Captain Don Juan Castañeda, a Mexican officer who had arrived in Alta California but a few weeks before with Don José Antonio Carrillo. It is possible that this choice was the result of a decision by Captain Zamorano, made in the hope the new captain might prove to be an effective officer in the field. In this he was doomed to disappointment, for the captain turned out to be a man of little force.

Captain Castañeda's instructions were dated March 10 and were transmitted to him on the same day. Both the instructions and the letter of transmittal have been preserved and, though signed by Captain Portilla as general commandant, are in Don Agustin's autograph.[46] According to these instructions, Castañeda was to hold the mission, to prevent the *norteños* from using its resources, to cut off all communication with Santa Barbara, and, if attacked by overwhelming numbers, to retreat. If he found the mission occupied by the enemy, he was to use his own discretion as to attempting to dislodge them.

The occupation of Mission San Buenaventura was effected without opposition. Captain Portilla, on March 16, from Los Angeles, wrote to Captain Castañeda that he had heard of that fact and that he should remain there until further orders.[47] On the same day, Por-

---

[45] Estudillo, J. A., to C. A. Carrillo, San Diego, February 25, 1838, in *San Diego Archives*, MS., 197; see also *ibid.*, 195, 211.

[46] Portilla to Castañeda, Los Angeles, March 10, 1838, MS., in *Vallejo, Doc.*, V, 38.

[47] Portilla to Castañeda, Los Angeles, March 16, 1838, MS., *ibid.*, V, 42.

tilla also advised Castañeda that a party of troops under Ensign Don José Antonio Pico was leaving Los Angeles to join him.[48] Both of these letters are in Captain Zamorano's hand and show that he did not accompany Castañeda's expedition.

On March 18, Captain Portilla, in a letter also written by Don Agustin, ordered Captain Castañeda to advance and take Santa Barbara before it could be reenforced by the enemy. He was to develop his own plan of attack but to move swiftly and to demand an unconditional surrender, as "no more consideration must be shown for those faithless rebels."[49] Later in the same day, Portilla instructed Castañeda to act quickly and attack Santa Barbara before Alvarado could arrive or the garrison escape. If the garrison should escape, he was to send fifty men in pursuit, but with orders not to go beyond Mission La Purísima Concepcion.[50] This letter is also in Don Agustin's handwriting.

Don José María Covarrubias, on the same day, March 18, wrote a letter of encouragement to Captain Castañeda in which he expressed his full confidence in the outcome of the latter's expedition.[51] This letter was endorsed by several friends in Los Angeles who took that means of expressing their agreement with the sentiments contained in the letter. Among those who signed this endorsement was Captain Zamorano. This signature is the last documentary evidence we have of Don Agustin's presence in Alta California until he returned in 1842.

A few days later, Captain Castañeda, in obedience to his orders, left Mission San Buenaventura at the head of about one hundred men and advanced on Santa Barbara, where he demanded the immediate surrender of that place.[52] Captain Don José Antonio de la Guerra y Noriega and *Padre Presidente* Fr. Narciso Duran came out to meet the captain and succeeded in persuading him to abandon his purpose.

[48] Portilla to Castañeda, Los Angeles, March 16, 1838, MS., *ibid.*, V, 44.
[49] Portilla to Castañeda, Los Angeles, March 18, 1838, MS., *ibid.*, V, 51.
[50] Portilla to Castañeda, Los Angeles, March 18, 1838, MS., *ibid.*, V, 52.
[51] Covarrubias, J. M., to Castañeda, Los Angeles, March 18, 1838, *ibid.*, V, 49.
[52] Bancroft, *op. cit.*, III, 550, says that Castañeda "left San Buenaventura probably March 17th." Since his instructions are dated Los Angeles, March 18, it could not have been before the 19th; he probably left on the 20th or 21st.

Three days later, he retired to Mission San Buenaventura. This flagrant failure to occupy Santa Barbara when it was defended by a garrison of but twenty-five men was a sore disappointment to Castañeda's supporters and many of the *sureños* convinced themselves they were the victims of deliberate treachery.

News of the events in the south had, in the meantime, reached Monterey where Alvarado acted with characteristic energy. Don José Castro was immediately on his way south with fifteen men to reenforce the garrison of Santa Barbara. On arrival there he added the troops stationed at that place to his force and, with a sufficient number of volunteers to give him about a hundred men, pushed on to Mission San Buenaventura. He approached the mission unnoticed, surrounded it, cut off communication with Los Angeles, shut off the water supply, captured the horses of the southern forces, and, on the morning of March 27, demanded the evacuation of the place within one hour. Captain Castañeda refused and soon the fight was on.[53]

Much powder was burned at the battle of San Buenaventura as Castro maintained a steady fire from five cannons on the mission buildings throughout the day. The church, which still stands, bore its scars of this battle for many years. In the night, under cover of darkness, the defending army fled on foot. The following day Castro's mounted men gathered in seventy prisoners. The single casualty of the battle was one man, in Castro's force, killed. This man, Captain Don Romualdo Pacheco and Don José María Ávila were the only men known to have been killed in all California's revolutionary warfare.[54]

When the tidings of the disaster at Mission San Buenaventura reached Los Angeles, Carrillo and Portilla retired hastily to San Diego. Presumably, Captain Zamorano accompanied them. Castro occupied the city on April 1 and after a stay of but a few days withdrew, on the eighth, to Mission San Fernando.[55]

---

[53] Many of the Californians mention this incident in their memoirs and histories, *cf.* Ord, *Ocurrencias en California*, MS., 108-10; Pio Pico, *Narracion Histórica*, MS., 63 *et seq*; del Valle, *Lo Pasado de California*, MS., 21.

[54] Castro to Alvarado, San Buenaventura, March 28, 1838, MS., in *Vallejo, Doc.*, XXXII, 155; also *Dept. St. Pap.*, MS., IV, 188.

[55] Castro to Alvarado, Los Angeles, April 1, 1838, in *Dept. St. Pap.*, MS., IV, 192; April 8, 1838, *idem*.

Remaining Years in California 249

At about the same time that Carrillo, Portilla and Zamorano reached San Diego, there arrived at that place, on April 4, Captain Don Juan José Tobar. He possessed a considerable reputation as an Indian fighter and *guerrillero*. He was accompanied by a small escort but came in no official capacity.[56] Captain Tobar was induced to assume the command of Carrillo's supporters, by what means I do not know, but we can be certain that Don Agustin hoped he might prove as good as his reputation and that they had found, at last, an effective field commander.

The next few days were spent in feverish activity in preparation of a new campaign. The new commander started north at the head of about one hundred men and was accompanied by Carrillo, Portilla and several other prominent persons. After passing Mission San Luis Rey, at Rancho de las Flores, they received reports that Castro was marching south from Los Angeles. Captain Tobar decided to make a stand where they were, and the adobe ranch house and an adjoining corral were fortified. Three pieces of artillery were placed so as to command all approaches, with the gunners protected by parapets built up of cowhides, pack saddles, and whatever else came to hand. Alvarado had joined Castro at Mission San Fernando and, after gathering volunteers, marched south with over two hundred men. He appeared before the fortified ranch house on April 21.

Not a single shot was fired in the battle of Las Flores. Don Carlos Antonio Carrillo, although freely charged with cowardice by his associates, declined to permit a gun to be discharged. Soon after the two armies were face to face, the rival claimants to the governorship met under a flag of truce. It is not clear which side sent it. Such proceedings were too much for Captain Tobar. He resigned his command on the spot and, with several companions, rode off to the south in disgust.[57]

Don Carlos was no match for Don Juan Bautista at the conference table. After two or three days of talk, they agreed to meet again at Mission San Fernando. For the relations between the two rivals during the next few weeks, the interested reader is referred to the works

[56] Pio Pico, *op. cit.*, 63, says that Tobar's sole purpose in coming to California was to visit him; see Bancroft, *op. cit.*, III, 557.   [57] *Ibid.*, III, 559.

of the general historians. We close our review of these events by noting that, on November 15, Captain Castillero returned to California, bringing the appointments, by the central government, of Alvarado as civil governor and Vallejo as general commandant, together with a decree granting amnesty for all political acts and opinions during the late troubles. He had succeeded completely in his mission and Alvarado and Vallejo were the unquestioned legitimate rulers of Alta California.

Unfortunately, I have been unable to ascertain definitely that Captain Zamorano was present at Las Flores. It would appear probable that he was. It would also appear probable that he was one of those who rode off in high dudgeon with Captain Tobar.

Likewise, very little is known about Captain Tobar's subsequent movements. By April 24, he had sufficiently recovered from his anger of the twenty-first to write Carrillo a note from San Diego, bidding him farewell and thanking him for his kindnesses. He said he was about to leave California.[58] Don Pio Pico says that he returned to Sonora.[59]

On June 20, 1838, Alvarado wrote Vallejo from Santa Barbara,

> It seems to me that in my former letter I told you Tobar, Zamorano, Don Pablo [*Portilla*], Joaquín Ortega, Requena and Trujillo went to Baja California. It is said that they await there the troops that Don Antonio and Don Carlos [*Carrillo*] have asked of Bustamante. I have told them that if any troops show themselves here to attack us, I will execute more than ten of their sympathizers before I go out to fight them.[60]

Alvarado's threat was probably based on rumors and is not to be taken as evidence that Captain Zamorano was on the southern frontier at that date. All we know is that soon after the "battle" at Las Flores Don Agustin went to Mexico.

[58] Tobar to C. A. Carrillo, San Diego, April 24, 1838, in *Dept. St. Pap.*, MS., IV, 203.
[59] Pio Pico, *op. cit.*, 70.
[60] Alvarado to Vallejo, Santa Barbara, June 20, 1838, MS., in *Vallejo, Doc.*, V, 98.

Chapter x.

ZAMORANO'S LAST YEARS, 1838 TO 1842.

I. In Mexico.

LITTLE is known definitely of the movements or activities of Don Agustin V. Zamorano during his sojourn in Mexico. From San Diego, he appears to have gone to La Paz, in Baja California. He was there in April 1839.

It will be recalled that Judge Don Luis del Castillo Negrete, following the Alvarado-Castro revolt in Alta California, had sailed from San Diego for Mazatlan on the *Leonidas* on December 29, 1836. He reached Mexico City early in the following spring and, in May 1837, was appointed civil governor of Baja California. He thereupon took up his residence at La Paz, the capital of that Territory. At about the same time, Lieutenant Colonel Don José Caballero, a brother of Fr. Felix Caballero, of the frontier mission, was appointed *comandante principal* of Baja California. This office was the military command of the Territory and corresponded with that of *comandante general* of Alta California, except that its occupant reported to the *comandante general* of Sonora and not directly to the War Department. Baja California had been torn by a series of small revolutions which had embittered its people and ruined its prosperity. The appointment of Don Luis del Castillo Negrete was an effort to remedy this situation. He ruled the Territory with great energy and wisdom from 1837 to 1842.

Early in 1839, Lieutenant Colonel Caballero, for reasons that are unknown to me, retired from the office of *comandante principal*. The civil governor, anxious that the new appointee be sympathetic with his policies, sent his secretary, who was also his brother, Don Francisco del Castillo Negrete, to the capital of the Republic to support his plans. It appears that the chief object of Don Francisco's journey was to obtain the appointment for Don Agustin V. Zamorano. On April 11, 1839, he made a confidential report to the Secretary of War and Marine on conditions in Baja California. After reviewing the situation that had prevailed before his brother took office and outlining the progress and improvements that had been made to date, he wrote that it was essential that the appointment of *comandante principal* should go to a person known to be in accord with the plans of the civil governor.

> Your Excellency, as one who is better informed in the matter than myself, will agree that Captain Don Agustin V. Zamorano, who at present is in this California [*Baja*], is the officer best qualified for the military command. He is the senior captain, the one who has rendered the greatest and most distinguished service, the only one who has consistently remained loyal to the national government and to his superiors, the one who, because of his long residence in those countries, is most familiar with the weaknesses of their inhabitants, the one who, because of his military ability and kindly, conciliatory disposition, enjoys the best reputation, the one most deserving of promotion because of his sufferings, service, and seniority, and the one who will receive the most favorable reception because he is already known and his ideas are in agreement with those of the civil governor. With the two authorities working in perfect harmony, peace will be attained, and with it prosperity.[1]

It appears that Don Agustin received the appointment as *comandante principal* and that he served in that office from some time in 1839 to late in 1840, when he was called to the War Department, in Mexico City, for staff duty. The details of this service have not been uncovered. Nor do I know when he received his promotion in rank, although it is probable that this occurred at the time he received the appointment as *comandante principal* of Baja California.

I have seen a written statement made by "The Citizen José María de Echeandia, Lieutenant Colonel of Engineers, Retired," that, while serving as civil governor and general commandant of Alta California, he extended certain privileges to Captain John R. Cooper, master of

---

[1] Francisco del Castillo Negrete to Secretary of War and Marine, Mexico, April 11, 1839, in *Legajo* 52-6-9-2.

the schooner *Rover*, in the harbor of San Diego. This statement, which is "Dated at Mexico on the seventeenth of February, 1841," is unquestionably, in my opinion, in the handwriting of Don Agustin.[2] It is probable that Captain Cooper needed this document for some purpose and obtained it while on a trip to Mexico; that Don Agustin was familiar with the matter because of his position as secretary of the Territory at the time and drew up this statement which Echeandia signed. It indicates that Don Agustin was in the City of Mexico on that date.

Rivera's *Guia de Forasteros Politico-Commercial de la Ciudad de Mexico* for the year 1842 lists Don Agustin as being on duty in the War Department, in the Cavalry Division, with the rank of lieutenant colonel.[3] His residence address is given as *Calle Inditas, Número 5*.

II. Brigadier General Don Manuel Micheltorena.

Don Juan B. Alvarado served as constitutional governor of Alta California for four years. His administration was, on the whole, an able and successful one. Its chief blight was that the secularization of the missions reached the period of its greatest scandal. These years are also significant because of the increased arrivals of foreign settlers within the Department; chief of these was Captain John A. Sutter, who settled at New Helvetia, on the Sacramento.

It was not long before serious differences of opinion developed between the governor and the general commandant, Don Mariano G. Vallejo. The chief cause of this dispute was their conflicting interests in the reorganization of the government and the apportionment of the departmental revenues between the two rulers. By the years 1840 and 1841, the situation had led to an open break between them and both finally appealed to the national government to adjust their differences. Vallejo, on several occasions, recommended to the central government that the civil and military commands be again united in the person of a strong Mexican officer, supported by a body of troops

[2] In the possession of Miss Frances Molera, of San Francisco, a granddaughter of Captain John R. Cooper.
[3] *Guia de Forasteros Politico-Commercial de la Ciudad de Mexico Para el Año de 1842. Con Algunos Noticias Generales de la Republica. Par Mariano Galvan Rivera*, 15.

sufficient to cause him to be respected. His suggestion was practically the same as that made many times by Don Agustin. It is evident that experience and responsibility had caused Don Mariano to progress far from the position he had taken in 1832 and again in 1836.

In January 1842, the central government decided to act on these recommendations. We can believe that it was influenced in this decision by Lieutenant Colonel Zamorano, then on duty in the War Department. Because of his many years service in California, Don Agustin probably took part in the many discussions on the subject and, since Vallejo's recommendations agreed so closely with his own urged their adoption. The officer selected to be the new governor of Alta California was Brigadier General Don Manuel Micheltorena then serving as adjutant general of the General Staff of the Mexican army. He was a cultivated gentleman with a pleasing personality and a long record of satisfactory service in various parts of the Republic. His appointment as *Gobernador, Comandante General e Inspector del Departamento de la Alta California* was dated January 22, 1842. His instructions, which were dated February 11, gave him extraordinary powers to reorganize and improve both the civil and military governments of California without waiting for approval from Mexico. The Californian authorities were notified of his appointment on February 22.

Lieutenant Colonel Zamorano received the appointment as adjutant inspector of Alta California and was expected to act as a general adviser to the governor. To Don Agustin this meant an opportunity to rejoin his family.

The new governor was to take with him an army of five hundred men, which was to be made up of two hundred regular soldiers and three hundred convicts. In February, the Minister of Justice issued a decree ordering the selection of three hundred men from the prisons for this service. How many were thus obtained is not clear but with his army of convicts, Brigadier General Micheltorena, accompanied by Lieutenant Colonel Zamorano, left Mexico on May 5 1842, and arrived at Guadalajara on May 22, after a very rapid march which is said to have been the quickest on record by that route. The general commandant of the state of Jalisco had orders to provide

Micheltorena with two hundred regular soldiers from his command. That officer took advantage of the opportunity thus presented to rid himself of all the undesirable, useless, and unmanageable men in his troops.

This army of about three hundred and fifty men, called the *Batallon Fijo de Californias*, was then marched to the coast at Mazatlan. Desertions on the way and at the port reduced their number to about three hundred, who embarked, on about July 25, 1842, in four vessels for California. We can imagine the disappointment and chagrin of Lieutenant Colonel Zamorano as he watched this troop of incorrigibles, clad in rags and tatters, file aboard the ships. They were not the well-disciplined, trained, and fully equipped corps that he and Vallejo had recommended as the solution of California's troubles. As his ship sailed, he was probably torn between anticipations of joy at again being with his beloved family and of dread as to what disasters this army of *cholos* might bring.[4]

III. Zamorano's Death.

After an interminably tedious voyage of thirty-one days, the first vessel of this expedition dropped anchor on the bar of San Diego harbor at one o'clock in the afternoon of August 25, 1842. On board were Brigadier General Micheltorena and Lieutenant Colonel Zamorano. The other ship arrived within the next ten days.

There was much suffering and many deaths on the trip. It is said the ships were chartered by the day and that their masters made the voyage as long as they could make their fresh water last. Don Agustin was very ill and, in a dying condition, was carried ashore to the arms of the family he had not seen for four years.[5] Don Antonio María Osío claims that his illness was due entirely to the sufferings endured on the long voyage.[6]

We know very little of Don Agustin's last days. His father-in-law, Don Santiago Argüello, with whom Doña Luisa and her chil-

[4] This section is based on Bancroft, *History of California*, IV, 285-91, and the sources cited there.
[5] United States *vs.* Limantour, Appendix No. 1, Archives Exhibit, Exhibit IV, No. 1.
[6] Osío, *Historia de California*, MS., 420-22.

dren had been making their home, then lived in Los Angeles. Therefore, I think it probable that he was carried to the house of his brother-in-law, Don Juan Bandini, and that there he died.

There is no documentary record preserved today of either his death or burial. His children often told his grandchildren that their father was so loyal to the Mexican Republic that he died on the Mexican national holiday, September 16. This is a sentiment so typical of the character of Don Agustin that, taken with its universal acceptance among his grandchildren, it leaves no grounds for doubt. He died, we may safely assume, in his forty-fifth year, on September 16, 1842.

Thomas Savage, Bancroft's assistant, examined the records of Mission San Diego in January 1878. He wrote in his notes that the last entry in the *First Book of Burials* was under the date of June 14, 1831, and that the *Second Book* was not present and must be lost. Twenty-six years later, Fr. Zephyrin Engelhardt, O.F.M., performed the same task and found the same situation.[7] I am informed that it continues to this day. Therefore, the record made of his burial at Mission San Diego by the priest who performed the last rites of the Church over his remains is not available.

Don Agustin's eldest son, then a boy of thirteen, often told his children that he distinctly remembered his father's funeral. He said that his father was carried, on the day following his death, from San Diego to the mission and buried, with the full military honors of his rank, in the mission church. He recalled that he was delighted with the soldiers marching, the flags flying, the band playing, and the salute that was fired. Not until he returned home and saw the grief of his mother did he realize the family's bereavement.[8]

Governor Micheltorena planned to be in Los Angeles for the celebration of the national holiday on September 16. There was, however, so much trouble and so many delays in finding quarters for the officers and men, transportation for their baggage and equipment, and provisions for their sustenance that the departure from San Diego was repeatedly delayed.[9] The governor, therefore, was present at the funeral of his friend and adjutant inspector. For the same reasons,

---

[7] Engelhardt, *San Diego Mission*, 290.   [8] Don Luis Agustin Zamorano.
[9] *Dept. St. Papers, Angeles*, MS., VII, 7-23.

Don Santiago Argüello, who was then prefect of the southern territory, was unable to leave Los Angeles and was not present. On October 23, 1842, Don José Antonio Góngora, *juez de paz* at San Diego, transmitted to Don Santiago some documents relative to Don Agustin's burial.[10]

The same son of Don Agustin also told his children that many years later his father's remains, and those of two others, were removed from within the mission church to a small cemetery close by. I have been unable to learn of a record of this reburial. The little cemetery is shown in early pictures of the mission but all trace of it has now disappeared.

There we must leave Don Agustin V. Zamorano. His remains lie in an unmarked grave, within or without Mission San Diego de Acalá. Let us hope that some day his last resting place may be identified and marked with a memorial of his services to his country and to California.

Governor Micheltorena's administration was not a successful one. Well meaning but ill advised, he undertook to undo policies that had become accomplished facts. He appears to have had a well developed talent for doing the wrong thing. By the end of 1844, much of the Department was in revolt against him. Again forces were in the field. Again bloodless battles were fought. Again a hated Mexican governor was sent, in March 1845, out of the country.

Don Pio Pico, whose home was in Los Angeles, as senior member of the legislature, became the civil governor and Don José Castro, who lived in Monterey, became the general commandant. Once more there was recognition by the national government of the existing order as the constitutional one. The old jealousy between the *norteños* and the *sureños* soon reappeared and the remainder of the period until the time of the American occupation was taken up by petty quarrels between the two divisions of the departmental government. These, in all probability, would have led to another bloodless civil war by 1846 if the civilized warfare of the American occupation, which was not bloodless, had not interfered.

[10] Góngora, J. A., to Santiago Argüello, San Diego, October 23, 1842, *idem*, 12.

Chapter xi.

ZAMORANO'S FAMILY: CONCLUSION.

WHEN Don Agustin V. Zamorano set out from San Diego for Mexico, in the spring of 1838, he left his wife and seven children in California. As he and his family had, since December 1836, been making their home with Doña Luisa's parents, he undoubtedly left with the full approval of Don Santiago Argüello. His father-in-law, and possibly his brother-in-law, Don Juan Bandini, must have assured him that Doña Luisa and the children would be cared for. Family relationships were so close in that time and place that there was nothing unusual in this arrangement.

In this connection it is interesting to note the several remarks of Don Juan Bautista Alvarado. He, very naturally, bore no love, especially in the years following the fall of the Monterey *presidio* in November 1836, for Captain Zamorano. He considered Don Agustin the chief reason for the consistent refusal of the *sureños* to accept him as governor. In his letters of the time and in his *Historia de California*, he never missed an opportunity to cast some reflection on his arch-enemy.

In a letter written to Vallejo from Mission San Fernando on August 18, 1838, Alvarado remarked,

> When I received your letter a moment ago the wife of Bandini was here with me, having come to implore aid for her children. I have always played the role of papa to the families of my opponents because as soon as they flee they leave them to me to provide for. That is what is happening to me now with Zamorano's family, etc., etc., and others whom I don't wish to mention as it makes me ashamed.[1]

[1] Alvarado to Vallejo, San Fernando, August 18, 1838, MS., in *Vallejo, Doc.*, V, 145.

It is possible that Alvarado's persecutions of the supporters of Don Carlos Antonio Carrillo, in the summer of 1838, caused Bandini and Argüello to seek refuge in the hills of Baja California—that was preferable to being transported as prisoners to Sonoma. Both men, as we have seen, suffered greatly from the Indian depredations in 1837. Both were in straitened circumstances in the summer of 1838. These are probably the reasons why Doña Refugia Argüello de Bandini, who was Doña Luisa's sister, felt obliged to ask Alvarado for assistance. Alvarado, in spite of his protestations of feelings of shame, probably found satisfaction in the estate to which he had reduced the families of his opponents.

In this same connection, the following passage appears in his manuscript *Historia de California*,

> It is no less true that some of the most prominent revolutionists [*he considers those who opposed him, and not himself, to have been rebels*], when they set out to organize a revolution in the extreme southern part of the Department, would send me letters telling me that urgent matters had obliged them to leave their homes without first making the necessary arrangements for the upkeep of their families and, being convinced as they were of my generosity, they left them confided to my "parental care." Although it may seem incredible, among the number of those revolutionary nuisances who left their families in the care of the man against whom they proposed to fight was the notorious [*celebre*] Zamorano, who left his family in Monterey without a single *peso* and without provisions. On my order, for almost two years, Señor Estévan Munrás furnished the family of Zamorano all that lady asked for. It is very probable that otherwise she and her children would have found themselves in great need.[2]

This, I believe, has the very minimum of foundation in fact. I have

---

[2] Alvarado, *Historia De California*, MS., IV, 82; Bancroft, *California Pastoral*, 771, writes: "There was a peculiar vein of generosity in Alvarado's character. He was not rancorous toward his opponents, nor did he visit upon their families any responsibility for hostile acts. Very often, while his political opponents were working in the south to oust him from power, he was protecting and providing for their families in the north. One of these men, a prominent officer, noted for his bitter hostility to Governor Alvarado, left his family in Monterey without provisions. His party having been defeated, he preferred to abandon California; and had it not been that Alvarado, through a third party, provided for the wife and children during two years, they would have suffered for the necessaries of life." Thus Alvarado's malicious fabrication has served to sully the memory of Zamorano and to glorify that of himself.

stated that I believed Don Agustin left Monterey as quickly as possible after the evacuation of the *presidio* there on November 6, 1836, and that he was not accompanied by his family. We have seen that he was at Santa Barbara on November 28 and I have given my reasons for believing he reached San Diego sometime between the 13th and 25th of December. Don Santiago Argüello, in his letter of August 22, 1837, to his brother in Mexico, said that Don Agustin brought, at great trouble, his family with him.[3] In addition, we have seen that Don Agustin, in his report of April 24, 1837, told the War Department that he could neither abandon his family nor transport it to Mexico for which reason he had removed to San Diego where he had greater resources for a livelihood. And finally, the Baptismal Register of Mission San Diego records, on February 6, 1837, the birth at San Diego of a daughter to Doña Luisa. Therefore, Alvarado's statement that he provided for Doña Luisa and her children for a period of almost two years because they had been left destitute by their husband and father must be labeled as false.

It is possible that Don Agustin, as he hurriedly left Monterey for Santa Barbara, did bespeak Alvarado's care of his family until they could leave to join him. He had known Don Juan Bautista for many years and as the life and property of no Mexican was safe in Monterey during the following week it was a natural and proper request to make and should have implied no restraint on his subsequent actions.

Another flaw in Alvarado's statement is that Don Estévan Munrás was a good and close friend of Don Agustin and I doubt that Doña Luisa needed an order from Alvarado to obtain whatever assistance he could give her during the few days she and her children remained in Monterey.

I. Doña Luisa.

Doña Luisa, although but a girl of fifteen, was already famous for her brilliant smile and sparkling vivacity when she became the bride of Ensign Don Agustin V. Zamorano. These characteristics she appears to have retained until her death. She entered into every occa-

---

[3] Argüello, Santiago, to Gervasio Argüello, San Diego, August 22, 1837, MS., in *Legajo* 52-6-9-2.

sion with great zest and enjoyed life to the fullest. Visitors were always welcomed at the quarters of the commandant of the *presidio* at Monterey and its commanding officer's wife was never so happy as when the old buildings were thronged with people. None of the Mexican governors who came to Alta California brought his lady with him and it often fell to Doña Luisa to fill the post of official hostess at the social affairs given at the *presidio*. All who visited the capital of the Territory fell victims to her gracious charm. She was popular with the officers and their families, loved by the soldiers, and respected by the townspeople.

Other than she was small in stature, no description of her appearance has come down to us.

Of Doña Luisa's movements after the departure of Don Agustin in 1838, very little can be learned. Her father became administrator of Mission San Juan Capistrano in 1838. Soon after, Don Juan Bandini became administrator of Mission San Gabriel. During the winter of 1839-1840, Doña Luisa and her children lived at Mission San Gabriel with Bandini and his family.[4] Don Santiago Argüello became prefect of the southern district in June 1840. His headquarters were in Los Angeles and he established his residence there. Thereafter, that city was Doña Luisa's home. A few months before her husband's return, on April 26, 1842, she applied for the grant of a small plot of ground, measuring eighty *varas* in each direction, "for the purpose of cultivating it and planting a small orchard." This ground was adjacent to the property of Martín Duarte and her application appears to have been granted.[5]

In September 1844, Doña Luisa was granted a pension of sixty *pesos* per month as the widow of Lieutenant Colonel Don Agustin

---

[4] Engelhardt, *Missions and Missionaries of California*, IV, 161, quotes letter of Fr. Esténega, the missionary at San Gabriel, dated in January, 1840, in which he complains of the number of *gente de razon* the mission has to support. He said, "During the last winter . . . besides Señora Luisa, the wife of Agustin Zamorano, with her six or seven children, have occupied the mission in grand style."

[5] Zamorano, M. Luisa Argüello de, to Prefect of Second District, Los Angeles, April 26, 1842, MS., in possession of Mr. Roger Dalton.

V. Zamorano.[6] This she seems to have drawn with a fair degree of regularity until her death.[7]

Thomas O. Larkin, the Monterey merchant who was United States Consul in Alta California, was captured by the Californians during the American occupation and taken to Los Angeles. In a letter to his wife, written on January 11, 1847, Larkin said that Doña Luisa had helped to make his captivity pleasant by giving him tea twice a day "besides two meals of 3 or 4 courses each".[8] On his release and return to Monterey, Larkin published a card of thanks to those who had befriended him. This appeared in the *Californian*, the first newspaper in California which was printed on the press Don Agustin had imported, in its issue for February 13, 1847. Doña Luisa Argüello de Zamorano is listed among those whom he thanked for their many courtesies.[9]

Doña Luisa died at Los Angeles, in her thirty-sixth year, on May 11, 1847, and was buried the next day from the Plaza Church in the old cemetery on North Main Street.

II. Zamorano's Children.

After their mother's death, the children of Don Agustin and Doña Luisa continued to make their home with Don Santiago Argüello. Their grandmother, Doña María del Pilar Ortega de Argüello, cared for them until they left to build homes of their own.

María Dolores, the eldest of the children, was approaching her fifteenth birthday at the time of her father's death and was, therefore, considered a young lady. In July of the following year, she became the bride of Captain Don José María Flores.[10] Captain Flores came to California in 1842 with Governor Micheltorena as a captain in the

---

[6] Batres, Antonio, to Treasurer of California, Mexico, September 14, 1844, in *Dept. St. Pap., Benicia*, MS., I, 89.

[7] See *Dept. St. Pap., Ben., Mil.*, MS., LXXXVI, 3; *ibid.*, LXXXVIII, 50; and *Dept. St. Pap., Ben., Commissary and Treasury*, MS., V, 5.

[8] Larkin to his wife, Los Angeles, January 11, 1847, MS., in *Larkin, Doc.*, V, 5.

[9] *Californian*, Monterey, February 13, 1847.

[10] The *Diligencias Matrimoniales* of Don José María Flores and Doña María Dolores Zamorano, in the possession of Mr. Thomas W. Temple, of San Gabriel, is dated Los Angeles, June 21, 1843. I have not been able to locate the record of their marriage.

ZAMORANO'S FAMILY: CONCLUSION 263

Batallon Fijo. He served the governor as secretary and was a prominent figure in California until after the American occupation. In 1844, and again in 1845, he made a trip to Mexico to solicit aid for the governor in the form of money and supplies. He played a conspicuous part in the resistance offered by the Californians in 1846 to the American forces. In September of that year, in the absence of Don Pio Pico, Captain Flores was made governor and, in October, general commandant. He directed all the operations of the final campaign of the war with great energy, skill, and patriotism under trying circumstances. In doing this, he committed the dishonorable act of breaking his parole. Much, however, can be said in extenuation of the final effort against the American forces. Captain Flores did not surrender but retreated in January 1847, to Sonora. He never returned to California and appears to have deserted his wife and three children. I know nothing of his subsequent career.[11] Very little appears to be known regarding the later years of Doña Dolores. Many years after 1847, she became the wife of Ventura Arnaiz, for whom she bore three children. She is said to have died at San Luis Obispo in about 1870.

Don Agustin's eldest son, Don Luis Agustin Zamorano, was married on November 7, 1882, at the Plaza Church, Los Angeles, to Doña Carlota Murphy. Of their eight children, four died in infancy. Don Luis died at San Diego, where he lived for many years, on January 13, 1907. His wife died on October 12, 1916.[12]

The third child and second son of Don Agustin was born at Monterey on September 15, 1831. He was baptised three days later in San Carlos Church by Father Abella, with Don Juan Malarin and his wife, Doña Josepha Estrada, as his godparents. He was named Gonzalo Nicomedez.[13] He died while a boy at San Diego.

María de Guadalupe was the name given to the fourth child and second daughter of Doña Luisa and Don Agustin. She was born at Monterey on December 18, 1832.[14] Her godparents were David E.

---
[11] Bancroft, *History of California*, III, 741; IV, 289; V, 309-25, 329-56, 389-410.
[12] Statement of Doña Luisa Ana Zamorano de Gilbert, of Tijuana, Baja California.
[13] Entry 3753, *Second Book of Baptisms*, San Carlos Church, Monterey.
[14] *Idem*, Entry 3818.

Spence and his wife, Doña Adelaida Estrada. At the Plaza Church in Los Angeles, on August 14, 1847, three months after the death of her mother, Doña Guadalupe became the wife of Henry Dalton and went as mistress to the great ranch house on Azusa Hill.[15] Her beauty is often mentioned. Henry Dalton was born on October 8, 1803, at London, England. As a boy of fourteen, he went to Lima, Peru. He came to California from Mazatlan as supercargo of the Mexican brig *Soledad*, which was on the coast from October to December 1843.[16] He became an extensive landholder in the country about Azusa. His last years were embittered by litigation, chiefly with squatters, over his holdings. He died at Los Angeles on January 21, 1884.[17] Doña Guadalupe was the mother of eleven children of whom seven lived to maturity. She died at Azusa on September 1, 1914.[15]

The fifth child of Don Agustin was born at Monterey on February 13, 1834.[18] Her godparents were Don Ignacio del Valle and Doña Ramona Carrillo, the widow of Don Romauldo Pacheco. She was baptised as Josepha María although she is remembered in the family as Josepha Rosa. She is said to have died at San Diego at about the age of seventeen, unmarried. She was a beautiful and vivacious young woman.

The sixth child was born at Monterey on September 6, 1835, and was named for his father, Agustin Vicente.[19] His sponsors at his baptism were Governor José Figueroa and Doña Soledad Ortega, the widow of Don Luis Antonio Argüello and the sister of Doña Luisa's mother. On January 7, 1865, at the Plaza Church, Los Angeles, this son married Doña María Leonora Jeantet, who was born at Taos, New Mexico, in 1842. He died on a ranch near Tijuana, Baja California, in 1872, and was buried in San Diego. His widow died at Azusa in 1879. They were the parents of three children.[20]

[15] Statement of the late Joseph R. H. Dalton.
[16] Bancroft, *op. cit.*, II, 773; IV, 400, 568.
[17] Baker, "Don Enrique Dalton of the Azusa," in *Publications of Historical Society of Southern California*, Vol. X, No. 3, 17.
[18] Entry 3886, *Second Book of Baptisms*, San Carlos Church, Monterey.
[19] *Idem*, Entry 3959.
[20] Statement of Agustin Vicente Zamorano 3d. Mr. Zamorano is the only living descendant of Don Agustin who bears the family name. As he is a bachelor, the name will disappear with his passing.

Zamorano's Family: Conclusion

The last child of Don Agustin and Doña Luisa was born at San Diego on February 6, 1837. She was baptised on the same day at Mission San Diego by Father Oliva, who had married her parents almost exactly ten years before. She was named Eulalia Dorotea and her godparents were Doña Luisa's brother and sister, Don Santiago Emidio Argüello and Doña María Concepcion Argüello.[21]

Don Agustin's three younger daughters are all remembered for their beauty but the youngest appears to have inherited more of her mother's vivacity and spirit than the others. Doña Eulalia was the pride of her doting grandparents and the belle of San Diego. On October 6, 1860, in the little church in what is now called "Old Town" at San Diego, she married Don José Vicente Estudillo. Don Vicente, who was a grandson of Captain Don José María Estudillo, the founder of the Estudillo family in California, was born at Rancho San Leandro on the 19th of February, 1833. He took his bride to the old family *rancho* on the east side of San Francisco Bay. He was a *ranchero* all his life and died, on November 9, 1893, at his place near San Luis Obispo. Doña Eulalia was the mother of twelve children, all but one of whom lived to maturity. She died at San Luis Obispo on March 24, 1909.[22]

III. Don Agustin V. Zamorano.

Our review of the public services of Don Agustin V. Zamorano has shown us a man endowed with no little natural talent, a steady patriot in times when it was by no means easy to be one, and a successful executive in a troublous period. He served as executive secretary of the territorial government of Alta California for eleven years—from October 1825 to November 1836. In that time he earned and received the friendship and confidence of every governor, excepting only the erratic Chico, who ruled the Territory. That he was a loyal, efficient and capable public servant is beyond question.

He appears, however, never to have pushed himself forward and he never took advantage of the many opportunities presented to

---

[21] *Book of Baptisms*, Mission San Diego.
[22] Statement of Mrs. M. Anaís Estudillo Throop.

increase his personal fortunes. He was probably the only man of any prominence in California of whom there is no record of his having received a grant of land. He never applied for one. His conception of the proprieties of his position would not permit him to increase his personal resources in a way that was common and accepted practice among public men of his time.

He was ambitious—what man is not?—but not in the sense as applied by Brutus to Caesar. Energetic and effective in an emergency, he was content, in normal times, to allow affairs to take their course uninfluenced by any action on his part. When the San Diego revolt broke out, in December 1831, he was slow to accept his responsibility, as the senior remaining loyal officer, to maintain the duly constituted government of the Territory. That duty once accepted, however, he acted with a promptness and effectiveness that compels admiration. His central policy was to preserve the peace of the country. Others might threaten war but he stood for peace. As perhaps the only officer in California who had ever been under actual fire, he knew, from his experiences in the Mexican Revolution, the cruelty and horrors of war. Therefore, he thought it sufficient to maintain the *status quo*, which he succeeded in doing, in the face of the opposition of the Californian politicians, until the arrival of Governor Figueroa.

When the new governor reached Monterey, Zamorano was happy, in all probability, to revert once more to the routine duties of his secretarial office and the command of the *presidio* at Monterey and to leave to others the risks and rewards of more spectacular duties.

Had Don Agustin been a man ambitious for personal advancement, he would have displaced the ineffective Portilla in the campaigns of 1837 and 1838, and the cause of the southern patriots might have been better served. He preferred, however, to remain loyal to the brother officer who was his senior.

When we turn from his public career to his private life and attempt to discover something of his personality, we are on difficult ground. Our efforts are handicapped by the complete absence of personal letters and memorabilia. The only personal letter known to have been preserved, which is but a brief note, is one written to Don Mariano G. Vallejo, in September 1835, urging him to come to

Monterey for the funeral of Governor Figueroa. With no help from Don Agustin himself, we are forced to work largely by inference.

In contrast to the social instincts of Doña Luisa, the gregarious impulse does not appear to have been strong in Don Agustin. His official position gave him an extensive acquaintance throughout Alta California but his circle of close friends was very limited. His dearest and closest friend was, without doubt, Don Romualdo Pacheco, whose ill-fated career we have reviewed. The void that resulted with the passing of Don Romualdo was never completely filled, but Don Juan Malarin, Don Mariano Estrada, Don Estévan Munrás, William E. P. Hartnell, David E. Spence, Don Ignacio del Valle, and Don Ignacio Coronel are known to have been his intimates and to have enjoyed his confidence. As a man's friends are an indication of his character, it is worth our while to note who and what manner of men they were.

Don Juan Malarin was a native of Peru who first came to California in 1820 as the master of the *Señoriano*. He married Doña Josepha Estrada in about 1826 and thereafter made his home at Monterey, although he continued to follow the sea for many years. He was a member of the council called by Zamorano at Monterey on February 1, 1832, and he stood as godfather to Don Agustin's third child. There are many indications that he and Don Agustin were very close friends. Don Juan is remembered as a quiet, unobtrusive person of steady character and much influence.

Lieutenant Don José Mariano Estrada, although a much older man, was Don Agustin's first acquaintance in Monterey. He and his wife, Doña Ysabella Argüello, a relative of Doña Luisa, were the godparents, in November 1827, of Don Agustin's first child. Don Mariano was a native of Baja California and came to Alta California in about 1798 as ensign in the Monterey Company. He retired from the military service in 1829. He was appointed *comisario subalterno* at Monterey, in October 1832, by Don Agustin while acting governor. Never a rich man and never occupying high position, he was, nevertheless, by force of character, one of the most important men in Monterey. Bancroft says that, "he was one of the most respected and influential men in northern California."

Don Estévan Munrás was a Spaniard and came to California in about 1820. He established himself at Monterey as a merchant and, for the time and place, built up a large business. He was active in the formation of, although not an officer in, the *compañia extranjera* in 1832. Thomas O. Larkin, in 1845, described him as a man of property and character.

William E. P. Hartnell, whose work in organizing the Company of Foreigners, in 1832, we have already noticed, was an Englishman. He was probably the most highly educated man in California at the time. In 1834, with the Reverend Patrick Short, he opened a school of higher education at Alisal which was known as the *Seminario de San José*. He occupied many positions of public trust until the time of the American occupation, when he was employed by the United States as official interpreter and translator. Bancroft describes him as, "a man who enjoyed and merited the respect and friendship of all who knew him, being perfectly honest and straightforward in all his transactions, of most genial temperament, and too liberal for his own interests. In some directions he was a man of rare ability, being a master of the Spanish, French, and German languages besides his own."

David E. Spence was a native of Scotland who came to California in 1824 from Lima, Peru, to superintend the meat packing plant of Begg & Company at Monterey. In 1827, he began business on his own account as a merchant and was prosperous from the beginning, being cautious, shrewd in money matters, and energetic. He married Doña Adelaida, daughter of Don Mariano Estrada, in 1829. He and Don Agustin early became close friends and he and his wife were the sponsors at the baptism, in December 1832, of the latter's fourth child.

Don Ignacio del Valle is said to have come to Alta California with Governor Echeandia in 1825 as a soldier. His father, Don Antonio del Valle, was in the Territory at the time as a lieutenant in the Mazatlan Company, commanded by Captain Portilla. Don Ignacio was made a cadet in the San Diego Company in 1828. In 1831, at the same time that Don Agustin was made captain of the Monterey Company, he was appointed ensign in that company. However, before he could join his new command at Monterey, the revolt of December 1831 broke out and he remained at San Diego as a supporter of Echeandia. His father, on the other hand, supported Zamorano and was present at Santa Barbara, in 1832, with Lieutenant Ibarra's army. After the arrival of Governor Figueroa, in 1833, Don Ignacio joined his company at Monterey and soon became the close friend and loyal supporter of his commanding officer, Captain Zamorano. He was the godfather of Don Agustin's fifth child, born in February 1834. After the fall of the Monterey *presidio*, in November 1836, he accompanied Zamorano south. He took an active part with the southern forces in the campaigns of 1837 and 1838 against Alvarado. Don Ignacio was prominent in public affairs both before and after the American occupation. He died in 1880 at Camulos Rancho, where he had lived for many years.

Don Ignacio Coronel was a Mexican school teacher who, with his family, came to California in 1834 with the Hijar and Padrés Colony. He opposed the Alvarado-Castro revolution in 1836 and, in 1837, moved his family from Monterey to Los Angeles, where, at the insistence of Don Agustin, so it is said, he started a school. He was a supporter of Carrillo in the campaign of 1838. In the years following, and in addition to teaching his school, he conducted a small store and served as secretary of the *ayuntamiento*.

As we review this group of Don Agustin's closest friends, we are impressed with the fact that none among them was a native Californian, that all were educated men, that four of them—Malarin, Munrás, Hartnell, and Spence, were foreigners who had become naturalized Mexican citizens and that all, with the exception of Estrada, were, comparatively, newcomers to California. None of these men was a politician and all opposed each of the revolutions that California experienced. Munrás and Spence were members of the territorial legislature in 1836 but did not approve the revolt of that year and were slow to give their half-hearted support to Alvarado's government, an action to which they were prompted by their commercial interests. All these friends of Don Agustin were of the most responsible element in the community.

There can be but little question that Zamorano had enjoyed the advantages of a superior education. The documents in his handwriting that have been preserved suggest that he was probably the best penman in the Territory. The clear, even, well-formed products of his easy flowing pen are easily recognized. The accounts of his presidial company were kept with accuracy. His memoranda to the governors, summarizing the correspondence on special subjects in the archives under his care, are models of brevity and point. There is a tradition that he possessed some knowledge of the English language.

Territorial politics were not nearly so attractive to Captain Zamorano as the hunting field. He was an inveterate hunter and spent many hours roaming the country about Monterey in search of game.

After hunting, Don Agustin's greatest avocation appears to have been the graphic arts. He enjoyed drawing and painting. There are many family traditions and a few contemporary references touching on his abilities as an artist but the only product of his brush of which there is record today is the self-portrait used as the frontispiece to this study. This was a water-color painting and was probably made sometime between the spring of 1830 and the autumn of 1836, for tradition states that it was done while he was living at Monterey. Telling his wife one day that he was going hunting for doves, he went instead to a favored spot, carrying a mirror, which he hung from the limb of a tree, and, by its aid, proceeded to make this self-portrait. On his return, he handed the finished picture to Doña Luisa with the remark, "Here is your dove." The portrait presently came into the possession of Don Agustin's younger daughter, Doña Eulalia Dorotea Zamorano de Estudillo, of San Luis Obispo. It was destroyed when her home there was burned about 1900. Fortunately, it had been photographed.

The wood-blocks, and later the small font of old-style type, that were part of the equipment of his office, probably proved very fascinating to Don Agustin. We can assume, I believe, that the pieces printed with this early equipment were largely the products of his hands. The extremely limited capacity and the worn condition of these facilities were possibly the reasons why he acquired and set up California's first printing press. He wanted to do larger and better work than was possible with the meager equipment at hand. How much time and attention he devoted to the work of the printing press we shall never know.

The complete lack of personal memorabilia is in itself indicative of the character of Don Agustin V. Zamorano. He made no effort to preserve for posterity a record of his accomplishments. His self-portrait was painted for his wife and not for succeeding generations. Therefore, he chose to picture himself in hunting costume and not in the regimentals of his military rank. He was a proud man but in no sense a vain one.

Born in Florida, educated in Mexico, statesmen, soldier, engineer, hunter, craftsman, and secretary of the territorial government, his position in California was a somewhat anomalous one. In the eyes of the native Californian chieftains he was a Mexican and therefore viewed with little sympathy and no little suspicion. However, as a man of character and honor, distinguished for his loyalty, probity, and independence, he guided his conduct by his own principles and, as he wrote to Echeandia on April 21, 1832, "those who wish to believe to the contrary can believe whatever they may wish."

The End.

SOURCES

Sources

THIS study is based almost entirely on contemporary manuscript material, or transcripts of such material, nearly all of which is available at the Bancroft Library, University of California, Berkeley. The greatest depository that ever existed for information concerning the history of California under Spanish and Mexican rule was the archives of the secular government of the Territory—the *Archivo de California*. This enormous collection of documents passed into the possession of the United States, and was, in time, bound in two hundred and eighty-nine stout folio volumes and placed for safe-keeping in the office of the United States Surveyor General, in San Francisco. H. H. Bancroft, while gathering material for his series of histories of the Pacific states, transcribed and summarized the documents in the archives into sixty-three folio volumes for his own use. His description of this herculean task follows,

> A room was rented near the surveyor-general's office, to which Mr. H. G. Rollins, then in charge, had kindly granted permission to have the bound volumes taken as required by the copyists. Tables and chairs were then purchased, and the needed writing-materials sent round. Then by a system of condensation and epitomizing, now so thoroughly understood that no time or labor need be lost, under the efficient direction of Mr. Savage fifteen Spaniards were able in one year to transfer from these archives to the library all that was necessary for my purpose. This transfer was not made in the form of notes; the work was an abridgement of the archives, which would be of immense public value in case of loss by fire of the original documents. The title of every paper was given; the more important documents were copied in full; while others were given in substance only. The work was begun the 15th of May, 1876. The expense was about eighteen thousand dollars; and when in the form of bound volumes these archives stood on the shelves of the library, we were just ready to begin extracting historical notes from them in the usual way [*Literary Industries*, 471].

The great fire that destroyed San Francisco in April 1906 brought to pass the very possibility of which the historian speaks. Nothing was saved of the archives. Its contents are available to the student of today only in Bancroft's transcripts. Of these, Bancroft wrote,

> For historical purposes these copies are better than the originals on account of their legibility, and the condensation effected by the omis-

sion of duplicates and suppression of verbiage in minor routine matters [*California*, I, 46].

Unfortunately, as the student soon discovers to his sorrow, this is not true. Many hundreds of documents are listed by title only, with no indication as to their contents, and other hundreds are summarized in a manner so incomplete that they are, at times, tantalizing to the point of distraction. There are innumerable instances, also, where the summarization or transcription of part of a document and the suppression of the remainder causes one to suspect the judgment, and even sincerity of purpose, of the Spanish assistants who did the actual work.

However, notwithstanding their obvious defects, these transcripts are all that is available of the great store the archives contained and every student of California's history is indebted to the great historian of the Pacific Coast for having made them, for no part of the history of California during the Spanish and Mexican periods can be written except on the foundation these transcripts provide. They have been consulted many times in the preparation of this study and as nearly every volume is cited in the notes, I attach a full list of them.

ARCHIVO DE CALIFORNIA.

Provincial State Papers, Vols. 1 to 22, in fourteen.
Provincial State Papers, Benicia, Military, Vols. 1 to 52, in three.
Departmental State Papers, Benicia, Military, Vols. 53 to 88, in three.
Provincial State Papers, Presidios, Vols. 1 and 2, in one.
Provincial Records, Vols. 1 to 12, in five.
Departmental State Papers, Vols. 1 to 16, in six.
Departmental State Papers, Juzgados, Vols. 17 and 18, and *Naturalization*, Vols. 19 and 20, in one.
Departmental State Papers, Angeles, Vols. 1 to 10, in three.
Departmental State Papers, Angeles, Official Correspondence, Vols. 11 and 12, in one.
Departmental State Papers, Benicia, Vols. 1 to 5, in two.
Departmental State Papers, Benicia, Commissary and Treasury, Vols. 1 to 5, in one.
Departmental State Papers, Benicia, Custom House, Vols. 1 to 8, in one.
Departmental State Papers, Benicia, Prefecturas y Juzgados, Vols. 1 to 6, in one.
Departmental State Papers, Monterey, Vols. 1 to 8, in one.
Departmental State Papers, San José, Vols. 1 to 7, in two.
Departmental Records, Vols. 1 to 14, in four.
State Papers, Missions, Vols. 1 to 11, in two.
State Papers, Missions and Colonization, Vols. 1 and 2, in two.
State Papers, Sacramento, Vols. 1 to 19, in three.
Superior Government State Papers, Decrees and Dispatches, Vols. 1 to 18, in one.

Sources

Superior Government State Papers, Vols. 19 to 21, in one.
Legislative Records, Vols. 1 to 4, in three.
Miscellany, Provincial State Papers-Miscellaneous-Benicia, Vols. 1 and 2, *Brands and Marks, Lower California,* Vols. 1 and 2, and *Actas de Elecciones,* all in one.
Unbound Documents, one volume.

In addition to the general territorial archives, Bancroft transcribed, in the same manner, the local Spanish and Mexican archives found in public offices at San Jose, Salinas, Santa Cruz, Los Angeles, and San Diego. These collections are still preserved and, with the exception of those at San Diego, have been examined by me. With a few exceptions, which are indicated, my references, however, are to the Bancroft transcripts. These are:

Archives of San José, Vols. 1 to 6, in one.
Archives of Monterey County, Vols. 1 to 16, in one.
Archives of Santa Cruz.
Archives of Los Angeles, Miscellaneous Papers, Vols. 1 to 3, in three.
Archives of Los Angeles, Miscellaneous Papers, Ayuntamiento Records, Vols. 4 and 5, in two.
Archives of San Diego.

The collection of transcripts made by Bancroft also includes copies and summaries of documents in the archives of the Archdiocese of San Francisco, and in private hands. The Spanish and Mexican documents in the archives of the Roman Catholic Archdiocese of San Francisco constitute one of the largest and most important collections of original documents relating to the period. They were gathered by the late Dr. Alexander S. Taylor and are preserved in five volumes, bound as seven. These I have been privileged to examine. My references to the originals are made to the Taylor, *Documents, Archives of the Archdiocese of San Francisco.* The Bancroft transcripts of these papers, in three volumes, are entitled *Archivo del Arzobispado de San Francisco.* The following transcripts are of a collection in private hands— Guerra y Noriega, José A. de la, *Documentos para la Historia de California,* seven volumes.

Of the many collections of original documents of the period at the Bancroft Library, I have had occasion to make citations to the following,

Bandini, Juan, *Documentos para la Historia de California.*
Carrillo, Domingo, *Documentos para la Historia de California.*
Coronel, Antonio Francisco, *Documentos para la Historia de California.*
Documentos para la Historia de California, 4 vols. Cited as Bancroft, *Documentos.*
Estudillo, José Joaquín, *Documentos para la Historia de California,* 2 vols.
Pico, Pio, *Documentos para la Historia de California,* 3 vols.

Pinto, Rafael, *Documentos para la Historia de California*, 2 vols.
Larkin, Thomas Oliver, *Documents for the History of California, 1839-1856*, 9 vols.
Vallejo, Mariano Guadalupe, *Documentos para la Historia de California*, 37 vols.

There is also at the Bancroft Library a small collection of modern transcripts made from the large collection of documents of the period of this study owned by Mr. John Gaffey, of San Pedro. My references to the Gaffey *Papers* are to these transcripts.

Of the large collection of manuscript histories and memoirs available at the Bancroft Library, I have used the following,

Alvarado, Juan Bautista, *Historia de California*, 5 vols.
Bandini, Juan, *Historia de Alta California, 1769-1845*.
Gómez, Rafael, *Diario de Cosas Notables en Monterey, 1836*.
Ord, Angustias de la Guerra, *Ocurrencias en California*.
Osío, Antonio María, *Historia de California, 1815-1848*.
Pico, Pio, *Narración Histórica*.
Valle, Ignacio del, *Lo Pasado de California*.
Vallejo, José de Jesús, *Reminiscencias Históricas*.
Vallejo, Mariano Guadalupe, *Historia de California*, 5 vols.

The preceding materials in the Bancroft Library have been available to the student since that collection was taken over by the University of California in 1906. Recently, however, there has become available transcripts of several hundred documents in the Archivo General y Público and the Secretaría de Guerra y Marina, Archivo General, in Mexico. Dr. George Tays, of Berkeley, spent most of the year 1929, under a Native Sons of the Golden West Traveling Fellowship in Pacific Coast History, in a search of the archives of the Mexican Government for historical material relative to the Mexican period in California's history. His efforts were richly rewarded and these transcripts are the results of his labors.

The documents that have served this study are nearly all in the Secretaría de Guerra y Marino, Archivo General, where they are preserved in numbered bundles, or *legajos*. My citations to *legajo* numbers are to the transcripts of these documents in the Bancroft Library. Although infinitesimal in bulk in comparison with the manuscript material previously described, the physical size of this collection of transcripts does not indicate its importance. The discovery of these documents has made necessary the rewriting of the history of California's Mexican period and has made possible this biography of Don Agustin V. Zamorano. As an indication of their importance, I would point out that in *Legajos* 52-6-6-7 and 52-6-6-10 was found the entire correspondence that passed between Zamorano and Echeandia during the years 1831, 1832, and 1833, their reports to the national government, and Governor

Figueroa's reports on conditions in California as he found them. These documents make it possible to present the history of the revolution of 1831 and 1832 in its proper prospective. In *Legajo* 52-8-7-1 were found the reports made to the Secretary of War and Marine by Governor Chico from Monterey on July 22, 1836, and by Governor Gutiérrez from Cape San Lucas on November 30, 1836. In *Legajo* 52-6-9-2 were found the reports made by Zamorano, Santiago Argüello, and Portilla on the resistance offered by San Diego and Los Angeles, in 1837, to the revolution of Alvarado and Castro. The existence of all these documents was previously unknown. Many of them I have had occasion to quote, in full or in part, in the course of this study.

The only previous use of these transcripts that has been made was by Dr. Tays himself. His doctoral thesis was a general political history of California from 1821 to 1848 and utilized the documents he discovered. It has been my privilege to read his manuscript and I have referred to it in the notes. He is now preparing his study for publication under the title of *Revolutionary California*.

Aside from the documents and transcripts in the Bancroft Library, my chief sources have been papers in the possession of descendants of Zamorano and the early registers of births, marriages and deaths at the Roman Catholic Cathedral, St. Augustine, Florida, San Carlos Church, Monterey, Our Lady of Sorrows Church, Santa Barbara, and Mission San Diego.

Two descendants only of Zamorano possess family papers of the period covered by this study. Curiously, there is not a single document among them that relates to Don Agustin himself. Mrs. Francis Horatio Throop, *née* María Anaís Estudillo, of San Luis Obispo, owns a collection of family documents that cover the entire official life of Don Gonzalo Zamorano and thereby disclose the antecedents of Don Agustin. It consists of nineteen separate items, of from two to eighteen pages each, which date from 1751, in Madrigal, Old Castile, Spain, to 1813, in Guanajuato, Mexico. I have referred to this collection as the Gonzalo Zamorano *Documentos*.

The first thirteen documents in Mrs. Throop's possession are certified copies of the proceedings in a judicial investigation into the ancestry and standing of Don Gonzalo Zamorano, which was a prerequisite to the issuance of a royal patent of arms by the king-at-arms of the Spanish Court. The *Certificacio de Armas de D. Gonzalo Zamorano y Gonzalez*, issued as the result of this inquiry, by Don Juan Felix de Rujula, King-at-Arms to Carlos III, at Madrid on June 4, 1777, is now in the possession of Mr. George Henry Dalton, of Tucson, Arizona. It is a magnificent manuscript on thirty-two vellum leaves, bound in tooled leather covers.

For notes from the James Hunnewell *Papers*, in Harvard College Library, I am indebted to Miss Adele Ogden, of Berkeley, and for notes from the *Escrituras* in the Spanish East Florida Archives, Manuscript Division, Library of Congress, to Miss Emily L. Wilson, of St. Augustine, Florida.

PRINTED WORKS.

Baker, C. C., "Don Enrique Dalton of the Azusa," in *Annual Publications Historical Society of Southern California*, 1917. Volume X, No. 3, 17.

Bancroft, Hubert Howe, *California Pastoral*, San Francisco, 1888.

Bancroft, Hubert Howe, *History of California*, San Francisco, 1886-90, 7 vols.

Bancroft, Hubert Howe, *History of Mexico*, San Francisco, 1883-88, 6 vols.

Bancroft, Hubert Howe, *North Mexican States and Texas*, San Francisco, 1884-89, 2 vols.

Barrows, David Prescott, "Romualdo Pacheco," in *Dictionary of American Biography*, Vol. XIV, 124.

Bernard du Hautcilly, Auguste, *Voyage autour du Monde, principalment à la Californie et aux Iles Sandwich, pendant les Années 1826, 1827, 1828, et 1829*, Paris, 1834-35, 2 vols.

Bolton, Herbert Eugene, *Guide to Materials for the History of the United States in the principal Archives in Mexico*, Washington, 1913.

Boston Type and Stereotype Foundry, *Specimen of Modern Printing Types and Stereotype Cuts*, Boston, 1826.

Boston Type and Stereotype Foundry, *Specimen of Modern Printing Types*, Boston, 1845.

Brevard, Caroline May, *History of Florida from the Treaty of 1763 to our own Times*, edited by James Alexander Robertson, Deland, 1924-25, 2 vols.

Briggs, L[loyd] Vernon, *History of Shipbuilding on North River Plymouth County, Massachusetts, with Genealogies of the Shipbuilders, and Accounts of the Industries upon its Tributaries, 1640-1872*, Boston, 1889.

Carter, Charles Franklin, translator, "Duhaut-Cilly's Account of California in the Years 1827-1828," in *Quarterly* of California Historical Society, June and September, 1929. Volume VIII, Nos. 2 and 3.

Colton, Walter, *Three Years in California*, New York, 1850.

Cowan, Robert Ernest, *Bibliography of the Spanish Press of California, 1833-1845*, San Francisco, 1919.

Dana, Richard Henry, Jr., *Two Years before the Mast*, Boston, [1911].

Duflot de Mofras, Eugène, *Exploration du Territoire de l'Orégon, des Californies, et de la Mer Vermeille, exécutée pendant les Années 1840, 1841, et 1842*, Paris, 1844, 2 vols. and atlas.

Engelhardt, Charles Anthony *(in religion,* Fr. Zephyrin), *Missions and Missionaries of California*, San Francisco, 1908-16, 5 vols. and index.

Engelhardt, Charles Anthony *(in religion,* Fr. Zephyrin), *San Diego Mission*, San Francisco, 1920.

Fairbanks, George R[ainsford], *History and Antiquities of the City of*

SOURCES

St. Augustine, Florida, founded A.D. 1565, New York, 1858.

Figueroa, José, *Manifiesto a la Republica Mejicana*, Monterey, 1835.

[Figueroa, José], *The Manifesto which the General of Brigade, Don José Figueroa, Commandant-General and Political Chief of A. California, makes to the Mexican Republic*, San Francisco, 1855. A translation of the preceding title.

Fisher, Lillian Estelle, *Viceregal Administration in the Spanish-American Colonies*, Berkeley, 1926.

Harding, George Laban, "A Census of California Spanish Imprints, 1833-1845," in *Quarterly* of California Historical Society, June 1933. Volume XII, No. 2, 125.

Hittell, Theodore Henry, *History of California*, San Francisco, 1885-97, 4 vols.

Hodge, Frederick Webb, editor, *Handbook of American Indians North of Mexico*, Washington, 1907, 2 vols.

Kelley, Hall J[ackson], *History of the Settlement of Oregon and the Interior of California*, Springfield, 1868.

[Kemble, Edward Cleveland], *History of California Newspapers*, New York, 1927. A reprint from the Sacramento *Daily Union*, December 25, 1858.

Kroeber, A[lfred] L[ewis], *Handbook of the Indians of California*, Washington, 1925.

Priestley, Herbert Ingram, *The Mexican Nation, a History*, New York, 1923.

Richman, Irving Berdine, *California under Spain and Mexico, 1535-1847*, Boston, 1911.

Rivera, Mariano Galvan, *Guia de Forasteros Politico-Commercial de la Ciudad de Mexico para el Año de 1842*, Mexico, 1842.

[Robinson, Alfred], *Life in California*, New York, 1846.

Royce, Josiah, *California, from the Conquest in 1846 to the Second Vigilance Committee in San Francisco*, Boston, [1886].

Transcript of the Proceedings in Case No. 548, José Y. Limantour, Claimant, vs. The United States, Defendant, for Four Square Leagues of Land in San Francisco County. Appendix No. 1, Archives Exhibits, San Francisco, 1857.

Whitaker, Arthur Preston, *The Spanish-American Frontier, 1783-1795*, Boston, 1927.

Zúñiga y Ontiveros, Mariano de, *Calendario Manual y Guia de Forasteros en Mexico para el Año de 1811*, Mexico, 1811. Also, for the years 1812 to 1821, inclusive.

NEWSPAPERS.

Alta California, San Francisco, October 20, 1851.
Californian, Monterey, February 13, 1847.
Daily Union, Sacramento, December 25, 1858.

APPENDIX

Genealogy

THE FAMILY OF
DON AGUSTIN VICENTE ZAMORANO

1798 May 5	Agustin Juan Vicente Zamorano *Born at St. Augustine, Florida* *Died at San Diego, California* 1827 Feb. 15 *married to*	1842 Sep. 16
1812 Mar. 5	María Luisa Joana Josepha de la Luz Argüello *Born at Santa Barbara, California* *Died at Los Angeles, California* *Their issue:*	1847 May 11
1827 Nov. 23	María Dolores Francisca Zamorano I *Born at Monterey* *Date and place of death not known* 1843 July *married to* José María Flores 1842 Aug. *came to California* 1847 Jan. *left California* *Their issue:*	
1844 June 9	José María Alberto Agustin Flores *Born at Monterey* *Died at Azusa*	1875 Mar. 12
1845 Dec. 4	José Alfredo Flores *Born at Los Angeles* María Luisa Flores *Became the wife of* Ventura Arnaiz *Their issue:* Ventura Arnaiz, Jr. Paulacion Arnaiz Francisca Arnaiz	
1829 Apr. 29	Luis Agustin Marcelino Zamorano II *Born at San Diego* *Died at San Diego* 1882 Nov. 7 *married to*	1907 Jan. 13

	Carlota Murphy	1916 Oct. 12
	Born at San Francisco	
	Died at San Diego	
	Their issue:	
	Four children died in infancy	
1885 Apr. 21	Luisa Ana Zamorano	*
1887 Feb. 10	Lula Dorotea Zamorano	*
1894 Oct. 12	Carlota Zamorano	*
1896 Dec. 13	Minnie Lucille Zamorano	*
1831 Sep. 18	Gonzalo Nicomedez Zamorano III	
	Born at Monterey	
	Died as a child, date unknown	
1832 Dec. 18	María de Guadalupe Zamorano IV	1914 Sep. 1
	Born at Monterey	
	Died at Azusa	
	1847 Aug. 14 *married to*	
1803 Oct. 8	Henry Dalton	1884 Jan. 21
	Born at London, England	
	Died at Los Angeles	
	Their issue:	
	Henry Edward Dalton	
	Died in infancy	
1850 June 14	Winnall Agustin Dalton	1917 Aug. 31
1852 Jan. 5	Ana Luisa Dalton	1887 May 29
1853 Nov. 2	Henrietta Dalton	1854 Mar. 27
1855 Apr. 5	Soyla Carolina Dalton	1933 Dec. 31
1857 Sep. 28	Elisa Dalton	1860 Feb. 15
1859 Nov. 30	Henry Albert Dalton	1860 Aug. 27
1861 July 15	Henry Francis Dalton	1933 July 20
1864 Aug. 22	Elena Dalton	1918 Nov. 29
1867 Feb. 14	Valentin Zamorano Dalton	1889 Feb. 22
1869 Dec. 17	Joseph Russell Henry Dalton	1934 Mar. 16
1834 Feb. 12	Josepha María Zamorano V	
	Born at Monterey	
	Died a young woman, unmarried, date unknown	
1835 Sep. 6	Agustin Vicente Zamorano VI	1872
	Born at Monterey	
	Died near Tijuana, Baja California	
	1865 Jan. 7 *married to*	

GENEALOGICAL TABLES

1842	María Leonora Jeantet *Born at Taos, New Mexico* *Died at Azusa* *Their issue:*	1879
1865 Nov. 20	Agustin Vicente Zamorano 3d	*
1867 May 9	María de Guadalupe Tiburcia Zamorano	1892 Feb. 20
1870 Apr. 9	Dolores Zamorano	1910 Jan. 2
1837 Feb. 6	Eulalia Dorotea Zamorano VII *Born at San Diego* *Died at San Luis Obispo* 1860 Oct. 6 *married to*	1909 Mar. 24
1833 Feb. 19	José Vicente Estudillo *Born at San Leandro* *Died at San Luis Obispo* *Their issue:*	1893 Nov. 9
1861 Sep. 1	José Joaquín Estudillo	*
1863 Mar. 13	Agustin Vicente Estudillo	1927 Sep. 30
1864 Sep. 7	José Vicente Estudillo	*
1866 Feb. 6	Eulalia Dorotea Estudillo	1933 Sep. 19
1867 Dec. 6	Josepha Rosa Estudillo	*
1869 Oct. 14	María Concepcion Estudillo	*
1870 July 29	Elena Ramona Estudillo	1903 Dec. 29
1872 Dec. 30	Enrique Ramon Estudillo	*
1874 Aug. 2	José Gonzalo Estudillo	*
1876 July 2	María Odulia Estudillo	*
1878 Jan. 31	Francisca Dalinda Estudillo	1884 Jan. 15
1882 July 13	María Anaís Estudillo	*

* *Living in September 1934.*

The Ancestry of
Don Agustin Vicente Zamorano

Third Preceding Generation

Gabriel Zamorano
   Lived and died at Horcajo de las Torres, Ávila,
     Old Castile, Spain
   Married to
Inés González
   Died at Horcajo de las Torres
   Their issue:

1707 June   Francisco Zamorano
        Baptised June 25, 1707

Francisco González
   Lived and died at Rasueros, Ávila, Old Castile, Spain
   Married to
María Lopez
   Their issue:

1710 May 2   Joaquína González

Second Preceding Generation

1707 June   Francisco Zamorano
        Born at Horcajo de las Torres
        Lived and died at Muriel, Ávila, Old Castile, Spain
        Married to

1710 May 2   Joaquína González
        Born at Rasueros
        Died at Muriel
        Their issue:

1740 Dec. 22   Gonzalo Zamorano y González   1820?
                Manuel Zamorano y González
                Antonio Zamorano y González

Felix del Corral
    Capitan de Navio in Royal Navy
    Lived at Havana, Cuba
    Married to

Genealogical Tables

Juana de Dios Garcia Menocal
Their issue:
Francisca Sales del Corral

First Preceding Generation

1740 Dec. 22	Gonzalo Zamorano y González	1820?

                  Born at Muriel, Ávila, Old Castile, Spain
                  1741 Jan. 4 *baptised*
                  Died at Guanajuato, Guanajuato, Mexico
                  1784 May 6 *married, at Cathedral of the Immaculate Conception, Havana, Cuba, to*
                  Francisca Sales del Corral
                  Born at Havana, Cuba
                  Died at Guanajuato, Guanajuato, Mexico
                  Their issue:

1785 Jan. 28	Francisca Sales Juliana Zamorano	
	Born at St. Augustine, Florida	
1786 June 29	Petrona Josepha de la Luz Zamorano	
	Born at St. Augustine, Florida	
1787 Dec. 17	María de la O. Lazara Vicenta Zamorano	
	Born at St. Augustine, Florida	
1791 June 12	Joseph Juan de Sahagun Zamorano	
	Born at St. Augustine, Florida	
1793 Mar. 30	Juana Olimaca Joaquína Francisca de Paula Zamorano	
	Born at St. Augustine, Florida	
1798 May 5	Agustin Juan Vicente Zamorano	1842 Sep. 16
	Born at St. Augustine, Florida	
	Died at San Diego, California	
1800 Jan. 6	Rafaela Melchoza Zamorano	1800 Sep. 24
	Born and died at St. Augustine, Florida	

Don Agustin V. Zamorano

The Ancestry of Doña María Luisa Argüello de Zamorano

Third Preceding Generation

  José Francisco Ortega   1798 Feb. 3
   Born at Zelaya, Guanajuato, Mexico
   1755 *Oct. 1 enlisted in the army*
   1769 *came to California with Portolá and Serra*
   Died at Santa Barbara, California
   Married to
  María Antonia Victoria Carrillo   1803 May
   1803 *May 8 buried at Santa Barbara*
   Their issue:

1759   José María Ortega

  Ygnacio Lopez
   Native of Baja California
   Married to
  María Fecunda de Mora
   Born at Tepic, Mexico
   Their issue:

1763   María Francisca Lopez

Second Preceding Generation

1753?   José Darío Argüello   1827?
   Born at Querétaro, Mexico
   1773 *enlisted in the army*
   1781 *July 14 arrived in California*
   Died at Guadalajara, Jalisco, Mexico
   1780? *married to*
  Ignacia Moraga   1829 Apr. 12
   Born at Altar, Sonora, Mexico
   Died at Guadalajara, Jalisco, Mexico
   Their issue:

1792 July 27   Santiago Argüello   1862 Nov. 9

1759   José María Ortega
   1779 *June 14 married to*

1763	María Francisca Lopez *Born at Loreto, Baja California* *Their issue:*	
1794 Oct. 12	María del Pilar Salvadora Ortega	1879?

First Preceding Generation

1792 July 27	Santiago Argüello *Born at Monterey, California* *Died at Tijuana, Baja California* 1810 May 30 *married to*	1862 Nov. 9
1794 Oct. 12	María del Pilar Salvadora Ortega *Born at Santa Barbara, California* *Died at Tijuana, Baja California* *Their issue:*	1879?
1812 Mar. 5	María Luisa Joana Josepha de la Luz Argüello	1847 May 11

INDEX

Index

INDEX TO DOCUMENTS QUOTED.

Alamán, Lucas, to
Secretary of War and Marine, Mexico, May 17, 1832, 133.
Alvarado, Juan Bautista, *Historia de California*, regarding
Zamorano's desertion of his family, 259.
Alvarado, Juan Bautista, to
Vallejo, Santa Barbara, July 12, 1837, 238-9.
Vallejo, Santa Barbara, July 17, 1837, 239-40.
Vallejo, Santa Barbara, June 20, 1838, 250.
Vallejo, San Fernando, August 18, 1838, 258.
Anderson, Stephen, to
Cooper, Santa Barbara, January 24, 1830, 41.
Argüello, Santiago, to
Secretary of Relations, San Diego, December 25, 1836, 214.

Carrillo, Carlos Antonio, to
de la Guerra y Noriega, Mexico, March 15, 1832, 145-6.
Castillo Negrete, Francisco del, to
Secretary of War and Marine, Mexico, April 11, 1839, 252.
Castro, José, to
Gutiérrez, Monterey, November 6, 1836, 176.
Bandini, Zamorano, Cabello and Ramírez, Santa Rita, June 17, 1837, 231.
Chico, Mariano, to
Secretary of War and Marine, Monterey, July 22, 1836, 173.
Council of February 1, 1832, Monterey, Minutes and resolutions of, 94-7.

Echeandia, José María de, to
Circular Letter, San Gabriel, December 9, 1831, 64-5.
Circular Letter, Los Angeles, February 25, 1832, 86-8.
Ibarra, San Diego, March 7, 1832, 105-6.
Ibarra, San Diego, March 8, 1832, 107.
Ibarra, Los Angeles, April 7, 1832, 116.
Secretary of Relations, San Diego, June 30, 1829, 48.
Secretary of War and Marine, Monterey, August 31, 1830, 43-4.
Zamorano, San Juan Capistrano, December 29, 1831, 78-9.
Zamorano, San Luis Rey, January 8, 1832, 81-3.
Zamorano, San Luis Rey, March 24, 1832, 110-13.
Zamorano, San Luis Rey, March 24, 1832, 113-14.
Zamorano, San Gabriel, April 16, 1832, 118-19.
Zamorano, San Gabriel, April 24, 1832, 125-7.
Zamorano, San Luis Rey, May 3, 1832, 129-30.
Zamorano, San Diego, June 19, 1832, 135.

Figueroa, José, to
Secretary of War and Marine, Monterey, March 26, 1833, 151-3.
Zamorano, Monterey, February 15, 1833, 149-50.

Ibarra, Juan María, to
Echeandia, Santa Barbara, February 23, 1832, 102.

Osío, Antonio María, *Historia de California*, regarding
battle at Cahuenga Pass on December 5, 1831, 63.

character of Ibarra's troops in February 1832, 101.
Plan of San Diego, San Diego, November 29 and December 1, 1831, 55-7.
Portilla, Pablo de la, to
Secretary of War and Marine, San Diego, September 12, 1837, 228-36.

Vallejo, Mariano Guadalupe, *Historia de California*, regarding
Zamorano's offer to surrender the command of the Monterey *presidio* in December 1831, 75.
Echeandia's forces at Paso de Bartolo in April 1832, 119.
Victoria, Manuel, to
Proclamation to Inhabitants of California, Monterey, September 21, 1831, 53.
Secretary of War and Marine, San Blas, February 5, 1832, 59-62.

Zalvidea, Fr. José María,
Circular Letter, San Gabriel, March 29, 1832, 114.
Zamorano, Agustin V., to
Circular Letter, Monterey, February 2, 1832, 100.
Commandant of San Francisco *presidio*, Monterey, January 14, 1833, 147-8.
Echeandia, Monterey, December 17, 1831, 74.
Echeandia, Monterey, December 29, 1831, 76-7.
Echeandia, Monterey, January 7, 1832, 79-81.
Echeandia, Monterey, February 12, 1832, 101-2.
Echeandia, Monterey, April 1, 1832, 115.
Echeandia, on the way to Santa Barbara, April 12, 1832, 117-8.
Echeandia, Santa Barbara, April 21, 1832, 120-5.
Echeandia, Santa Barbara, April 26, 1832, 127-8.
Echeandia, Santa Barbara, May 8, 1832, 130.
Echeandia, Monterey, July 7, 1832, 136.
Proclamation to Citizens of Los Angeles, Monterey, March 11, 1832, 108-9.
Proclamation to the Inhabitants from Santa Barbara to San Francisco, Santa Barbara, May 9, 1832, 131-2.
Proclamation to the Inhabitants from Santa Barbara to San Francisco, Monterey, July 7, 1832, 136-7.
Secretary of War and Marine, Monterey, June 6, 1832, 134-5.
Secretary of War and Marine, Monterey, November 16, 1832, 141-3.
Secretary of War and Marine, Rancho de Ti Juan, April 24, 1837, 219-21.
Secretary of War and Marine, San Diego, June 5, 1837, 224-8.
Zamorano, Agustin V., and Juan María Ibarra to
Echeandia, Monterey, December 16, 1831, 72-4.
Zamorano, Gonzalo
Baptismal entry of, Muriel, Old Castile, Spain, January 4, 1741, 10.

General Index

Abella, Fr. Ramon, 35, 67, 263.
Agustin I, Emperor of Mexico, *see* Iturbide, Agustin de.
Alamán, Lucas, 45, 133, 145.
Alamitos Rancho, 230.
Alert, 32.
Alhóndiga de Granaditas, 15.
Alta California (newspaper), 181, 182.
Alva, Manuel, 147, 176.
Alvarado, Francisco, 216.
Alvarado, Juan Bautista: his opinion of Echeandia, 22; secretary of deputation in 1832, 84; mentioned, 157; his statement of Zamorano's advice to Figueroa regarding succession, 166; leader in the revolt of November, 1836, 175-7; Bancroft's comments regarding, 175, 259; southern opposition to in 1837-8, 211-50; recognized as governor at Santa Barbara, 215; meeting with commissioners from Los Angeles and San Diego, 216; meeting with *ayuntamiento* of Los Angeles, 217; Zamorano's report on activities of, 219; relations with Castillero, 232-3, 237, 238, 239, 250; as constitutional governor, 234-5, 237, 238, 250, 253; on succession to *comandancia general*, 238, 239; antipathy for Zamorano, 239, 250, 258-9; delay in delivering office of civil governor to Carrillo, 242-3; at Las Flores and negotiations with Carrillo, 249.
Alvitre, Ysidoro, 221.
Amao, Domingo, 218, 221.
Americans in California, 141, 220-1, 234.
Amesti, José, 93.
Anderson, Dr. Stephen, 41.
Archivo de California, 178, 275-7.
Archivo General y Público, Mexico, 278.
Archdiocese of San Francisco, Archives of, 277.
Argüello, Gervacio, 44, 241.
Argüello, María Ignacia Moraga de, 27, 290.
Argüello, José Darío, 5, 26, 27, 290.
Argüello, Luis Antonio, 1, 6, 20, 26, 67, 264.

Argüello, María de la Concepcion Marcela, 5, 26.
Argüello, María Concepcion, 265.
Argüello, María del Pilar Ortega de, 27, 38, 262, 291.
Argüello, María Luisa: marriage to Zamorano, 25-7; first child, 34-5; second child, 38; mentioned, 260; character of, 260-1; her later years, 261-2; her children, 262-5; genealogy, 285, 290-1.
Argüello, Soledad Ortega de, 264.
Argüello, Santiago: ensign in San Diego Company, 23, 24; youth and parentage, 26-7; mentioned, 38; objected to Echeandia's secularization decree of January 6, 1831, 50; member of deputation, 52, 84, 103; signed Plan of San Diego 1831, 56-8; mentioned by Victoria, 59; his promotion to captain, 71; member of Council at San Diego, March, 1832, 103; provided home for Zamorano and family, 211; his efforts in opposition to Alvarado in 1837, 212-15, 218; the Plan of San Diego, 1837, 222-7; his protest against Castillero's actions, 237; mentioned, 255; prefect of southern district, 257, 261; administrator of Mission San Juan Capistrano, 261; provided home for Zamorano's children, 262; genealogy, 290, 291.
Argüello, Santiago Emidio, 213, 222, 223, 265.
Argüello, Ysabella, 35, 267.
Arithmetic, 207.
Arnaiz, Francisca, 285.
Arnaiz, Paulacion, 285.
Arnaiz, Ventura, 263, 285.
Arnaiz, Ventura, Jr., 285.
Atzcapotzalco, battle of, 18, 44.
Avila, José María, 63, 154, 248.
Aviso al Publico, 1834, 196.
Ayacucho, 68.

Baja California, 2, 38, 251-2.
Bancroft, Hubert Howe: quoted on secularization of the missions, 46; on Council of February 1, 1832, Monterey, 98;

on character of Figueroa, 158; regarding Alvarado, 175, 259; regarding Hartnell, 268; his transcripts of territorial archives, 275-6.
Bancroft Library, 179, 275-9.
Bandini, Juan: his part in persecution of Herrera, 34; elected alternate deputy to congress, 44; his part in promoting Plan of San Diego 1831, 54-8; mentioned by Victoria, 59; as *comisario subalterno*, 95, 97, 139; member of Council at San Diego, March, 1832, 106; connection with the Hijar and Padrés Colony, 160, 161; mentioned, 168; as commissioner to Los Angeles in 1836, 213; his part in Plan of San Diego 1837, 222-4, 227; mentioned, 231, 244; death of Zamorano at home of, 256; his wife appealed to Alvarado for aid, 258-9; administrator of Mission San Gabriel, 261.
Bandini, Refugia Argüello de, 259.
Baptist Foreign Missionary Society, 194.
Barker, R. S., 93.
Barragan, 169, 174.
Barroso, Leonardo Diaz, 61, 62, 103, 109, 115, 117.
Batallon Fijo de Californias, 254-5.
Bee, Henry, 93.
Begg & Company, 268.
Bonifacio, Juan B., 92, 93, 94, 97.
Boston Type and Stereotype Foundry, 197.
Bourne, Jonathan, 195.
Bourne Memorial Whaling Museum, 195.
Bradshaw, John: master of *Franklin*, 35-6; of *Pocahontas*, 66; of *Lagoda*, 191-4.
Brannan, Samuel, 181.
Bravo, Juan D., 93.
Brooklyn, 181.
Brotherhood of the Most Holy, 11.
Burns, John, 93.
Bustamante, Anastacio, 7, 17, 18, 45, 145.

Caballero, Fr. Felix, 229, 251.
Caballero, José, 251.
Cabello, Martín Sánchez, 218, 221, 231.
Caguenga Rancho, 117.
Cahuenga Pass, battle of, 58-63.
California, the name, 2.
California Star, 181, 182.
California State Library, 179.

Californian, 180, 182, 208, 262.
Callejo, General, 15.
Cañada de los Sauzes, 233.
Campo, see Perez del Campo.
Campo, Antonio, 144.
Campo de la Palma, 222, 229.
Carrillo, Anastacio, 62, 100, 152, 230.
Carrillo, Carlos Antonio: elected to congress, 44; correspondence with J. A. de la Guerra y Noriega, 144-6; mentioned, 168; recognized Alvarado as governor, 215; as Castro's envoy, 232-3; claimed civil governorship, 241-50.
Carrillo, Domingo, 41, 42, 72, 100, 112, 121, 127.
Carrillo, Joaquín, 25.
Carrillo, José Antonio: exiled by Victoria, 51; promotes Plan of San Diego 1831, 53, 59, 62, 63; mentioned, 75; supported C. A. Carrillo as governor, 241-4.
Carrillo, María Antonia Victoria, 290.
Carrillo, Ramona: marriage to Romualdo Pacheco, 24-5; marriage to John Wilson and later years, 68-9; godmother of Josepha María Zamorano, 264.
Carlos III, 11.
Castañares, Ana González de, 170-1.
Castañares, José María, 170-1.
Castañeda, Juan, 246-8.
Castillero, Andrés, 176-7, 229-41, 250.
Castillo Negrete, Francisco del, 169, 251-2.
Castillo Negrete, Luis del, 176, 212, 214, 242, 251.
Castro, José: mentioned, 49; license to hunt otter, 139; acting civil governor, 157, 164-5; a leader in revolt of November, 1836, 174-7; campaign of 1837, 229-32; capture of Mission San Buenaventura in 1838, 248; at Las Flores, 249; as general commandant, 257.
Castro, José Tiburcio, 52, 53, 54.
Catalina, 147, 148.
Catecismo De Ortologia, 207.
Causes of strife in Alta California, 7-9.
Cruz, Doña, 169, 171.
Centralism, 168, 169, 237, 238.
Certificacio de Armas de D. Gonzalo Zamorano y Gonzalez, 11, 277.
Cervantes, Andrés, 39, 57, 58, 103.
Chevrette, Pierre J., 93.

INDEX

Chico, Mariano: mentioned, 157; as governor, 168-73; remarks regarding Zamorano, 173; his proclamation of May 3, 1836, 204-5; his proclamation of May 11, 1836, 205; his *Discurso* of May 20, 1836, 205; his *Discurso* of May 27, 1836, 205-6; his proclamation of July 24, 1836, 206-7; his report of July 22, 1836, 279.
Christo de las Injurias, El Santisimo, 11.
Clementina, 172, 177, 207, 212, 222.
Colton, Walter, 180, 208.
Columbia *Star*, 181, 209, 210.
Comandancia general, succession to in 1837, 235-6, 238, 239, 240-1.
Commerce, laws regulating, 35, 205.
Compañia extrangera, 92-3, 150.
Compañia Cosmopolitana, 160-4.
Company of Foreigners, see *Compañia extrangera*.
Contaduria General de Exercito y Real Hacienda, 12.
Cook, James, 93.
Cooper, John B. R., 41, 93, 252.
Coulter, Thomas, 93.
Council of February 1, 1832, Monterey, 93-7.
Council of November 4, 1836, Monterey, 176.
Council of March, 1832, San Diego, 103-8.
Coronel, Ignacio, 211, 267, 269.
Corral, Felix del, 12, 288.
Corral, Francisca Sales del, 12, 289.
Corral, Juana de Dios García Menocal de, 12, 289.
Covarrubias, José María, 247.
Cowan, Robert Ernest, 189, 190.
Crespo, Manuel, 176.
Cuba, 12.

Dana, Richard Henry, Jr.: his description of Monterey in 1835 quoted, 30-2; his mention of Captain John Wilson, 68; his description of the *Lagoda* quoted, 194.
Dalton, Ana Luisa, 286.
Dalton, Elena, 286.
Dalton, Elisa, 286.
Dalton, George Henry, 279.
Dalton, Henrietta, 286.

Dalton, Henry, 264, 286.
Dalton, Henry Albert, 286.
Dalton, Henry Edward, 286.
Dalton, Henry Francis, 286.
Dalton, Joseph Russell Henry, 264, 286.
Dalton, María de Guadalupe Zamorano de, 263-4, 286.
Dalton, Soyla Carolina, 286.
Dalton, Valentin Zamorano, 286.
Dalton, Winnall Agustin, 286.
Declaration of independence of November 6, 1836, 177.
Deputation: the first, 6; election of deputies to, 1827, 27; election of deputies to, 1828, 37; election of deputies to, 1830, 44; Echeandia's plan for secularization of the missions submitted to, 48; Victoria's relations with, 52-3; the Plan of San Diego, 1831, 56; convened by Echeandia, 65; mentioned, 75; sessions in 1832 and its relations with Echeandia, 83-8, 108; its election of Pico as acting civil governor, 84; position of Council of February 1, 1832, Monterey, regarding, 95; provisions regarding in truce of 1832, 112, 121, 124, 131; Zamorano's position on election of deputies in 1832, 138; its sessions in 1834, 159; its *Reglamento*, 200; its relations with Chico, 170; its part in revolt of November, 1836, 177, 215; Alvarado as senior member, 235, 237, 239.
Dios y Libertad, 7.
Dixon, Joseph, 93.
Doak, Thomas, 93.
Dolores, El Grito de, 15, 16.
Dominguez, Elena, 37, 67.
Dominguez, Manuel, 109.
Douglas, D., 93.
Duarte, Cristóbal, 221.
Duarte, Martín, 261.
Duckworth, Walter, 93.
Duflot de Mofras, Eugène, 179, 180.
Duhaut-Cilly: on character of Echeandia, 22; his description of Santa Barbara quoted, 28; of Monterey, 29.
Durán, Fr. Narciso, 25, 68, 215, 240, 247.

East Florida, province of, 12-14.

Echeandia, José María de: his appointment as governor of Californias, 1, 18; his arrival at San Diego in 1825, 2, 19-20; his mission policy, 8, 48-50; character of, 22-3, 40, 41-2, 51; his persecution of Herrera, 33-4, 41-2; relieved of military command of Baja California, 38; his conduct during the Solis Revolt, 39-42; recommended Zamorano for promotion to captain of Monterey Company, 43-4; his secularization decree of January 6, 1831, 46-50; statement regarding Spanish friars, 48; his part in Plan of San Diego 1831, 55-8; his interview with Victoria at Mission San Gabriel on December 9, 1831, 61, 64; his circular letter of that date, 64-5; his circular letter of December 21, 1831, 75-6; urged Zamorano to accept Plan of San Diego 1831, 77-9, 81-3; his intimidation of deputation, 83-8; circular letter of February 25, 1832, 86-8; offered governorship to Zamorano, 88; refused to recognize Zamorano as acting governor, 102-8; on Council of February 1, 1832, Monterey, 103-4; his Council at San Diego, March, 1832, 103-8; raised an army of Indians, 109-10, 114, 115, 119, 124, 132; negotiations with Zamorano in 1832, 110-32, 135-6; Alamán's statement regarding, 133; his relations with Figueroa, 148-9; his departure from California, 149; Figueroa's report on affairs in 1831-2, 151; his claim as acting governor in 1832, 154-6; mentioned, 252.

Ejército Trigarante, 17, 18.

Elections: in 1827, 27; in 1828, 37; in 1830, 44; Zamorano's position regarding in 1832, 138.

Elizalde, Antonio, 221.

Engelhardt, Fr. Zephyrin, 256.

Engineer's Corps, 18, 19.

Espinosa, Salvador, 93, 94, 97, 104.

Estrada, Adelaida, 264, 268.

Estrada, José Mariano: commandant at Monterey, 34; godfather of María Dolores Zamorano, 35; mentioned, 43; appointed *comisario subalterno* at Monterey by Zamorano, 139-40; repri-

manded by Chico, 172; friend of Zamorano, 267.

Estrada, José Ramon: obtained license to hunt otter, 139; claimant of Rancho El Toro, 166; as *alcalde* of Monterey and troubles with Chico, 171-2.

Estrada, Josepha, 263, 267.

Estrada, Nicanor, 222, 227, 235, 241.

Estrada, Patricio, 2, 20, 176, 177.

Estrada, Ysabella Argüello de, 267.

Estudillo, Agustin Vicente, 287.

Estudillo, Elena Ramona, 287.

Estudillo, Enrique Ramon, 287.

Estudillo, Eulalia Dorotea, 287.

Estudillo, Eulalia Dorotea Zamorano de, 265, 270, 287.

Estudillo, Francisca Dalinda, 287.

Estudillo, José Antonio, 246.

Estudillo, José Gonzalo, 287.

Estudillo, José María, 23, 265.

Estudillo, José Joaquín, 287.

Estudillo, José Vicente, 265, 287.

Estudillo, José Vicente, Jr., 287.

Estudillo, Josepha Rosa, 287.

Estudillo, María Anaís, 279, 287.

Estudillo, María Concepcion, 287.

Estudillo, María Odulia, 287.

Facio, Secretary of War and Marine, 45.

Farías, Valentin Gómez, *see* Gómez Farías, Valentin.

Ferguson, Daniel, 93.

Fernández de San Vicente, Agustin, 6.

Figueroa, José: expected arrival of, 135, 137, 141; arrival of in Alta California, 143-8; takes office as governor, 147; his relations with Echeandia, 148-9; his commendation of Zamorano's services, 149-50, 151-2; report on situation in California, 151-3; mentioned, 157; as governor, 158-64; Bancroft quoted regarding, 158; his relations with Hijar and Padrés Colony, 159-63; his death, 164; his *Manifiesto de la Republica Mejicana*, 1835, 164, 202; printed announcement of his arrival January 16, 1833, 189-90; his proclamation of August 6, 1834, 200; his proclamation of August 9, 1834, 201; godfather of Agustin Vicente Zamorano, Jr., 264.

Fijo de Hidalgo, 2.

Index

Fling, Guy F., 93.
Flores, José Alfredo, 285.
Flores, José María, 262-3, 285.
Flores, José María Alberto Agustin, 285.
Flores, María Dolores Zamorano de, 262-3, 285.
Flores, María Luisa, 285.
Flores, Rancho de las, 249.
Font, Francisco, 12.
Foreigners in Alta California, 141, 234, 253.
Fort Ross, 162.
Foster, Seth and Samuel, 194.
Franklin (ship), 35-6, 66, 192.
Funchal, 41.

Gálvez, Bernardo de, 12.
Gálvez, José María de, 3.
Garner, William, 93.
Genealogy, 285-91.
Gil y Taboada, Fr. Luis, 27.
Gómez Farías, Valentin, 160, 162.
Gómez, José Joaquín, 93, 94, 95, 97, 104, 105, 106, 139.
Gómez, Rafael, 93, 94, 97, 104.
Góngora, José Antonio, 257.
González, Francisco, 11.
González, Francisco, 10, 288.
González, Inéz, 288.
González, Joaquina, 10, 288.
González, M. M., 176.
González, Miguel, 2, 19, 34, 43.
González, Rafael, 147, 170.
González, Theresa, 10.
Goodwin, Osias, 192.
Gore, G. W., 209.
Gorman, John, 93.
Graham, Isaac, 175, 215, 217, 220.
Gralbatch, William, 93.
Guadalupe (ship), 143.
Guanajuato, 14-17.
Guerra y Noriega, José Antonio de la: elected deputy to congress, 27, 37; Duhaut-Cilly's visit to, 28-9; induced Victoria to take additional troops with him, 59; Victoria's letter to from on board the *Pocahontas*, 66; protector of Pacheco's family, 68; recognized Alvarado as governor, 215; Alvarado's remarks to Vallejo regarding, 238, 239, 240; induced Castañeda to retire from Santa Barbara, 247.

Guerrero, Vicente, 7, 16.
Guijarros, Point, 24, 36.
Gunn, Dr. L. C., 209.
Gutiérrez, Nicolás: arrival in California, 147; mentioned, 157; in command of troops in south, 163, 173; as acting governor, October 1835 to May 1836, 165-8; August to November 1836, 172, 173-7; his departure from California, 176-7; mentioned, 207, 219; his report of November 30, 1836, 279.

Hartnell, William E. P.: formed Company of Foreigners, 91-3; at Council of February 1, 1832, Monterey, 93-7; thanked by Figueroa, 150; friend of Zamorano, 267, 268, 269.
Harvard College Library, 191, 277.
Havana, 12.
Héros, 22.
Herrera, Ildefonsa González de, 170-1.
Herrera, José María: his arrival as *comisario subalterno* in 1825, 20-1; Zamorano's investigation of conduct of office, 33; his persecution by Echeandia, 33-4, 41-2; prepared *pronunciamiento* for Solis, 39; mentioned, 51; *causa célebre* of Castañares and his wife, 170-1.
Hidalgo y Costilla, Fr. Miguel, 15.
Hijar, José María, 160-3.
Hijar and Padrés Colony, 159-64, 180, 201-2, 207, 269.
Hijos del pais, 9, 22, 47, 98.
Hopkins, Rufus C., 179.
Horcajo de las Torres, 10, 288.
Howell, John, 184.
Hoz, Juan José de la, 12.
Hunnewell, James, 191.
Hunnewell, *Papers*, Harvard College Library, 191, 277.
Huntington, Henry E., Library, 179.

Ibarra, Juan María: member of court martial that tried Fr. Luis Martínez, 42; mentioned by Victoria, 62; rejects Plan of San Diego 1831, 72-4; member of Council of February 1, 1832, Monterey, 93-7; in command of northern forces in 1832, 100, 105-6, 107, 109, 110-19; character of troops, 101; mentioned, 126; commended by Figueroa, 152.

Iglesias, José, 93.
Iguala, Plan de, 17.
Immigrants, undesirable, from Mexico, 8, 21.
Indian, Californian, 4, 47-8.
Indian disturbances: in 1832, 140, 143; in 1834, 161; at San Diego in 1837, 222-3, 224, 225, 228, 232, 240.
Inquisition, Holy Office of the, 11.
Iturbide, Agustin de, 6, 7, 16-7, 18.

Jamul, Rancho de, 54, 225.
Jeantet, María Leonora, 264, 287.
Johnson, William, 93.
Johnstone, Andrew, 69.
Joven Victoria, 135.

Kemble, Edward C.: his "History of California Newspapers," 181; his career in California, 181-2; his history of California's first printing press, 183, 193; his translation of Zamorano's *Aviso al Publico*, 196; his description of the press, 198; his description of Chico's proclamation of May 3, 1836, 204-5.
Kinlock, George, 93.

Lagoda, 68, 191-5.
La Paz, 251.
La Pérouse, 5.
Las Flores, Rancho de, 249.
Las Oncaladas, 10.
Larkin, Thomas O., 262, 268.
Leandry, Juan B., 93.
Legislature, *see* deputation.
Leiba, Alipas, 221.
Leiba, Santiago, 221.
Leonidas, 212, 214, 219.
Leonor, 43, 169.
Letterheads: printed from wood-blocks, 184-6; printed from type before July 1834, 186-7.
Lewis, William, 195.
Littlejohn, David, 93.
Lobato, Miguel G., 42.
Lopez, María, 288.
Lopez, María Francisca, 290.
Lopez, María Fecunda de Mora de, 290.
Lopez, Ygnacio, 290.
Loriette, 68.
Loriot, 163.

Los Angeles: founding of, 5; mentioned, 40; accepts Zamorano as acting governor, 108-9; wavering allegiance in 1832, 117, 119; neutral territory under the truce of 1832, 121, 124, 126, 132, 152; uprising at in March 1835, 163-4; made capital, 168, 215, 242, 243; opposition to Alvarado in 1837, 212, 213, 215-16; Alvarado accepted by, 216-17, 219; accepts Plan of San Diego 1837, 223-4; Portilla's campaign in 1837, 228, 230-1, 232; recognized Carrillo as civil governor, 242, 243, 246-7.
Lugo, Antonio María, 232.

McCarty, William, 93.
McCulloch, Hartnell & Company, 91, 92.
McCullough, John, 195.
McKinley, Santiago, 93.
Madrigal de las Torres, 11.
Maitorena, José Joaquín, 37, 67.
Malarin, Josepha Estrada de, 263, 267.
Malarin, Juan: member of Council of February 1, 1832, Monterey, 93-7; godfather of Gonzalo Nicomedez Zamorano, 263; friend of Zamorano, 267.
Manifiesto de la Republica Mejicana, 164, 201-3.
Marriage of junior officers, 37.
Martínez, Ignacio, 67, 97.
Martínez, Fr. Luis, 42, 51.
Mead, Samuel, 93.
Medrano, José María, 94, 95, 97.
Menocal, Juana de Dios Garcia, 12, 289.
Micheltorena, Manuel, 253-5, 256, 257.
Mier, Francisco de, 10.
Mier y Teran, José María, 218, 221.
Miles, John, 93.
Missions: the mission system, 3-5; secularization of, 8, 46-50;
Bancroft quoted on, 46-7; Echeandia quoted on, 48.
Mission La Purísima Concepcion, 29, 41, 247.
Mission San Buenaventura, 29, 232, 233, 246, 247, 248.
Mission San Carlos Borromeo, 3, 8, 49.
Mission San Diego, 3, 8, 24, 25, 38, 119, 256, 257, 260.

Index

Mission San Fernando, 60, 119, 216, 217, 219, 230, 231, 237, 248, 249, 258.
Mission San Francisco Solano, 161, 220.
Mission San Gabriel, 28, 49, 50, 61, 63, 64, 65, 70, 71, 113, 114, 116, 119, 129, 135, 235, 245, 261.
Mission San José, 114, 140.
Mission San Juan Bautista, 163, 175.
Mission San Juan Capistrano, 109, 114, 117, 119, 229, 261.
Mission San Luis Obispo, 35, 42, 49.
Mission San Luis Rey, 66, 102, 109, 110, 113, 119, 129, 229.
Mission San Miguel, 35, 50.
Mission San Rafael, 140, 161.
Mission Santa Barbara, 8, 27, 40, 68, 110.
Mission Santa Clara, 140.
Mission Santa Inéz, 29, 214.
Mission La Soledad, 35.
Mofras, *see* Duflot de Mofras.
Monsoon, 194.
Montenegro, Eugenio, 218, 221.
Monterde, Mariano, 45.
Monterey: described by Dana, 30-2; by Duhaut-Cilly, 29-30; by Alfred Robinson, 30.
Monterey Bay, 3.
Monterey Council of February 1, 1832, 91-102.
Monterey *presidio*, 5, 166-7, 176.
Mora, María Fecunda de, 290.
Moraga, María Ignacia, 27, 290.
Morelos, 19, 21, 161.
Munrás, Estévan: member of *Compañia extranjera*, 93; mentioned by Alvarado, 259; friend of Zamorano, 260, 267, 268, 269.
Muñoz, Juan Antonio, 135, 138, 173, 176, 177.
Murphy, Carlota, 263, 286.
Murphy, Timothy, 93.
Muriel, 10.

Natalia, 161.
Navarrete, Bernardo, 147, 176, 177.
Negrete, *see* Castillo Negrete.
Nietos, Rancho de los, 63, 230.
Nieves, 20.
Noriega, *see* Guerra y Noriega.
Offices, authority by which held, 99.
Old Dartmouth Historical Society, 195.

Oliva, Fr. Vicente Pascual, 26, 38, 265.
Oliver, William, 192.
Olvera, Agustin, 199.
Orcajo de las Torres, *see* Horcajo de las Torres.
O'Reilly, Fr. Miguel, 13.
Ortega, José Francisco, 3, 27, 290.
Ortega, José Joaquín, 52, 53, 54, 84, 87, 219, 250.
Ortega, José María, 27, 290.
Ortega, María Antonia Victoria Carrillo de, 290.
Ortega, María del Pilar, 27, 38, 262, 291.
Ortega, María Francisca Lopez de, 290.
Ortega, Soledad, 264.
Osío, Antonio María: Member of deputation, 52, 53, 54, 84; his *Historia* quoted on battle at Cahuenga Pass, 63; quoted on character of Ibarra's troops in 1832, 101; mentioned, 106, 217; quoted on number of Echeandia's troops at Paso de Bartolo in April 1832, 119; as envoy to treat with Alvarado, 216, 219; his statement regarding Zamorano's death, 255.
Otis, Thomas, 194.
Otter, 5.

Pacheco, Francisco, 94, 95, 97.
Pacheco, Mariano Martín, 67, 69.
Pacheco, Ramona Carrillo de, *see* Carrillo, Ramona.
Pacheco, Romualdo: his youth and arrival at San Diego, 2, 18-20; his expeditions to the Colorado River in 1825-6, 24; assistant to the executive secretary, 24; his marriage to Ramona Carrillo, 24-5; a witness at marriage of Zamorano, 25; made acting commandant at Monterey, 34; made acting commandant at Santa Barbara, 37; disciplined for his marriage, 37-8; his part in suppressing the Solis Revolt, 40, 41; mentioned, 43, 59, 71, 245, 248; summary of his career, 66-9; his death at battle of Cahuenga Pass, 60, 63; Victoria's grief at, 62.
Pacheco, Romualdo, Jr., 68, 69.
Padrés, José María: appointed adjutant inspector of Californias, 19; as Echeandia's deputy in Baja California, 20; appointed governor of Alta California, 38;

his arrival in Alta California, 42-3; Bancroft quoted on his character, 46; as acting executive secretary, 48-9; exiled by Victoria, 51; mentioned, 98; the Hijar and Padrés Colony, 159-64.
Palomares, Dolores, 37.
Palomares, Ignacio, 229.
Paso de Bartolo, 115, 117, 119, 230.
Peña, Cosme, 240.
Pensacola, Spanish expedition against, 12.
Perez del Campo, José, 21, 42.
Petaluma, Rancho de, 162.
Peyri, Fr. Antonio, 66, 145, 193.
Pico, Andrés, 63, 229, 231.
Pico, José Antonio, 247.
Pico, Pio: member of deputation, 52, 53; as one of the originators of the Plan of San Diego 1831, 54-8; elected acting civil governor by deputation, 84-8, 99, 154; appealed to by Echeandia, 103; as commissioner from San Diego, 216, 217, 219; destruction of his Rancho de Jamul, 225; mentioned, 230, 231, 238, 239, 244; as civil governor, 257, 263.
Piedra Blanca Rancho, 69.
Pilgrim (ship), 30, 68, 194.
Placer Times, Sacramento, 208.
Plaza Church, Los Angeles, 262, 263, 264.
Pliego, Rodrigo del: arrival in California, 2, 19; second in command at Santa Barbara, 40; suggested for commandant at Monterey, 44; accompanied Victoria, 54, 59, 61, 62; departure from California, 66; mentioned, 145.
Pocahontas, 62, 65-6, 83, 84, 193.
Pombert, Luis, 93.
Portrero, Juan, 10.
Portilla, Pablo de la; commandant at San Diego, 23, 54; signed the Plan of San Diego 1831, 57, 59; at battle at Cahuenga Pass, 58, 60-1, 63; interview with Victoria, 61, 64, 65; mentioned, 96, 109, 163; offered governorship by Echeandia, 88, 106; at Council of War, San Diego, March 1832, 103; at Council of War, November 4, 1836, Monterey, 176, 177; called to acting governorship by Plan of San Diego 1837, 223, 224, 226; his report on campaign of 1837, 228-36, 237; mentioned by Alvarado, 238, 239, 250; as military commander in the south in 1838, 244, 245, 246, 247, 248.
Portolá, Gaspar de, 3.
Printing Press: contemporary references to, 178-84; Kemble's history of, 183, 196, 198, 209-10; printing before June 1834, 184-91; the *Lagoda*, 191-5; the press and its equipment, 195-8; Zamorano's first printer, 198-203; Zamorano's second printer, 204-8; later history of, 208-10.

Quixote (ship), 176.

Rainsford, John, 93.
Ramírez, Angel, 240.
Ramírez, José María, 2, 20, 37, 38, 57, 58, 59, 61, 103, 109, 176, 231.
Raymore, Thomas, 93.
Reglamento Provicional, 159, 199-200.
Requena, Manuel, 220, 244, 250.
Rezánof, Nikolai Petrovich, 5-6.
Richardson, William A., 143.
Rincon, El, 232, 233, 235.
Roach, John, 93.
Robinson, Alfred: description of Monterey quoted, 30; regarding Echeandia, 22; regarding Victoria, 46.
Rocha, Juan José: arrival in California, 2, 20; his marriage to Elena Dominguez, 37, 38; imprisoned by insurgents during Solis Revolt, 39; member of court martial that tried Fr. Luis Martínez, 42; signed Plan of San Diego 1831, 57, 58; mentioned by Victoria, 59; godfather of Mariano Martín Pacheco, 67; at Council of War, San Diego, March 1832, 103; mentioned, 109, 230, 244; in command at San Gabriel in 1837, 212, 216, 217; arrested by Alvarado, 220.
Rocque, Mariano de la, 13.
Roe, Charles, 93.
Romero, José Mariano, 176, 207.
Roper, John, 93.
Rosa, 163.
Rover, 253.
Ruiz, Francisco María, 2, 23.
Rujula, Juan Felix de, 11, 279.
Russians in California, 161.

INDEX

Sacramento *Daily Union*, 181, 182, 183.
St. Augustine, Florida, 12-14.
Salazar, Juan, 103, 211, 212, 221.
San Antonio Abad, Rancho de, 218.
San Buenaventura, battle of, 248.
San Carlos Church, Monterey, 30, 35, 66, 263.
San Diego Council of War, March 1832, 103-5, 107-8.
San Diego, Plan of, 1831, 54-8, 145, 154.
San Diego, Plan of, 1837, 223-6, 229.
San Diego *presidio*, 2, 15, 23-4, 211.
San Francisco Bay, 3.
San Francisco *presidio*, 5.
San Francisquito, Rancho de, 166.
San José de Guadalupe, 5.
San José, Seminario de, 268.
San Leandro, Rancho, 265.
Sánchez, José, 76, 78, 97, 112, 121, 140.
Sánchez, Fr. José, 61.
Santa Ana Rancho, 229.
Santa Anna, Antonio Lopez de, 145, 160, 161, 206.
Santa Anna y Farías (town), 162.
Santa Barbara *presidio*, 5, 28.
Santa María de Castillo (church), 10.
Savage, Thomas, 256.
Sealed-paper headings, 187-9, 199.
Secretaría de Guerra y Marina, Archivo General, 278.
Sectional jealousy, 9, 211-12, 242-4, 257.
Selidonio, 109.
Semple, Robert, 180, 208.
Señoriano, 267.
Sepúlveda, José, 216, 219.
Serra, Fr. Junípero, 3.
Shaw, Thomas: supercargo of *Pocahontas*, 66; mentioned by Kemble, 183; supercargo of *Lagoda*, 191-4.
Short, Rev. Patrick, 268.
Silva, Francisco, 221.
Smith, Charles R., 93.
Smith, Jedediah, 192.
Solá, Pablo Vicente de, 6.
Soledad (ship), 264.
Solis, Joaquín, 21, 39-42.
Solis Revolt, 39-42, 82.
Sonora *Herald*, 181, 208, 209-10.
Soto, Joaquín, 221.
Spanish East Florida Archives, Library of Congress, 279.

Spear, Nathan, 93.
Spence, Adelaida Estrada de, 264, 268.
Spence, David E., 263, 267, 268, 269.
Star and Californian, 182, 208.
Stearns, Abel, 51, 53, 59.
Stockton *Times*, 208.
Sutter, John A., 253.

Tablas Para Los Niños, 207-8.
Talamantes, Tomás, 63.
Taylor, Alexander S., 277.
Taylor, William, 93.
Tecate, Rancho de, 227.
Tepotzotlan, seige of, 44.
Texas, 206, 221.
Thomas Nowlan (ship), 42.
Thompson, John, 93.
Three Years in California, 180.
Ti Juan, Rancho de, 218, 227.
Tijuana, Baja California, 218.
Tobar, Juan José, 220, 249, 250.
Toro, Rancho el, 166-7.
Treaty of Paris, September 3, 1783, 12.
Trujillo, Manuel, 250.
Two Years before the Mast, 30-2, 68, 194.

Vallejo, Mariano Guadalupe: his opinion of Echeandia, 22; mentioned, 43, 121, 266; imprisoned by insurgents during Solis Revolt, 39; member of court martial that tried Fr. Luis Martínez, 42; member of deputation, 52, 53, 54, 72, 75, 84, 86; his *Historia* quoted on Zamorano's offer to relinquish command at Monterey, 75; at Council of War, San Diego, March 1832, 103, 107; quoted on Echeandia's forces at Paso de Bartolo in April, 1832, 119; quoted on Echeandia's position in 1832, 154; granted Rancho de Petaluma, 162; his part in revolt of November, 1836, 175-7; as revolutionary general commandant, 177, 220, 221, 222, 236, 238, 239, 244; as constitutional general commandant, 250; his recommendations to central government, 253.
Valle, Antonio del, 268.
Valle, Ignacio del: signed Plan of San Diego, 1831, 57, 58, 59; at battle of Cahuenga Pass, 63; at Council of War, San Diego, March, 1832, 103; at Coun-

cil of War, Monterey, November 4, 1836, 176, 177; godfather of Josepha María Zamorano, 264; friend of Zamorano, 267, 268-9.
Vancouver, George, 5.
Venegas, Francisco Xavier, 15.
Verdugos, Rancho de los, 231, 232.
Victoria, Manuel: appointment as governor and his arrival in Alta California, 45-6; Alfred Robinson's remark regarding, 46; as governor, 50-4; at battle of Cahuenga Pass, 58-62; his departure from California, 62, 65-6, 83; his relations with Zamorano, 70-1; mentioned, 72, 145, 193.
Vignes, Louis, 92, 93.
Villavicencio, José María, 240.
Virmond, Henry, 144, 145, 146.
Viva el estado libre y soberano de Alta California, 174.
Volunteer, 42.

Watson, Edward, 93.
Watson, James, 93.
Webb, William, 93.
Wilson, John, 68.
Wilson, John, Jr., 68.
Wilson, Juanita, 68.
Wilson, Ramona Carrillo de, *see* Carrillo, Ramona.
Wilson, Ramonsita, 68.
Wilson, Ygnacia, 68.

Xavaleta, Aniceto María, 222.

Yoalgo, Sánchez, 145.
Yorba, Tomás, 84, 86.

Zacatecan friars, 147.
Zalvidea, Fr. José María, 110, 114, 117.
Zamorano, Agustin Vicente:
  Antecedents and youth:
    his father's career, 10-16; his birth and baptism, 13; commissioned a cadet, 17; his experiences during the Mexican Revolution, 17-18; friendship for Romualdo Pacheco, 17, 18; education, 18, 270; his promotion to ensign, 18.
  Arrival in California:
    appointed executive secretary of the Californias, 19; the trip to Alta California, 19-20; arrival at San Diego, 1-2, 20.
  Echeandia's administration:
    his marriage to María Luisa Argüello, 25-6; district elector in 1827, 27; his investigation of Herrera's conduct of office, 33-4; the birth of his first child, 35; his attempted investigation of the activities of the *Franklin*, 35-6; district elector in 1828, 37; disciplined for his marriage, 37-8; his promotion to lieutenant, 38; the birth of his second child, 38; his part in suppressing the Solis Revolt, 39-42; recommended for captain of the Monterey Company, 43-4; candidate for congress, 44.
  Victoria's rule:
    his absence from Monterey in December, 1830, and January, 1831, 48-9; his reactions to Echeandia's secularization decree of January 6, 1831, 50; left in command at Monterey by Victoria, 54; his relations with Victoria, 70-1; his promotion to captain of the Monterey Company, 71.
  Plan of San Diego:
    his and Ibarra's statement of December 16, 1831, 72-4; his request for passports, 74; his offer to relinquish the command of Monterey to Vallejo, 75; his reply to Echeandia's circular letter of December 21, 1831, 76-7; his reply to Echeandia's letters of December 29, 1831, 79-81; Echeandia's offer of the acting governorship, 88.
  As Acting Governor:
    his decision to maintain the territorial government, 90-1; the formation of the *Compañia extranjera*, 92-3; the Council of February 1, 1832, Monterey, 93-7; criticisms of his motives, 98-9; as *comandante general accidental*, 99; he sends Ibarra south, 100; Echeandia's recognition refused, 102-8; his negotiations with Echeandia, 108-30; his proclamation of May 9, 1832, 131-2; his report of June 6, 1832, to central government, 134-5; his refusal to discuss the situation

INDEX

further with Echeandia, 136; his proclamation of July 7, 1832, 136-7; his offer of the command to Muñoz, 138; his enforcement of regulations, 139; granted license to hunt otter to Castro and Estrada, 139; his appointment of José Mariano Estrada as acting *comisario*, 139-40; Indian disturbances in 1832, 140; his report of November 16, 1832, to central government, 141-3; Bustamante's decision to appoint him governor, 145; C. A. Carrillo's opposition to, 145-6; his claim to having been acting governor in 1832, 154-6.

Figueroa as governor:
  Figueroa's praise of his services, 149-50; Figueroa's report of March 26, 1833, to central government, 151-3; his relations with Figueroa, 159; his trip north of San Francisco Bay in 1834, 162; Figueroa's *Manifiesto*, 164; Figueroa's death, 164.

Gutiérrez as acting governor:
  Alavarado's statement regarding his advice on succession, 165-6; his defense of the presidial company's grazing lands, 166-7.

Chico as governor:
  his difficulties with, 169, 171-2; Chico's comments regarding, 172-3.

Gutiérrez again:
  his transfer to the command of San Diego, 173; the Council of War of November 4, 1836, Monterey, and fall of the *presidio*, 176-7.

The printing press:
  Kemble's history of coming of, 183; printing in Alta California before June, 1834, 184-91; Kemble's translation of his *Aviso al Publico*, 196; his first printer, 198-203; his second printer, 204-8.

Remaining years in California:
  his removal to San Diego, 211, 259-60; his report of April 24, 1837, to central government, 218-21; called to acting command by Plan of San Diego, 1837, 222-4; his report of June 5, 1837, to central government, 224-8; the campaign of 1837, 228-36; Portilla's report of September 12, 1837, to central government, 236-7; called Portilla's director by Alvarado, 239; his support of Carrillo and campaign of 1838, 244-9; at Las Flores, 249; departure from California, 250.

In Mexico:
  as *comandant principal* of Baja California, 251-2; on staff duty in War Department, 252-3; appointed adjutant inspector of Alta California, 254; his return to California, 254-5.

Conclusion:
  his death and burial, 255-7; his family, 258-65; the man and his friends, 265-71; genealogy, 285-91.

Zamorano, Agustin Vicente, Jr., 264, 286.
Zamorano, Agustin Vicente, 3d, 264, 287.
Zamorano, Alonzo Jimenez, 11.
Zamorano y González, Antonio, 288.
Zamorano, Carlota, 286.
Zamorano, Carlota Murphy de, 263, 286.
Zamorano, Dolores, 287.
Zamorano, Eulalia Dorotea, 265, 270, 287.
Zamorano, Francisca Sales del Corral de, 12, 289.
Zamorano, Francisca Sales Juliana, 289.
Zamorano, Francisco, 10, 288.
Zamorano, Francisco, 11.
Zamorano, Gabriel, 288.
Zamorano y González, Gonzalo: his early career, 10-14; as treasurer of Guanajuato, 15-16; his *Documentos*, 279; genealogy, 288, 289.
Zamorano, Gonzalo Nicomedez, 263, 286.
Zamorano, Joseph Juan de Sahagun, 289.
Zamorano, Joseph María, 264, 286.
Zamorano, Juana Olimaca Joaquina, 289.
Zamorano, Luis Agustin: birth, 38; his memories of his father's funeral and burial, 256, 257; his marriage and death, 263; genealogy, 285-6.
Zamorano, Luisa Ana, 286.
Zamorano, Lula Dorotea, 286.
Zamorano y González, Manuel, 288.
Zamorano, María Dolores, 35, 262-3, 285.
Zamorano, María de Guadalupe, 263-4, 286.
Zamorano, María de Guadalupe Tiburcia, 287.

Zamorano, María Leonora Jeantet de, 264, 287.
Zamorano, María Luisa Argüello de, *see* Argüello, María Luisa.
Zamorano, María de la O. Lazara Vicenta, 289.
Zamorano, Minnie Lucile, 286.
Zamorano, Petrona Josepha de la Luz, 289.
Zamorano, Rafaela Melchoza, 289.
Zéspedes, Vicente Manuel de, 12.

Printed by Bruce McCallister
Los Angeles 1934

THE CHICANO HERITAGE

An Arno Press Collection

Adams, Emma H. **To and Fro in Southern California.** 1887

Anderson, Henry P. **The Bracero Program in California.** 1961

Aviña, Rose Hollenbaugh. **Spanish and Mexican Land Grants in California.** 1976

Barker, Ruth Laughlin. **Caballeros.** 1932

Bell, Horace. **On the Old West Coast.** 1930

Biberman, Herbert. **Salt of the Earth.** 1965

Casteñeda, Carlos E., trans. **The Mexican Side of the Texas Revolution (1836).** 1928

Casteñeda, Carlos E. **Our Catholic Heritage in Texas, 1519-1936.** Seven volumes. 1936-1958

Colton, Walter. **Three Years in California.** 1850

Cooke, Philip St. George. **The Conquest of New Mexico and California.** 1878

Cue Canovas, Agustin. **Los Estados Unidos Y El Mexico Olvidado.** 1970

Curtin, L. S. M. **Healing Herbs of the Upper Rio Grande.** 1947

Fergusson, Harvey. **The Blood of the Conquerors.** 1921

Fernandez, Jose. **Cuarenta Años de Legislador:** Biografia del Senador Casimiro Barela. 1911

Francis, Jessie Davies. **An Economic and Social History of Mexican California** (1822-1846). Volume I: Chiefly Economic. Two vols. in one. 1976

Getty, Harry T. **Interethnic Relationships in the Community of Tucson.** 1976

Guzman, Ralph C. **The Political Socialization of the Mexican American People.** 1976

Harding, George L. **Don Agustin V. Zamorano.** 1934

Hayes, Benjamin. **Pioneer Notes from the Diaries of Judge Benjamin Hayes, 1849-1875.** 1929

Herrick, Robert. **Waste.** 1924

Jamieson, Stuart. **Labor Unionism in American Agriculture.** 1945

Landolt, Robert Garland. **The Mexican-American Workers of San Antonio, Texas.** 1976

Lane, Jr., John Hart. **Voluntary Associations Among Mexican Americans in San Antonio, Texas.** 1976

Livermore, Abiel Abbot. **The War with Mexico Reviewed.** 1850

Loyola, Mary. **The American Occupation of New Mexico, 1821-1852.** 1939

Macklin, Barbara June. **Structural Stability and Culture Change in a Mexican-American Community.** 1976

McWilliams, Carey. **Ill Fares the Land:** Migrants and Migratory Labor in the United States. 1942

Murray, Winifred. **A Socio-Cultural Study of 118 Mexican Families Living in a Low-Rent Public Housing Project in San Antonio, Texas.** 1954

Niggli, Josephina. **Mexican Folk Plays.** 1938

Parigi, Sam Frank. **A Case Study of Latin American Unionization in Austin, Texas.** 1976

Poldervaart, Arie W. **Black-Robed Justice.** 1948

Rayburn, John C. and Virginia Kemp Rayburn, eds. **Century of Conflict, 1821-1913.** Incidents in the Lives of William Neale and William A. Neale, Early Settlers in South Texas. 1966

Read, Benjamin. **Illustrated History of New Mexico.** 1912

Rodriguez, Jr., Eugene. **Henry B. Gonzalez.** 1976

Sanchez, Nellie Van de Grift. **Spanish and Indian Place Names of California.** 1930

Sanchez, Nellie Van de Grift. **Spanish Arcadia.** 1929

Shulman, Irving. **The Square Trap.** 1953

Tireman, L. S. **Teaching Spanish-Speaking Children.** 1948

Tireman, L. S. and Mary Watson. **A Community School in a Spanish-Speaking Village.** 1948

Twitchell, Ralph Emerson. **The History of the Military Occupation of the Territory of New Mexico.** 1909

Twitchell, Ralph Emerson. **The Spanish Archives of New Mexico.** Two vols. 1914

U. S. House of Representatives. **California and New Mexico:** Message from the President of the United States, January 21, 1850. 1850

Valdes y Tapia, Daniel. **Hispanos and American Politics.** 1976

West, Stanley A. **The Mexican Aztec Society.** 1976

Woods, Frances Jerome. **Mexican Ethnic Leadership in San Antonio, Texas.** 1949

Aspects of the Mexican American Experience. 1976
Mexicans in California After the U. S. Conquest. 1976
Hispanic Folklore Studies of Arthur L. Campa. 1976
Hispano Culture of New Mexico. 1976
Mexican California. 1976
The Mexican Experience in Arizona. 1976
The Mexican Experience in Texas. 1976
Mexican Migration to the United States. 1976
The United States Conquest of California. 1976
Northern Mexico On the Eve of the United States Invasion:
   Rare Imprints Concerning California, Arizona, New Mexico, and Texas, 1821-1846. Edited by David J. Weber. 1976